Politics
in
Palestine

SUNY Series in The Social and Economic History of the Middle East
Donald Quataert, Editor

Politics
in
Palestine

Arab Factionalism and
Social Disintegration, 1939-1948

Issa Khalaf

State University
of New York
Press

Published by
State University of New York Press, Albany

For information, address State University of New York Press,
State University Plaza, Albany, N.Y., 12246

Production by Marilyn Semerad
Marketing by Bernadette La Manna

Library of Congress Cataloging-in-Publication Data

Khalaf, Issa, 1955-
    Politics in Palestine : Arab factionalism and social
disintegration, 1939–1948 / Issa Khalaf.
        p.   cm.—(SUNY series in the social and economic history of
the Middle East)
    Based on the author's thesis (doctoral)—Oxford.
    Includes bibliographical references (p.) and index.
    ISBN 0-7914-0707-1 (cloth).—ISBN 0-7914-0708-X (pbk.)
    1. Palestine—Politics and government—1929-1948.   2. Palestinian
Arabs—Politics and government.   3. Palestinian Arabs—Social
conditions.   4. Jewish-Arab relations—1917-1949.   I. Title.
II. Series.
DS126.4.K432 1991
956.9402'2—dc20   90-10167
                                                            CIP

10   9   8   7   6   5   4   3   2   1

To the memory of my father
and to my mother,
and
to all those Palestinians
of their generation

Contents

List of Illustrations

Tables

Maps

Preface

In the academic year 1980/81 I arrived in Oxford to start my doctoral work, enthusiastic to undertake research on some aspect of contemporary Arab politics or political economy, either comparative in nature or focusing on Syria or 'Iraq. Determined to produce an original and fresh work, theoretically sound and replete with the kind of scientific methodological armament I was equipped with from my American graduate training, I spent the first year to this end, trying to develop a thesis proposal. However, the required research would have involved travel to secretive states—one of which plunged itself into a most destructive and prolonged war with its neighbor, while the other became embroiled in conflict over Lebanon with the most powerful state in the Middle East—where I had to seek sensitive documents and ask sensitive questions dealing with regimes and parties. I began to realize that such an enterprise would require more funds than I had, and might involve a lengthy amount of time, not to mention the uncertainty of obtaining the information I wanted and, perhaps, some potential danger.

So I began to think of archival research, pushed in that direction by a friend who, having done research in Lebanon for his thesis, strongly suggested that the archives would be less hazardous, less costly for research, and certainly more convenient. But he also insisted that Palestine would be a good topic, even though I felt then that I did not want to do anything on mandatory Palestine because, I reasoned, the subject was already too saturated with literature. Moreover, I really did not know very much about the period. However, after a preliminary trip to the Middle East (Israel and the occupied territories), the encouragement of friends, and, needless to say, because of my own background, I became increasingly fascinated with the idea. Particularly so since I knew a study on Arab Palestine in the mandate period would help me learn much about Palestinian politics or the Palestine question today.

Having done some secondary research, I found that the period 1939-48 was inadequately treated. My plunge into archives in London and Jerusalem brought home to me the historical value of what I was doing, in addition to breaking down my reluctance to do a work historical in nature. Furthermore, the archives gripped my attention and I wanted

xi

to find out more and more about the British mandate's last decade. From an interest in factionalism in Palestinian politics, I increasingly began to ask the bigger question: What political, sociological, socio-economic, and politico-military factors led to the disintegration of Palestinian society?

I couldn't answer this question by maintaining a narrow focus on a theme like factionalism, constrained by theoretical constructs. I wanted to do a work much broader and more inclusive in nature, and Oxford provided the flexible interdisciplinary tradition to enable me to do so. Also, the archival material available for the period under study was, not surprisingly, very preoccupied with political/diplomatic events. Thus, my task was set: to understand the reasons for the dissolution of Arab Palestine in 1948, I had to take into account the multiplicity of variables enumerated above, in addition to the roles played by the colonial state, Jewish settlement, and the Arab states. The archives, as well as the unique situation of Palestine, defined and shaped what I would do, nudging me to new directions and conclusions.

The end result is a broad work which examines all the factors that converged to perpetuate factionalism and social fragmentation and so caused the disintegration of Palestinian Arab society. It is narrow and specific, yet simultaneously general and encompassing. Therefore, the work is self-consciously historical and, when it needs to be, it is empirical/ conceptual, interpretive, and descriptive. It adheres to no particular theory nor does it preoccupy itself with hypothesizing, proving propositions, etc. Methodologically, it is eclectic. Though it combines features of both, it is systematic more in a historical than in a social scientific sense. It is, really, a work of history on Arab Palestine in the last decade of the mandate, trying to weave together the socio-economic and the political.

*   *   *

This book is based on a balance between Public Record Office and Israel State Archives (which includes Arabic documents) material, other primary sources such as newspapers (mainly Arabic), and secondary works, in English and Arabic. It was actually written before the recent publication of what might be called revisionist works, such as B. Morris's *The Birth of the Palestinian Refugee Problem* or A. Shlaim's *Collusion Across the Jordan*, which also focus on the late forties. However, their concerns are not mine, though obviously we do overlap on some aspects. On those aspects, I found that I needed to revise very little of what I had written, and thus maintained my findings and conclusions.

The work utilizes many of the recent documents which became available at the archives that shed new or fresh light on the forties, particularly 1948. Nevertheless, it may be limited in insight, angles, or emphases because it certainly does not exhaust all the archives, some of whose material may enrich it even more. Moreover, my topic and investigation being so inclusive of a multiplicity of variables, some themes may take yet much more detailed treatment, while others probably get too much. Still, I am confident its documentation and findings are solid, while its interpretations and conclusions are sound, regardless of any limitations, faults, or errors, for which, if the customary disclaimer is even needed, I willingly assume responsibility.

*   *   *

I am grateful to the staff and librarians at the PRO and ISA (most of whom, particularly those of the PRO, I never met), at the Middle East Centre of St. Antony's College, Oxford, and at the Arab Studies Society in Jerusalem.

The manuscript readied for publication has changed in some dramatic ways, mostly organizationally and in terms of length, from the original D. Phil thesis. My primary appreciation goes to those anonymous individuals who read the manuscript for the publisher. They gave insights and made suggestions that were invaluable in assisting me to make the work more clear, coherent, and manageable. I would also like to express my gratitude to Kenneth W. Stein, at Emory University's Carter Center, for being extremely helpful in more ways than one. The current product, however, basically reflects an individual effort, which even went much beyond what was suggested by the readers.

I am especially thankful, however, to those who were instrumental in the putting together of the dissertation itself without which this book wouldn't exist. First to Roger Owen, who served as my supervisor at Oxford, and whose opinions, suggestions, and questions were extremely helpful in constructing a coherent theme. To Donald Quataert and James Jankowski, of SUNY-Binghamton and the University of Colorado, Boulder, respectively. Both lent moral support, gave of their time to read material, offer opinions, and ask questions. Lastly, I would particularly like to mention the friendship of Ms. Norma Masriya, who at the time worked at Bir Zayt University. She was always willing to volunteer her time in helping me locate archives, material, and persons when I was doing field research in the occupied territories and in Israel, and she continually suggested sources for my perusal.

Certain family members, who had the misfortune to be around at a seemingly indefinite stage in my life, gave generously of themselves. To these people, I should like to record my thanks and deep appreciation: Randa and Riad Ajluni, my sister and brother-in-law, George and Hessie Chahin, my in-laws, Ghada Hamdan, my other, but not forgotten, sister, and Khalil (Charlie) Khalaf, my brother.

Above all, my wife Rebecca, offered her unfailing patience, support, and encouragement, motivating me during some difficult times, serving as an unofficial advisor, putting up with my idiosyncratic quirks, insomnia, and obsessions, and reading, editing, and helping me type a seemingly endless number of drafts. This product is also hers in a very personal way. My daughter and son, Rasha and Darik, were always there to remind me, by their presence and insistence on their inalienable right to share my time equally with the book, that the world and things in it are after all much larger than my world.

Map Acknowledgments

The preparation of the maps was made possible by the permission and help of the following institutions and individuals:

Map 1 is based on Walid Khalidi, *Before Their Diaspora, A Photographic History of the Palestinians, 1876–1948* (Washington, D.C.: IPS, 1984), p. 307. It is used with the permission of Professor Khalidi and the Institute for Palestine Studies, for which I am grateful.

Map 2 is reproduced with the kind permission of Avi Shlaim, *Collusion Across the Jordan* (New York: Columbia Univ. Press, 1988), p. 63.

All the maps (1–5) were prepared with meticulous care, detail, and artistic talent by Ms. Cynthia Boland, Loras College senior and Studio Arts major.

Ms. Norenne K. Masbruch, graphic designer at Loras's Publications Department, also worked on the map preparations on her computer and made the resources of her office readily available.

(The figures on the refugees for Map 5 are from Laurie A. Brand, *Palestinians in the Arab World* (New York: Columbia Univ. Press, 1988), table 1.1, p. 9.)

A Note on Transliteration

I have avoided burdening the reader (and more myself) with any dia-
critical marks except 'ayns and hamzas. These marks are indicated at
the beginning, middle, or end of each word and are used in the following
form: 'ayn=('), e.g., 'Abdullah, Sa'id, or al-Difa'; hamza=('), e.g., Fu'ad, mu'assasat, insha'i. I have tried throughout to be consistent in transliterating
Arabic words and names by avoiding the use of common spellings and
adhering to purity, although I hope I was successful. Where the same term
is transliterated differently in Arabic and Turkish (e.g. wali/vali), the Arabic
is used. Lastly, with few exceptions, I have simply added an "s" for Arabic
words that are used in plural form.

Acronyms*

AAC	Anglo-American Committee of Inquiry
AHC	Arab Higher Committee
AHE	Arab Higher Executive
AHF	Arab Higher Front
ALNL	Arab League for National Liberation
CO	Colonial Office
CS	Colonial Secretary
DC	District Commissioner
FATU	Federation of Arab Trade Unions
FO	Foreign Office
FS	Foreign Secretary
HC	High Commissioner
HMG	His Majesty's Government
ISA	Israel State Archives
MC	Military Committee (Arab, Damascus)
NC	National Committee
NDP	National Defence Party
PAP	Palestine Arab Party
PAWS	Palestine Arab Workers Society
PG	Palestine Government
PRO	Public Record Office
UNSCOP	United Nations Special Committee on Palestine

---

*It should be noted that, in my notes, I do not indicate "PRO" in making references to British archival material. Thus, when I refer to "CO" and "FO," it should be understood that these are records found at the Public Record Office in London. The other archival codes are explained in the bibliography.

Introduction

Despite the voluminous literature on mandatory Palestine, the latter part of the mandate, 1939–48, has been largely ignored by historians and social scientists. Much of what has been written is concerned with such topics as British-Jewish-Arab relations and policies[1] and the development of the Palestinian Arab national movement and its confrontation with the Zionists and British.[2] The tendency to delimit Palestinian political and social history to 1939 is understandable enough: the late thirties is a convenient historical stopping point as, after the Palestinian Arab rebellion of 1936–39, the fate of Palestine was largely influenced and shaped by external events and powers. The last decade of the mandate was characterized by diplomacy more than anything else and the activist radical nationalism of the thirties was missing or largely quiescent. This had to do mostly with the harsh suppression of the rebellion and the nationalist rank and file and the enforced exile of the leadership, followed by restrictions on political activity and the press during the course of the Second World War.

But there occurred rapid social and political changes during the forties and up to the time of the disintegration of Arab Palestine in 1948, that have not yet been fully investigated. This period is crucial to understanding the origins and nature of the complex factors that led to the destruction of the Palestinian Arab people. Although these factors are multifaceted, internal and external in source, the main thrust of this work is concerned with an examination of changes and events that are *internal* to Palestinian Arab politics, while external variables are analyzed in relation to their effect on these politics.

If there is one characteristic feature of Palestinian politics and society during the mandate, it is the pervasiveness of factionalism. Factionalist politics continued to hold sway until 1948. This factionalism is a manifestation of traditional, largely agrarian societies dominated by vertical cleavages, identities and divisions. In Palestinian society, the central cleavages were based on family, kinship, and clan. In this regard, part of my interest is to look at the evolution of such cleavages in light of the changes that were affecting the very basis of this kind of social framework. Thus, the central theme or thread is continuity and change in factionalist

1

politics, the role of internal and external factors which perpetuated and exacerbated it, and how this led to the undoing of Palestinian society in 1947–48. The focus is on the social, economic, political, and sociological factors that made Palestinian society more fragile and vulnerable to dissolution.

Factionalism as used here is based on two conceptual levels of analysis. One level deals with factionalism as it affected the social structures. That is, I look at how socio-economic changes in Palestinian society might have contributed to the fragmentation, fragility, and vulnerability of the traditional social structures and organizations at all levels, but particularly at the lower social levels. The other level of analysis of factionalism deals with the conflict of the traditional elite over power and leadership. Thus the first refers to *structural* factionalism, while the second refers to *political* factionalism.

Factionalism at these two levels was affected both by internal and external factors. While the analysis of changes internal to Palestinian politics is meant to shed light on the extent of the society's cohesion/ fragmentation (that is, on the extent of factionalist conflict and divisions) at the mandate's end, this cannot be understood in isolation from external influences. The colonial state and Zionist settlement, while secondary to our focus, form an integral and underlying part of the work. They are central to an understanding of the content of change in Arab social structure and the evolution of factionalist politics. They also partly help to explain why the Palestinian urban notable elite was able to hold on to its power. These external influences affected Palestinian structural factionalism by inhibiting and blocking the full potential of socio-economic changes in Palestinian society and by aggravating political factionalism by posing formidable political challenges and pressures.

The foregoing focus on the dialectical effects of internal and external influences on Palestinian politics and society form the core of the analysis in Part One, which is meant to be an introductory background to the rest of the book. It contains three chapters. After setting out the nature of Arab society and politics in late Ottoman Palestine, the first chapter then examines the evolution of the urban notable elite that was to play a dominant role throughout the mandate. This chapter also analyzes and defines the social basis of factionalist politics, which continued through the mandate. It ends with an overview of the socio-economic, political, and cultural impact of the colonial state on Palestinian Arab society.

Chapter 2 then leads into the impact of social change on the lower levels of society: the village and countryside, rural migrant wage labor, and the formation of a working class in the urban centers. The purpose is to show how internal changes—social differentiation, the intrusion of nationalism in the countryside, the development of a working class—

might have affected factionalism, patronage ties, and vertical cleavages. The final chapter of Part One continues with the theme of continuity and change in factionalist politics, particularly at the elite level, by analyzing the impact of social change on the urban notable elite. It examines the question as to whether there was social differentiation within such an elite, whether a new elite was developing, and, if so, why that elite was unable to challenge the power of the notability.

The common thread of these chapters is the evolution of political and structural factionalism and vertical identities and cleavages from the upper to the lower levels of society. Zionism and colonial policies will form a part of this analysis as these two external sources had more of a direct effect on Palestinian society than factors indigenous to the Palestinians.

Even though this book is concerned with the years 1939–48, much of Part One, while concentrating on the last decade, also takes into consideration the evolution of social change throughout the mandate, particularly the 1930s (beginning of the mandate's latter half). This was unavoidable, for it would not be very intelligible to talk of the situation during and after the war period without setting that period in its historical context. Thus, there is continual reference and comparison between the first and second halves of the mandate. The rest of the book (Parts Two and Three), however, maintains a detailed focus on my period of interest and investigation.

Part One attempts to trace the changing social context of factionalism and is concerned with assessing whether such social change—from vertical cleavages to more horizontal stratification patterns—undermined the very basis of factionalist politics and identities. While showing the extent of social structural change, it concludes that, one, the full potential of change at the elite level was blocked by extraneous sources and, two, these sources directly contributed to the unevenness, fragility, and fragmentation—structural factionalism—at the lower levels of Palestinian Arab society. Though historical patterns of factionalism were rapidly changing, they were continually reformed by the severe external socioeconomic and political challenges.

Part One sets the tone for what follows in Part Two, which focuses on factional politics within the traditional elite. It prepares the way by explaining why the urban notables retained their preeminence despite the significant social changes that were occurring and indicates that these disjointed changes, particularly in the countryside where traditional agrarian cleavages were made insecure by uneven development, were to play an important role in the rapid disintegration of Palestinian society in 1948.

Much of Palestinian politics during the forties was elite politics. Though the uprooting and dislocation of the peasantry was an ongoing process which, as just implied, contributed significantly to their fragmentation and vulnerability, they did not play an important role in politics in the forties as they had done in the 1936–39 period. Despite the changes, the majority of Palestinians lived in the countryside. The peasantry was not only exhausted by the rebellion of the late thirties, but the post-war period saw the increasing radicalization of the national movement, toward nationalist expression more than organization or popular participation, and the peasantry believed that its interests were being represented by the notability. Any intrusions into elite politics in the forties came from the young, educated, middle class, and commercial elements, and from the urban workers. Unlike the thirties, however, the notability went on with its infighting with little connection to or influence on the lower classes or lower class politics. Therefore, a good part of this book looks at politics from the top, as Palestinian politics in the forties were very much shaped by the urban notables. It is mostly a history of those who make politics.

Paradoxically, then, there was more lower class intrusion into elite politics in the thirties than in the forties, despite the rapid social changes of the latter decade. As Part One concludes and Part Two illustrates, this was made possible by the anti-colonial, anti-Zionist (synonymous in the eyes of the Palestinians) nationalist struggle. My contention is that, though there was significant social change and differentiation, particularly in the urban centers, which posed a potentially serious challenge to the urban notables and therefore to factionalist politics, traditional authority and legitimacy were sustained, however precariously, because the notability was at the forefront of the nationalist, anti-colonialist movement. Therefore, there are political reasons for the notability's control of politics, in addition to the sociological reasons given in Part One. There is then a sharp change of focus from the socio-economic, or a discussion of social change and differentiation, in Part One, to the political, or elite factionalism and infighting, in Part Two.

The nationalist struggle cannot be underestimated as a factor that prolonged notable domination. Because the Palestinian Arabs were not allowed a national government like the surrounding Arab states, the Palestinian notability, never having been given the opportunity to run the state (mainly because of the British commitment to Zionism), was not tainted with having collaborated or cooperated with the colonial regime. Palestine, unlike the surrounding Arab countries, was unique in this case. Almost all the regimes in the Arab countries were challenged by nationalist elements. In Palestine, the notability was at the forefront of the nationalist sentiment, thus deflecting internal (leadership) change and discontent among other classes and groups.

The implications of this for national integration were profound. Despite a vibrant nationalism, mobilization of the Palestinians, particularly the peasantry, was done through more traditional, factional means.

The notables suppressed the existence of independent nationalist parties and groups, yet their brand of politics was rooted in their generation and their social background. Therefore, the national movement was fragmented because of the very factionalism of the traditional elite who led it. This helps explain why the Palestinian Arab national movement, nationally and culturally conscious and enjoying widespread support, was unable to transcend factionalism even in the face of grave threats to Arab Palestine's existence.

Part Two, containing four chapters, illustrates this thesis. Chapter 4 provides the backdrop to the opening of the forties. The first three to four years were dominated by the relationship between London and the Palestinians over the White Paper. This chapter analyzes the aspects of the White Paper and also looks at the attempted come-back of the opposition and the organization of the dominant parties.

The following three chapters, 5, 6, and 7, focus on the political reasons for the notability's ascendancy, the futile attempts at political unity, nationalist leadership, and preparations to meet the Zionist challenge. They show how the urban notable elite, insecure under an eroding patronage system and leading a society that was rapidly changing, appropriated nationalist sentiment, highly focused on Zionism, in order to maintain its position. The essence of these chapters is that the notability helped intensify fragmentation in Palestinian society, particularly as the external challenges became more severe. Though the old elite was nationalist in its own way, its vision was limited by its own social background.

Because of their monopoly on leadership, the urban notables served as an impediment to wider national integration, particularly because they were determined to block out the participation of middle and working class elements or individuals representing a new commercial elite. These groups increasingly criticized and challenged the notability's dominance. Chapters 5-7 bring to light the frustrating inability of the leaders to achieve unity among themselves and therefore in the nationalist movement as it struggled to meet the Zionist challenge.

During the forties, with the progressive immobilization and ineffectiveness of the national movement due to the factional divisiveness of the elite who led it, the Arab states became increasingly involved in Palestine affairs and Palestinian politics. This intrusion of the wider inter-Arab politics, particularly after 1945, also had the effect of exacerbating Palestinian political factionalism. The Arab states influenced not only the nature, direction, and outcome of the Palestinian response to the dynamic Zionist challenge, but inter-Arab politics and intervention in Palestinian affairs had an impact on the way the notability held and organized political power and how it led its people into the last crucial few years of the mandate.

Part Three, therefore, examines the factors and events that led to the fall of Arab Palestine in 1948. It emphasizes the role of outside forces in contributing to internal collapse and disintegration. Chapter 8 in this section analyzes inter-Arab politics and the Palestinians. Its purpose is threefold: to examine the goals and motivations of the various Arab states, particularly the Hashemites, towards Palestine; to show how and why they came to dominate the Palestinians and how they weakened the position of the Mufti, al-Haj Amin al-Husayni; and to explain their role in stripping the AHC of all power and independence. The central point here is that the predominant divisions and intrigues furthered disorganization in Palestinian society and politics.

Chapter 9 in Part Three, the last chapter, analyzes the consequences of all the internal and external factors on events in Palestine during the Palestinian Arab/Jewish war of 1947–48. It is the climax. It mainly focuses on two variables as determinants of Arab Palestine's collapse and disintegration: one, Zionist motives and tactics; and two, the nature and role of Palestinian and Arab (the volunteers) politico-military organization. The second variable looks at the internal reasons for collapse. To illustrate these internal factors, the characteristics of Arab politics and defense of Haifa and Jaffa will be used as small case studies. Chapter 9 also offers a sociological analysis of societal weakness and compares traditional social organization to industrial society. British withdrawal and the vacuum left behind, in authority and administration, forms the background to this chapter.

An extended conclusion is then offered, focusing on the reasons for the persistence of Palestinian factionalism within the context of the main themes postulated in this book.

Palestine is a unique case in modern history, if not the only case, in terms of the relentless combination of factors, events, and forces that converged upon it to cause its collapse and to deny its people national self-determination. These variables, reflecting socio-economic, sociological, military, political, and diplomatic dimensions, were at once multifaceted, interconnected, and concurrent. This book is an attempt to weave all these dimensions together in order to offer a coherent picture of how and why Palestinian society disintegrated in 1948 and of the origins of a tragic problem that still seems to elude resolution and of a people whose aspirations are yet to be fulfilled.

Part One: Introduction

*The Changing Social Basis and Context of
Palestinian Arab Factionalist Politics:
The Dialectical Effects of Internal and
External Socio-Economic Factors*

1

State, Society and Politics in Late Ottoman and Early Mandatory Palestine

---

Almost any discussion of Palestine Arab society and politics must start with late Ottoman Palestine. This is a period that began with the restoration in 1840 of Ottoman authority over the country, after less than a decade of occupation by the Egyptian Muhammad 'Ali. From that time on a series of political, economic, financial and state reforms were instituted by the Ottomans in an attempt to centralize and consolidate power.[1] These reforms had a gradual impact upon Palestinian Arab social structures and, therefore, power relationships.

Administrative Structure

Ottoman Palestine in general differed in its regional history and characteristics (particularly between north and south), thus making it difficult to speak of Palestine as a political/territorial unit.[2] Until the turn of the twentieth century, it was known in the consciousness of many as the southern part of *Bilad al-Sham* (Greater Syria). Palestine in the second half of the nineteenth century encompassed various administrative units. Regionally, there were two *wilayas* (provinces, Beirut and Damascus), governed by a *wali*. The Beirut *wilaya* incorporated most of the country (at least up to the 1870s when the Jerusalem district became independent), and was divided into four *sanjaqs* or *mutasarrifiyas* (districts), each under a *mutasarrif*. These were the *sanjaqs* of Beirut (comprising, in addition to what is today central-south Lebanon, the very northern part of Palestine), Acre, Nablus and Jerusalem. At the local level there were the *qada*s of Acre, Haifa, Nazareth, Safad, Tiberias, Jenin, Nablus, Tulkarem, Beersheba, Gaza, Hebron, Jaffa and Jerusalem, each led by a *qa'im-maqam*.

In the ever-changing Ottoman administrative boundaries, the *sanjaq* of Jerusalem held a distinctive place. In 1873 the district was established as an autonomous unit, directly responsible to Istanbul and comprising: one *markaz al-liwa (al-Quds* or Jerusalem itself); three *qada*s (Jaffa, Gaza,

Hebron); and two *nahiyas* (sub-districts after *qadas*), which included Bethlehem and Ramle.[3] This shrunk the lines of the Beirut *wilaya* to a point north of Jaffa. Before this, two districts were sometimes ruled by one governor. In the early sixteenth century, Gaza and Jerusalem were amalgamated; from the second half of that same century, Nablus and Gaza were sometimes annexed to Jerusalem; and the same was done in the 1850s.[4]

Before 1918, then, Palestine was a vague geographical entity. As recent as the late nineteenth century, a peasant living north of the *sanjaq* of Nablus (in Acre) most probably felt himself to be a resident of the province of Beirut, and if he lived south of the Dead Sea, a resident of the Syrian province.[5] Economically, the Galilee (*sanjaq* of Acre) was more a part of the southern and western regions of *Bilad al-Sham*, more akin to what is today southern Lebanon. Sidon and Acre were particularly important as ports for the export of agricultural commodities (cereals, grains, and, during the sixteenth through eighteenth centuries, cotton[6]) from the Syrian interior. In particular the Galilee (and the Jabal Nablus) was dominated by rural shaykhs, beduin chieftains, or local rural families and strongmen.[7]

The southern part of the country was more cohesive administratively, economically, religiously, and socially. The district of Jerusalem was a unifying factor, which encompassed by the late nineteenth century much over half of the country (that is, of the borders that later constituted mandatory Palestine). Internal trade, production and contact were more pronounced in the Jerusalem district, hence the studies on agricultural exports of southern Palestine. This helped unify, in a cultural sense, the rest of the country. This is demonstrated by Y. Porath.[8] First, the area of jurisdiction of the Jerusalem *qadi* exceeded the geographical area of the Jerusalem *sanjaq* and included the *sanjaq* of Nablus as far as Haifa. Second, there was cooperation in the military sphere between the *sanjaq*s of Jerusalem and Nablus. There were feudal armies (*sipahis*) organized in every *sanjaq*. The Nablus and Jerusalem *alay beyis* (commanders of their *sipahis*) were required to protect pilgrims and often cooperated. For example, some of the tasks of the Jerusalem *alay beyi* were carried out by Nablus residents. Third, popular religion and worship of saints contributed to the development of ties between the various sections of southern and central Palestine as far as the Jezreel Valley. There were many occasions for pilgrimages to tombs and sancturies where festivals and celebrations were held. The outstanding event was the one celebrating al-Nabi Musa, an annual pilgrimage to the mosque located on the site of Moses's tomb near Jericho. People from all over the country came together. Fourth, the social order in the rural regions of Hebron, Jerusalem, Nablus and Carmel was similar. One of the characteristics of the social order was the split between *Qays* and *Yaman,* ancient tribal and fictive alignments dating back to pre-Islamic conquests. The continually shifting clan alliances produced ties between the various regions. Fifth, Christianity and its institutions played a very important part in the creation of the Arab concept of *Filastin.* Even before the turn of the century, the idea that *Filastin* was a separate unit from Syria was already evident.

Rural Society and Elites: From Shaykhs to Notables

Despite the regional differences, the land regime and related socio-economic conditions have often been described in the following terms. Late Ottoman Palestine was essentially an agrarian society in which land constituted the main form of capital.[9] Much of what the rural population produced was for itself and a good portion of the surplus was appropriated by the Ottoman state through tax-farmers and later directly through landowners.[10] The peasant (*fellah,* pl. *fellahin*) thus was heavily burdened with taxation in kind through government officials, officers, merchants, and rural shaykhs who, at annual public auctions, bought rights to tax-farming (*iltizam*). The tax-farmer (*multazim*) usually squeezed what he could out of the peasants and, after paying to the state the taxes assessed for his area, kept the rest for himself. The state gave him the authority to employ troops if necessary and at times he used his own private army and took over many of the police duties of government. While the tax-farmer's rights were over the peasants and not the land, his position tended to become hereditary.[11] The status, power, and authority of the dominant shaykhs derived from their role as *multazims* and the state's recognition of their position, as long as they collected the taxes.

Extensive tracts of land were held by the state and some by large landowners.[12] Village land, particularly on the hills, was usually individually owned and cultivated. Many villages and large tracts were cultivated on the basis of crop-sharing arrangements, such as share-cropping, joint farming, and share rent contracts, wherein the landlord provided land, seed, and ploughing stock in progressively decreasing proportion parallel to the order of mention of these three types of share contract.[13] Finally, a significant portion of village land was held in *musha'* land tenure. This was land held in common under which shares were divided into parcels, or collections of parcels, which were then periodically redistributed between the different members of the village.[14] In general, a large amount of state and private land was cultivated by the peasants.

By the early part of the nineteenth century in particular, village life was characterized by insecurity, beduin raids, and endemic factionalism. From the eighteenth to the mid-nineteenth century, the weakness of central power over *Bilad al-Sham* resulted in a shrinkage of the cultivated

area (along the coast and plains) and an expansion of the territory dominated by the beduin. Beduin raids and their virtual encirclement of the hill
regions, plus malaria, pushed the population to the central hills.[15] Only in
the mid-nineteenth century did the Ottomans begin to push back the
nomadic frontiers. Until then and even in the latter part of the century, the
hills were more heavily populated. Many of these villagers, particularly
the peasants who moved to the mountains, maintained continuous contact with plain lands and made use of these lands by descending—in
times of security—to sow, reap and carry to the threshing floor. As a
result, satellite villages developed, called *khirbes* and *nazlas*, the former
occupied on a seasonal basis, the latter on a temporary (harvesting) basis.
These satellite villages began to grow as the population again began to
drift westwards in the latter part of the nineteenth century.

Before the rise of the urban notables and the institution of reforms,
the whole central range extending to the Jezreel Valley in the north was
divided into administrative sub-districts, the *nahiyas*, headed by the local
shaykhs already referred to. The *nahiya* shaykhs and their families held
authority over other village shaykhs in their sub-districts. From the
Hebron to the Jerusalem to the Nablus areas there were no fewer than
eighteen *nahiyas* each with its ruling clan.[16] The basis of the shaykhs'
power and prestige was the extended and partriarchal family system.
Each village prided itself on its family and sub-clan ties and relations. The
family and village played a central role in the cultural psychology and
consciousness of the peasants. The weakness of central power and
general insecurity reinforced the village unit as a secure and (concretely)
defensive haven for the peasantry, while in the family the peasant felt
protection and belonging.[17] Social control, self-government, collective
responsibility, sanctions and ostracism were exercised through the
extended family and its heads. Under these conditions, the shaykhs were
all-powerful.

The shaykhs and their clans preserved their identities and power for
many generations, forming and unforming alliances according to wider
divisions known as *Qays* and *Yaman*. All clans traced their origins to one of
two tribal groups originating in northern (*Qays*) and southern (*Yaman*)
Arabia before the Islamic conquests. These factions were pervasive
throughout Syria and Lebanon. Because *Qays* and *Yaman* loyalties were
based on fictive origins and descent, clan alignments were their medium
of expression. Therefore, divisions were expressed through clan alliances
that cut across district, regional, urban, sectarian, and religious lines, and
that produced solidarity on the basis of common ties. Two clans of the
same sect and religion could belong to either faction. Christian and
Muslim families belonged to the same moiety. These divisions and alliances were used by the shaykhs to preserve the vertically segmented

social structure rooted in patronage networks and their position as tax-farmers and, in many cases, moneylenders. They were also used by the wealthy landlords who moved to the towns, such as Nablus and al-Khalil, to control the peasantry and protect their land (through their village clients) against the depradations of inter-clan and inter-family conflict.[18] Again, the clan alliances reinforced the relationship and reciprocal loyalty between patron and client through the pervasive pride in common descent.

Ottoman restoration and reforms beginning in 1840 led to the start of the decline of the rural shaykh. Through the *tanzimat*, the state sought to centralize administrative control and develop institutions to foster growth and efficiency—in other words, to build an effective state. A strong impetus for these reforms was the increasing penetration of Western capitalism into the Ottoman Empire and the consequent increasing debts. New ways had to be found to increase revenues, whose burden would fall most heavily on the peasantry. Campaigns were launched against the beduin and private, local armies.[19] The purpose was to restrain the military power of the shaykhs, who were also deprived of judicial powers.[20] An attempt was also made to simplify the complex laws and customs in the land regime and fiscal system and to provide a definite tenure system and so encourage or increase productivity.

In 1839 the *Hatti Sherif* of Gulhane announced the abolition of tax-farming which, although it did not succeed until the First World War, managed to change the character of *iltizam* and weaken the authority of the shaykhs. The government began to entrust the leasing of *iltizam* to the newly created *majlis al-idara* (administrative council) of the district. The government leased the collection of *iltizam* to the highest bidder, in return for a sum determined in advance which the lessee paid into the treasury.[21] The tax-collector, usually hailing from among the urban notables on the *idara*, kept for himself whatever taxes he managed to collect. The tax-collector collected the taxes in cash or kind with the aid of gendarmes who accompanied him or his emissaries. Cash payments for taxes reinforced the dependence of the peasant on the moneylenders/merchants (usually one and the same) who advanced loans at crushingly high rates of interest. This system gradually led to the weakening of the administrative status of the *nahiya* shaykhs and the transfer of the powerful function of tax collecting to other, more influential men.

The growing *a'yan*, or urban notables, had been consolidating their strength in the Ottoman Empire since the eighteenth century. The decline in power of the central government and degeneration and struggles with-in the imperial forces encouraged the rise of autonomous local powers such as the urban *a'yan* and local ruling families. The urban notables were those merchants and landowners who increasingly moved to towns and coastal cities, investing their capital in the seaborne related trade with Europe. They comprised powerful town-dwelling families from all over the Syrian province, the rich and influential families of Beirut and Damascus, and, to a lesser extent, Jerusalem, Acre, Jaffa, Gaza and other sub-district capitals.

The growth of agricultural production and trade and the increasing population of towns paralleled the rise of the urban notables to power. Beginning around the time of the Ottoman reforms and accelerating in the latter part of the nineteenth century, the fertile coast and plains of Palestine were increasingly cultivated and the towns grew in population. Although there were no dramatic changes in the agrarian and urban economies and hence in the social structure before 1882, that is, before significant colonization via European missions and Jewish immigration, merchants, big landowners, and tax-farmers were still investing their capital in trade and agriculture. Jaffa, Haifa and Acre served as important export points for external trade, while Nablus remained the most important center "for local and regional trade and for the manufacture of soap, oil and cotton goods."[22] Jaffa exported the produce of southern Palestine, mainly wheat, barley and dura, olive oil and soap, oranges and other fruits and vegetables. These went mainly to France but also to Egypt, England, Asia Minor, Greece, Italy, Malta and northern Syria. To many of these countries also wheat, barley, dura, sesame and olive oil were exported through Haifa and Acre. A good part of the wheat shipped through Acre came from the Hawran in Syria. Acre and Jabal Nablus were among the most important cotton growing districts of Syria, exporting to France the surplus that was not marketed internally. Finally, internal regional trade in craft manufacture was carried on between Hebron, Jerusalem, Nablus and Bethlehem. Jaffa, together with Ramle and Lydda, formed a center of soap and oil production second in output to Nablus.

Table 1.1: Increase in Town Populations, 1840–1922[23]

City	1840	1880	1922
Jerusalem	13,000	30,000	62,500
Haifa	2,000	6,000	24,600
Jaffa	4,750	10,000	47,700
Gaza	12,000	19,000	17,500
Nablus	8,000	12,500	16,000

In many of the towns, then, agriculture flourished, the population of those towns grew, and villages dotted the plains near the major centers. The figures in table 1.1 on selected towns indicate the steady increase in their populations between 1840 and 1922 (although one of them, Gaza, saw a slight decline between 1880 and 1922). These figures included Jews. The Arab population of the mixed towns in 1922 was: Jerusalem, 28,607; Haifa, 18,804; and Jaffa, 27,524.[24] The coastal towns, particularly Jaffa and Haifa, registered dramatic growth.

Aside from changes in economy and social structure, Ottoman reforms augmented the power of the *a'yan*. The local administrative councils previously mentioned were established in various districts to advise the governor. The councils, rather than strengthening the central government, were used by the *a'yan* to strengthen themselves. They advanced themselves and checked the *wali*'s attempts to introduce reform that was liable to affect their status, particularly as they were obviously more familiar with local affairs. Another factor that strengthened the notables was the abolition of the hereditary *iltizam*, as was indicated. Because the leasing of taxes came under the authority of the councils which they dominated, they facilitated the transfer of the function of tax collection to themselves.

In order to counter the growing power of the *a'yan* and their autonomous role as regional officials and tax collectors, the *Wilayet* Law of 1864 redefined the role of the administrative councils. But instead of controlling these councils, the law added to the power of the *a'yan* by stipulating that candidates for local councils had to pay a yearly direct tax of 500 piastres.[25] Furthermore, the Law vested the councils with authority over land and land taxation. With the institution of the Ottoman Land Code before it (1858), members of the Councils "authorized the assessment and collection of taxes, approved land registration, decided on questions of landownership, and expressed influential opinions about the ultimate fate of lands that reverted to the state."[26]

A big impetus to notable aggrandizement and power was the process in which this stratum accumulated large tracts of land in a short time. The Land Code of 1858 and Law of 1867 strove to increase taxation (in cash rather than kind) through individual land registration, extension of rights of inheritance, and the break-up of communal ownership. Villagers' fears of conscription and higher taxes prompted many to register their lands in the names of clan heads and they continued to farm on a communal basis. The local landowner, merchant, moneylender or other notable was also able to record *musha'* shares in his name, with village inhabitants continuing to practice the *musha'* system on a tenure or cultivation basis.[27] These notables were able to reduce the financial pressures of the peasants by redeeming their debts and paying their tax arrears.[28] The powerful *a'yan*, living mainly in coastal cities (in and outside Palestine, particularly in the *sanjaq* and *wilaya* of Beirut), were able to take advantage of high debts and dispossess the peasant or acquire large tracts of land at very low cost, much of it in the Galilee and the coastal plain.[29] Land appropriation also took place in some uncultivated and uninhabited land, since the small land tax these families paid was sufficient to entitle them to rights of ownership.[30] Finally, the indebtedness of the peasants and small land-owners to these men also brought about transfer of ownership. They registered in their names extensive tracts of land in Syria and Palestine. However, though the following examples show that major transformations occurred in landholding patterns, they also indicated that the peasants retained possession of the majority of cultivable lands.

According to an estimate made in 1907, some "20 percent of the land in Galilee and 50 percent in Judea was in the hands of the peasants."[31] In 1909, 16,191 families cultivated 785,000 *dunum*s (one *dunum* equals one-fourth of an acre) in the *sanjaq*s of Jerusalem, Nablus, and Acre, or an average of 46 *dunum*s each. The great majority of the peasants in the *sanjaq*s of Jerusalem and Nablus—67 percent and 63 percent respectively—were in possession of less then 50 *dunum*s to a family.[32] In 1920 a land register listed 144 large estate owners in possession of 3,130,000 *dunum*s, an average of 21,736 *dunum*s each.[33] Of these 3,000,000 *dunum*s, however, 2,000,000 consisted of tribal grain-growing lands (with very little rainfall) around Beersheba and Gaza, leaving 1,000,000 for the Sultan and absentee owners like the Sursuqs and other large (Palestinian) landowners. This would seem to indicate that little of the central range was yet incorporated into large estates.[34] Additionally, at the end of 1932, out of 3,200,000 *dunum*s in the coastal and Acre plains, some 80 percent (2,560,000 *dunum*s) belonged to *fellahin* and the rest (640,000 *dunum*s) belonged to large land-owners.[35]

Regarding big landowners, the absentee Sursuq family of Beirut owned 230,000 *dunum*s near Nazareth and in the Marj Ibn 'Amr (Esdrae-lon). Close to another 250,000 *dunum*s in the Jezreel Valley were in the hands of the Khury family of Haifa, the Twayni family of Beirut, and other wealthy families.[36] They held this amount after selling at least the equivalent to the Zionists in the years before 1919. The non-Palestinian absentees held and sold some of the most fertile and cultivable land areas of Palestine.

Of the influential Palestinian Arab families who are reputed to have possessed significant amounts of land, the following are examples. The Husaynis owned, in various parts of the Jerusalem district, Gaza and Trans-Jordan, some 50,000 *dunum*s; the 'Abd al-Hadis held about 60,000 *dunum*s in the Nablus and Jenin areas; the al-Taji al-Faruqis possessed close to 50,000 *dunum*s in the south of Palestine (around Ramle); and the al-Ghusayns (Ramle) owned tens of thousands of *dunums*.[37] There were numerous other influential village families who made their homes in neighboring towns and cities: the Beydases from al-Shaykh Mu'annis (near Tel Aviv); the Abu Khadras (in the Jaffa and Gaza districts); the al-Khalils (Haifa); the al-Shawwas (from Gaza, reputed to have owned over 100,000 *dunums*); the Hanuns (Tulkarem); the Beyduns (Acre); the al-Fahums (Nazareth); the al-Tabaris (Tiberias); and the Jarrars and al-Nimrs (Nablus).

By 1919, thirty-two Palestinian Arab families from all the districts except Beersheba owned a total of 455,000 *dunums*, or an average of slightly over 14,218 *dunums* per family. Seventeen non-Palestinian (i.e., those residing outside of the geographical boundaries of Palestine) families owned (in all districts) 405,000 *dunums*, or an average of slightly over 23,823 *dunums* per family.[38] Of course, the averages conceal wide variations in ownership. However, the proportions give a rough indicator of ownership between the two groups.

A final reason for the rise of the *a'yan* was their access to empire-wide administrative bodies set up by the Ottomans towards the end of the nineteenth century. While land accumulation gave the *a'yan* families power and prestige, they used their resources to send their sons to relatively modern Ottoman schools concerned with the civil service and the military. Their members increasingly became part of the Ottoman aristocracy.[39] They comprised the educated sector and from this stratum emerged the *'ulama* and other religious functionaries. With the promulgation of an Ottoman Constitution in 1876, the urban notables of the various districts dominated nomination and access to that higher body. Bureaucracy and landownership coalesced, giving the notables their political influence despite the fact that this class held no formal or recognized role in the political structure. These notable families pervaded local politics in the Ottoman period and continued to do so in the early part of the mandatory period.

The British colonial administration, although it denied the Palestinian Arabs effective self-government from the national to the local level, nevertheless strengthened the notability stratum by giving it recognition and legitimacy in social and religious affairs, and by accepting its members as the leaders and representatives of the Arabs. At this early juncture, it was almost given that the British should cement their alliances with the socially dominant stratum in Palestinian Arab society. Thus the urban-mercantile class, the religious functionaries, and the socially dominant village families, all retained their positions under the British. The British pursuit of the status quo in the land regime, agrarian situation, and peasant social organization, as we will see in the next chapter, only reinforced the relationship of the urban notables to the countryside.

The British policy of alliance with the town's notability was especially pursued in regard to Jerusalem, which helped that city's notability
achieve decisive preeminence in Palestinian politics. For example, during
the military occupation, Kamil al-Husayni, the Mufti of Jerusalem, was
elevated to the head of the Central *Waqf* (religious endowment) Committee and President of the *Shari'a* (Islamic legal system or code) Court of
Appeal in that city. The British also secured him the new title of grand
mufti.[40] In 1922 al-Haj Amin al-Husayni became president of the newly
created Supreme Muslim Council, which was granted wide ranging powers over collection and disbursement of *waqf* funds (and which Haj Amin
used to build a patronage network). In addition, the urban landowning
notables in Jerusalem and all other towns dominated the local municipal
councils and mayoral posts. Just as in late Ottoman times, the notables
continued to serve as intermediaries between the state and society.

Factionalism and Clientelism in Early Mandatory Palestinian Politics and Society

Within the socio-economic conditions that predominated in late
Ottoman Palestine, it is no surprise to find that, with British rule, the
dominant political culture was one based on clientelism and its attendant
form of political action, factionalism. From a comparative perspective, it is
widely assumed that because pre-modern, developing or Third World
countries are not fully industrialized, a social structure having power
bases in well-developed, organized, and conscious classes is usually elusive and vaguely defined. Ethnic, religious, familial, or linguistic cleavages
and identities are the dominant features of such societies.[41] These vertical
political cleavages are manifested through factionalism, the faction leaders fighting for power and status.

The social framework is characterized by a system of patronage in
which the faction heads act as mediators, allocators, and arbiters.[42] The
essence of the patron-client relationship is the idea of exchange: a good or
service is exchanged for support or participation. Clientelism itself is characterized by the following factors. One, there is the concept of unequal
interaction or asymmetry. Here the patron is usually higher in wealth,
status and political power. Two, there is the concept of reciprocity. The
patron is expected to make tangible economic and administrative favors
in return for support and votes. Three, clientelism inherently involves
informal face-to-face contact between patron and client.[43]

Because vertical cleavages dominate in such societies, it should not
be assumed that there are no class divisions. Clientelism actually exists
because there are sharp class and wealth differences, as existed in manda-

tory Arab Palestine. There, the landowner-merchants were the dominant class over the peasantry. In addition, professionals, bureaucrats, clerics, workers, and nomads were all part of the class system. What patron-client ties did was to encourage personalist and dependent relationships, and thereby perpetuate the status quo of inequality in power, status, and wealth. For the patrons (notables) and, therefore, faction heads, political factionalism meant the preservation of the social framework and their adaption to change through shifting alliances and manipulation of both nationalist and traditional symbols and appeals.

What was the nature of Palestinian factionalism and the clannish political culture? Palestinian society constituted a sort of pyramidal structure in which political ties were maintained from the peasant villages to the towns to the "national" elite through a network of clan alliances headed by the major urban notables in Jerusalem. The smaller extended family wove this clan network together. In the village and town it constituted the basic social and economic unit, as in many Middle Eastern and Third World countries.

The dominant vertical cleavage in Palestinian society, then, was the clan. The *hamulah* structure with its familial and clan consciousness served well the interests of the landowning urban notables who naturally viewed patronage as the most appropriate form of political action in order to preserve their dominant role, power and status. Mobilization of peasants, therefore, was not based on ideological or class consciousness but on personalities, clan appeals and connections. David Waines, in an article on the nationalist resistance during the mandate, sums up Palestinian politics very well:

> The political life of the country was ... atomized, and vertical lines of alliance were its most common feature. Thus the head of a hamula in a small village would align himself with a larger and more influential clan in the same district, and this in turn might be linked to one of the more powerful landowning families which formed part of the urban upper classes. Political alliances, therefore, rather resembled factions centering around the chief personalities of one or another of these major landed families.... The object of political rivalry was the acquisition of power and, thereby, the dispensation of patronage by which means power could be maintained.[44]

But the urban notables did not represent a stable or cohesive network of vertical alliances. Many of the provincial and lesser town notables were relatively strong and secure within their respective areas of influence and thus inhibited the growth and influence of a unified elite rooted in a coherent socio-economic institutional setting. There were powerful and prestigious "leading" families who remained neutral and whom the urban notability, particularly those of Jerusalem, continually attempted to recruit (when needed) to their factions in order to maintain the "balance of power."[45] Also, the powerful potentates of villages aligned themselves with either faction and were able to maintain a strong position in their villages,[46] which illustrates the continuing power of some rural families even throughout the mandate. Shifting, temporary alliances gave a dynamic to factionalism, which was exacerbated by town frictions and local family divisions. Thus, each notable family was, in a concrete respect, autonomous, and the urban notables as a group held no overall or national control over Palestinian society.

The sources of legitimacy and power of the urban landowning classes were their hold over the peasantry, their administrative, professional and religious positions, and their high political offices. Public office was used as a means for political and economic advancement, prestige and influence. The notables used their role as allocators and arbiters and as the accepted spokesmen (intermediaries) for their people to maintain their power and status. For example, they protected villagers against bandits and arbitrated family feuds. They also obtained favors for the villagers from government, such as tax remission, release of prisoners, and clerical jobs in the bureaucracy.[47]

Descent also played a central part in the position, prestige and status of the notability. Descent claims referred to religious, historical or military origins. The first claim referred either to direct descendance to the Prophet, his family or tribe or the existence of a relationship between the family's ancestry and a religious figure. The second claim referred to descent from a military figure who came with the Muslim conquests or who fought against the Crusades, and the third claim referred to the history of the family in the country.[48] While not all these were really verifiable, they were accepted and gave prominence to the families. Many of the claimants to religious and military origins lived in the central range while practically all of Jerusalem's families claimed descent from all three origins, hence giving that city a special prominence. For example, out of some one hundred and twenty prominent families, forty claimed religious origins, sixteen to twenty claimed military origins, and sixty claimed historical origins.[49]

In the towns and cities, the various urban quarters served as power bases for the notables, with each family maintaining its influence in the particular quarter. The urban masses, such as artisans, wage earners, daily laborers, and porters, were easily mobilized through the factional system. "The family promoted an informal style of association by encouraging a plethora of socioeconomic groups. . . . to seek consultation, favors, loans or any other services."[50] Furthermore, the Muslim urban elite developed connections with Christian sects of Palestine. For example, the Khalidis had generally held a close relationship and had reciprocal loyalty with the Greek Orthodox community, while the Dajanis had a similar relationship with the Armenians[51] (of course, an ethnic as well as a Christian group). The *diwan,* or outer salon or reception room, was used either for the Christian minorities or for patronage/social purposes in general, and for settling personal conflict, rendering advice, or intervening with the tax collectors. This reinforced the personal links, connections, and reciprocal loyalties. It should also be mentioned that the educated sons and family members of the uper classes—the *effendis*—who constituted the upper range of the professions such as doctors, lawyers, civil servants, merchants, and real estate investors, strengthened patronage through their roles as creditors, whether in the urban areas or rural countryside.

But it was not just the urban notables who used the town and its public and administrative offices to maintain influence over their clients. We have seen how rural autonomy decreased beginning with the Ottoman reforms. Influential village families were able to amass large portions of real estate (particularly through the break-up of *musha'*), bringing many peasants under their control. Many rural based families (and their patriarchs) eventually (as late as the 1920s) moved to the cities[52] to take advantage of economic, political, educational, and administrative opportunities whether for themselves or their sons and relatives. Like the urban notables and merchants before them, the village families used public office and their connections to their land (as absentee landlords and rentiers) to reinforce the patronage system. Questions of taxes and legal cases were referred by the peasants to the absentee landlord.

For the upper stratum as a whole, then, land ownership and the interest accruing from it, as well as trade and manufacture in grain and agriculturally related products, were their sources of wealth. The tenancy arrangements, in particular the crop-sharing agricultural relations of production, provided patronage-factionalism with much of its vitality. Those who resided on or near the land they owned (as some of the rural potentates) directly looked after their interests. But if the landowner lived in the market towns of his region or was an urban notable (i.e., was an absentee landlord), he employed a *wakil*, or agent, to look after his interests, the latter either a manager or subcontractor. In this way, the social basis of clan power became dependent on the amount of land controlled by a clan head and the system of patronage concluded with peasant sharecroppers. Again, it also depended on his ability to act as creditor, and his accessability to public office, therefore providing goods and services to his clients (loans, work, and administrative connections in the city) in exchange for support in factional conflicts, especially municipal elections during mandatory times.[53]

Municipal elections, competition for mayoral posts and for control of institutions such as the Supreme Muslim Council (located in Jerusalem) actually became particularly intense during the mandate. As will become clear in Part Two, this intensity was most visible in Jerusalem, where the Husayni family and what rapidly became its main rival, the Nashashibis, jockeyed for power and sought and created countrywide factionalist alliances. Jerusalem's religious importance conferred prestige and status on the family that could become the city's preeminent leader (a position which eventually reverted to the Husaynis). Therefore, despite the decline and disappearance of the old fictive tribal divisions (*Qays-Yaman*) and active physical conflicts, elite factional conflict and the more extensive (clan) identities it appealed to helped give new vigor and vitality to a familiar and dominant cleavage in Palestinian society—the family.

What therefore changed by the time of the mandate was that it was no longer fictive alignments that mattered, but the aligning of a traditional society behind various notables and their ostensible (and similar) nationalist goals. Just as the shaykhs decades before them used (consciously or unconsciously) tribal divisions among the clans in order to perpetuate their privileged positions in rural society, the notables used family, clan, patronage and class connections also to maintain their privileged positions. The significant difference was that, under the mandate, nationalism and rapid social change increasingly were intruding into the secure domain of the notability. How these two elements were used and dealt with by the urban notables is the story of Palestinian Arab politics throughout the mandate. Before proceeding to the next chapter, it is important to set the mandate period in perspective by indicating the broad nature and contours of change under British rule.

Socio-Economic and Political Change During the Mandate

With the advent of British colonial rule, many economic opportunities were opened up as Palestine became increasingly tied to the international market and the cash economy became pervasive. In the twenties and particularly by the mid-thirties the strategic role of Palestine for the British became of central importance. British fiscal policy was almost strictly based on the ability of the mandatory country to pay its own way. Its expenditures were focused on its strategic needs (i.e., ports, roads and communications infrastructure) and internal factors of defense (i.e., roads, prisons, security, and police stations constructed mainly to control Arab dissidence and rebellion), with social services relegated to the bottom of the scale. In fiscal year 1937–38, for example, these types of expenditure swallowed 73.9 percent of the budget.[54]

But, it was these strategic and defense requirements that necessitated projects on roads, camps, airfields, and ports, which brought about economic expansion, urbanization, migration to a growing coastal area, and a growing wage labor class. The standard of living increased, some peasants (during WWII) were able to free themselves from indebtedness, and Arab financial assets multiplied and were invested in a growing citriculture industry and small scale manufacturing, which was producing differentiation in the notable landowning elite as a nascent bourgeois class was developing.[55] There was also the growth of a large professional and administrative middle class which was becoming increasingly vocal in Palestinian nationalist thought.[56] Cultural nationalism was now made available to the literate public through growth in magazines, newspapers, and other publications.[57]

Demographic and urbanization trends, too, reflected the fast-paced changes between 1922 and 1944, during which time the Arab population increased from 660,541 to 1,061,277.[58] Between 65 and 70 percent of the Arab population was rural in 1944, as compared to 75 to 80 percent in 1922. The Christians numbered 71,464 in 1922, one-quarter of whom were rural, and increased to 134,547 in 1944, one-fifth of whom were rural.[59] Or, by 1944, 80 percent of the Christians were urban based (concentrated mainly in Jerusalem, Jaffa, and Haifa, which encompassed 53 percent of the Christian population). The increase of the Muslim population was larger in the towns than in the rural areas: In the towns it increased 48 percent between 1931 and 1944, and 42 percent in the rural areas for the same years.[60] In terms of urbanization, there was dramatic increase in the Arab populations in nearly all the towns.

Table 1.2: Arab Population Growth in Selected Towns, 1931 & 1944[61]

City	1931	1944
Jaffa	44,666	70,000
Acre	7,897	12,360
Gaza	17,046	34,170
Lydda/Ramle	21,671	30,940
Hebron	17,531	24,560
Nablus	17,189	23,250
Jerusalem	39,281	60,080

Cumulatively, between 1931 and 1944 the Arab population of the eastern (hill) districts grew from 414,935 to 540,700 (or 30 percent) while the western (coastal) districts grew from 340,581 to 518,750 (or 52 percent).[62]

Urbanization, then, was proceeding rapidly. It was producing new structural relationships in the coastal cities of Jaffa, Haifa, and Acre as these grew at a pace faster than the natural birth rate and at a higher percentage than inner mountain cities such as Nablus and Hebron. More rapid economic development in the sub-districts of the coastal plain resulted in a reduction in mortality, a rise in the rate of natural increase, and migration from other, mainly mountainous, sub-districts.

*   *   *

The question to be asked regarding all this is: what difference did it make for factionalist politics? While there is no doubt that significant social change took place, the traditional elite also remained the dominant group in Palestinian politics. It is important to ask why this was so. We therefore need to examine precisely the extent of social disruptions and changes in order to understand more fully why factionalism continued to be prevalent in Palestinian society, what forms or permutations it underwent, and how this paradoxically led, at the mandate's end, to factionalist politics that were carried on at the "higher" levels with little challenge from or interaction with "lower" politics. To do this, and thereby to clarify the continuities and discontinuities in Palestinian politics and society, it is necessary to analyze social change and factionalism at the rural, urban working class, and elite levels, aspects with which the rest of Part One is concerned.

2

Socio-Economic Change During the Latter Part of the Mandate: Peasants, Workers, and Factionalism

---

Despite the fact that parochial divisions remained a dominant feature of Palestinian society, they were not immune to the influences of urbanization, progress in education, and important economic and social structural changes. Also, a growing Palestinian nationalism and identity, influenced by the nationalist, anti-colonialist movements in the Arab East and the challenge of the Zionist enterprise, played as big a role as socio-economic change in shaping the evolving political perceptions and behavior of various strata in Palestinian society, particularly the peasantry and nascent urban working class. How these elements, along with the push and pull of external factors beyond Palestinian control, coalesced to influence the identities and loyalties of these two strata, is the focus of this chapter. This will help us sort out the interaction between nationalism, social and class change, and factionalism, and to assess the extent of cohesiveness or integration in Palestinian society. This in turn is crucial for understanding the developments in the last few years of the mandate, which saw the disintegration of the Palestinian social structures.

Rural Impoverization and Dislocation: The Role of Arab Landowners and Zionist Settlement

Almost all writers on the subject of the Arab agrarian economy agree on the very difficult plight of rural society during the mandate. There were opportunities outside the peasant economy, yet simultaneously these opportunities were blocked by a combination of endogenous and exogenous factors which exacerbated conflict and factionalism. The extreme poverty and frustration that the peasants were experiencing, worsened as these were by external factors, contributed to a growing realization of their inferior and oppressed situation, of their social position.

25

Peasant difficulties destabilized patronage relationships even though the erosion of the social basis of rural factionalism was slow. However, the ongoing social dislocation in the countryside led to increased structural factionalism, fragmentation and insecurity, and a more fragile rural society.

The peasantry's perception of and response to its situation were shaped by its objective (socio-economic) conditions as much as by a growing (communal) awareness and identity. This section offers an analysis of the rural situation, or rural social economy, in order, one, to clarify the changing conditions that were leading to vulnerability in the countryside and, two, to set the context for the following section, which discusses the interaction between social change, peasant response, state policy, and the effects these had on a wider national identity.

The British inherited from the Ottomans a complex system of land tenure and a difficult peasant situation. Tax collection, interest on loans to moneylenders, insecurity, lack of state support, and difficult soil and climate conditions placed a heavy burden on the shoulders of the *fellahin*. By 1918, WWI compounded Palestine's difficult situation and caused much hardship because of such factors as conscription and the destruction of trees (mostly olive) by Turkish troops.

Various complex factors combined during the mandate to perpetuate the peasants' condition and create an endemic rural surplus of workers. The first of these was the internal socio-economic dynamics of the Arab agrarian economy. In 1930, it was found that the average annual income of a *fellah* family owning its own land was about LP35 while tenant farmers' annual income was much less.[1] The peasant's yearly income was swallowed up by taxes and debts (interests alone averaged 30 percent a year) and he was vulnerable to the fluctuations in world prices and changes in weather. During the early thirties, for example, successive poor harvests, droughts, cattle, locust and field mice plagues, and a glut in the world market, caused the collapse of prices and the production of cereals to plummet. Money for interest, rent, and taxes was hard to come by.

The agrarian situation was also aggravated by population increases. By the end of 1947, the Arab population was 1,319,434, with between 700,000 and 800,000 living in the countryside.[2] Furthermore, bigger proprietors were buying into *musha'* and some better-off peasants gained bigger shares.[3] Finally, the Islamic influence on inheritance rights (i.e., equal shares for the sons) tended to progressively break up the land into ever smaller plots, while the rapid multiplication of the Arab extended family increased the number of owners.

It is not clear how big of an impact inheritance, family growth (which means population increases), and *musha'* had on the peasant situation. While they all certainly contributed to congestion and parcelization (and communal tenure did not encourage growth in production and effi-ciency), they could be seen also as peasant adaptations to poverty and land scarcity. In additioin to tenancy arrangements, co-cultivation between family members and the continuing prevalence of *musha'* helped alleviate poverty. *Musha'* holdings did decrease from 56 percent in 1923 to 46 percent in 1930[4] to 40 percent in 1940.[5] But this slow decrease obviously served the interests of the landowning classes who were able to maintain influence over the peasantry. However, resistance to parcelization of *musha'* did not just necessarily reflect the unwillingness of the landowners to give up their leverage (i.e., they were unwilling to sell) or peasant igno-rance and fears of the tax implications of individual registration. Both "communal tenure and equal inheritance [could be seen as] a way of coping with poverty, through which both resources *and* poverty are fairly equally distributed throughout a peasantry, which thereby is enabled to stay on the land."[6]

Because the size of peasant landholdings became increasingly smaller, many peasants turned to tenancy arrangements with landlords to sustain themselves. These tenancy, or rent, arrangements were adapta-tions, both by the landlord and tenant, to difficult and changing rural conditions and to changes in market conditions. They enabled some land-lords to maintain their influence (patronage) and ties to the peasant, who was increasingly attracted to work outside agriculture, and to meet changing demands in the commodity market, by determining which crops were produced.[7] Thus, tenancy arrangements provided some relief to the landless peasants (and those with land, although small). Politically, the effect of these tenancy arrangements strengthened patronage rela-tions.[8]

Generally, then, Arab landowners did not invest substantially in agricultural enterprise. The cultivated area did increase substantially from about five million *dunum*s in 1921 to at least eight million *dunum*s in the early forties. Aside from the enclave of citrus, however, no other branch in agriculture utilized significant intensive farming methods. No fundamental changes or transformations in agricultural production took place. Many peasants had to seek work outside the rural countryside in order to supplement their meager agricultural income.

Indigenous socio-economic processes inhibited increased produc-tivity, created a large rural surplus of workers and squeezed the peasants continually. However, Zionist land purchases also played a central role in aggravating and accelerating those indigenous processes. The negative Zionist contribution affected the peasantry in four interlocking ways: it contributed to land scarcity, congestion, landlessness, and land aliena-tion. In 1920, land in Jewish possession was 456,003 *dunum*s. In 1930 that figure reached 987,600; in 1940, 1,322,338; and by 1945, 1,393,531.[9] From the time of the 1929 Wailing Wall disturbances all commissions and investigative bodies (Shaw Commission, Johnson-Crosbie, Hope-Simpson, Lewis French, the Peel Commission) were in agreement over the scarcity of land. Estimates of total cultivable land ranged from 9 to 11 million *dunums*. Minus the plain of Beersheba (and minus state land, of which over 900,000 *dunums* were cultivable), the total cultivable land was between 6.5 million and 7 million *dunums*. By 1930, "the inescapable fact remained that there was an increasing scarcity of unoccupied land or partially occupied land."[10] Out of the 26.3 million *dunums* that made up Palestine's land surface, it is generally considered that up to a third was cultivable.

Loss of land to Jews and the consequent eviction contributed to congestion in both the coastal plain and central hills. During the 1943 discussions on partition, Colonial Secretary Oliver Stanley submitted a memorandum to the Cabinet in support of partition. In it the Colonial Office compared national congestion rates between Arabs and Jews. The memorandum used the lot viable categories into which rural land was divided by the 1937 Palestine Royal Commission for taxation purposes. It was found that the rural land in Arab ownership (all citrus, banana, and "other" plantations, taxable and untaxable cereal land, and uncultivable land, equalling 10,325,833 *dunums*) was capable of supporting a rural population of 342,979 but was *actually* supporting a population of 676,150, or nearly twice the economic number.[11]

There is intense controversy over the number of Arabs made landless by Jewish land purchases. The large purchases from non-Palestinian and Palestinian landowners in the early part of this century and in the twenties saw the eviction of thousands.[12] From the early thirties, many smallholders sold part or all their lands to the Jews. Between 1933 and 1942, a total of 6,207 sales/purchases were transacted. Of these, 5,713 (or 92.04 percent) involved sales of less than 100 *dunums*.[13] However, the Zionist organizations estimated that by 1936 the Palestine Land Development Company had purchased 89 percent of its holdings from large landowners (non-Palestinian absentees and Palestinians) and only 11 percent from peasants.[14] Those peasants were usually the better-off ones.

Smallholder sales were made for a variety of reasons: to improve holdings and invest in new equipment (particularly in the citrus belt), to maintain families, or to pay back loans to moneylenders. They sold their land mainly because of need, unlike large landowners, who sold their land for conspicuous consumption, greed, and for obtaining capital and thereby maintaining their socio-economic standing.

Eventually, many smallholders were left penniless and joined the ranks of the landless and urban poor. Once land was purchased it was permanently alienated and Jewish ownership increasingly denied Arab laborers access to land they formerly tilled. The policy of Jewish labor,

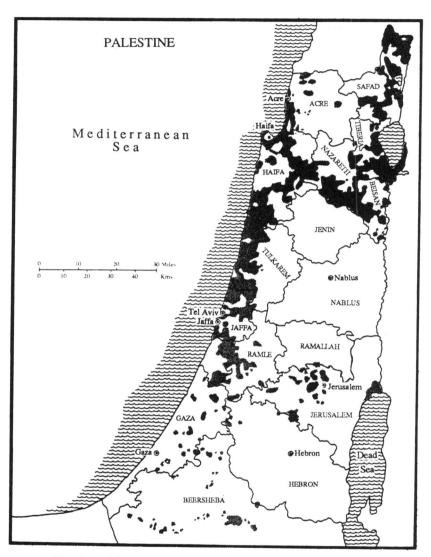

Map 1. Jewish Landholding Patterns by 1945 as They were Located Within and Across Administrative Subdistricts

begun in the 1920s, was "ferociously" implemented by Jewish authorities and the *Histadrut* (Jewish labor federation) between 1931–35 because of the dramatic increase in immigration.[15] It should also be mentioned that, unlike the process of expropriation and landlessness during the mandate, in the late Ottoman period large landowner appropriation usually meant that the peasant continued to cultivate his land.

The internal and external factors combined to impoverish the rural population. In a detailed survey of five villages in 1944, it was found that 75 percent of the parcels were smaller than 10.5 *dunums*, while parcels over 51 *dunums* constituted only 3 percent of the total.[16] As concerns the landless, as early as 1930 the Hope-Simpson *Report* stated that "of the 86,980 rural Arab families, 29.4 percent are landless" (or about 20,000 families).[17] It was estimated in the forties that some 80,000 farms were 50 to 100 *dunums* in size (i.e., subsistence).[18] If we multiply this by an average of five to a family, it would mean some 400,000 people out of a rural population of 800,000 (by the late forties), or 50 percent, were barely making ends meet.

These statistics could be used as rough indicators of the proportions obtaining in the latter part of the mandate. In more general terms, the majority of rural Palestinians were owner-occupiers of insufficient holdings, practically all (including laborers) owned a house and its surrounding gardens in the village, a large number were agricultural laborers (perhaps 25–30 percent of the rural population), and many were tenants (there were close to 13,000 tenants in the early thirties).

Finally, the shrinkage of peasant land holdings did not necessarily translate into a continued process of big owner appropriation. On the contrary, big owner appropriation was slowed down under the mandate because of the more coherent presence of the state—that is, British control over the land regime (land registration) and tax collection checked the ability of the landowning classes to accumulate land. Like peasant landholdings, large holder ownership also decreased during the mandate because of land sales and because the same processes that affected the shrinkage of peasant land (inheritance, extended family) affected large holdings. It would be reasonable to assume that by the forties there were very few families possessing "huge" amounts of land (i.e., 15,000–20,000 *dunums*).[19]

The difficult social conditions of the peasantry, then, shaped by influences outside the Arab agrarian economy, contributed greatly to dislocation, vulnerability, disjointed change, and rural frustration. This situation had a direct effect on the peasants' awareness and political discontent, directed at both the Zionist enterprise and Arab landowners. Despite the pressures in the countryside, however, the British pursued policies that tried to preserve the status quo in the rural areas and thereby helped aggravate tension and conflict.

Factionalism, Social Conflict, and Nationalism among the Peasantry

British policies were based on the cautious notion of continuing with past, or historical, patterns of rule and administration. Therefore, it is well to recall that the Ottoman state reinforced traditional social organization through its administrative, political and economic policies. It encouraged divisions, whether regional, familial, local or social. Administrative reform and the rise of notables only perpetuated the existing social divisions, parochial tendencies and patronage politics. The insecurity, weak state authority, and regional identities produced by Ottoman administrative divisions, all served to hinder integration and the development of a broader communal identity. The *millet* system also was central in sustaining communal religious identities, although this system began to erode with reforms, European privileges, and the continuing slide into disintegration of the Ottoman Empire.

Inasmuch as Palestinian society remained splintered by these divisions during the mandate (though, except for family and clan segmentation, to a much lesser degree), British practices contributed to them significantly and thus erected barriers to wider integration and sociopolitical unity. The colonial state actually was intent on maintaining the traditional rural social structure. From the beginning of the mandate, the British aimed at achieving administrative stability without altering existing social relationships. "Priority was given to public order and efficient collection of taxes."[20] Innovation was resisted and policy was formulated within Ottoman precedents and norms. Social, economic and educational programs and services were limited by the more broadly colonially inspired policy of having Palestine pay its own way. Though some long term plans for the development of the rural countryside were formulated, particularly in the late 1920s and early 1930s (Lewis French reports, Hope-Simpson's inquiry), very little eventually came out of them. Policy was short-term, limited, and intended to meet immediate contingencies. The central propelling motive of British policy throughout the mandate was to maintain existing rural life and *stability*. It was understood that changes would, and did, produce social and economic mobility within villages that would increase migration, occupational differentiation, rising expectations, and, as a result, conflict and instability.

British policy in local administration, politics and education therefore sought to perpetuate a social structure that was itself rapidly changing.[21] In village government the principles of collective responsibility, based on custom and local village authority, were sustained. The government also attempted to enhance the power of the *mukhtar*, as its representative in the village, even though his authority was declining because of villagers' increasing distrust in his role. Villages and village leaders were responsible for village works through contribution of male labor and/or taxation; collective punishment recognized a system of social control based on traditional norms and not on individual responsibility and legal justice; and the familial and religious basis and divisions in village councils (the few that existed—there were only 24 by 1946) were recognized and encouraged. A sort of familial proportional representation was allowed to operate in these and larger urban municipal councils, despite elections.

Finally, educational policies showed the marked disparities between British goals and Arab expectations. The village people were eager for education and saw it as the best avenue towards social mobility and advancement in the face of little concrete service.[22] Emphasis in all schools was placed on religious instruction and identification, which "undermined the concept of national education."[23] In the face of a highly nationalistic and ideological Jewish deucational system, Arab leaders and intellectuals were outraged at government neglect of Arab history, culture and identity. They wanted more extensive Arabization in both control over education and curriculum content as well as rapid expansion.[24] Political and urban intellectual leaders, the middle class in the civil service and the rural people themselves saw education as a primary tool in preserving and enhancing national identity and aspirations. However, "The British ...sought to use education...to maintain a stable social order and to transmit what seemed to them universal values [i.e., citizenship and character]. They hoped thereby to immunize the population against the nationalist emotions that seemed threatening to their concept of order and stability."[25]

While the state therefore sought order, it reinforced segmentation and factional conflict in rural society. However, this conflict was exacerbated in the face of contradictory processes: Urbanization, generational change, increased literacy and the press, education and Western administrative practices all were slowly eroding the legitimacy of traditional rural organization and political authority. Also, despite mandatory emphasis on preserving rural social structure and a policy of interacting with it as little as possible (except for taxation purposes), Palestine was no longer ruled by a distant and ineffectual Sultan. The presence of district commissioners and officers, with their seeming efficiency and control, was close by. The state and its bureaucracy were pervasive and in control of a small and (geographically) defined country. This had a progressive impact on the perceptions of the peasantry. Increasingly they came to expect more from their rulers—education, development, stability, self-government— yet the rulers were unwilling to meet expectations, though they refused to relinquish control.

There were also more concrete socio-economic processes that had a severe impact on stratification in rural society. Especially beginning in the 1930s the social and economic dislocation that was taking place enhanced conflict at all levels. The urban notables were slowly losing influence over large parts of the peasantry as many of these were attracted to jobs in the urban centers along the coast and in citrus plantations. Some of those who were penniless and landless settled in the shantytowns of large cities.[26] Most were temporary, seasonal, or short-term migrant laborers. As will be seen in the next section, they had no chance of being integrated into the urban social economy, whether because of the ineffectiveness of nationalist societies, the social differences and values of the urban dwellers, or because of the inability of the Arab urban economy to absorb them.

The peasantry was progressively disenfranchised and frustrated with its poverty and position. Control over access to land became increasingly important as Jewish purchases decreased its availability. These purchases and Jewish immigration compounded already complex problems. Social conflict, factionalism, and nationalism became intermeshed in the minds and behavior of the peasantry. In the 1936–39 revolt (see chapter four), peasant anger was directed at the landowning classes as it was at the state and its perceived pro-Zionist policies. The stagnating agricultural situation in the early thirties, the general economic crisis engendered by the war atmosphere in 1936, and the growing number of Jewish immigrants caused thousands of Arabs to lose their jobs and added to the resentment and anger.

The peasants, then, were experiencing the severe pressures of objective (i.e., class, socio-economic) and subjective (i.e., transformation into a broader communal identity, nationalism) processes. The latter process had been evolving since early in the century and was the result of a combination of growing Arab nationalism and anti-Zionism.

Arab nationalism was given an impetus by the Young Turk Revolution of 1908, headed by the Committee for Union and Progress. Many urban notables, and some intellectuals from these families, at first supported a decentralized empire whereby Arab ethnic and national identity would enjoy the fruits of autonomy within the confines of Ottomanism.[27] These wanted to preserve their power and privileges within the empire. However, the CUP's adherence to Turkification increasingly alienated those Arabs who called for decentralization and reform. The CUP progressively adopted a Turkish nationalist program and emphasized the supremacy of the Turkish language and culture. This contributed to the growth of secret societies composed of educated young men from Palestine, Syria and Egypt (mainly Syrian emigres) who embraced a more Arab nationalist program that became dominant after WWI. It also led to the adoption of Arab nationalism by the Palestinian notability after the break-up of the Ottoman Empire.

After the British occupation, Arab nationalism in Palestine and else-where was given added strength by the growing intelligentsia, particu-larly its Christian component. Because of a maturing Arab identity, the relative religious homogeneity of Palestinian society, and the role of the Christians in the nationalist awakening, any serious sectarian trends were, early on, effectively precluded. To be sure, subtle Christian/Muslim differences, dislikes and suspicions did exist. Social contact was pervasive at all levels of society yet love and intermarriage were vehemently (and at times violently) opposed by both sides. In addition, some Christians maintained a distance from Muslims and assumed a sense of superiority, engendered, perhaps, by contact with Europe. Finally, in the early part of the mandate, there were occasional Muslim protests against excessive empolyment of Christians in the civil service.[28]

Beyond this, however, Christian/Muslim differences in Palestine had historically been negligible and, in fact, did not evolve into fundamental divisions. Additionally, the Zionist threat led to an irreversible Palesti-nian nationalist consciousness and Christian-Muslim cooperation, both of which took root after the establishment of the mandate. But even between 1908 and 1914, the newspapers in particular, through their strong anti-Zionist reactions, played a pivotal role in setting the tone and context of Palestinian Arab nationalism throughout the rest of the man-date, though it should be made clear that the press during this period reflected a Palestinian *patriotism* within a larger Arab context.[29]

From the time of the issuance of the Balfour Declaration in 1917, there was a growing fear of Zionist political and economic domination and displacement of all classes. (Before WWI, too, Jewish immigration and land purchases, with their consequent dispossession of the peasantry, caused increasing opposition to Zionist political ambitions.) The wides-pread feeling was that Zionism would deprive everyone of livelihood and country. The villagers were responsive to incitements and anti-government agitation from the towns. The townspeople, including mer-chants, traders, artisans, and migrant laborers, complained throughout the mandate about Jewish competition, the high cost of living, and the preference shown for Jewish labor, whether in Jewish-owned enterprises or government concerns.[30]

The press and nationalist leaders made the issue of landlessness and the plight of the peasantry of central importance, particularly in the 1930s. The obvious hypocrisy of those leaders who sold land yet carried the nationalist banner was not lost on the press or peasantry.[31] The press played a vigorous role in getting the message out to the masses, through the medium of the more educated men (teachers) in the villages. Also, the landless and middle class elements (in the late twenties and early thirties) discredited the ineffective Arab Executive (many of whose members sold land) headed by aging Ottoman-educated landowners. The more serious the land problem became, the more the "radical" elements (the *Istiqlal,* Haj Amin's PAP) became vocal and eventually took over the nationalist movement. Zionist land purchases, immigration, and territorial ambitions were all connected in the minds of the Palestine Arabs. They were crucial to a perception of a threat to national existence, a perception which permeated Palestinian society at all levels.

Nationalism, then, had for various complex reasons penetrated the countryside by the 1930s. The Shaw Commission commented that "The Arab fellaheen and villagers are . . . probably more politically minded than many of the people of Europe."[32] But nationalism was unable to overcome the factionalism and sectional differences in the countryside. Part of this weakness was due to British policies which tended to intensify confusion and conflict. Secondly, the peasantry was suspended between its growing broader identity and its localized identity. Peasant society, in general, is very localistic and social habits tend to be tied to the village—kinship and land are linked to the geographic and social history of a particular town and region. And the roots and local loyalties are strong. Peasant society, however, can sustain a multiple sense of loyalties and political community —in order of priority, from the family to the village to the territorial entity. The fact that Palestinian society exhibited a criss-crossing mesh of vertical cleavages and horizontal stratification patterns does not negate the point that there existed a national awareness, but does serve to weaken and fragment the society.

This weakness was worsened as the peasantry was unable to turn either to the government or the national movement for help or protection of its interests. The government did not show much interest in the peasantry until they rebelled. The national movement was unable or unwilling to make use of the growing national identity of the peasantry. It failed functionally and organizationally in the countryside and in the urban centers. It could not offer anything to the peasantry—neither rural security nor the prospect of urban integration or acceptance of the migrant laborers. It also failed because of its own factionalism.

An important attribute of the national movement was that it *did not* try to overcome traditional kinship patterns but worked within such a societal framework to maintain and preserve its dominant role. What this means is that the notability simultaneously led the national movement yet used it to protect its narrow social/class position. Power, position, and privilege took precedence over the nation. Therefore, factionalism remained prominent and led to the severe weakening of Palestinian society. By 1939 the revolt and its aftermath served to intensify the fragmentation because of all the bitterness it caused and because it weakened and exhausted communal unity.

Wage Labor and Partial Transformation:
The Background and Context of the Arab Urban Workers

The potential reserve or labor pool in the countryside was reflected throughout the mandate in the eagerness of Arab villagers to seek work outside of their villages. Starting in the 1920s and continuing into the thirties, particularly with the general industrial boom between 1932 and 1935, there were thousands of Arab migrant workers employed in various sectors of the economy. The construction industry employed 7,000 workers.[33] Arab citriculture employed up to 15,000 in the busy months, and Arab-owned industry employed around 4,400.[34] Also, the government employed thousands on its public works (railway, posts and telegraphs, Haifa harbor) projects, while some Jewish companies and citrus plantations and "mixed" British-Jewish undertakings employed additional thousands.[35]

The reasons for the economic growth were many. The completion of the Haifa harbor in 1934, the establishment and growth of concessions, the oil pipe line leading from 'Iraq to the Haifa refineries, the growth of citrus, various industrial undertakings in towns, quarrying and road work, and Jewish immigration drew ever-larger numbers of peasants to seek the largely unskilled wage labor available. Until the start of the Second World War, however, this labor pool contracted and expanded with the fluctuations in the economy, returning to the villages when recessions hit. Most undertakings, including Arab, therefore took advantage of the erratic and plentiful labor pool by using it to fit their needs and keep wages low. The lower wages of rural migrant workers, even lower than the Arab urban worker, reflected the fact that recruitment patterns were informal (based on village connections) and employers assumed the villager needed less to live on, given his reliance on his small plot of land.[36] This was a kind of cultural conception which determined wage scales.

The years during the Second World War witnessed the tremendous expansion of wage labor. Excluding agriculture, the number of persons employed went up from 169,000 to 285,000 between 1939 and 1944 (including 23,000 members in the armed forces).[37] In 1939, some 183,000 males (Arabs and Jews) were employed in agriculture, while in 1944 that figure decreased to 126,000. The number of rural male Arabs deriving a livelihood from agriculture in 1939 was 180,000, decreasing to 100,000 by 1944,[38] leaving about 80,000 Arabs employed in the war economy. The usual figure given for employed Arabs during the war is between 80,000 and

100,000. In addition to these there were some 30,000 non-manual workers, including those engaged in personal service. The great majority of the peasant workers employed in the war economy were unskilled.

The rural economy was witnessing increased prosperity as never before. Despite the inflationary prices which pressed heavily on the poorest rural and urban strata, the high prices paid by the government for agricultural produce during the war alleviated the peasant's lot substantially. The index of Arab farm prices rose from a base of 100 in 1938–39, to 320 in 1941–42, to 450 in 1942–43, and to 560 in 1943–44.[39] Wage rates in agriculture, as in migrant wage labor, steadily climbed. Finally, the government started a drive early during the war to modernize and intensify agricultural production.[40] Because of all these factors, rural indebtedness declined somewhat between 1939 and 1945, in some areas more than others.[41]

Along with the factors that bettered the lot of the rural migrant worker, there were factors militating against his transformation into a permanent wage laborer. As mentioned already, most of the labor was unskilled. Despite the rising wages, the Arab laborer continued to earn wages below urban workers, craftsmen and Jewish workers. Because the explosion in village migrant wage labor took place over a very short time-period and under extraordinary circumstances (the years during WWII), the recruitment of villagers into wage labor was necessarily "incomplete and inconsistent"—that is, hasty and temporary. Migrant labor was employed largely on a casual (and unskilled) basis, which impeded the development of occupational differentiation and a distinct identity. The rural concentration of the work force and erratic recruitment patterns because of the instability of wartime employment militated against a general working class identification.[42] It should be added that the Arab urban economy obviously would be unable to absorb the tens of thousands of rural migrants (i.e., provide them with proper jobs) despite its relatively impressive growth in the forties.

Dislocation of Arab society in the forties was, then, on a huge scale. The rural economy could not have reabsorbed so many people. With the reduction or elimination of war-related employment, there was a potential floating element of tens of thousands of rural migrants throughout the country. Because of these dislocations, the countryside was rendered unstable, structurally factionalized, and vulnerable at a very crucial time in Palestinian history.

On a much larger scale than the thirties, some migrant laborers in the forties remained in the towns and cities. Urbanization, while more pronounced along the coast, was also a countrywide phenomenon. Growth in the forties was directly related to location of wartime employment in the public sector. Thus many rural migrants also settled in smaller

Arab towns such as Tulkarem, Nazareth, and Majdal, where an expansion of traditional or small industry also took place.[43] In the Arab urban social structure in general, many worked in the service industry and many others continued to be mobile in their search for temporary jobs.

The fast growth and uneven absorbtion and development meant that a large number of marginalized migrants lived in wretched slum conditions, particularly in bigger coastal cities. For example, by 1945, 70 percent of Jaffa's population of 72,000, and 41 percent of Haifa's Arab population of 65,000, were living in slum conditions.[44] With the spectacular increase of migrant wage labor, then, the social structures of the Arab towns, again particularly along the coast, were being rapidly transformed into a mosaic of class and parochial identifications. It is next of interest to note the growth of urban labor organization, its class cohesion, and its ideological outlook.

Formation of Working Class Organization: Cohesion, Class Interests, and Nationalism

In the forties, a distinctive urban working class population was beginning to rapidly emerge and proliferate. Of course, the primary cause was the economic transformation of Palestine brought about by the war. But there was an additional factor that affected its growth, particularly the growth of the largest labor union, the Palestine Arab Workers Society (PAWS) led by Sami Taha.[45] By the early forties the government adopted a policy of encouraging the formation of labor unions. It was felt by both the Palestine government and the Colonial Office that the establishment of Arab unions was necessary to combat their position of inferiority in relation to Jewish workers and employees in general.[46]

There were two principal trade union organizations: PAWS and the Federation of Arab Trade Unions (FATU). In addition to these there was the independent Nablus Arab Labor Society (Nablus and surrounding villages), claiming a membership of 1,013, and labor societies at Nazareth and Ramallah; also, the Labor League claimed a membership of 500 but was affiliated to the *Histadrut*.[47] The Nablus Society was more of a trade union, embracing numerous small retailers and independent craftsmen.

PAWS was the oldest, established in 1925 in Haifa. It was social-democratic in orientation. It had branches in Jerusalem, Jaffa, Acre and the villages of the coastal plain and Galilee. By 1939 its membership did not exceed 2,000. However, by January 1943, at the peak of war-related employment, its membership reached 4,500 and by the end of the same year had jumped to over 9,000. Its membership principally came from Jerusalem and the coastal towns.

Table 2.1: PAWS Membership by Branch, 1943[48]

Branch	Membership
Haifa	4,000
Jaffa	1,700
Jerusalem	1,234
Nazareth	400
Bethlehem	90
Tulkarem	182
Acre	800
Ramle	300
'Anabta (near Tulkarem)	200
Salama (near Jaffa)	100
Ramallah	100
Total	9,106

There were other small branches in the villages near Acre, Sarafand, Safad and Qalqilya. By late 1945, PAWS had a membership of some 15,000, almost doubling over a period of less than two years.[49]

In 1946, when the government announced its intention to hold municipal elections (suspended since the revolt), PAWS was vigorous in asking for changes in the Municipal Corporation Ordinance laws on voting rights. In particular, it complained that a large number of persons were excluded from exercising their rights to vote by the stipulation that they should pay an annual registration fee of LP1. PAWS requested that it be dropped to a nominal annual rate of 100 mills and that persons who were exempted from payment on account of poverty should also be allowed to vote.[50] PAWS had actually made this request for reforms in response to the government's announcement that the public should submit proposals or ideas on change in local self-government.

However, the PAWS leadership was also beginning to become more involved in politics. It viewed the elections as an avenue of gaining support and strength through local municipal and council elections. Although there is no evidence that any of PAWS's local leaders were elected to the municipalities in 1946, PAWS nevertheless began a renewed drive in that year to recruit members in the small towns and villages, particularly those of the Galilee, Acre subdistrict. Between June and October 1946, it managed to recruit hundreds of members in such towns and villages as Mi'laya, Suhmata, Bayt Jan, Zib, Tiberias and Safad. In Safad alone, PAWS had over 500 members, that branch having been established there since the late thirties.[51]

The members of the administrative committees of these rural or village branches were young (the majority between the ages of 25 and 35) and predominantly small farmers with a sprinkling of teachers, barbers, small merchants, laborers, (i.e., carpenters, mechanics, stone crushers), drivers, tailors, and clerks.[52] This drive by PAWS, perhaps, was an attempt to recruit members as a counter-weight to its slipping influence with its Jaffa and other southern branches, which, in the summer of 1945, had pretty much become autonomous societies and whose policies were more in line with FATU. It also reflected a renewed awareness of the need to counter traditional forces of political influence in the countryside, despite the odd fact that most of its members in the villages were farmers and some belonged to the petit bourgeosie. But the fact that such elements joined PAWS, indicates the dissatisfaction of many of the young with the local clan leaders.

The war economy and the relative prosperity it brought to villagers, generational change and changes in social structure, were factors which influenced a change in village perceptions of authority, in some regions more than others. Younger and more educated men began to complain about the illiteracy, incompetence, or corruption of some of the *mukhtars* and domination by single families.[53] In the forties, "villagers began to assert their own priorities, to request councils, and to question the legitimacy of electoral lists."[54] The urban working class organizations were trying to recruit these disaffected elements in the face of little initiative from notable-led national parties. PAWS's influence in the villages, however, was concentrated in the Galilee area, reflecting the fact that Haifa was its central stronghold and that a high proportion of migrant workers who worked in the Haifa industrial zone hailed from that area.

The activities of PAWS and its independence from factional politics, like the other labor unions, attracted to it the largest number of workers. In addition, its nationalist stand, reflected in a speech delivered on May Day by Executive Committee member Hanna 'Asfur, made it popular: "Wage increase is no longer our principle aim. Our normal and legal obligation is to support the Arab cause entirely. The success of a nation depends on the intense efforts of its united workers....Imagine what power and what influence you can have if it were possible for each of you to induce 5 persons to join the Society."[55]

The second largest and rival union, FATU, was communist-led. It had split from the ranks of PAWS in November, 1942, following a Nablus conference of PAWS. It was led by more radical intellectuals who were dissatisfied with PAWS's conservatism. They criticized PAWS for devoting too much attention to developing *Histadrut*-like institutions and neglecting the organization of workers in large industrial undertakings of the north, and for being altogether too timid in its union policy.[56] FATU concentrated on skilled workers and was comprised of individual members and affiliated registered associations from Shell, IPC, Consolidated Refineries, Ltd., and Nazareth Arab Workers Society. Workers were organized at Haifa harbor, the Royal Depot at Haifa Bay, the Public Works Department in Haifa, and Steel Brothers, transport contractors for the government. In addition, FATU had influence with PAWS branches in Jerusalem, Jaffa, and south Palestine (e.g., Ashdod). FATU's membership was around 4,500, although paid-up membership was 2,000.[57]

From the time of the reformation of PAWS in 1942, its organizational structure was based on an autonomous and decentralized branch system. This reflected the nascent nature of the workers movement as well as that of the wider society. From the beginning, the various PAWS branches were heavily influenced by the radical activism, organization and coherence of FATU. The Nazareth branch and the southern branches of Jaffa, Jerusalem and Gaza were especially led by leftists and communists: Khalil Shannir, Rafiq al-Asfar, Sa'id Qabalan, and Musa Quaydar were active in the Jaffa branch; Fahmi al-Salfiti led the Gaza branch, Mukhlis 'Amr led the Jerusalem branch; and Fu'ad Nassar was secretary of the Nazareth branch. There was close contact between these branches and the only organized Arab leftist party, the communist-influenced Arab League for National Liberation (ALNL), led by Haifan Emile Tuma and boasting a membership of 5,000.[58] Significantly, another group which had close ties to both FATU and the ALNL was the Arab Intellectuals League. Led by radicals Musa Dajani and Mukhlis 'Amr, it was strongly nationalist in outlook and had an estimated 2,000 members.[59] Thus, by 1946 PAWS was challenged by rival bodies which were radically influenced.

It would seem that no substantial integration of rural migrant labor within the urban working class organizations was achieved. PAWS and FATU's memberships of 17,000–18,000 (15,000 for PAWS and 2,000–3,000 for FATU) by the end of 1945 could indicate the accretion of some rural migrant wage laborers that resided permanently in the towns. However, there were over 8,000 workers in the Arab manufacturing industry. If we add the transport, railway, port, War Department, and municipal employees, mainly urban, the figure of 17,000–18,000 appears reasonable. Also, FATU's membership was small and mainly skilled, composed of long time urban workers, while PAWS neither made attempts to recruit rural migrants, nor were many of its member societies—bakery, municipal, transport, refinery, and port employees—reflective of rural migrant wage laborers. The latter worked mostly on roads, buildings, camps, and airfields. If there was any accretion from the 80,000–100,000 rural migrant workers to the dominant labor unions, it could not have been more than a few thousand.

Arab labor at the end of the mandate scored impressive gains, as

witnessed by its growth, activism, and independence. There is no doubt
that it had succeeded in forging a relatively strong class consciousness
and a working-class culture. There were, however, forces that simultaneously weakened the movement. First, an ambivalence between nationalism and class organization existed. Given the peculiar situation, the labor
movement emphasized national solidarity and contact with national
leaders. Secondly, antagonism, division and competition between the
two groups weakened their effectiveness. But here again, both groups'
total membership was not great and labor protest was more relevant to
the governmental and international employers than it was to the weak
Arab bourgeoisie.

The temporary nature of the war economy made for weak labor
organization. Given its weakness, labor attempted to strike a balance
between class opposition and greater participation in the national movement. However, the alliance between the national leaders and labor was
not consistent, given the former's attempts to submerge labor and labor's
determination to maintain independence. The political and ideological
conflict and disharmony was made clear with the assassination of Taha in
late 1947. Nevertheless, because of the antagonism between Arabs and
Jews, Arab labor's nationalist sentiment is hardly surprising. Even here
Arab labor distinguished between Jewish workers or people and Zionism
and imperialism.[60] This, in itself, was a cause of friction with the national
leaders. Lastly, it is surprising that Arab labor was able to achieve the class
cohesion and representation that it did.

The central factor that militated against the Arab labor unions was
government policy. Indeed, government did nurture the growth of Arab
unions. However, its policies were predicated on a philosophy that proved
to be detrimental to Arab labor.[61] Government policy, as in the countryside, emphasized social order and harmony and minimum intervention. It
resisted progressive social legislation though it was willing to help labor
unify industrial relations standards and improve labor conditions. Thus,
the Labour Department encouraged peaceful conciliation and cooperation between Arab employees and employers. But it feared legislation
dealing with social policy. The government did not help or encourage
workers to fight for wages and refrained from framing laws governing
trade unions and the conciliation of trade disputes. Most of all, the
government failed to create labor exchanges. This would have meant
political involvement and expenditures. During the war, the Arabs were
at a strong disadvantage in the face of a developed Jewish exchange and
were particularly affected at the close of the war.

The absence of progressive labor legislation maintained the temporary character of labor relations and heightened Arab labor's ambiguous
position. The urban drift was viewed as a first step towards unemploy-

ment, social disaffection, and politicization. Government encouragement created labor expectations for guidance and help yet government immobility also caused much frustration and, after the war, gradual friction between it and labor. Despite this contradictory policy, the war economy precipitated irreversible social change. However, change was uneven, as was government policy, which refused to pursue social legislation or programs that would solidify labor's achievements and class transformation. This paradox, as in every sector of Arab society, was the result of an interplay of internal and external forces which left Arab society weakened and fractured. The weakness of Arab labor is illustrated by its simultaneous need for self-assertion yet its dependence on the colonial government.

Labor's dependent position weakened the ability of unions to establish strong or viable working-class parties. The only organized party was that of the Arab wing of the Communist party, led by the ALNL.[62] The ALNL was founded by Tuma in March 1944. Although theoretically not communist, Communists such as Emile Habibi, Bulus Farah, Radwan al-Hilu, and Mukhlis 'Amr were dominant within it.[63] The Communist element was merged with the left-wing and merely liberal elements on the ALNL bound together by nationalist feeling and by impatience with the negative attitude of the older Arab political parties. The Communists had joined with Tuma after the split between the Arab and Jewish sections of the Palestine Communist Party in 1943, the main causes being national differences. Moreover, Tuma himself, through al-Ittihad, openly made the labor newspaper a protagonist of Soviet Communism. The ALNL's program contained a mixture of nationalist goals and radical socio-economic changes. It called for an end to Jewish immigration, abrogation of the mandate, and complete independence.[64] It also condemned British imperialism and "Zionist aggressive penetration"—i.e., immigration and terrorism —and called for a free, democratic Palestine in which Jews would be guaranteed their civil and democratic rights.

The composition of the ALNL's membership reflected the growing and vocal young, as well as educated and professional groups in urban centers, such as the members of the Arab Intellectuals League referred to earlier. Its spread attracted a considerable number of educated young men who not only desired to keep their distance from factional politics, but, perhaps, felt that the existing socio-political regime blocked their participation in the system and did not give them the opportunities to which their abilities and education entitled them. In other words, a large body of the Arab professional class was frustrated by the existing political framework. Their opposition to the notability, although not fully crystallized or organized, found expression in the more radical elements such as the ALNL, which was about the only party to openly oppose the Mufti and the Arab Higher Committee.

*   *   *

It is clear that the changes that took place among the "lower" social classes, while contributing to the nascent formation of new groups, simultaneously and just as importantly led to widespread disruption and dislocation in the agrarian economy. These socio-economic processes, induced by a combination of colonial state policies, Zionist settlement, and internal Arab dynamics, had a profound effect on exacerbating social structural unevenness, fragility and factionalism. The countryside's vulnerability, being caught in the transition between the agrarian economy and the growing urban, modern economic sector, was to have a direct effect on the dissolution of Arab society in 1947–48. The disruption of traditional social organization had been ongoing since late Ottoman times. Zionist settlement and the colonial state enormously magnified and accelerated the process, ensuring a severely disjointed development.

The emerging working class, as will be seen in Part Two, attempted to play a relatively aggressive, though sporadic, role in Palestinian Arab politics. Nevertheless, as was just seen, this class did not have a solid (industrial) base that would ensure its growth and consolidation. Though its socio-economic development was feeble, however, it was remarkably socially-conscious and politically aware. Much of this awareness, inevitably and not surprisingly, was due to the strong sense of Palestinian nationalism, the effect of the aggressive Zionist enterprise on Palestinian working class awareness, and the example of the Jewish labor federation.

But while the urban workers attempted to intrude into elite politics, they depended on an Arab bourgeoisie to give them structural backbone and longevity. What, then, was the nature of the Arab "bourgeoisie," if any such class indeed developed? The next chapter examines the nature and extent of the development of a new elite in Arab society.

3

Notables, Merchants, and Capitalists in the Arab Political Economy

During the mandate, because of the expanding population, economy, and purchasing power, particularly among the urban population, a large commercial class had become established in the urban centers, especially along the coast. This class reflected capital invested in both commerce and manufacture by traders and merchants. Most of its members were the products of urban expansion and consumption who came from middle-size families long resident in the towns who made their money through their own initiatives. Their dramatic growth in the forties was due to the economic opportunities opened during the Second World War. They were not dependent on the hinterland for power and economic expansion as the mandate offered many among this group the opportunity to expand in light manufacturing.

But whether their capital was invested in commerce or manufacture, they were beginning to develop into an independent, entrepreneurial class. They were continually referred to (by the government or other Arabs) as the modern businessmen or business interests. In the eyes of many at the time, they were the bourgeoisie as opposed to the landowning urban notables and politicians. Their views were considered progressive by the government, in particular because they were tied to the vibrant coastal economy which was increasingly dependent for its growth on the world economy. They constituted an emergent segment that was slowly and under difficult conditions investing in industrial production, regardless of its relative backwardness.

Thus, my contention is that, contrary to the dominant assertions on the subject in the literature, the urban notables did not constitute an all-pervasive rentier class whose economic and political power reached from town to countryside. *Economically*, they did not continue to dominate because a commercial elite began to replace them, most notably along the coast. But the fact that they were losing their economic base, and therefore patronage control, did not translate into political power for the new commercial elite. Economic power and political power did not necessarily coincide and in fact began to diverge in the forties.

The focus of this chapter is to look at the development of this new elite. Its purpose is threefold: to examine the nature of the bourgeoisie, or commercial class, to show how it differed from the urban landowning elite, and to explain why it was unable to take control from that old elite. Thus, some of the central questions being asked are: What was the socio-economic basis of the new elite? Can it be perceived as a class? Why was it unable to cohere into a social class and gain control of Palestinian politics from the urban notables? What was its structural relationship with the urban landowning class?

These questions cannot be answered without first outlining the impact of the war economy on the Arab manufacturing sector, the sector which is assumed to give rise to a bourgeoisie that is not connected to a landowning rentier class. In turn, the development of this sector cannot be understood without a consideration of the presence of a competing Jewish industry, to which due weight will be given.

The Arab Manufacturing Sector in the War Economy

The reasons for the relatively dramatic transformation and economic growth that began with the advent of British rule have already been discussed in the previous chapters. In particular, the geostrategic and communications centrality of Palestine in the Middle East, especially in relation to India, determined the priority of British spending throughout the mandate.

But even by the First World War, there already was a diverse range of local industries, from flour milling and soap making to weaving, pipe making and metal shops.[1] In fact, by 1927 there were 3,505 industrial establishments, 2,269 having been established since 1918. Of the 2,269 enterprises, 60.5 percent were Arab, representing an investment of LP613,000.[2] Finally between 1920 and 1935, Arab capital investment reached LP2,000,000.[3] By the late 1930s this capital represented relatively large tobacco, cardboard, soap, and milling factories, with a growing textile industry.

In addition to the colonial impact and its stimulation of a growing Arab manufacturing sector, the stream of Jewish immigrants, bringing with them new skills and capital, played a central role in facilitating Arab capital accumulation and investment. Much of the expansion in the boom period of 1932–35 was fostered by the large influx of Jews during that period.[4] Between 1932 and 1936 Arabs sold LP4,510,000 worth of land to the Jews.[5]

But despite some positive effects of Jewish capital on Arab development, the Palestine economy (and society) fundamentally exhibited dual characteristics. There were profound differences in political structures, social organization, wage structures and industrial development. Also, the intrinsic character of the colonial state ensured the long term growth of the mainly Jewish capitalist sector at the expense of the agrarian Arab economy. This was achieved through indirect taxation (derived from customs duties on mainly subsistence necessities), a tariff assisted industrial sector, and rural property taxation, all of which placed a heavy burden on the peasants in proportion to their meager incomes.[6]

Between 1933/34 and 1940/41, 56 percent of local revenue originated from indirect taxation, principally customs duties (45 percent), 9 percent from direct taxation (urban, rural property taxes and animal taxes), and 35 percent from fees, ports and marine, posts and telegraph, and so on.[7] In 1946, 48.5 percent of revenue came from indirect taxes and 26.2 percent from direct taxes (including income tax).[8] The peasant in the late thirties felt the pinch in the rising cost of living by paying as much as 10 percent in taxes on his total net income through indirect taxes via customs and excise duties.[9] Arab labor received lower wages as a result of Jewish immigration and they also were victims of rising prices.[10]

On the other side of the argument, some say that a significant portion of the revenue came from Jews as the greater part of import and excise duties fell on them.[11] Also, during the forties direct taxation through income tax became a principal form of government revenue to which the Jews contributed by far the greater share.[12]

Such a topic has almost endless potential for see-saw economic arguments. What is more certain is that colonial policies of tariff assistance and exemption of import duties on raw materials nurtured the growth of Jewish-owned industry to the detriment of the fledgling Arab industrial sector. The intrinsic government bias in favor of large-scale industry already present before the Second World War was especially magnified in view of the need to exploit the potential of Palestine industry so as to supply military needs and a vulnerable civilian market. "At the same time, official policies proferred little inducement for Arab entrepreneurs to reinvest their capital..., so that the gulf between the capitalist sector and the traditional economy was sustained."[13] Furthermore, the interdependence of the Palestine economy never did resume at its pre-revolt levels.

Government policies during the war benefited the Jewish manufacturing sector at the expense of the Arab manufacturing sector in three main ways. First, military orders involved Palestine industry in practically every branch of manufacturing, especially metals. In 1942 alone, these orders were valued at LP8,000,000, and provided a considerable range of inventory for the Defense Authorities in Turkey.[14] By 1945, military orders reached a total of over LP28,000,000.[15] Of course, part of this rise in value is attributable to inflation.

Much of this production was made possible by the relatively large amount of raw material Palestine was allowed to import during the war, which constitutes the second way the government benefited Jewish industry. Not only was there practically no competition during the war as a result of the almost total cessation of imports, but the majority of raw materials were imported duty free. In 1944 alone, for example, non-dutiable imports used mainly for manufacturing amounted in value to LP17,264,590. And raw materials and semi-finished goods, used by local industry, constituted an ever increasing proportion of total imports during the war and fundamentally restructured the import trade: In 1939 raw materials alone constituted 10 percent of total imports while by 1943, that figure rose to 40 percent.[16]

Third, the demand of the domestic market also helped mainly Jewish-owned industry. Because of the monopoly on the civilian market and the colonial policy of strict regional trade during the war, local industry was further artificially stimulated to meet the demand in these guaranteed markets. Jewish manufactured goods in textiles, leatherware (shoes), confectionary, and pharmaceuticals were in abundance in Arab markets. Also, since the military was not supplied with any foodstuffs other than oranges and jams and marmalades, the civilian market absorbed the whole of the local products including canned foods.[17] More than this, varied manufactured products as diverse as lavatory seats, mattress cloth, brass primas stoves, burners for primas stoves, gasoline pressure lamps, china plates and meat mincing machines, besides crockery, cutlery and general domestic ware,[18] found their way to the mainly urban market, both Arab and Jewish.

The result of this situation for Arab industrial development was that Jewish-owned industry grew in those light industries in which Arabs were trying to make headway. Thus, the Jewish sector came into direct competition with Arab industry. Jewish manufacturers were guaranteed access to the Arab consumers in Palestine and the Middle East, magnifying the paradoxical predicament in which the Arabs found themselves.

The huge disparity between Arab and Jewish industry is illustrated by the following figures. In 1939, there were 872 Jewish industrial establishments (firms engaging more than three) which employed a total of 13,678 workers.[19] Handicrafts and small businesses such as laundries, small workshops, printing presses and garages employed another 18,000,[20] while the three Jewish concessions (Palestine Electric, Palestine Potash, and Palestine Salt) employed 2,619.[21] By 1942 there were 1,907 establishments (firms engaging more than three) employing 37,773.[22] Handicrafts and small businesses employed 26,000,[23] while the three concessions employed 3,400.[24] Capital invested in Jewish industry jumped from LP4,390,552 in 1939 to LP12,093,929 in 1942.

By contrast, in 1939 there were 339 Arab industrial establishments which employed 4,117 persons, while by 1943 there were 1,558 establishments employing 8,804.[25] Capital invested jumped from LP703,565 in 1939 to LP2,131,307 in 1942. In terms of total horsepower, Arab industry in 1942 stood at 3,812 while Jewish industry horsepower in that year was 57,410. Statistics on Arab industry, however, were usually incomplete. The Arabs did not have any organization comparable to the Jewish Agency to compile statistical records and the government showed more interest in the more significant Jewish industry. Arab industry, however, was most advanced in tobacco and cardboard manufacturing, textiles, and milling but made advances in metals, cement, chemicals, leather, beverages, and quarrying.

The effect of colonial tariff, fiscal and economic policies in Palestine and the Middle Eastern region was strong protection for the most advanced sector in the Palestine economy. The basic pattern of bias in favor of the more advanced Jewish sector accelerated during the forties. Despite these fundamental drawbacks, however, the Arab industrial sector made significant advances. In fact, the war not only caused boom conditions that substantially increased the Arab buying potential,[26] but there was a psychology of growth, of entrepreneurship at every level. Arab entrepreneurs were being fully awakened to the need for and advantage of investing capital in industrial concerns. It would, therefore, be correct to assume that Arab industrial development would have achieved even greater proportions during the forties had it not been for colonial policies and Jewish competition.

New Elites and Old Elites

As in the countryside and among urban workers, a combination of internal and external factors, mediated by the colonial state, profoundly affected the development of the Arab political economy. Unevenness in structural development continued to fragment Arab society by way of inhibiting the growth and congealing of the Arab economies. Moreover, it directly affected the rise of an elite rooted in a new socio-economic setting.

These facts have led many observers to conclude that the old urban-dwelling, landowning elite continued to hold economic, hence political power. One writer, for example, suggests that a bourgeoisie did not crystallize as a class because it was "organically linked" to the landowning classes (that is, the bourgeoisie in many cases were from the very same landowning class and both were connected through marriage and patronage alliances); while others argue that the urban notables' "property, money, income and power were spread throughout the country.... "[27] Thus, landowning families were able to achieve total socio-political control.

There is, then, little disagreement over the political changes, or lack of them, that occurred within the dominant urban notability as a result of the rapid socio-economic changes in the forties. However, this agreement is based on two assumptions: first, that the bourgeoisie could only come from the landowning urban notables, with the term bourgeoisie itself left undefined; and, second, that the landowning families controlled the hinterland—hence the emphasis on a political-economic continuum, rather than dichotomy, between town and country. Both of these assumptions are innacurate.

It is not true that landowners and bourgeoisie are necessarily the same people. It is always difficult to assign notables to a single socio-economic category when they seem to obtain their income from so many sources—i.e., trade, rent, mercantilism. Furthermore, because the vast majority of the top elite belonged to wealthy landed families, it is important to distinguish between extended family wealth and individual income. It is best, therefore, to speak of the *principal* occupation or source of income of a particular notable.

In one study of the principal occupational backgrounds of the 32 men who dominated the Arab Higher Committee from its founding in 1936 until 1948, it was found that 3 (or 9.4 percent) were landowners (i.e., absentee landlords), 2 (or 6.3 percent) were religious functionaries, 7 (or 21.9 percent) were bureaucrats, and 18 (or 56 percent) were professionals (e.g., engineers, doctors, lawyers, journalists).[28] These 18 were also from the major landed families who attended institutions of higher learning.

In another study with a much larger sample of the elite (100 men), it was found that 35 men were in "private enterprise": 6 were big merchants, 23 were landowners, 5 were big merchants/landowners, and one was a clerk.[29] (It seems the last was a clerk in a company or business and was, therefore, not necessarily a man of means.) Twelve were employees in the Supreme Muslim Council, 24 were in the bureaucracy or civil service (in higher posts), 36 were from the intelligentsia (teachers, journalists), and 24 were from the professions. The sample encompassed every individual active in Palestinian politics and political institutions throughout the mandate (e.g., parties, Arab Executive, Supreme Muslim Council, Islamic-Christian societies, National Committees, the Arab offices, AHC, delegations to the United Nations). Therefore, the appearance of a more liberally representative "elite," particularly among the middle classes, is not the same as a fundamental shift of power from old to new groups or classes or a change in political behavior.

Notwithstanding the study's conclusions, it is clear that the thirty-five men of the elite loosely subsumed under "private enterprise" could not have represented a significant element in the manufacturing sector, which employed over 8,000 people. Furthermore, the elite was not particularly wealthy, as the same study makes clear.[30] In the period between 1939–48, 28 men out of a sample of 34 (or 82.4 percent) belonged to the "poor, middling, and well-to-do." The poor (1 man) were those who "experienced serious economic difficulties" in life; the middling (14 men) had a "definite source of income" but lived on a modest budget; and the well-to-do (13 men) enjoyed "a moderate surplus income" for luxury consumption or savings. The rest in the sample (6 men, or 17.7 percent of the total) were wealthy (4 men), and very wealthy (2 men). The wealthy were able to live in affluence and spend freely; the very weatlhy "constituted a social elite within the wealthy."

It is obvious that factional leadership did not translate into wealth. The extended family's prestige and financial support, however, helped maintain factional heads in power. Lastly, it is incorrect to assume that intermarriage in the elite kept it "organically" (financially, socially, and politically) linked. Unlike the very wealthy families of 'Iraq or Syria, there is no empirical evidence of great family alliances among the Palestinians (and very few great families). Intermarriage is of miniscule importance in understanding either the circulation and investment of capital, or class differentiation in the Palestinian notability.

There is widespread confusion displayed in employing the term bourgeoisie. Because the term is inexact, it is open to controversy and debate, whether it is applied to Western or Middle Eastern history. However, bourgeoisie as generally understood in its European context refers to the middle class entrepreneurial capitalists who belonged to the upper stratum in the towns. In the Palestinian situation, it is not only implicitly accepted that bourgeoisie and landowners are the same people, but also the meaning of the former is restricted to the manufacturing segment. Trade and mercantilism (commerce) are viewed as the non-productive (i.e., non-capitalist) pursuits of landowners, a Marxist influenced assumption based on the proposition that in traditional societies mercantile activity and trade involve the rapid turnover of capital and, therefore, the circulation of wealth rather than its investment in industrial activity. This viewpoint assumes that merchants cannot be bourgeoisie who constitute the transforming medium from pre-capitalism (under-development) to modern capitalist economies.

The meaning and conception of bourgeoisie and other social classifications is influenced by the political and national context in which it is being examined. Strict economic-structural causality does not account for the wide national variations. In a Middle Eastern context, Orientalist scholarship correctly maintains that merchants and traders constituted a bourgeois middle class in Islamic towns,[31] in addition to the clerical and bureaucratic middle classes. Commerce was not, then, the absolute domain of the landowning notability. Thus, I do not adhere to the notion that merchants and traders are, intrinsically and by definition, incapable of industrial investment. In the case of Palestine, the bourgeoisie constituted more than those engaged in manufacturing (i.e., industry).

Therefore, the definition proposed here is broader. Aside from those individuals who acted as agents of foreign trade, merchants, traders, small manufacturers, businessmen, and even the professional middle class comprised the Arab "bourgeoisie" elements situated in the urban centers. Bourgeoisie is not only defined in economic terms, but also in terms of similar occupational and socio-economic backgrounds. This definition implies socio-economic changes in addition to changes in the social and political culture, in the habits, tastes, and outlook, of a variety of middle and upper groups and classes who lived in the towns and cities.

The nature of the new entrepreneurial elements is borne out by looking at the economic growth of Jerusalem and Jaffa. It can be seen by comparing, firstly, Jerusalem's manufacturing and related businesses for the years 1938 and 1947, as indicated in Table 3.1. The 1938 data is from a report on Arab industrial activity during the Arab revolt compiled by the district commissioner.[32] The list for the year 1947 is from the Arab Chamber of Commerce of Jerusalem.[33]

The forties illustrate the phenomenal growth not only of a manufacturing bourgeoisie, but also of the Arab commercial class. For Jerusalem's Chamber of Commerce membership list includes a total of 528 businesses and companies.Thus, in addition to the primarily manufacturing businesses recorded in Table 3.1, there were some 260 general commission agencies, importers of luxury goods and appliances, retailers and wholesalers (in cereals, food-stuffs, vegetables, and textile piecegoods, which accounted for about 125 businesses), and automobile, automobile spare parts, and tire dealers. And there were also close to 150 retail and/or service businesses such as pharmacies, laundries, advertising companies, transport and travel agencies, and insurance companies.

Table 3.1's data, of course, confirms the strength of the commercial and trade sectors over the manufacturing sector. However, the point being made is that the economy was diversifying and not just dependent on the import/export of cereals, the sale of construction materials, and milling factories, businesses most associated with the branches of investment of the urban notability. Not only was there a growth in light industries, but related businesses were created at a fast pace. Lastly, Jerusalem's economy seems to have depended heavily on the sale and

Table 3.1: Jerusalem Businesses and Companies, 1938 and 1947

1938		1947	
Bakeries	11	Bakeries	5
Jam and preserved fruit establishments	6	Carpet manufacturers	3
Flour or corn mills	3	Cigarette and tobacco manufacturers	3
Oil mills	11	Flour mills	6
Factories for canning, curing, or preserving meat or fish	1	Oil presses and edible oils	3
Ice factories	1	Confectionary and macaroni factories	7
Potteries, brickworks and tile making industries	1	Building contractors	20
Candle factories	1	Ice gazeuze (soda water) and mineral water factories	5
Establishments employing power driven machinery	50	Building and assembly of car bodies	3
Establishments employing steam under pressure	0	Diamond cutters	2
Total Enterprises	85	Car repair garages and shops	7
		Shoemakers and factories	17
		Stationary and printing presses	9
		Textile factories	7
		Tire repairs and reconditioning	3
		Watchmakers and opticians	2
		Building materials, brass and sanitary equipment factories	16
		Total Enterprises	118

trade of manufactured goods and agricultural products produced in the district and the Arab economy—in other words, it served as a big market center for locally produced goods and services.

The membership list of the Jaffa Chamber of Commerce in the late forties reveals much the same pattern. However, Jaffa was more heavily dependent on external trade, consistent with its importance as a port city. There were a total of 670 businesses listed in Jaffa (at least those that were members of the Chamber of Commerce, which we assume were the majority), though Table 3.2 records manufacturers only.

Table 3.2: Number and Kind of Factories in Jaffa, 1946[34]	
Alcoholic drinks	2
Brick and cement	5
Bus bodies	3
Dairy products	3
Aerated water	2
Embroidery	1
Flour mills	10
Flour mills stones	1
Fruit essences	1
Furniture	8
Jam	1
Perfumery	1
Shoemakers	12
Refreshments	1
Sweets	1
Soap	8
Textiles	4
Total Enterprises	64

There also were 40 small enterprises, such as contractors, machinery repairers, and printers. And it should be emphasized that Jaffa contained big metal and other type factories that are not recorded in the Chamber of Commerce list. Two examples are the Palestine Brass Foundry, which employed 40 people, and the Building and Construction Company.[35]

In the trade and commercial sector, there were close to 500 businesses dealing with an incredible array of goods. The businesses ranged from citrus fruit exporters (41) to importers of products and items such as building materials, automobiles and automobile spare parts, chemicals, drugs, electrical appliances, bicycles, glassware, agricultural machinery, cereals, iron, paints, timber, clothing, and yarns. In addition to these, there were, of course, a number of grocery retailers (13), transport businesses (i.e., taxi services) (8), bus companies (3), hotels, banks, etc.

The main light industry of Jaffa was in the categories of soap, textiles, flour milling, beverages, furniture, leather, metals, and building materials such as cement, concrete and tiles, typical of the growth of the Arab economy as a whole. The majority of businesses were, predictably, in the realm of trade and commerce and, secondarily, manufacturing. Also, the marketing of citrus and related services and industries constituted a major sector of Jaffa's economy, not to mention the wage labor, particularly at the port, that was dependent on the citrus industry. A striking revelation is the variety and vastness of the luxury and non-luxury goods imported, which is an indication of the rapid growth of the domestic market in the forties.

The growth of the Arab economy towards trade, commerce, light manufacture and services was a typical pattern for many colonial dependencies or semi-dependencies. Colonial societies usually experience growth in light industry, a segment of the economy that is dependent on the metropolitan country for finished and semi-finished products and materials.[36] Thus, a commercial economy is what basically develops, with emphasis on trade and light manufacture.

The investment in manufacturing represented the capital of the more enterprising merchant families. More than landowning urban notables, merchants are apt to expand their activities in manufacturing because of their exposure to and experience in the world market. Moreover, merchant capital not connected with the urban notables was not as economically, politically, and culturally tied to landowning. Merchants, rooted in the urban economy, were more mobile and entrepreneurial than the conservative landowning class.

A very similar process took place among the merchants of 'Iraq, those more enterprising investing their capital in light manufacture of consumer products.[37] The 'Iraqi pattern was largely determined by the dominant presence of foreign companies. In Palestine, the government protected the more developed and dominant Jewish industry, which helped determine the pattern of Arab investment in commerce and light manufacture.[38]

The sheer number of businesses reveals the extent to which industry, trade and commerce were hardly the preserve of landowners and their mercantile activities. The vast majority of businesses reflected the growth of a *mid-level* sector dominated by entrepreneurs and families who were not particularly influential in landowning or who even had no connections with income from it.

Out of the 670 businesses of Jaffa, a mere 23 belonged to individuals who carried the surnames of the great families of Jaffa and vicinity (Ramle and Lydda). The families of Ghusayn, Bitar, Abu-Khadra, Taji, Sa'id, Abu-

Kishk, 'Abd al-Rahim, and Beydas can hardly be said to have dominated the commercial, manufacturing, trading and mercantile activities in the Jaffa district. On the Executive Committee of the Jaffa Chamber of Commerce, only two, Haj Zafir Dajani and Sa'id Beydas, represented notable family names. The first had interests in foodstuffs, textiles, and citrus growing; the second in citrus growing, cereals and, significantly, the manufacture of dairy products. The 23 individuals had interests in clearing and general agencies and in citrus, cereal, colonial goods and edible oil importation. The vast majority of commerce, trade and manufacture was in the hands of smaller middle class families such as the Kayyalis, Tamaris, Himmos, Hanuns, Nijms, Can'ans and Hajjars.

Out of Jerusalem's 528 businesses, only 56 (or 10.6 percent) belonged to individuals who carried surnames of influential or notable families of the city. (The notable landowning families included the Husaynis, Nashashibis, Khalidis, Dajanis and Da'udi Dajanis, 'Alamis, Nusaybahs, Barakats, and Jarallahs.) There were ten Dajani family members in such businesses as commission agents, electrical appliance and cereals and foodstuffs retailers; there were five Da'udi Dajanis and three Nashashibis in similar businesses; one Khalidi and one Nusaybah were commission agents; and there were eighteen Barakats in textile piecegoods. There were two Husaynis and one Nashashibi listed as landlords and farmers and no great family member had any representation in the flour mill business. It should be reiterated that a notable surname does not translate into landed wealth; there were many members of the extended families who were not wealthy —for example, as retailers. On the Executive Committee, a Barakat, a Dajani, a Nashashibi, a Khalidi, and a Da'udi Dajani were members and one Dajani was vice-president. Ahmad Hilmi Pasha, who played a leading role in Palestinian politics in the forties, was honorary president.

Although there were those urban notable landowners/merchants who invested in modern industry, their capital was predominant in traditional, small scale manufacture. Moreover, most of this small scale industry was located in the central range, as opposed to the bigger enterprises in the coastal area. In the wage census of 1947, for example, 15 percent of a sample of 339 Arab establishments (or over 50 establishments) employed 52 percent of the 4,841 workers enumerated (or 2,517 workers), averaging 50 workers per establishment.[39] There was a marked discontinuity or disjunction between the few relatively large industrial undertakings and the majority of small-scale manufacturing. The latter type of industry was located throughout the country but predominant in the towns of the central range. "Many of the largest Arab workshops were located in Haifa, Jaffa and Jerusalem...."[40]

Thus, those from among the landowning class who invested in small and traditional (i.e., soap, milling) enterprises were more common in the interior or central range towns and districts (other than Jerusalem), such as Hebron, Nablus, or small towns in the Galilee. In the inner mountain cities, the economic and political power of the landowning notability may have more neatly corresponded. This justifies Sara Graham-Brown's conclusion about the town of Nablus in which "trade was dominated by a small number of families. The composition of the Executive Council of the Nablus Chamber of Commerce in the mid-1930s is more or less a summary of the most important merchant families in the town."[41]

An example that reflects the political economy of the towns of the interior is the occupations of the directors of the Tiberias Chamber of Commerce.[42] There were a total of 28 directors and members. All 28 were landlords and possessors of property; and they were one and the same, whether as landlord and merchant, landlord and farmer, doctor and landowner, millowner and farmer, or commissioner and landowner. Every director of the chamber was connected with the land and income derived from it, particularly through rent. Capital was invested in basically nonproductive or non-enterprising pursuits—i.e., in mills, education, and grain related merchant activity.

Conclusion to Chapter and to Part One

It should be clear that the rigid picture of a landowning rentier class dominating throughout the mandate the mainly agriculturally related enterprises in the urban centers is innacurate, at least as far as the 1940s are concerned. There were large segments in the Palestinian political economy that were not tied or related to the urban notability or to landowning and the rent and income derived from it. Their role in factionalist politics was minimal and they formed part of the middle and upper middle class *economic* elite in the urban social structure, particularly along the coast. The vast majority of businesses were in the hands of entrepreneurs and urban families who neither had control over the peasantry, nor contact or familial affiliation with the notables. While they reflected a growing social class, they did not have much influence or ties with the other middle classes sharing the same space with them—i.e., the professional middle groups. But notable influence or control was pervasive neither in the urban centers nor with these elements.

The diversity in social history and political economy in the different regions of Palestine (i.e., north and south, mountains and coastal plains) renders the proposition of a pervasive urban notability (in a socioeconomic sense) questionable at best. Socially and politically, there were regional variations of the landowning elite in Palestine that simply did not fit into a neat picture of complete urban notable control. In Jerusalem, for example, the urban notables did not have close contact with the peasantry. The national notability of Jerusalem, in fact, had little concrete (e.g., economic) power in the hinterland. Jerusalem's economic vitality came from building contracting, religiously related handicrafts and workshops, trade, and commerce. In the coastal cities of Jaffa and Haifa, light industry such as metal works, textiles, quarrying, mining, tobacco and matches as well as a growing citriculture industry meant that patronage or the landowners' political control was not so tightly knit, particularly as these cities contained a heavy representation of a complex social strata. The Jabal Nablus area (along with the central range in general) perhaps came closest to classical patronage relations as the relationship of landowners to the peasantry was based on a historically continuous cultivation and settlement of the area,[43] with some of the influential families having actually remained in their original villages.

The notability, then, was playing an increasingly smaller role in the political economy of Palestine. The rapidly growing cities of Jerusalem and the coastal plains contained new economic elites that were gaining ascendancy in terms of wealth. The old, landowning rentier elite was still the group with wealth in the mountainous towns such as the Nablus and Hebron areas. But if this conclusion is accurate, than why did the urban notables continue to dominate factional politics? If landownership and therefore patronage was the basis of factionalist politics, why did factionalism remain a strong feature of Palestinian society despite the fact that its social basis was rapidly being lost?

The first explanation is a socio-economic one. The various segments of the emerging entrepreneurial class were economically too distinct to represent a cohesive and integrated social class. Merchants, citrus growers, and manufacturers did not have any occupational similarity with each other, despite the fact that most of them were not linked to the notability. The development of this business elite should be distinguished from any class differentiation in the notability. Those from the notable families who invested in commerce, manufacture, or citrus continued to identify and belong to the landed elements. This further contributed to the lack of social integration in the new elite. Furthermore, the lack of integration was due to the fact that the new elite was a class in the making and had therefore not enough time to cohere before the abrupt dissolution of Palestinian society in 1948.

Lastly, the growing bourgeoisie was not able to develop independent political power because of competition from British economic enterprises and Jewish concerns, especially in wage scales. Thus, the Arab workers streaming from the villages to the growing coastal regions were "fed" into a variety of "institutional settings," that is, into British (and, in some cases, Jewish) infrastructural projects and firms rather than Arab firms and infrastructural projects.[44] This further helped weaken the influence of the new economic elite.

A second explanation is socio-political. Despite the fact that the notables' economic power and control of the hinterland eroded significantly, the notable families continued to attract loyalty and prestige. Wealth was not the only criterion of power. Social and religious prestige were important criteria for maintaining loyalty. Also, the fact that many of the families had been in important political positions for decades (as mayors, civil servants) helped legitimize their dominant role. Thus, ascription was a central part of notable political influence, Jerusalem being an example. The religious, military, and historical origins of its families and the religious significance of the city contributed to its central role. Its factionalist influence was determined more by its generally nationalistic stand and the *perception* of many, particularly the peasantry, that its notables had prestige, stature, and national influence. Its leaders' influence, moreover, was due to an established administrative tradition whereby the city became the preeminent center and symbol of a Palestinian national identity.

Closely related to ascription is that, while the urban notability *did not* form a continuous and all-pervasive *socio-economic* link and chain to the hinterland, it had familial, kin, and clan connections, which was the way of doing things for the vast majority of those in the countryside. The peasantry was still mobilized on a personal, familial, and patrimonial basis. Its very nationalist idiom was also traditional, reduced and understood through the lens of the village. The non-urban, provincial and local notable families helped provide the political and socio-cultural ties to the urban notability. Although the new elites were beginning to predominate economically in the cities, they did not have the traditional ties (more socio-cultural than economic) to the countryside, as did the urban notables. Thus, the urban notables maintained influence despite the fact that by the mid–1940s they no longer constituted a rentier class hierarchically connected to the countryside and in control of Palestinian society and economy.

But the most compelling explanation for the continued domination of the urban notables, notwithstanding their weakened economic position, was nationalism. Despite the growth of an administrative, professional, and educated middle class, of new commercial ties, of a promising urban working class, and of dramatic disruptions in agrarian society, of patronage ties, the traditional elite attempted to deal with its slipping authority through tireless nationalist appeals. Because of the social changes and the old elite's inability to bring the new groups and classes, particularly those in the urban centers, under its patronage wing, its leadership of the Palestinian national movement put it in a position of either intimidating or coopting its challengers.

Nationalism served to maintain in power those elites who otherwise most probably would have faced serious challenges from the other groups and classes. To the peasantry, the urban notables appealed on the basis of a nationalist-populist-religious idiom; to the urban middle classes and intelligentsia, and to some in the commercial elite, the notability used secular nationalist themes, very much rooted in an anti-colonialist, anti-Zionist appeal, in addition to using cooptation in national organizations, intimidation, and, at times, violence.

Though the urban notables were genuinely nationalist, at least most of them, they protected their class and social position through the nationalist weapon, thereby placing self interest over the wider national interests. In that sense, they actually limited the existing potential to unite Palestinian society and mobilize it on national grounds.

All this, not surprisingly, did not encourage a more cohesive and united society—at least one that would effectively and definitively transcend other parochial loyalties. Combined with the structural fragility and disruption throughout Palestinian society in the forties, this did not bode well for the ability of the Palestinians to withstand external military pressures.

The foregoing concluding statements form the main themes of Part Two. The practical impact of the notability's factionalism on Palestinian politics and society, and the sporadic but real intrusion into political activity of labor, the professional/educated middle classes, and some individuals from the commercial segments, will be the subject of the following chapters.

Part Two:

Urban Notable Political Leadership:
Factionalism and Its Effects on
National Integration

4

The Backdrop:
British Policy and Palestinian Politics
in Regard to the White Paper, 1939–41

Because to the vast majority of Palestinians, Zionism was synonymous and identifiable with colonialism—that is, the forced imposition of the colonial state and rule—the notability's anti-colonialist, nationalist agitation, as led by the Mufti, put them at the forefront of the nationalist movement. This movement, as throughout the Arab world, was largely nihilist—that is, its existence and impetus derived from its opposition to alien domination and it therefore lacked a coherent social, economic, and political program or ideology.

But there was a uniqueness to the Palestinian case even in this matter of anti-colonial nationalism. In the Middle East, most states at the time were led by dynastic, status quo regimes who were identified by urban segments and young nationalists with the colonial state and thus lacked legitimacy. In this region—and indeed throughout the Third World —traditional authority was being undermined by nationalists who eventually (after decolonization) formed the nationalist successor regimes. It was nationalist, westernized elites, not traditional elites, who took power.

In Palestine, the notability, particularly the Mufti and Husaynis, played the role that the young nationalists did in the Middle East and other parts of the world. This is because the Palestinian traditional elite never wielded national and state power under the sponsorship of a colonial regime, as in Egypt or 'Iraq, for example. Except for the opposition led by the Nashashibis and those that were involved with land sales to the Zionists—who largely came from the opposition—the Palestinian notables, especially the Mufti, were not tainted with collaboration or identified with the colonial state. The legitimacy of the Mufti, for example, was enhanced precisely because of his irrepressible anti-colonialism.

While the professionals and intelligentsia therefore articulated nationalism, they were unable to gain control or power or lead the national
movement because of the notability's relative radicalism in this regard.
This reinforced, to some degree, the traditional authority and legitimacy
that the notables always held. In this sense, neither the new elite nor the
middle classes could offer a political alternative to the notability.

Nationalism, therefore, was overriding. Yet, the superficiality of national unity was clear because the society was fragile and divided both by
vertical cleavages or loyalties and identities and by horizontal stratification patterns that were becoming sharper. Narrow loyalties were reinforced by the notables at the same time that social change was taking
place. Although they desired to unify the Palestinians, particularly in
preparation for the conflict with the Zionists, their limited outlook,
methods, and own narrow factionalist bases served as impediments to a
more integrated society and unified political leadership. These peculiari-
ties and contradictions informed Palestinian society and politics in the
forties.

Additionally and as importantly, these facts and the increasing intensity of Palestinian/Jewish conflict in the forties enabled the notability to
carry on its politics without much contact or interaction with lower
classes in the countryside. And because the end of the mandate was
dominated, particularly after 1945, by diplomatic and political initiatives
emanating from Britain and other powers, "lower" politics, that is, the
mass of people and their interests, hardly figured in the politics of the
notables. The complex and tangled situation of the Palestine problem was
left in the hands of the elite to solve. Though patronage connections
between notables and countryside were getting slimmer, the rural population put its trust in the hands of its recognizable leaders. Its fate was tied
to the politicking of the elite, who seemed, from their rhetoric, to be in
control of things and events.

This traditional elite politicking and nationalist politics were increasingly being played out in Jerusalem, more so in the forties than at any
previous time during the mandate. For reasons that will be seen, Jerusalem and its elite became in that decade the definitive center of national
politics. It contained a national leadership—Husaynis, Khalidis, Nashashibis, Ahmad Hilmi Pasha, Musa al-'Alami—in the sense that national
direction and policy were increasingly set in Jerusalem.

Connected to Jerusalem's importance is the role of the Mufti of
Jerusalem, al-Haj Amin al-Husayni. Despite his physical distance from
Palestine (he escaped from British hands during the revolt), he became,
particularly for the peasantry which could easily identify with his person-

alist, familial, Islamic-populist appeal, the preeminent Palestinian leader. This rural support and popularity deflected any vigorous challenges to the Mufti, who really represented the notable social class. Even other notables paid deference to him in the Post-WWII period.

These assertions are analyzed in detail in this and the following chapters, whose underlying focus is on the attempts of the Palestinian Arab national movement, as led by the traditional elite, to achieve its aims between the years 1939 and 1948.

The Setting

Britain's commitment to a "Jewish National Home" under the Balfour Declaration of 1917 had proved to be a continuous saga of protests, disturbances, and rebellions (1920, 1921, 1929, 1936–39) as the Arabs made clear their fears and objections to its implementation and their demands for national self-determination. The slow conquest of Palestine was taking shape through Jewish immigration and land purchases under British aegis, and there seemed to be very little the Arabs could do to counter the political influence of the Zionist movement in Palestine and outside it, particularly in London. It was quite clear to the Palestinians (and Zionist leaders hardly veiled their aims and aspirations), that Zionism was out to create more than a national home; an objective that, from its inception and logic, would lead either to the Palestinians' permanent subjugation in their own patrimony or, as it turned out, the destruction of their national existence. The loss of Palestine was practically insured with the rapid increases of Jewish immigrants who came on the heels of trouble in Europe. The dramatic growth of the Jewish population in the 1930s in fact helped set the stage for the Jewish rebellion of the 1940s.

Caught between Palestinian Arab rebellion and its support of Zionism, Britain's policy towards Palestine during the first two decades of colonial rule had continually fluctuated between numerous solutions, depending on the source from which pressure was emanating. With each successive wave of Arab unrest, the British felt compelled to make a move either on immigration or self-government, later to retreat on various pretexts in the face of Zionist pressure and/or Arab vacillation. London's policies fluctuated so regularly between pressures for self-rule for the Arabs and commitment to the Balfour Declaration that its behavior became almost predictable. In the twenties the controversy concerned legislative councils, in the thirties and forties it had to do with partition versus unitary schemes, the irreconcilable demands of the two communities in practice resulting in London's paralysis.

By 1939, after a bitter and bloody rebellion in Palestine and the shadow of war looming over Europe, the conservative British government attempted to come to a definitive conclusion on Palestine policy. The White Paper was the result, a policy statement that emphasized a unitary solution and that was mindful of the need of not alienating the wider Middle East interests and peoples.

The White Paper was never to be implemented, initially because of Cabinet opposition and then because of preoccupation with the war effort. However, 1939 and the first two years of the war saw a quiet, low key dialogue between the government and Palestinians who were ready to accept the White Paper. But the government's intention was to keep the Arabs placated, encourage the moderates, and continue to talk but promise very little, particularly on the constitutional provisions contained in the White Paper.

There were some among the Palestinian moderates who genuinely saw the positive aspects of the White Paper. Others were interested in office and power; while still others, landowners who led the opposition to the Husaynis, were more interested in combining with the government to destroy the political influence of their nationalist rivals.

Because the British really had no intention of carrying through with the White Paper, they pretty much destroyed any chance for a settlement with moderate elements. They also drove the Mufti, who might have accepted the White Paper if the British were willing to commit themselves to it, towards the Axis and into anti-British propaganda and agitation during the course of the war.

While the political parts of the White Paper therefore did not have a chance of being implemented, traditional opponents of the Mufti and Husaynis were more concerned with obtaining British acquiescence and assistance in weakening or destroying the organizational and financial sources of the Mufti's political influence in the country. Since the Mufti and most of the lower level nationalist leaders and activists were out of the country, the opposition attempted to attain power in the vacuum. They even tried to cooperate with the more genuinely nationalist moderate individuals who also felt antipathy towards the Mufti. However, neither this shaky cooperation nor the opposition's bid for power worked, not least because the government did not desire to be openly associated with the unpopular opposition. These early years of the war, then, represented the opposition's final serious try to inject itself into Palestinian politics.

British policy in the opening years of the forties, which basically translated into an unwillingness or inability to move in any direction, determined the tone of colonial policies for the rest of the decade. The consequences were that the Husayni-led Palestine Arab Party was able to wait quietly in the wings until it could openly agitate for leadership of Palestinian politics. This eventually meant the continuation of urban notable factionalist politics that blocked out wider participation and, therefore, a more united leadership, as the rest of the war years were to attest.

Palestine at the Closing of the Revolt

In addition to British suppression of Palestinian political and national aspirations during the mandate, immigration, as we noted in chapter two, was having negative economic consequences on many Arabs. It made the plight of the peasantry increasingly acute as many became landless because of the sale of lands. Most of these peasants were not allowed to work on the land they farmed for generations because of the increasing practice of employing only Jewish farm laborers. Additionally, the tenet of exclusive Hebrew labor, which began in the 1920s (and which was given an impetus in the 1930s by the world depression and the flood of immigrants that needed to be absorbed), had a negative impact on Arab workers employed mainly in the construction industry, many of whom found themselves without jobs. These economic dislocations, plus the growing urbanization centered in the coastal area of Palestine, were creating an ever-larger urban-peasant proletariat in slums such as those of Jaffa and the "tin" town of Haifa. These political, economic, and social factors, coupled with seeming British determination to bring about the Jewish National Home, set the ground for the 1936–39 Arab revolt against the mandatory power and the Zionist settlers.

The spark that set off the revolt was the killing of two Jewish settlers on the Tulkarem road in April 1936. The Jewish reprisals (killings) against Arabs which led to mass rioting in Jaffa clearly revealed the tension and frustration building up in the last fifteen years of British rule.[1] The mass-based general strike and the rebellion which followed came as a shock to British officials because of its spontaneity and widespread popularity. In the town the strike was politically coordinated by locally based national committees, and in the countryside the rebellion was carried on in the main by bands of peasant guerrillas who acted independently of the traditional leaders.

The revolt was so strikingly peasant-based and led, that the traditional elite which precariously coalesced under the umbrella of the AHC, felt the threat of loss of power and influence as the guerrilla commanders became increasingly popular. Their fear of losing control and positions under the mandatory, and also of being deported by the British, as most of them eventually were, prompted a fairly moderate stance, thus increasing their activity on the pan-Arab level to bring the strike to an end. The first stage of the strike and rebellion came to an end in October 1936 after an appeal by Arab states.[2]

The British sent yet another committee of inquiry, the Royal (Peel) Commission, and in the summer of 1937 it recommended partition. Palestine was to be divided into three parts: A Jewish state, an Arab state, and a mandatory zone.[3] The Jewish state would be comprised of the Galilee, the Jezreel Valley and the coastal plain to a point midway between Gaza and Jaffa. The Arab state would be composed mostly of the remainder of Palestine (the central hills and the Negev), including Jaffa, and Trans-Jordan. The mandate zones, or enclaves, would include a corridor linking Jerusalem-Bethlehem to the Mediterranean (through Jaffa), Nazareth, Sea of Galilee (Lake Tiberias), and an enclave in the northwest corner of the Gulf of 'Aqaba—in other words, the Holy Places and strategically important areas. (Map 2 indicates the Jerusalem enclave only.) The Jewish state would assist the Arab state with an annual subsidy of L2 million.

Despite the small size of the proposed Jewish state (less than 20 percent of the country), it would contain the most fertile parts of Palestine and substantial numbers of Arab-owned industry and include Arabs living in the coastal areas.[4] In fact, half of the Jewish state's population would have been Arab. The Arab state, considered economically non-viable, would be joined with Trans-Jordan under the Amir 'Abdullah's rule. This state would receive a grant of L10 million from Britain. Finally, a plan was formulated to transfer the Arab populations. Most notable under this plan would have been the forced eviction of the 250,000 Arabs of the Galilee. The partition recommendation set the precedent for subsequent such proposals, whether suggested by the British or international community. It gave legitimacy to the Zionist claim, despite its inherent anomaly or unfairness.

The partition proposal stunned practically everyone. It elicited widespread outrage and disbelief from the Palestinian Arabs. Particularly outrageous to them was the proposal for the fusion of the Arab part with Trans-Jordan and the prospect of population displacement. The AHC and the Arab states condemned partition after a pan-Arab conference at Bludan, Syria in September 1937. Thus, the revolt was rekindled and, in the same month, the Acting District Commissioner of Galilee, Lewis Andrews, was assassinated.

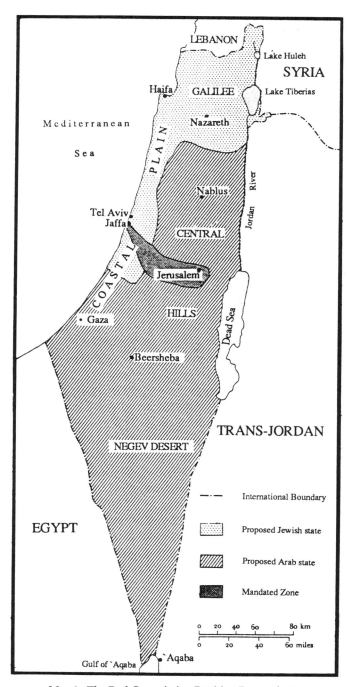

Map 2. The Peel Commission Partition Proposal, 1937

This time many members of the AHC were deported and the Mufti, who headed that body, escaped to Lebanon in October 1937. This British action led to an open break between the Husaynis and Nashashibis in the erstwhile coalition, the latter not only distancing themselves from the rebellion but subsequently taking an active role against their factional rivals. Even though many of the guerrilla commanders gave the revolt its success, the factionalism and clan rivalries of the notables made more frequent assassinations, blackmail, destruction of property, and threats against fellow Arabs by factional groups who acted independently of the main nationalist guerrilla bands and who served their own ends. This represented an effort on the part of the divisive notability to regain control and dominance over "the forces they have set in motion."[5] To regain this control, the notability attempted to organize local bands where their clientelist influence was strong and to use these bands to balance the politico-military strength of each other.

Not only, then, was the rebellion beginning to regress into factional violence by the end of 1938, but throughout 1938 and into 1939, especially in the latter part when the Round Table conference was rumored as imminent, British military and security policy became more severely repressive, and included collective punishment, brutality, the demolition of homes, searches of villages, and mass arrest. Jewish supernumerary police (6,000 of them) were recruited and used in the towns and villages for guard and watch duties and many took the opportunity to humiliate Arab detainees or those in collective custody.[6]

These British measures, plus the growth of extortion, threats, and violence against villagers and townspeople at the hands of factional bands, particularly those supported by the Husaynis, began to erode popular support to the point of some villages organizing themselves for defense with the active assistance, in some cases, of the Nashashibi faction. The revolt, then, was coming to an end by the spring of 1939, a time when the London talks were taking place, although sporadic engagements with the British, plus factional violence, continued throughout 1939 and into 1940.

The White Paper and British Interests

Before Britain called a conference in London in 1939, it was aware that, given the Munich crisis the year before and the need to settle the grave security situation in Palestine, there would be a further explosion in Palestine and in the Arab world if the Woodhead Commission (formed in

January 1938) concluded that partition was the only feasible solution (which it did, but it reduced the Jewish state's boundaries to tiny proportions). The lesson after the Royal Commission Report had been clear to the British government, especially those in the Foreign Office and the Chiefs of Staff—partition was "likely to weaken Britain's position in the Middle East."[7] London was in a dilemma and uncertain whether to impose partition or to establish a unitary state.[8]

With Foreign Office opposition and grave soundings from Britain's representatives in Arab capitals about the depth of Arab opposition to partition, Malcolm MacDonald, some four months after taking his post at the Colonial Office in May 1938, had decided that partition must be abandoned in favor of a new policy. He began to formulate this new policy after September 1938, when the Munich crisis occurred, deciding, in effect, to call a conference which London knew neither Arabs nor Jews would be likely to accept and that therefore would leave Britain free to impose its own policy. And since one of the major ramifications of the Palestine revolt was the involvement of the Arab rulers, who had outdone each other in support of the Palestinians because of public feelings, the "convening of the conference was designed mainly to placate the Arabs by giving them the chance to air their grievances, and to create the impression that due regard had been given to their fears and susceptibilities."[9]

The White Paper, although finally setting a limit to Jewish immigration (stoppage after five years during which time 75,000 were to enter) and restricting land sales in various zones or categories of land areas, was not as clearly committal on political matters. Here, London tried to strike a balance between essential British interests, Palestinian acceptance, and Jewish acquiescence, although ultimately none of these aims was achieved. The White Paper specified that "as soon as peace and order have been sufficiently restored" Palestinians would be put in charge of government departments at a ratio of two Arabs to one Jew with the assistance of a British adviser and subject to the control of the High Commissioner.[10] It also stated that, five years into the transitional period, a body representing the people of Palestine and the British government would be set up to review the working of the constitutional arrangements and recommend the constitution of the independent state.[11]

M.J. Cohen argues in his book, *Palestine: Retreat from the Mandate,* that the White Paper went so far to appease the Arab states that it promised that Britain would consult not only the Council of the League of Nations, but also the neighboring Arab states in case postponement was necessary after the maximum ten year time limit on the transitional period had been achieved. It also omitted the Jewish veto on an independent Palestine state originally offered at the London Conference.[12]

Cohen fails to mention that the White Paper clause on postponement was qualified by the stipulation that the League Council, the neighboring Arab states, *and the Palestine people* would be invited to cooperate in framing further plans.[13] Palestine people fairly clearly denotes Arab *and Jewish* consent. Further, the postponement clause stipulated that "establishment of an independent state and complete relinquishment of mandatory control would require such relations between Arabs and Jews as would make good government possible" (para. 10), which could be interpreted to mean that independence was to be conditional on *Jewish cooperation*. As will be seen later, this was one of the reasons why the Mufti rejected the White Paper. The White Paper also made clear that the representative body appointed at the end of the five year period to consider the constitution of the independent state would be free to recommend any device for reconciling and safeguarding the essential interests of the two communities—in other words, the form of the independent state would not be imposed on the Jews who would be free to demand parity in representation.

Finally, Cohen suggests that, through the unofficial Anglo-Arab negotiations after the London Conference, the original St. James proposals of an establishment of an Advisory Council, which would be possibly replaced by an elected Legislative Council after two years, had been changed as the White Paper left open the option of election to a Legislative Council.[14] The fact is the 'Iraqi model that the Arab states were pressing for in private talks at the London Conference, that is, the appointment as a first step of a Council of Ministers with executive powers and, as a next step, the election of a constituent assembly for the purpose of drawing up a constitution, had been emasculated by the final White Paper proposal. The White Paper substituted a limited number of Palestinian heads of departments for the Council of Ministers; denied any executive function to such heads; and, as has already been mentioned, left the drawing up of a constitution for the independent state to a representative conference of the people of Palestine.[15]

Of course, substantial concessions were made to Arab demands. The continuation of immigration after five years was subject to Arab consent; and the original proposal at St. James for parity in representation *during the transitional period only* was whittled down first from 3:2, then 2:1 (although the fundamental issue of the form of representation in an independent state was left open). London also agreed to place a ten year limit on the transitional period and to invite Arab cooperation in the event of postponement. Most of these agreements were reached between Britian and the Arab states after the London Conference in the form of proposals forwarded from London to Cairo where the Arab states' delegations had gathered after leaving London.[16] As regards restriction on immigration and land sales, the White Paper went a long way in meeting Arab demands. Politically, although at first glance seemingly promising, it really did not constitute a radical departure from past offers for legislative or council proposals. Also, it was obvious Jewish consent on various aspects would not be forthcoming.

British policy in 1939 was, therefore, partially based on coming to terms with the nationalist aims of the Palestinian Arabs, as London clearly sensed the majority of the people were sympathetic to the rebels although they were weary of a bitter and bloody rebellion. And with the ever-increasing prospect of war looming over Europe, the British wanted to put a quick end to a rebellion which took some 20,000 troops, two air squadrons, and the use of the naval fleet to quash. A political settlement of the Palestine problem, or at least some statement that would bring the revolt to an end and allay Arab feelings over Palestine, was felt to be urgently needed.

The British High Command and government officials viewed Palestine as the nerve center of the Empire's geo-strategic and economic life-line, and especially as a communications center to the Middle East and India. By 1939, with the rise of the USSR and the American challenge, the British were reluctant to lose their dominant position in a crucial area of the world over a policy in Palestine that was causing tension between Britain and the Arabs, and was proving to be a source of deepening political difference. Furthermore, Palestine had a continuing emotional effect on public opinion in Arab countries which gave rise to nationalist opposition groups that the British saw as dangerous to their interests. It was, in the complicated and tormented inter-war period, preferable to protect British interests rather than continue pushing a policy by force of arms because of Zionist political activity and pressure in London and Washington.

The White Paper was the result of this kind of thinking on the part of Colonial Secretary MacDonald and Prime Minister Chamberlain. The White Paper might, thus, be seen more as the logical end to British aims and interests and less as an act of appeasement to Arab pressure. Naturally, the two are impossible to separate in a practical way in that the British interests called for some degree of cooperation from Arab states, cooperation which the British could not afford to alienate completely. Finally, the White Paper was not necessarily issued because of a continuing rebellion and general Arab pressure in the face of war in Europe, as the rebellion had pretty much ceased to be of military significance by the spring of 1939. The dilemma was to settle a problem that could prove to be detrimental to British long-term interests, whether in time of war or peace. The White Paper was supposedly the clear expression of British policy to that end.

Palestinian Politics and the White Paper in 1939

As we already noted, the revolt began to rapidly degenerate by 1939. Some moderates in the by then defunct AHC were questioning the wisdom of maintaining the struggle in the face of the political gains made through the White Paper and the Mufti's campaign of escalation to gain the maximum out of the British. The leading moderates in the Husayni-dominated nationalist coalition of the AHC were: 'Awni 'Abd al-Hadi, one of the founders of the Palestinian branch of the pan-Arab *Istiqlal* (Independence) party and member of a big landowning family in the Jenin sub-district; Ahmad Hilmi Pasha 'Abd al-Baqi, head of the Arab Bank and *Istiqlal*ist leaning; Ya'qub al-Ghusayn, head of the Young Men's Congress Executive or Youth Congress (*Mu'tamar al-Shabab*) and a member of another big landowning family with citrus interests in the Jaffa area; and 'Abd al-Latif Salah, local Nablus area notable, landowner and head of the National Bloc (*al-Qutla al-Wataniya*) party. Also in opposition to the Mufti's policies were Rashid al-Haj Ibrahim, a Haifa businessman and *Istiqlal*ist; Dr. Husayn Fakhri al-Khalidi, former mayor of Jerusalem and head of the *Islah* (Reform) party; Fu'ad Saba, a Christian Arab from Jerusalem and former secretary to the AHC; and George Antonius, former civil servant in the mandatory administration and a widely known intellectual and author on Arab nationalism. He served as secretary general to the Arab delegation at the London Conference.

The political differences within the AHC actually existed as early as January 1939, when the Seychelles exiles and others met with Haj Amin at Junieh (Lebanon) to map out strategy for the London Conference. At this meeting the AHC passed resolutions containing the maximum demands of the Palestinians (independence and complete stoppage of immigration and land sales), and the Mufti made sure that the struggle would continue both before and after the London Conference.[17] However, privately, the moderates influenced the Mufti to accept a set of minimum demands (which remarkably paralleled what the White Paper finally offered). And they were opposed to the idea of escalating the "struggle" which, in many cases, meant violence against Arab opponents.[18]

It was not until the White Paper had been officially rejected by the AHC at the end of May, that the political differences between the moderates and the Mufti came to the fore. The White Paper was rejected on the basis that it did not put an immediate stop to immigration, that the land policy "comes too late with imperfect remedies," and that the condition on independence (i.e. that Jewish cooperation was required) was unacceptable.[19] The rejection was mostly the work of the Mufti and rebel leaders and excluded some of the moderates. Of course, the Mufti was sincere and committed in his desire for independence and colonial withdrawal and, in that sense, reflected the feeling of the vast majority of the Palestinians.

Nevertheless, there were further reasons for his uncompromising attitude. He calculated that escalating operations in Palestine might gain the Palestinians further concessions from London. Also, he surrounded himself with radical nationalists who tried to conduct the rebellion from Beirut and Damascus—intellectuals, professionals, and experienced nationalist activists such as 'Izzat Darwaza, Amin al-Tamimi, Wasif Kamal, Akram Zu'aytar, and Mu'in al-Madi. These were mostly men who hailed from modest provincial landowning families and who therefore did not have as much to lose as the traditional heads within the AHC who were inclined towards cooperation with Britain. They, numerous rebel leaders, and the Mufti were indefinitely excluded from Palestine and this was an added reason as to why Haj Amin rejected the White Paper without leaving an open door. Then, too, the Mufti wanted to forestall any claims by the Nashashibis to the effect that their influence had resulted in a cessation of hostilities.

But the Mufti's rejection of the White Paper was not just due to intransigence. In fact, his actions were motivated more by nationalist principles than the motivations of some of the moderates. During the post-London Conference talks among the Arabs in Cairo, 'Abd al-Hadi tried to convince his fellow Palestinian delegates to be flexible towards the White Paper, specifically those clauses which made Palestinian independence after the transitional period dependent upon Jewish cooperation and consent. He argued that the Palestinians had very little choice. He makes clear in his memoirs that the delegates did not budge "one hair in their decision to reject the White Paper from its beginning to its end...."[20] Thus, it was hypocrisy mixed with confusion (because of all the pressure) that the moderates subsequently tried to strike a deal on the White Paper with the British.

To be sure, the moderation of many of these men even before the London Conference was due to the fact of their increasing political eclipse during the rebellion and of their fear of losing their properties through sabotage.[21] Also, perhaps particular moderates, such as Ahmad Hilmi and 'Abd al-Latif Salah, opposed the Mufti because they were passed over as delegates to the London Conference.[22] There were those, like Ghusayn, who also were lured to the prospect of being the men to whom the Palestine government would turn when making its appointments.[23] On the other hand, some saw the White Paper as offering of the best the Palestinians could hope for. In particular, 'Abd al-Hadi felt that, despite the fact that the White Paper did not meet Palestinian Arab nationalist goals, it went some ways in "freezing" Zionist political goals.[24]

Throughout 1939 and into 1940, then, Palestinian moderates tried repeatedly with the help of Arab heads of state to gain some sort of clarification from London concerning the constitutional provisions of the White Paper in order to strengthen their hands against Haj Amin and enable them to publicly accept British policy with the endorsement of the Arab states. London, for its part, kept contacts open through the Palestine government which had an intermediary in Cairo, one Kingsly Heath, Assistant Head of Palestine Police.

The Palestinians who were mainly active in this regard were 'Abd al-Hadi, Ahmad Hilmi, and Ghusayn, having originally approached 'Ali Maher Pasha to act as an intermediary with the British in June 1939. The main theme of these men was that they were prepared to cooperate on the lines of the White Paper and urge Haj Amin to do so and, if he refused, to break with him. In order to do this, they argued that they must have something of an apparent concession to the Arabs such as an interpretation of the Departmental Heads provisions (when and how it would be implemented and over which departments) or a statement on whether Britain even intended to carry out the White Paper.[25] They also asserted that they never opposed the White Paper and did not sign the manifesto of rejection issued by the AHC. This, Ahmad Hilmi claimed through a message sent to the High Commissioner from Lebanon which said that he was also speaking for Dr. Khalidi and Fu'ad Saba.[26]

The most interesting and revealing views were those of 'Awni 'Abd al-Hadi. In his series of private meetings with Arab heads of state and British officials, 'Abd al-Hadi said the rejection of the White Paper proposals was a mistake and that his views were shared by Egyptian Prime Minister Muhammad Mahmud Pasha, 'Ali Maher Pasha, Nuri al-Sa'id Pasha, and Amir Faysal.[27] He said that the Arab states had virtually promised to adhere to the Palestinian views and could not openly dissent from their decision of rejection. But in Egypt and 'Iraq, government leaders were anxious not to give the opposition "a stick to beat them with" and found it "easier" to reject. He maintained further that the AHC's reply was made without the knowledge of him or Ahmad Hilmi, Ghusayn, 'Abd al-Latif Salah, Dr. Khalidi, Fu'ad Saba and Rashid al-Haj Ibrahim.

There were various reasons why these men could not declare publicly their readiness for cooperation and their acceptance of the White Paper. For one, they could not openly repudiate the decisions of the Arab states and the Palestinian delegation. And it certainly was impossible at the time for any leader with any sort of nationalist reputation to return to Palestine and support a policy against the Mufti.[28] Secondly, they could not stand up against the Mufti and risk the loss of political influence (or even physical harm) as the Mufti's financial resources and widespread organization in all Arab countries were "formidable."[29] Thirdly, they needed some sort of declaration interpreting the White Paper on certain points as they themselves, with the Arab states, were not sure whether London intended to implement its declared policy in the constitutional realm. And lastly, they feared they would be discredited if they openly accepted the White Paper and the Palestine government did not introduce into the administration "non-party" Arabs of "serious stamp" and not men of the "Nashashibi type."[30]

The Role of the Opposition in the Absence of the Husayni Dominated AHC

Simultaneously with the internal talks between the Palestine government and the Palestinian moderates, Jamal al-Husayni, a distant cousin of the Mufti, and other AHC members in 'Iraq were trying to get London to indicate its willingness to implement the constitutional provisions of the White Paper. Jamal had shown an inclination to accept the White Paper from its inception. In July 1940, Colonel Stewart Newcombe, a British officer well acquainted with the Middle East and Arab leaders, was sent to 'Iraq by Lord Lloyd on a mission of propaganda, as any political concessions were ruled out.[31] Newcombe went to Baghdad without anything of substance to offer. His visit was unofficial and he was given a sum of money for securing influence (i.e., bribes). Newcombe was instructed to resist any suggestions for modification of the White Paper and was told the Mufti (who had escaped to 'Iraq in October 1939 and had become a popular and influential figure with the nationalists there) would not be allowed to return to Palestine.[32]

At the time, through the mediation of 'Iraqi Nuri Pasha al-Sa'id, Jamal broadly agreed that the step that needed to be taken by Britain towards self-government was fulfillment of paragraph 10 (4) of the White Paper (Heads of Departments) as a gesture of British commitment towards independence, in return for Palestinian Arab cooperation. Jamal told Newcombe: "Remove the fear of Zionist domination and we will stop our anti-British propaganda and cooperate with you." Jamal assured Newcombe that the Mufti was willing to remain in Baghdad and not interfere in Palestine if London and Jamal came to terms.[33] But the British responses to Palestinian overtures were negative, which drove the final wedge between London and the Mufti.

For a short time in 1939–40 the Mufti attempted, under pressure from Jamal and the rest of the AHC, to show a more compromising side. To be sure, Newcombe's visit to 'Iraq in the summer of 1940 and Jamal's acceptance and initialing of the White Paper (in Nuri's house, with Musa al-'Alami, Jamal's brother-in-law, present) incurred the Mufti's rancor. Although the Mufti at first strongly opposed the agreement, he later gave his reluctant consent, partly to see what would come out of the agreement (he did not trust Britain to keep its word) with Newcombe and partly because of his weakened position.[34] Once Newcombe was recalled and the scheme had collapsed, the Mufti's influence again acquired a dominating position and Jamal and 'Alami became permanently alienated from him, especially in his subsequent turn to the Axis.

Ever since the publication of the White Paper and especially after the start of the war, Arab political activity was relatively mild in contrast to the period before 1939. This was, first of all, due to many obvious external factors. Harsh British measures during the rebellion such as exiling and silencing practically all the leadership had a devastating effect on the orientation of internal political activity and on the national movement. Palestinian society was, in effect, left leaderless. The groups or classes that existed in the late thirties (labor, businessmen, professional middle class) were as yet just beginning to loosely coalesce as alternatives to the dominant elite. Too, the rebellion had marked the beginning of official Arab states activity on behalf of Palestine, which deflected the importance of internal political activity. This was magnified by the fact that the person who had the overwhelming support of the Palestinian peasantry, Haj Amin, was outside of Palestine and therefore had to work within the context of Arab states politics in his attempt to gain the nationalist objectives of the majority of the Palestinian people. Lastly, there was the fact that the British had banned any political activity for the duration of the war so as to naturally control any problems concerning the Palestine government's authority.

The main channel of opposition to the Husayni dominated PAP (led by Jamal al-Husayni) prior to 1939, was the Nashashibi dominated National Defence Party. The NDP had ceased to be a political force in the country after the rebellion, partly because it was discredited in its association with the colonial authorities, partly because of the terror of the Husayni bands, and partly because of the self-imposed exile of its major personality, Raghib Bey al-Nashashibi. While Raghib Bey was in Cairo during the rebellion, it was mainly his corrupt cousin, Fakhri al-Nashashibi, who attempted to resuscitate the NDP after it had fallen into apathy by late 1938.[35] Raghib Bey tried to dissociate himself from his cousin, "a young blackguard whose energies are chiefly devoted to self-interest and who is believed to be in Jewish pay,"[36] as he saw Fakhri being the biggest handicap to a party trying to regain credibility at a time when it had a small following and commanded little respect.[37] And despite the fact that the NDP under Fakhri tried to take advantage of the anti-rebel reaction of the late 1930s by providing some sort of leadership, their allies were usually more anti-Mufti than pro-Nashashibi. For example, the only "representative" of the NDP in Acre and a traditional foe of the Husaynis, Shaykh As'ad al-Shukayri, was especially embittered when a Husayni band under the command of Abu Mahmud had assassinated a member of the family, Dr. Anwar al-Shukayri.[38] Also, it was widely felt that the Nashashibis were "working as much for their own advancement as for the country's good."[39]

When the White Paper was issued it was mainly the NDP that had expressed acceptance and pronounced itself grateful to Britain.[40] It not only expressed its desire to cooperate with the Palestine government by every means in carrying out the White Paper but agreed with High Commissioner Harold MacMichael that the matter of the constitutional provisions should evolve slowly. It also informed the High Commissioner that it had no wish to "force the pace" and was ready to cooperate with "moderate Jews" who held "similar desires."[41]

The NDP tried to take advantage of the leadership vacuum by attacks against the Husaynis. It not only propagandized against the violence the Mufti's men were committing against their "Arab compatriots" (claiming that the loss in property due to sabotage amounted to a million pounds), but also lobbied against a general amnesty that might include persons who had committed the "basest crimes against the Arabs of Palestine."[42] Naturally, the NDP also claimed in all its correspondence and public statements that it represented the sentiments of the majority of the Palestinian Arabs. The High Commissioner commented that "It would be easy to overestimate the importance of the Defence Party as such at the present juncture" as the majority of the people were more interested in the direction the AHC would take (regarding the White Paper).[43]

Beyond this kind of activity the NDP remained a party so long as Raghib Bey wrote letters to the Palestine government signed in the capacity of party president. Notables identified with the party in the past, such as Sulayman Tuqan of Nablus, 'Abd al-Ra'uf Bitar of Jaffa and Shukri Bey Taji al-Faruqi of the Ramle sub-district, were now staying on its outskirts in an effort to regain some legitimacy for themselves. With the gradual return of exiles such as Rashid al-Haj Ibrahim (February 1940), and Hilmi Pasha (April 1940), discussions took place between these men and supporters of the NDP to form a new party, either independent of the NDP or by its whole or partial absorption. What brought about the coming together of these disparate elements was opposition to the Husaynis, private acceptance of the White Paper, and an attempt to cooperate with the government.

The first initiatives for talks with the government came from Sulaymen Tuqan, Shukri Taji, and Shaykh 'Abd al-Qadir al-Muzaffar. Muzaffar, who resided in Jaffa, was formerly a member of the old Arab Executive under Musa Kazem Pasha al-Husayni and featured prominently in all nationalist activity until he became voluntarily inactive in 1933, after two years imprisonment. He became a sworn enemy of the Mufti on account of the destruction of his orange groves during the rebellion. It was his idea to form a new party in February 1940 when he came out into the open and contacted Amir 'Abdullah and other Husayni opponents to get support to form the party which he thought would cooperate with the government in opposition to the Husaynis for the duration of the war.[44] The High Commissioner had arranged their meeting with British Minister to Trans-Jordan, Alec Kirkbride in June 1940.

At the meeting which took place at Shukri Taji's house,[45] the three said they did not intend to blackmail Britain at such a critical time and were not interested in personal advancement, but thought it essential to gain some gesture on the part of the Palestine government concerning the progressive application of the White Paper so as to have something on which they could rally other individuals (meaning disaffected nationalists) to the party and gain popular support. They said that it was better to stay away from the word "party" for the time being as the creation of a new party would almost certainly arouse the jealousy and active opposition of existing parties, or what remained of them; that "parties," as such, were discredited in Palestine; and that a non-party movement would stand a better chance of attracting influential people of differing opinions. Shukri Bey said if there was a chance the government would meet some of their requests, he was confident he could get the support of many of its former opponents and members of the opposition. He cited as examples Hilmi Pasha, al-Haj Ibrahim, and Subhi al-Khadra, formerly appointed by the Mufti as legal adviser to the Supreme Muslim Council and a nationalist from Safad. He was imprisoned in Palestine from 1937 to 1940, until Amir 'Abdullah made representations on his behalf and Hilmi Pasha paid a LP500 bond for his release.

The three submitted a program in which the government would initiate "reforms" that would mainly result in their benefit—in essence they wanted the government to help them politically eliminate the main pillars of influence of the mainstream nationalists led by the Husaynis. They attempted to take advantage of the anti-nationalist and anti-Mufti colonial policies then prevailing by asking for the following:[46]

a. To appoint Palestinians to certain heads of departments;

b. To purge the Supreme Muslim Council offices, shari'a courts, awqaf administration, imams, and preachers throughout the country so as to make the SMC an "effective" body which could influence people in "the right way instead of being purely negative";

c. To permit them and their supporters to work with the government against a "fifth column" by assisting in organizing and conducting propaganda and maintaining public security by organizing local "vigilance" committees in villages and towns to keep "an eye open for any subversive activities";

d. To have a "trustworthy" Arab colleague to assist and advise every responsible British official, preferably sons of families with a long tradition of responsibility and leadership and not young men of families "no one had ever heard of" as they lacked the background and respect necessary for usefulness;

e. To stop forced sales of property in settlement of loans, taxes or debts as the value of property was very low and much hardship was being caused; and

f. To speed up loans to muncipalities and pay compensation for losses incurred during the rebellion.

From these requests, it is clear that the notability of the fragmented opposition was trying to gain government support for a whole gamut of political, administrative, military, economic and religious programs that would ensure its ascendency over the nationalists at a time when the AHC leadership and hundreds of other middle and low grade local activists were outside of Palestine. What is striking in their requests was that it revealed the fear of much of the traditional notability of being emasculated in their socio-political power by the Mufti, the middle class nationalists (e.g. *Istiqlal*ists) who articulated opposition to colonial rule, and the peasantry, who did not relish the thought of being subjected to the kind of economic and political domination by the landowners that existed before the rebellion. Thus, they were partly motivated by instincts of self-preservation in the aftermath of the rebellion and partly by personal ambition. They also desired to "freeze out Haj Amin and company." These motives especially apply to Tuqan and Taji Bey, as Muzaffar was probably more interested in revenging the Mufti for destroying his property and hitting "on his weakest spot—his pocket." Muzaffar also hoped his activities "may result in some financial benefit as he always managed to combine politics and profit to himself."[47]

The opposition, therefore, attempted between 1939 and 1941 to make a comeback. There was no coherent political program to bring these individuals together beyond factionalism and personal ambitions, although this should be qualified by the observation that the opposition to the AHC represented an effort to reassert its clientelist socio-political power in the face of the uncertain political conditions produced by the rebellion and the economic conditions that were being produced by the war.

In mid-1940, Britain was facing a critical situation in the war. By June, Italy had entered the war and France had surrendered. In addition, German and Italian propaganda was concentrating its efforts on Arab nationalist sentiments and on the situation in Syria and Palestine. For this reason, Colonial Secretary Lloyd encouraged the idea of having contact with the "three Arabs" (Tuqan, Shukri Taji, al-Muzaffar). In August 1940 he wrote MacMichael that he was sympathetic to their requests for some gesture on the part of the Palestine government on which they could acquire popular support. Lloyd thought "moderate" Arab opinion should be encouraged for need of a formation of a representative Arab body through which London could make contact and through which the discouragement of "extremist" hopes for the Mufti's return could be facilitated.[48]

Lloyd suggested, in the face of Cabinet opposition to progress on the White Paper, that MacMichael might set up some sort of Arab advisory committee as a "provisional measure" as some machinery for continuous contact with Arab opinion was necessary. The committee would have no official status and its advice would be limited to economic matters of importance to the Arab community.[49] This was, in effect, an attempt to gain a double advantage by making no moves on the White Paper and yet trying to pacify nationalist demands for progress on the constitutional provisions through "moderates" who accepted British policies and who might gain some popular legitimacy. And in the vacuum of Arab politics, made especially so because of Britain's hostility towards nationalist demands, an acceptable body to deal with was needed to further weaken the Mufti and nationalists.

After a second meeting between the High Commissioner and Tuqan, the latter promised to enlist the support of the Arab notability for the government's policies. He warned MacMichael, however, that it would be difficult to find many men willing to cooperate with the government as they were deterred by the fear that they would be accused of trying to take advantage of the difficult circumstances of the AHC, which would render them open to a campaign of vilification and possibly intimidation and violence by the Mufti and his supporters. Tuqan told MacMichael that he had attended a meeting at Hilmi Pasha's house in which Raghib al-Nashashibi, 'Abd al-Ra'uf al-Bitar, 'Umar Effendi al-Bitar, Ya'qub Effendi Farraj (all associated with the NDP), and Rashid al-Haj Ibrahim were present.[50] Al-Haj Ibrahim raised the question of the status and powers of the advisory body which the government proposed. He insisted that this question was important because if they were going to cooperate with the government and risk popular criticism, they must have power which would enable them "to do something." Hilmi Pasha had apparently supported al-Haj Ibrahim's position.[51]

Tuqan and his supporters liked neither al-Haj Ibrahim nor his views. Tuqan felt that al-Haj Ibrahim was an opportunist who was certain to put up impossible proposals ("to advertise himself") and withdraw as a protest against the rejection of his demands. Tuqan included al-Haj Ibrahim in the discussions because he was aware of the "desirability" of having men "from the other side."[52] They informed MacMichael that they were content with the government's proposals on an advisory body and were ready to leave aside questions of constitutionality until circumstances permitted further application of the White Paper. The government of course desired a more broadly based body, and MacMichael made it clear to Tuqan and his associates that those who had expressed willingness to cooperate were largely members of the NDP and that it was essential the government should not identify itself with any particular party.[53]

Tuqan had by March 1941 canvassed the support of some thirty-five

men representing the notability, middle farmers, businessmen, and bourgeoisie in Palestinian life. They included influential men from the various
districts of Palestine who identified with the NDP and PAP, as well as men
of neutral persuasion.[54] Raghib al-Nashashibi, Ahmad Hilmi, Ya'qub Farraj (member of the NDP and a Greek Orthodox and Deputy Mayor of
Jerusalem), Sulayman Tuqan, Rushdi al-Shawwa (Mayor of Gaza), 'Abd
al-Ra'uf al-Bitar (member of the NDP and Mayor of Jaffa), and Shaykh
'Abd al-Qadir al-Muzaffar all attended the consultations with the High
Commissioner. What had happened was that the government had successfully deflected the political aims of moderate PAP men and anti-
Husayni men and had channelled their cooperation into periodic discussions of harmless social, educational, and economic issues. Many who
attended were neither PAP nor NDP men, but were interested in gaining
favorable economic policies through direct contact with the government.

It was not that the Colonial Office and MacMichael did not desire to
see the formation of a political party that would gain some popular support and legitimacy and that would serve as a strong challenge to the PAP.
The problem was that, because London was unwilling to move on the
White Paper, it certainly could not meet the request of Tuqan and his
friends for a practical government gesture on constitutional matters to
help gain popular support. And what they initially wanted from the government in terms of the White Paper did not radically differ from what
Palestinian moderates within the AHC asked for. The difference was that
they were more conciliatory towards colonial rule and were ready to arrive at solutions that were also acceptable to "moderate" Jews, although
not at the cost of Zionist domination.

No political party was, then, formed, and the few discussions on social and economic matters which subsequently took place produced nothing of significance and did not serve to satisfy the political demands of the
Arabs. The discussions between the NDP men and Hilmi Pasha and al-Haj
Ibrahim did not come to a constructive conclusion, although Hilmi Pasha
did attend the subsequent meetings with the High Commissioner, as was
seen. It is of interest to note that al-Haj Ibrahim and Hilmi Pasha were
business associates, both identified with the *Istiqlal* party, and were related through the marriage of their children. It should also be pointed out
that, while al-Haj Ibrahim was carrying on discussions with the NDP, he
was active in nationalist politics. It was only in June and September 1940
that he approached Amir 'Abdullah on behalf of the Mufti about gaining
his support for Palestinian aims as it regarded the constitutional provisions of the White Paper.

It might therefore be concluded that al-Haj Ibrahim carried on discussions with the NDP in the hope of gaining some personal power. He indeed stressed to Tuqan that if he were to risk cooperation with the Palestine government he needed "powers" to look effective and legitimate. But to be fair to al-Haj Ibrahim, there was never much harmony between his *Istiqlal*ist beliefs and the PAP, and it is doubtful whether he cared much for the Mufti. In a sense, he did display a certain consistency in his political activity. In 1939 he was among those Palestinians in the AHC who privately voiced their support for the White Paper; in mid-1940, he contacted 'Abdullah on the basis of making progress on the constitutional provisions of the White Paper. In his discussions with NDP notables his interest was to get a government commitment on the provisions. The fact that he talked and cooperated with formerly sworn political enemies and indicated a willingness to start the nucleus of some form of political body, however, does illustrate an opportunistic side to him. In any event, by 1943, as the next chapter will show, he was active in trying to set up a nationalist political party as an alternative to the dominant PAP. As to the NDP, it never was able to rejuvenate itself and make a comeback and its role for the rest of the mandate did not go beyond writing letters.

*   *   *

The examination of Palestinian notable politics in the following chapters must be set against the background of the organizational context of the political "parties" (or, more precisely, the factionalist blocs) that they dominated. The following section identifies these parties, discusses their origins, bases of support and organization, and compares their effectiveness between the 1930s, when they were created, and the 1940s, when most of them remained largely inactive.

The Organizational Context and Background of the Dominant Parties

Unlike the more active period of the thirties, party organization in the forties was almost non-existent, despite the fact that notables continued to speak and bargain in the name of their factions. By the mid-forties, the PAP was the only party among the traditional factions that made a serious effort to reestablish itself. The NDP, the other faction that had some influence beyond the locality of the family that led it, and the

Istiqlal, a political organization that can more truly be called a party, remained largely defunct and existed in name only. The NDP, as already shown, had pretty much lost its influence in Palestinian politics after 1939. The problem with the NDP from its inception (in 1934) was its demogoguery. Its official pronouncements always differed from its private programs. Although anti-Zionist in rhetoric, its leaders maintained contact with the former and were willing to accept the status quo with regard to Jewish immigration—i.e., it accepted British regulation of immigration on the basis of economic absorptive capacity.[55] The second major weakness of the NDP was its lack of reference, as compared to the PAP and *Istiqlal,* to pan-Arab ideals. Thirdly, the NDP, whose strength was based on its majority in some important local councils and the support of the richest families (Nabulsi, Taji),[56] was discredited throughout the thirties not only for its Zionist contact but also because the majority of those who sold land to the Zionists hailed from its ranks. Finally, the party's collaboration with 'Abdullah (e.g., in 1937 when the latter accepted partition) and its general willingness to support the unity of Palestine and Trans-Jordan under 'Abdullah's crown, had further alienated it from the public.[57]

In the late thirties and early forties, the NDP's belated involvement in Palestinian politics centered on the initiatives of Raghib Bey al-Nashashibi who, in any case, largely stayed away from political maneuvering until, in his perception, an opportune moment presented itself for his participation. But the party was too weak, its supporters hesitant to come out into the limelight, and Raghib Bey too old to be actively involved in politics, although he was sporadically active throughout the war years.

It was the *Istiqlal* that had the potential of challenging the PAP and factional politics, as it did in the thirties. Its emergence in the early thirties (1932) reflected the growth of young, educated men who were ideologically (pan-Arabist) motivated and who desired to keep at arm's length from family divisions.[58] The founders were activist professionals who achieved status on their own. They included bankers and businessmen (Ahmad Hilmi Pasha and Rashid al-Haj Ibrahim), journalists (Hamdi al-Husayni and the eidtor of *al-Difa',* Ibrahim Shanti), lawyers ('Awni 'Abd al-Hadi), and schoolteachers (Akram Zua'yter). Its founders also included such men as Mu'in al-Madi and Fahmi al-'Abbushi, sons of provincial landowning families. Another active member was 'Izzat Darwaza. From its beginning the party's membership reflected its non-Jerusalemite (i.e., the center of factionalism) character.

In the 1930s the party initiated full scale campaigning and found a favorable response among the public—particularly the young. It had a core of leaders who encouraged political debate in the newspapers, clubs, and urban political gatherings.[59] It was active in the revolt; connected with the populist movement of Shaykh 'Izz al-Din al-Qassam; was influential with boy scouts, youth, and the Young Men's Muslim Association; and provided the initiative and leadership for the National Committees during the strike.[60]

But the party began to weaken even before the revolt. It was ridden with personal quarrels, financial problems, and the hostility of the Mufti, who created the rival PAP in 1935. Just as important, it never organized itself among the grass roots. That is, it never attempted to establish a mass base or network of rural and urban branches. It mostly wrote and debated.[61] Furthermore, a strong factor in its influence was due to the contacts of one of its more influential members, 'Awni 'Abd al-Hadi, with the various Arab leaders (particularly the Sa'udis) of the surrounding Arab countries. However, these external connections by themself could not sustain the party in Palestine. Finally, the *Istiqlal*'s platform was challenged by the platform of the more vigorous PAP. The *Istiqlal* called for the complete independence of the Arab countries, which it viewed as an indivisible unity, adhered to the view that Palestine as an Arab country was a natural part of Syria, demanded the abrogation of the mandate, and advocated the establishment of parliamentary Arab rule in Palestine.[62] The PAP, while also pan-Arab in character, was more strongly Palestinian nationalist, as we will note below.

Perhaps *Istiqlal*'s advocacy of complete unity between Palestine and Syria as part of a united Arab world overlooked the Palestinian nationalist component in Palestinian politics, which the PAP reflected more closely. Thus, the *Istiqlal*, although somewhat active in the forties, did not command any appreciable following to make it a credible force in Palestinian politics nor did it ever become active in organization and recruitment. For the Palestinians, the threat of Zionism was a matter of their potential destruction. *Istiqlal*'s emphasis on Arab unity and its lack of a vigorous Palestinian nationalist program ensured its marginal role in the forties.

Unlike the *Istiqlal*, the NDP and the other parties (Reform of Khalidi, the Youth Congress of Ghusayn, and the National Bloc of Salah), the PAP from its inception created a strong party organization. In 1935 it established seventeen branches in various towns and elected local branch committees. It also established several branches in villages around Jerusalem and in the lower Galilee.[63] Furthermore, it paid attention to organizing youth groups and scouts. It strongly featured the educated groups, Muslim religious functionaries and some notable rural families. Whereas the Husaynis "closed their ranks in one party, their more moderate opponents were split among various competing parties, thus damaging their position and influence."[64]

The Mufti's association with the PAP in the forties and Jamal al-Husayni's keen protection of the party placed it at the front ranks of those Palestinian parties that confidently challenged the growing and strident Jewish nationalism. Part of the party's strength in the thirties was due to the influence of the Mufti. His prestige and connections in the Arab and Islamic worlds, plus the use of the considerable funds of the Supreme Muslim Council to create a patronage network, sustained the influence of the PAP. Also, the party had wide backing because of its nationalist program. Besides calling for Palestinian independence, the abolition of the mandate, the safeguarding of the Arab character of Palestine, and the resistance to the Jewish National Home, the PAP advocated connecting Palestine with the Arab countries through a "completely independent national and political unity."[65]

Again in the forties, the party depended on the prestige of the Mufti, capitalizing on his influence among the Palestinian Arabs while the Husaynis reorganized and extended it. In the spring of 1944, the party formally reconstituted itself under the acting chairmanship of Tewfiq Salih al-Husayni (Jamal's brother). However, it was under the effective direction of Emile al-Ghury, who again (as in the thirties) became its secretary.[66] The PAP re-established its organization in all the major towns, including Jerusalem, Jaffa, Gaza, Nablus, Tulkarem, Jenin, Haifa, Acre, and Nazareth, with whom the headquarters in Jerusalem maintained frequent contact.[67] However, this time the branches were based in districts which did not parallel British administrative organization. There was the "district" of Jerusalem and al-Khalil (Hebron); the Jaffa "district"; the southern "district" (Gaza area); the "district" of Nablus, Tulkarem, and Jenin; and the northern "district" (Galilee), all of which, by 1945–46, were represented by seventy-two members from relatively influential families.[68] There was an executive committee of thirteen: Tewfiq Salih, Ghury and eleven others, who represented the five districts plus individual towns.[69]

The PAP constantly called for the return of Jamal al-Husayni and Amin al-Tamimi (interned in Southern Rhodesia) and for the release of Palestinian activists imprisoned by the authorities. It also dogmatically held to the position that constructive unity among the factions could only be achieved when the exiled duo were permitted to return. The party found in Palestinian nationalist fears of Zionist ambitions an avenue to gain publicity by continually making protests to Western leaders and appealing to Arab states. With the growing strength and belligerent proclamations of the Zionists, the PAP's militant nationalist stand served to ensure and revive its influence in the country. It also sought to ensure that an effective "hold" be put on Palestinian politics until its leading men returned from exile. Thus the PAP, in organization, activity, and political agenda, managed to slowly reassert its domination over the disorganized national movement and intensify factionalism. None of the other parties, including the *Istiqlal*, reorganized themselves in the country as did the PAP.

However, before 1944, when the PAP was able to become openly active, the other parties tried to take advantage of its temporary weakness. With the Mufti definitely on the side of the Axis and Jamal al-Husayni in exile, the Husaynis did not get involved in overt political activity but were "clandestinely" engaged in preserving the "nucleus" of their "organization" in Jerusalem.[70] In effect this meant the Husaynis and a few of their supporters in Jerusalem kept the PAP alive among themselves. In reality there was not even a nucleus before 1942, when early in that year Tewfiq Salih and Emile al-Ghury were allowed to return to Palestine.[71] Although PAP supporters still existed all over Palestine, these were largely quiescent. The Husaynis' immediate aim up to 1944 was to preserve themselves as a political faction in the hope that the opportunity might occur for them to head the national leadership. And even that was not possible until Jamal's return to Palestine in 1946. In the meantime, the Husaynis were determined to obstruct all schemes in which they would not hold the majority or controlling interest.

5

Notable Politics I:
Futile Exercises in Leadership

Between 1942 and 1945, despite the growing Zionist threat, the Palestinian elite was unable to unite or at least evolve a common program. Though the radicalization of the national movement forced the notability to temporarily fuse their parties into the Arab Higher Committee in 1936, the aftermath of the revolt again intensified factionalist conflict. Zionist pressure did bring about increased Arab political efforts to form a common front, although these usually ended in fruitless maneuvering and further political tension and alienation.

Rashid al-Haj Ibrahim continued, sometimes independently, at other times in concert with fellow *Istiqlal*ists, his efforts to form a political body independent of the PAP and the Husaynis. Many other groups and individuals, particularly from the middle classes, also were actively trying to form independent parties and cohesive fronts, however weak their efforts may have been. But although there was a growing consciousness among the Palestinians of the need for a united front and a clear-cut program in the face of the discussions on wider Arab unity and post-war settlements, the PAP blocked all efforts at constructive leadership. As Zionist political aspirations became increasingly vociferous, the Husayni dominated PAP, with its nationalist cries, had supremely manipulated this potent emotional weapon to cow its traditional challengers into submission. Zionism became the single most important weapon in its hands for isolating and eliminating any opposition and factional rivals. The factional leaders were able to use the external threat to deflect potential and actual middle or working class opposition and, conversely, to appropriate power to themselves.

Palestinian discussions regarding factional unity during the war period, then, rapidly developed into a tug-of-war between the PAP and a loosely knit group of opposition leaders led by Ahmad Hilmi, 'Abd al-Latif Salah, Ghusayn, and al-Haj Ibrahim, the last tending to reflect the attitudes of the new middle and upper-middle classes. Throughout the period before Musa al-'Alami, a respected neutralist, was sent to Egypt to attend the preparatory conference on Arab unity in late 1944, Palestinian politics continued to be characterized by jealousy, distrust, jockyings for power, and the fruitless movement from town to town of various emissaries and mediators carrying proposals and counter-proposals. Increasingly, there was a tendency to rely on neighboring Arab rulers to champion the Palestinian cause. This tendency was enhanced by popular frustration towards the inability of the Palestinian Arabs to organize themselves politically on constructive lines. It was also enhanced by the advice of leading Arab politicians, outside Palestine, such as Egyptian Prime Minister Mustafa Nahhas Pasha and 'Iraqi Prime Minister Nuri Pasha al-Sa'id (who also variously held the post of foreign minister), as to the importance of Palestinian representation among the Arab states or in regard to the outside world.

But even this outside intervention had its limits, as witnessed by the fact that factional divisiveness in Palestinian politics did not stop at the top. All practical efforts at effective measures to challenge Zionist aims, such as in the area of land, were also riddled with factionalism. Banks, constructive schemes, and national funds, initiated, organized, and controlled by the dominant leaders, became the arenas for political struggles, contention and control. The leadership's rivalries only exacerbated the lack of organization, coordination, and unity in Palestinian society. Although, as shall be seen in later chapters, by 1947 the Mufti achieved some success in putting a brake on such fragmentation, the destructive pattern of factional rivalries actually continued into the last days of the mandate.

While the Palestinians were thus futilely trying to manage their internal affairs, much was happening in London. The British, too, were busily attempting to formulate some long term policy for Palestine. Between 1942 and 1945, many schemes were proposed among the governmental departments concerned, but the British government could not achieve a consensus on any one of them.

British indecision invited outside, basically American, intervention. This resulted in an attempt at Anglo-American cooperation after 1945, which eventually led to inconclusive results, culminating in an almost meaningless Arab/British/Jewish conference in London at the end of 1946. London's paralysis, the Zionist drive for a state, lack of impartiality by the United States, and Palestinian disunity, all, almost inevitably, turned out to be disastrous for the Palestinain Arabs.

Palestinian Politics between 1942 and 1945

During the early period of the war, Palestinian politics did not transcend the largely quiet individual political maneuverings that were discussed early in the previous chapter. These activities were concerned with the White Paper. By 1942, the pre-revolt trend of Palestinian politics began to revive. Mainly, this took the form of sporadic attempts by the leaders of the dominant parties to create a political body to represent the interests of the Palestinian Arabs. These attempts were characteristically informal. At times they were single-party initiatives and at other times two or more parties were involved. In 1941 when the prospect for cooperation between anti-Husayni men and Rashid al-Haj Ibrahim (of the *Istiqlal*) was fading, the latter maintained his efforts to create an alternative political party to the PAP and the other parties. In the vacuum of Palestinian politics at this time, al-Haj Ibrahim hoped to become a leader of national stature. Further, with virulent Jewish attacks on the government, the *Istiqlal*ists thought that the atmosphere was suitable for starting a new movement. But most importantly, with the question of Arab federation increasingly being probed by Arab politicians, it was perhaps a conducive time for political activity on the part of the *Istiqlal*ists.

The men of the party, mainly 'Awni 'Abd al-Hadi, al-Haj Ibrahim and (less so) Ahmad Hilmi Pasha, were interested in Nuri al-Sa'id's activities towards Fertile Crescent unity throughout the war period. In January 1943 Nuri wrote a "Note on Arab Independence and Unity" to Richard Casey, the Minister of State in Cairo, in which he advocated semi-autonomy for the Jews within the context of a broader Arab state (Greater Syria) encompassing Syria, Lebanon, Palestine and Trans-Jordan.[1] Anthony Eden's Parliamentary reply on Arab federation in February 1943 encouraged Nuri's initiatives.[2] In this atmosphere, al-Haj Ibrahim sent a message to Nuri in early 1943 "suggesting the calling in the near future of a 'representative Arab Conference' which would discuss Arab Unity."[3] About the same time, 'Abd al-Hadi wrote Nuri a stirring letter from Jerusalem concerning the need for unity and the inseparability of Palestinian and 'Iraqi interests.[4]

Nuri corresponded with Arab nationalists and encouraged these kinds of initiatives, hoping to form a semi-official or popular consensus for his scheme. At the beginning of his consultations with Nahhas Pasha over the formation of a regional body, Nuri had been hoping that 'Iraq and Greater Syria would form a natural geographic and economic entity within a league (headed by the Hashemites) which Sa'udi Arabia and Egypt could join after its formation. The *Istiqlal* leaders hoped to unite the Palestinian Arabs among themselves and behind Arab unity. Nuri supported their internal activities.

Private discussions took place between al-Haj Ibrahim and 'Awni 'Abd al-Hadi and Ahmad Hilmi Pasha, who were interested in initiating a new beginning for the *Istiqlal*.[5] Their initiatives, however, were not necessarily coordinated nor cohesive. In December 1942, at a conference of Arab chambers of commerce held at Haifa, al-Haj Ibrahim, in his capacity as chairman of the Haifa Chamber of Commerce, introduced the idea of forming a political body to represent Arabs. It was normal for the Arab chambers of commerce to pass political as well as economic resolutions. In the fragmented and colonially repressed atmoshpere of Palestinian politics, almost any organized body of whatever purpose linked politics with its other interests. Moreover, the chambers represented many of the new commercial elite. The chambers' conference decided to convene a general conference of leading Palestinians to "create an Arab political body by electing an Executive Committee to represent and speak for the Arabs of Palestine."[6]

A conference was held in Haifa in February 1943, attended by a large number of the leading men of Haifa. Al-Haj Ibrahim was elected the head of a committee which was charged with organizing and convening a general Arab meeting to elect a permanent executive body to speak on behalf of the Palestinians. This was a clear attempt on the part of al-Haj Ibrahim to take the wind out of the PAP, although he was careful to call for a general Arab consensus. But the fact that the February conference was mainly attended by Haifa men suggested the area of al-Haj Ibrahim's influence and his limitations in inspiring unity among the factions. Al-Haj Ibrahim's efforts eventually came to nothing, especially as the PAP claimed that the Haifa meeting was sanctioned by the local authorities and attacked the movement as being one of "puppet opposition" to the mandatory government. The PAP partisans managed to terminate the movement at its conception, and the people of Haifa distanced themselves from al-Haj Ibrahim.[7] The weight of activity shifted to the secretary of the defunct *Istiqlal*, 'Awni 'Abd al-Hadi, and to other faction leaders.

At about the same time that al-Haj Ibrahim was active in early 1943, discussions and consultations took place in Jerusalem between 'Abd al-Hadi, Dr. Husayn Fakhri al-Khalidi of the Reform party, Ahmad Hilmi Pasha, and Ya'qub al-Ghusayn of the Youth Congress, over the formation of a representative political committee that would encompass the leaders of the various factions.[8] The secretary of the PAP, Emile al-Ghury, made it clear that the PAP disagreed with any political initiative at that time. He insisted that the Mufti's and Jamal's absence from the country did not mean these men forfeited their right to be the active heads of any political movement, and that any political initiative emanating from any other party was based on acceptance of the White Paper, which the PAP considered as a treasonous act.[9] 'Abd al-Hadi and the others tried to convince the PAP that their efforts to reestablish a political organization did not have any connection with the White Paper. They argued that it was imperative to form a committee that would represent the Palestinians at the impending Arab unity discussions.[10]

There is no evidence that al-Haj Ibrahim's initiatives were covertly sanctioned by the colonial authorities nor that 'Abd al-Hadi and the others desired to form a political body for any reason connected with acceptance of the White Paper. Although the PAP made such allegations to weaken any challenges to it, the Husaynis were not aware of the discussions al-Haj Ibrahim had with NDP men in 1941, nor of 'Abd al-Hadi's and Ghusayn's secret contacts with the British in 1939 concerning their acceptance of the White Paper. In all probability the main concern of these men was to form a united front, mixed with personal ambitions. However, the mandatory authorities were not against any alternative or opposition challenge to what they regarded as Husayni intransigence. After 1941, British support for such opposition did not take the form of intervention, active assistance or consultations. Simply, the authorities hoped that the PAP would lose influence in Palestinian politics. As for the PAP, although it attacked the White Paper or anyone who supported it, the fact was Jamal al-Husayni had indicated his willingness to accept it in 1939.

Further, most thoughtful Palestinians had by 1943 supported and adhered to the White Paper, regarding it as their best hope in the face of Zionist aggressiveness. It was clear from Arab leaders talking to the British on behalf of the Palestinians that the Arabs in and outside of Palestine feared any other alternative to the White Paper. It was also fairly clear that Husayni tactics were to use the White Paper, identified by the mass of people with evil colonial designs, as an intimidatory weapon against any potential opposition. For while Jamal may have been more amenable to moderation, Haj Amin's uncompromising nationalism still prevailed. Though the Mufti was out of the country, the strength of his influence was great and would grow greater still as Zionist statements and terrorism became more provocative.

During October 1943 Nuri Pasha, in an effort to help unite the Palestinian factions in time for the Arab unity discussions, came to Jerusalem and met with, among others, Ahmad Hilmi Pasha, Raghib al-Nashashibi, 'Awni 'Abd al-Hadi, Dr. Husayn al-Khalidi, Rafiq al-Tamimi, and Musa al-'Alami. Nuri's efforts were unsuccessful as the PAP, which was not invited but took part after finding out about the meeting, insisted on having the majority of representation in any new political body. Nuri's was a brief effort and was more in line with his scheme to get the Palestinians, along with Syria and 'Iraq, to sign a memorandum he proposed to prepare and submit to London, asking for the early formation of Greater Syria (i.e., Syria, Trans-Jordan, Palestine, Lebanon). It was for this reason that some of those Palestinians (other than the PAP men) who met with Nuri were amenable to some of his pan-Arabist concepts.[11]

Before a new Arab Higher Committee (the old AHC being disbanded by the authorities in 1937) was constituted in November 1945 and the Mufti again became a dominating force by late 1946, there were a few more spasmodic attempts at forming a political body. At the initiative of al-Haj Ibrahim, a popular meeting was held in Jaffa on 8 May 1945 for the purpose of organizing an Arab Front. The movement arose from the rivalry between the National Bank of Ahmad Hilmi Pasha and the Arab Bank of 'Abd al-Hamid Shuman, his father-in-law, and was an attempt at promoting unity among the factions.[12] The Front, which was short-lived, called for three things: the coalescing of all "general affairs" and social, cultural and economic "clubs" in Jaffa under a "national pact"; the unity of all factions in Palestine and the creation of an AHC to represent the Palestinians at the Arab League; and the "defense" of the Palestine question under a "national pact."[13]

The Front was the second attempt by al-Haj Ibrahim, after his Haifa initiatives in 1943, to start a popular movement for unity. The members who attended the first and only session of the Front were men of lesser families who reflected the impatience of a younger generation with factional politics. Two other meetings were held in Jaffa in the same month by other groups. A meeting with the same declared object was actually held on 4 May in the house of Ya'qub al-Ghusayn, chairman of the Youth Congress Party, and on 11 May representatives of the Arab clubs of Jaffa held a gathering at which a note for unity was sounded.[14]

In late 1945, an attempt was made to set the ground for the creation of a *Hizb al-Sha'b* (People's Party). Before it was launched, *al-Wihda* (The Unity) newspaper published what was intended by the People's Party to be a secret document containing details of their convention.[15] The weekly newspaper was founded by Emile al-Ghury in mid-1945 as an official organ of the PAP.[16] The document had fallen into the hands of a member of the *Istiqlal* through a discontented dissenter.[17] The party was composed of younger people not too closely allied to any of the existing parties and was quietly preparing itself in the guise of sports and cultural clubs and private discussions.[18] For example, the Nablus branch members of the party, Dr. Salih Din al-'Anabtawi, Muhammad al-'Awad and Malik al-Masri, all were members of the local Sports Club.[19]

After the activities of the People's Party became public and were received with hostility by the existing parties, in particular the PAP, its promoters were frightened and denied any connection with it.[20] Finally, in October 1945 a meeting was held at the Alhambra cinema in Jaffa for the purpose of promoting party unity. All political parties, except the PAP, were represented, and a delegation from neighboring Arab states also attended. There was a great deal of oratory but no concrete results were achieved.[21]

It should be noted that during 1944 a new "party" was formed, the Palestine Arab *Taqaddum* (Progressive) Party. The party called for a vague program of self-government as a preliminary step towards independence, thus implying a moderation consistent with the White Paper.[22] The party was centered in Nablus, where its president, Ihsan al-Nimr, lived. Al-Nimr was a member of one of the better known families in the Nablus area.[23] The ineffectiveness and limited outlook of the party is illustrated by some of the representations it made to the High Commissioner. In one complaint, al-Nimr called on the High Commissioner to abolish the "Jewish" place names of the various administrative districts (for example, the Galilee district should revert to its Ottoman place name, *mutasarrifa* of Safad), as the existing place names would "badly affect British officers and others."[24] In another representation al-Nimr reasoned that the Arabs of Palestine were "highly cultured and not less civilized than the other Arab peoples in intelligence" and therefore ready for independence.[25]

During November 1945, Syrian Prime Minister Jamil Mardam Bey, like Nuri Pasha almost two years before him, was sent to Palestine by the Arab League Council to help the Palestinians form a united party or body. Mardam Bey was chairman of the then current session of the League Council, which sat continuously from 31 October to 14 December 1945. The Arab initiative did not arise out of a vacuum. Throughout 1945, with the Palestinians unable to achieve agreement, there was continuous correspondence (letters, telegrams) between the dominant parties and Arab politicians. The Palestinian notables increasingly began to appeal to the Arab states and politicians for help in sorting out their affairs. Mardam Bey's visit actually was encouraged by the Husayni dominated PAP, which in November 1945 sent two telegrams to him asking the Arabs to help the Palestinians achieve a representative body.[26]

Initial agreement between the parties was again made difficult by the PAP's insistence on its right to have the majority of members. However, the deadlock was broken when the parties asked Mardam Bey to appoint a higher committee from among them, implying that they would abide by his choices. Mardam Bey wisely chose the leaders of the six factional parties and left the rest up to them. A new Arab Higher Committee was announced in late November, consisting of twelve members.

Table 5.1: Representation on the AHC Formed In November 1945[27]

PAP: Tewfiq Salih al-Husayni, Rafiq al-Tamimi, Emile al-Ghury, Yusif Sahyun, Kamil al-Dajani

---

Table 5.1: (cont)

NDP: Raghib al-Nashashibi
Youth Congress: Ya'qub al-Ghusayn
National Bloc: 'Abd al-Latif Salah
Reform: Dr. Husayn al-Khalidi
Istiqlal: 'Awni 'Abd al-Hadi
Independent Members: Ahmad Hilmi Pasha, Musa al-'Alami

The AHC would have a rotating chairman, chosen at each AHC session. Also they were allowed three representatives at League sessions, agreeing among themselves to rotate their delegates for each League meeting.

The AHC did not last very long because it was based on compromises that neither the PAP nor the other parties genuinely wanted to make. Although the PAP had five members on the AHC, the rotating chairman and the positions of Hilmi and 'Alami as independents had put a check on the party's dictatorial ambitions. Likewise, the other parties were resentful that one party should represent almost half the members of the AHC.

If anything, these desultory attempts at political unity and party creation illustrate the limited social outlook of the dominant classes. The emotional issue of Zionism, used by the Mufti and the Husaynis to snuff out any opposition, had compelled most Palestinian Arabs to rally around the dominant symbols and institutions that were in active opposition to Jewish nationalism—Arab nationalism, the AHC, the Arab National Fund, Musa al-'Alami's Arab Offices, and the Arab Bank. In the urban centers a restless younger generation was anxious and impatient with the fruitless activity and intrigues of the dominant leaders, as witnessed by the attempted creation of the People's Party and the Arab Higher Front. But they were weak in the face of demogogic opposition from the dominant parties.

Increasingly, as the Mufti's influence was rising (especially with the peasantry) upon his return to the Middle East in 1946, the PAP began to gain the upper hand. Its sheer energy, constant activity, and persistence of theme had exhausted and overshadowed the other traditional challengers. They, too, began to succumb to a party that maintained a vigorous facade of strength, unity, and energy. By 1945, any person or party had to voice protestations similar to those of the PAP to survive. For instance, Ghusayn's Youth Congress, the *Taqaddum* Party, the Reform Party and the National Bloc made continual representations to the High Commissioner that called for an end to illegal immigration and land transfers, that pointed out the Zionist threat to Arab national existence, and that called for disarmament of the various military organizations of the *Yishuv,* the Jewish colony.[28]

The immediate issue of the Zionist threat became overriding, and the frustration of being unable to unite, made so especially because of Husayni opposition, played into the hands of an intransigent PAP. In a national meeting the party held in Jerusalem in June 1945 (the party claimed 5,000 attendants), the following resolutions were passed: the party's attachment to the Mufti's leadership and a request for the return of Jamal al-Husayni; independence and the establishment of an Arab government; Arab unity; abolition of the Jewish National Home; and the stopping of immigration and land sales.[29] These demands reflected the basic wishes of the majority of the Palestinian Arabs and for that reason sustained the popularity of the PAP. The PAP's consistency in voicing these demands and its aggressively confident posture in the midst of a disorganized and disunited social milieu converged to demoralize its challengers. By 1947, almost all the other dominant party leaders were paying homage to the Mufti.

Banks as Factional Fronts:
The Bankruptcy of Political Organization

The appointment of Musa al-'Alami as the all-party representative at the Arab unity talks raised hopes that it would be followed by a modicum of cooperation. Even before 'Alami's return from Cairo in March 1945, however, new lines of cleavage began to appear whose fronts, oddly enough, were based on banks rather than parties. The issues continued to be based mostly on personal ambitions rather than political principles. On the one side stood Ahmad Hilmi Pasha, the Arab National Bank, the National Fund (*Sanduq al-Umma*), *Filastin* newspaper, and a group of leaders opposing the Husaynis: 'Awni 'Abd al-Hadi, Dr. Husayn al-Khalidi, 'Abd al-Latif Salah, Sulayman Tuqan and others. On the other side was the Palestine Arab Bank under 'Abd al-Hamid Shuman working in tacit alliance with the PAP, and their supporter, *al-Difa'* newspaper.[30] In the midst of the chaos of Palestinian Arab politics in mid-1945, Ahmad Hilmi, chairman of the National Bank and president of the National Fund, launched a campaign to catapult himself to a dominant position in Arab political life through the medium of the Fund.

The National Fund had been in existence since the thirties. It was established in 1932–33 as a central fund raising body of the national movement and became a land buying company on behalf of the Arab Executive. Its main purpose was to prevent Arab land from falling into Jewish hands and to generally function like the Zionist land buying organizations of the Jewish Agency. In July 1935 it was officially registered as a company, its declared objective then being to purchase, acquire and manage lease land

and immovable property in order to cultivate and build upon it.[31] Its reactivation in 1935 was mainly due to the personal efforts of Ahmad Hilmi Pasha. The Fund, however, was limited through faulty organization, internal disagreement, and an apathetic public.[32]

Although the Fund became inactive at the outbreak of the revolt in 1936, in 1944 it was again revived by Ahmad Hilmi in the face of intensified Zionist activity to purchase land. In the Gaza district alone, for example, 13,000 *dunum*s of land had passed into Jewish hands by 1945 (that is, since the Land Transfer Regulations took effect in 1940).[33] Manipulation of the provisions in the Land Regulations was commonly practiced by brokers and middle men acting between Arab landowners and Jewish buyers. Such transfers not only caused animosity towards families who sold their land to the Zionists, but local committees of the Fund were independently formed which issued pamphlets attacking brokers and openly threatened reprisals.[34]

In addition, many independent, extremist groups sprang up from among the marginalized poor and migrant workers and populist elements in the towns and villages. Besides the socio-economic causes, these groups were a radicalized response to Zionist terrorism, Jewish immigration, and Arab land sales. Two organizations in particular, the *I'tissam* (guardian) Society and the underground "Arab Blood Society," not only preached against the Zionists but against land sales and brokers.[35] These two were religious-nationalist organizations which, although tiny, were fanatical in their inculcation and beliefs. The Arab Blood Society in particular was an underground organization which came into existence specifically for the intimidation of land brokers. It was active in the Jaffa and Tulkarem areas, and was particularly strong among the poorer sections of Jaffa.[36] A number of cases of land broker murders in fact occurred, starting in February 1945, along with various acts of violence, intimidation, and extortion from merchants who were thought to have dealings with Jews.[37]

Associated with the two above were a host of minor organizations such as "The Committee for the Revival of the Arab Days," "The Committee of the Quran Councils,"[38] and "The Iron Hand," the latter located in Galilee. The Iron Hand in 1945 sent out pamphlets to land brokers, inscribed with a revolver and flaming torch, warning them of land sales to the Jews.[39] In the Galilee district especially, there were long-standing disputes between cultivators and absentee landowners (e.g. there was a dispute with the Sursuq family of Lebanon over 10,000 *dunum*s of land east of Nazaerth) that embittered the peasants.[40] And in the Huleh area, it was common knowledge that the Lebanese Khury family, who owned thousands of *dunum*s at the village of Zabuba, was considering selling 3,000 *dunum*s of the area to the Jews at a price of some LP300,000.[41] These land sales and potential land sales rendered the Fund and its director highly popular.

The Fund's board of directors in 1944 reflected the efforts of Ahmad Hilmi and the opposition leaders to use it as a vehicle towards gaining political influence and power. While in 1935 the board of directors included Jamal al-Husayni and Fu'ad Saba (treasurer to the AHC and a PAP man), in 1944 it was reconstituted as follows: Ahmad Hilmi, Rashid al-Haj Ibrahim, 'Umar al-Bitar, 'Awni 'Abd al-Hadi, Ya'qub al-Ghusayn, Rushdi al-Shawwa (Gaza), and Dr. 'Izzat Tannus (Jerusalem), all men opposed to the PAP. The board also contained non-party men who leaned towards opposition to the Husaynis.[42] By 1945, Ahmad Hilmi and his allies decided to separate the administration of the Fund from the National Bank and to appoint paid officials.[43] This step was taken because there still was a Husayni presence on the board of directors of the National Bank and it coincided with Ahmad Hilmi's initiative of consulting with opposition leaders to form a new AHC. Conversations to that end took place in Jerusalem with 'Abd al-Hadi, Dr. Khalidi, Ghusayn, and 'Abd al-Latif Salah.[44] In March 1945, Sulayman Tuqan (then still mayor of Nablus), Dr. Khalidi, and 'Issa Effendi al-'Issa (proprietor of *Filastin* newspapter in Jaffa) joined the board of directors of the National Bank, of which 'Abd al-Hadi was also a member, in addition to his position on the Fund.[45] Significantly, these men were given salaries of L400 a year although they had no banking experience.

The new AHC never materialized, primarily because Ahmad Hilmi was unable to weaken or detach from the National Bank Husayni members of the PAP. It also failed because Raghib al-Nashashibi, still titular head of the NDP, was unwilling to cooperate or to allow Sulayman Tuqan to effectively act in his place.[46]

Between these maneuverings stood Musa al-'Alami. The unexpected personal success of 'Alami in Egypt, and especially his meetings with Kings Faruq and Ibn Sa'ud, aroused the opposition of some Palestinian notables, especially men such as 'Abd al-Hadi, Dr. Khalidi, and Ghusayn. ('Abd al-Hadi and PAP man Emile al-Ghury had in fact left for Egypt during 'Alami's mission to renew their own contacts with Arab statesmen gathered there.[47]) Perhaps part of the reason for these men's alignment with Ahmad Hilmi and his Fund was their personal dislike of 'Alami, who gained popularity in Palestine and had a reputation as being above party factionalism and who was initially supported by the PAP.

'Alami's popularity began to sink upon his return to Palestine in March 1945, and he became the object of criticism by these notables. The publication of the Covenant of the Arab League caused public disenchantment at the mildly worded Special Annex on Palestine to that document.

Most Palestinian Arabs had expected that one result of the Arab unity talks at Alexandria would be some form of immediate and positive assistance to their cause. Specifically, the Annex recognized Palestine's *de jure* national independence but added that, as "special circumstances" prevented its *de facto* exercise of independence, the League Council was made responsible for selecting a Palestinian delegate to participate in its proceedings.[48] In other words, Palestine was not accorded full representative status because of its semi-independent legal status.

The Annex highly disappointed and dashed the hopes of the Palestinians who thought that the long Palestinian struggle for independence from mandatory rule should have been reason enough to grant them full representative status.[49] The nationalists felt that Palestine irrefutably was an Arab country and part of the Arab nation and should have been accorded, despite British objections and pressure, equal membership in the League of Arab States.[50] That kind of recognition, they thought, would help in putting political pressure on Britain to grant Palestine independence as an Arab country in the form of a unitary state. Furthermore, some Palestinians, such as Dr. Khalidi, 'Abd al-Hadi and their supporters, felt there was no clear Arab states plan to support Palestinian national rights. 'Alami's land development scheme and propaganda offices proposals made at the Alexandria conference in late 1944 were perceived by these men and others as innocuous substitutes for more effective action. The schemes also were believed to be in accordance with British wishes in the sense that they did not in any way challenge Britain's position that Palestine's legal and political future was not within the domain of rights of the Arab states.[51]

The land development scheme, more widely known as the constructive scheme (*al-mashru' al-insha'i*), aimed at preserving Arab land and at alleviating the social and economic lot of the peasant. The scheme envisioned assisting the *fellahin* to pay off their debts, to improve agricultural methods and carry out village construction, to promote village industries, and to facilitate the marketing of village products.[52] Thus, the intention of the scheme was not to buy land (although that is indeed what it ended up doing) but to raise the status of the *fellah* by increasing production and raising the standard of living in the villages.

The Arab League had in principle agreed with 'Alami's scheme, which was to be based on a contribution of LP1,000,000 a year for five years to a land development company.[53] However, the Arab states were reluctant to pay. Because of their reticence and delay 'Alami started the scheme on his own by December 1945. He was able to do this through an 'Iraqi contribution of LP150,000, which money he received after a visit he made to Baghdad (in May 1945) as a personal guest of 'Abd al-Illah. The money was deposited with the Palestine Arab Bank of 'Abd al-Hamid Shuman which eagerly served as a financial repository for any collections or subscription for the scheme. The Arab Bank also offered financial support to 'Alami and hoped to extend its activities to the neighboring Arab countries. 'Iraq's action prompted 'Abdullah to contribute LP50,000 to the National Fund.[54]

The Arab offices, on the other hand, were to be opened in Jerusalem, London, and Washington for the purpose of representing the Arab view on Palestine to the Western public, media, and public officials. Even though the Arab states promised LP2,000,000 for the offices project, eventually money came in trickles and the offices were underfinanced and understaffed. But the offices fared better than the constructive scheme, which ultimately received nothing from the Arab states (except 'Iraq, which continued to finance 'Alami).

Besides the criticism levelled at 'Alami's schemes, he himself was directly criticized. He was attacked for being in control of large sums of money and Dr. Khalidi, an old friend of his, inferred that 'Alami collaborated with the British and Arab League to produce ineffectual and meaningless programs for Palestine.[55] Khalidi sarcastically remarked that it would take thirty to forty years to implement 'Alami's constructive scheme in all the villages of Palestine.[56] Once it was obvious 'Alami's schemes had a semblance of concrete Arab support, especially from 'Iraq, Khalidi attempted to involve himself with him. Although both tried to reach an understanding, Khalidi wanted a voice in the Palestinian appointments to the Arab offices in London and Washington,[57] perhaps to install men whose political views coincided with his. 'Alami's resolute rejection of this request deepened the schism between them.

Ahmad Hilmi also had attacked 'Alami. He wrote to the Secretary General of the League, 'Abd al-Rahman 'Azzam Bey, criticizing 'Alami's constructive scheme project for hampering his own work through the National Fund.[58] In turn 'Alami complained that the Fund was not only not buying land but selling it at a profit, and suggested the Fund was likely to end in the division of its assets among its directors (from which he promptly resigned).[59] This prompted the PAP to publicly announce its withdrawal from support of the National Fund, accusing Ahmad Hilmi of adopting a dictatorial attitude in matters concerning its administration and policy.[60] The PAP defended 'Alami's scheme and its purposes stating Hilmi Pasha was using the Fund to strengthen his party (i.e., the abortive AHC).[61] Emile al-Ghury of the PAP announced in June 1945 that if the Fund could not be reformed (i.e. if the PAP were not admitted to its control), the PAP would support 'Alami's constructive scheme.[62]

By late 1946, with the return of Jamal and the Mufti (the latter to the

Middle East), the PAP, as we shall see, actually would reverse its position towards 'Alami, with the Mufti in continual conflict with him. By that time also, a Mufti dominated AHC attacked 'Alami's Arab offices, alleging that 'Iraq was behind the idea for the purpose of furthering Nuri's Fertile Crescent dreams. (How that conclusion was arrived at was not made clear.) It also charged that the offices worked with Western, particularly British, intelligence.[63] Thus, even at the most critical time in Palestinian history, the Palestinian Arab leaders could not agree as to the most expedient method of protecting Arab land from alienation.

The rivalry among the Palestinians eventually frustrated the prospect of financial assistance from the Arab states who did not need much incentive to withhold their contributions. The Arab League in July 1945 sent Taki al-Din al-Sulh, Counsellor to the Lebanese Legation in Cairo, to Palestine to gauge public opinion on the rival schemes. Sulh recommended support for both schemes, the Fund to buy endangered land and 'Alami's scheme to provide Arab farmers with machinary and capital.[64] But the Economic Committee of the League decided that a total capital of LP1,000,000 would not only be sufficient, but would be released after a further mission was sent to Palestine to examine the best way to spend the money.[65]

In November 1945, Sulh and Khayr al-Din al-Zarkaleh, Counsellor to the Sa'udi Legation in Cairo, went to Palestine but again failed to reconcile the rival Palestinian schemes. By the time (in April 1946) a Technical Committee decided on the safest project (investing the capital in an agricultural bank which would assist the *fellahin* with special allowances), the Arab governments did not feel compelled to contribute to the scheme because 'Alami had launched his project without the League's consent or assistance. The effectiveness of independent Palestinian efforts was bound to be limited. Up to late 1945, the area of land owned by the Fund was some 12,800 *dunum*s, while 'Alami's scheme was still foundering in 1946.[66] Divisions and bitter rivalries hampered the effectiveness of the projects. Resources, efforts, and manpower were not united into a coherent plan. More importantly, there were no funds forthcoming from the Arab states to sustain the ambitious projects. The PAP mouthpiece *al-Wihda* had acidly suggested that the leaders should either come to an understanding or let others take their places, meaning young PAP activists and Husaynis.[67]

*   *   *

While the Palestinians were preoccupied with issues that degenerated into intransigent individual positions, the war was coming to an end, promising many changes. The post-war period saw an increase in the tempo of

British policy in Palestine, and the divisive issues began to shift from an emphasis on creating a consensus leadership to disorganized preoccupation with outside challenges. These challenges were in the form of British and Anglo-American policies which called for radical political and territorial reconstruction of Arab Palestine. It is, therefore, not fruitful to continue discussing (in the following chapters) Palestinian factional politics, without first sketching the wider colonial and international policy initiatives to which the Palestine problem was being subjected.

British Schemes for Settlement During the War

Between 1940 and 1945, much of British policy centered around the staunch pro-Zionism of Winston Churchill, who was Prime Minister during those six years. Churchill actually was the main pillar of opposition to the White Paper from its very beginning, even though the Palestinians and Arab states came to accept it before 1945. Churchill therefore succeeded in checking the fundamental, though implicit, promise of independence contained in the White Paper.[68] He usually went at loggerheads with the Foreign Office, which was highly aware and sensitive to Britain's wider interests in the Arab world, in his support of Jewish aspirations for a state. Churchill felt that American Jewry was invaluable in enlisting American help in the war and that the Arab states would be useless in that war.[69] The conflict over this matter between him and the Foreign Office was especially tense up to 1942.

By 1942–43 there were a number of factors which were leading towards the consideration of solutions other than the White Paper. First, Churchill's emphatic opposition in the Cabinet to any hint of White Paper implementation was leading to paralysis. Although there was no wish in government circles to revive any controversies while the war continued, there still were various times in which either the Colonial Office or the Foreign Office undertook some form of movement on the constitutional clauses of the White Paper. These conflicting perceptions only aggravated Britain's anxiety over its position in the Middle East.

Second, in light of the scale of atrocities against the Jews of Europe that were slowly becoming known, the Zionist clamor for a Jewish state increased. Zionist objectives were made public in 1942 when Zionist leaders, congregating in New York, issued the Biltmore program which made clear the Zionist aim of creating a Jewish "commonwealth" over Palestine, containing a Jewish majority.[70]

Third, the Zionist lobby was becoming an entrenched and potent foreign policy interest group in the United States. Its pressures steadily increased in the latter years of the war. This was partly due to anxiety that with the war's imminent climax crucial decisions would be taken over

Palestine and partly to the projected White Paper deadline on immigration in March 1944.[71] During the 1944 presidential elections, considerable pressure was exerted on both the Democratic and Republican candidates and parties.[72] Also, in that year, resolutions were introduced into both houses of Congress calling for unrestricted Jewish immigration and the reconstitution of Palestine as a Jewish commonwealth.

This pressure led to government efforts to consider and formulate a long term policy. However, between 1942 and 1945 the British privately spawned a number of schemes and policies for Palestine. This is because there were deep divisions in the Cabinet over solving the Palestine problem. These factors, coupled with external pressures, eventually (by 1945) led to five plans for a Palestine settlement including the White Paper which wasn't abandoned as an option until after 1945. The first was proposed by the War Cabinet Committee on Palestine (WCCP) which was instructed by Churchill to start by examining various partition schemes. Five out of six members were sympathetic to Zionism and a Jewish state.[73]

The WCCP report, submitted to the War Cabinet in January 1944, was accepted in principle. It was an exaggerated variant of the Peel Commission report in 1937. The plan, in short, would have created three states: a Jerusalem state, a Jewish state, and a state of Southern Syria, to which the Arab parts of Palestine would be attached.[74] (The idea of a Southern Syria state grew out of the notion that, after Syria's liberation from France, the Arabs of the Levant States would be agreeable to a Greater Syria. The conception was that the first steps towards such a federation would be the partitioned Palestine Arab state's incorporation into Trans-Jordan, whose Amir 'Abdullah had ambitions to be king of Greater Syria.)

The report's presentation was met by opposition from various quarters, including the Foreign Office, the military chiefs, and the High Commissioner for Palestine, Sir Harold MacMichael. In fact, these held a conference in Cairo in April 1944, which was called by the Minister Resident to the Middle East, Lord Walter Moyne. The conference warned of the grave consequences for British interests if partition were implemented.[75]

Churchill, sensing the problems a policy of partition would create in the Middle East, thought it prudent to wait until the war's end. By the end of 1944, however, Lord Moyne was murdered by Jewish terrorists, which pushed an emotionally shaken Churchill to decide that it was impossible to consider partition until terrorist actions were brought to an end. From this point on, Churchill's advocacy and defense of Zionist goals were on the wane, and by 1946, with increasing Jewish terrorism in Palestine, his sentiments for a Jewish state were transformed into indifference or unconcern.

In late 1944, a new Minister Resident, Sir Edward Grigg, was installed in Cairo and, in Palestine, Lord Gort replaced MacMichael as High Commissioner. These two were strongly opposed to partition. Along with the service commanders, they unanimously felt that partition could not be implemented without serious disorders, involving heavy military commitments in Palestine and throughout the Middle East. A further difficulty was introduced into the situation as a result of the trusteeship agreement reached at the San Francisco Conference between April and June 1945. Partition could not be effected without alteration of the mandate and no such alteration could be made without British consulation with the newly created United Nations, which was to administer Palestine under international trusteeship.

Grigg advocated international involvement, particularly the involvement of the United States. He also felt that the Jewish Agency, in addition to convincing the Arabs of the Zionists' aggressive and expansionist aims, had largely undermined the mandatory administration and prevented progress towards self-government. Faulting the British mandate for its recognition of the Jewish Agency on terms which enabled the Jews to set up a "shadow" government with their own armed forces and autonomous society and economy, he emphasized the need for the severe curtailment of the Agency's powers and, perhaps, its abolition.[76]

In the spring of 1945 he offered his solution for a settlement, based on a local autonomy scheme originally proposed by MacMichael in 1938. This formed the second plan for a Palestine settlement. His scheme held that there would be elected local rural and urban councils, Arab-Jewish central councils in each of the five districts, and a legislative council formed from the central district councils, on which there would be established parity of representation.

Although Grigg's scheme was meant primarily to protect British geo-strategic interests, it was obvious to old hands in the Foreign Office and Colonial Office that, first, neither the Jews nor Arabs would accept the legislative council proposals, the Arabs insistent on their democratic right as a majority and the Jews bent on a Jewish state. Second, the Arabs adhered to the White Paper. Thirdly, it would, in all likelihood, have been impossible for the international body to control immigration in a way that would not encroach on British interests or Arab sensibilities.

Because of the indecision and conflicting views, the Foreign Office and Colonial Office were plunged into an acrimonious debate over which department had the responsibility of preparing a long term solution.[77] This situation pushed the Colonial Office to produce a new, or third, proposal for a Palestine settlement. It was clear that neither partition nor Grigg's scheme could be put into operation without a revision of the mandate, and it would have been impossible to give immediate effect to them under such strictures.

The Colonial Office scheme, proposed by Sir Douglas Harris, was called provincial autonomy, or cantonization, being based on one of the schemes put forward by the Royal Commission in 1937.[78] The essence of the plan was that there would be officially defined areas in which Jewish land buying and settlement could take place. The scheme envisaged the division of Palestine into an Arab and a Jewish province, each being autonomous in such matters as public works, health, education, and general administration, including control of land sales and immigration. A central mandatory government would retain control over such matters as foreign relations, defense, customs, railways, posts and telegraphs, and so on. The cities of Bethlehem and Jerusalem would be excluded from the provinces and administered directly by the mandatory. Local legislatures might be empowered to legislate certain subjects and collect revenue from such sources as property, income and excise taxes.

Harris reasoned that provincial autonomy would leave any decision on a final solution open and at the same time would offer some of the advantages of partition while avoiding its inherent difficulties. It was an ingenious middle solution which contained aspects of both one and two state solutions, and therefore, theoretically solved any revision of the mandate until the trusteeship arrangements were put into effect. When that time came, provincial autonomy could either lead to a partition, unitary, or even federal solution.

Lord Gort offered the only definitive rejection of provincial autonomy. His emphasis on the status quo actually constituted a fourth alternative. Gort showed an ongoing concern with dividing Palestine in any form. He saw Harris' scheme as entailing most of the disadvantages of partition while not relieving the mandatory of the burden of responsibility for major matters of contention such as immigration and tariffs.[79] It is interesting to note that Gort strongly emphasized Arab-Jewish coexistence and economic and political interdependence and the need for Palestine to remain a united administrative unit. He also put major blame on the Jewish Agency for frustrating "all efforts to establish any sort of regime under which collaboration between Jews and Arabs would have been possible."[80]

By late 1945, then, there were altogether five alternatives put forth to British policy: to continue governing Palestine with or without the consent or cooperation of the governed (as Gort in essence wanted), the White Paper plan, the partition plan, the international plan put forward by Grigg, and the provincial autonomy plan. The vast amount of paperwork and energy invested in what seemed to cover the entire gamut of solutions only indicated the futility of British policy, based, as it was, on a dual obligation that could not be reconciled. This clearly ridiculous and untenable situation, in which there was no clear idea as to Britain's ultimate intentions regarding Palestine, prompted Colonial Secretary George Hall to comment in despair that:

> We have governed on these lines for nearly a quarter of a century, a period marked by inter-racial strife with a major outbreak every few years, and, in the result, we now find ourselves faced with a situation which is little short of chaotic. It is not that our policy has failed; the failure is due to the fact that we have never had a policy....[81]

Between 1942 and 1945, no definitive policy was formulated by the British government. This state of affairs was to continue until the end of the mandate, indicating quite clearly that the British reacted to events more than initiated policy in Palestine. They essentially muddled through, creating a confused situation that was to have disastrous consequences for the Palestinian Arabs.

British Policy and Anglo-American Cooperation in the Postwar Era

London's paralysis was a result of conflicting pressures that it could not reconcile. These were, on the one hand, Zionist demands backed by American pressure and growing Jewish terrorism in Palestine and, on the other, growing Arab nationalism regarding Palestine and the Middle East. The sense of urgency in government towards a policy for Palestine therefore was constant. The situation was aggravated by President Harry Truman, who took the helm at Roosevelt's death in April 1945. When Truman came to power, he saw Palestine as a "side show" to the more pressing problems of postwar Europe. Beyond a vague idea of what was happening in the Middle East, he was against the idea of creating a religiously identified (Jewish) state that excluded Arabs from political power.[82] However, unrelenting Jewish pressure and the advice of two of his closest aides (David K. Niles, an ardent pro-Zionist, and Judge Samuel J. Rosenmann, presidential counsel until mid-1946 and pro-immigration) influenced Truman's turn towards his pro-Zionist policy.

His insistence, beginning in July 1945, that London rescind the immigration policy of the White Paper and his subsequent statements in favor of the immediate entry of 100,000 displaced (European) Jews into Palestine, caused embarrassment and consternation in British government circles. Truman, ignorant of the complexities of the Palestine issue, was not above hypocrisy in his dealings with the British over Palestine. In the formulation of Palestine policy, domestic pressure groups took precedence over the national interest.[83]

Despite these facts, Truman avoided advocating Jewish nationhood in Palestine. He did not believe that his position on Jewish immigration related to the more fundamental aspect of a political settlement in Palestine. Still, he set the stage for the firm connection of Jewish displaced persons in Europe with Palestine. This put immense pressure on Britain. With the climax of Zionist outcries over the human suffering of the European Jews and their insistence on Palestine's central role in solving the problem of displaced persons, Ernest Bevin, The Labour Foreign Secretary who assumed office in July 1945, felt that a proposal for joint Anglo-American action was essential. Bevin's plan to involve the Americans officially linked Palestine to European Jewry, something the British had previously resisted.

The result was the creation, in late 1945, of the Anglo-American Committee of Inquiry (AAC), which was given a time limit of 120 days to make its full recommendations, largely at American insistence. The main problem for Britain was its anxiety over the anticipated difficulties that would arise if the Committee had made recommendations viewed as deterimental to British interests.[84] The final recommendations of the AAC produced precisely such difficulties. Politically, the report recommended that Jews shall not dominate Arabs or *vice versa;* that Palestine shall be neither a Jewish nor Arab state; that the form of government ultimately to be established shall fully protect the rights of all three faiths and accord all inhabitants the fullest measure of self-government; and that the mandate shall continue pending a trusteeship agreement at the United Nations.[85] These vague political recommendations came as a relief to London, especially since they precluded American pressure for a political solution. But the AAC also recommended that Britian should grant the immediate authority for the entrance of 100,000 Jewish displaced persons into Palestine and that it rescind the Land Transfer Regulations of 1940 (a White Paper policy). This proved to be an obstacle to Anglo-American agreement. Needless to say, the Arab states, the Palestinians and the Zionists rejected the report, although the latter was interested in the 100,000 proposal.

Before London made its opinion clear regarding the report, Truman, reacting to Jewish pressure, unilaterally released a statement announcing his pleasure at the 100,000 proposal, emphasizing that it was a request he initially made and also that he was "pleased" the AAC recommendations in effect abrogated the White Paper.[86] It was clear that Truman's concern was with the 100,000. But the British did not feel they could accede to

American pressure without placing the 100,000 within the context of an overall, comprehensive settlement that both countries might agree upon. Such a project would involve military and financial responsibility, not to mention its implications for wider Middle East interests.

By July 1946, seven months after the AAC began its mission, an Anglo-American experts' meeting convened in London to discuss the financial and military aspects of the AAC report. The British made certain that the experts' committee would discuss all of the political, economic, social, military and logistics issues related to the AAC report. In their list of items sent to the Americans in May, the technical details ensured that a genuine, comprehensive agreement would have to be reached between the two countries.[87] The British strongly felt that since the Americans were not ready to commit themselves militarily in Palestine, they would not fall into the trap of devising policy constricted by American desires, which were largely motivated by domestic politics. While the Americans agreed to the agenda, they also insisted on an advance party to begin immediate discussions on the 100,000 issue, to which the British conceded.[88]

The British had entered the discussions with the intention of submitting the provincial autonomy scheme originally proposed by Sir Douglas Harris, a proposal the Americans ended up accepting. Thus, not only were constitutional and political proposals worked out in detail, but a plan was also devised for the 100,000 to be transported from Europe to Palestine.[89] However, Washington was unhappy that the American team accepted the British conditions that action on the 100,000 begin only after the entire plan (political settlement and the immigration of the 100,000) was accepted by both Arabs and Jews.[90] This was contrary to Truman's wishes, who wanted to implement the immigration plan immediately and relieve himself of the burden. Thus, the Anglo-American experts' discussion ultimately proved inconclusive.

The Americans, not without some justification, were distrustful of British motives, seeing in them attempts to cause further protraction. It was taken as a given in British government circles that the immigration proposals would cause a fundamentally adverse Arab reaction, and clearly both Arabs and Jews rejected provincial autonomy. But in fairness, the British had averred their intentions of consultations and agreements even before the AAC inquiry was launched. Furthermore, it was Truman who had weakened the AAC report because of his singular insistence on the 100,000. Truman had instructed the American team to take the position in London that the United States was unwilling to make military commitments to enforce any agreement. He also did not want to deal with a fundamental solution in the Middle East.[91] On the other hand, the British logic for submitting the provincial autonomy scheme was based on the fact that the AAC report did not provide a solution to the Palestine problem nor did it recommend any long term solution.[92]

British hopes were finally dashed in light of Truman's refusal to endorse the experts' report, known as the Morrison-Grady scheme, just as he had refused to endorse the ACC report. Though he privately thought the provincial autonomy scheme was a "correct solution," the Zionists exerted tremendous pressure against the report. The Jewish lobby and its partners in the Democratic party as well as some Republican senators had successfully checked the President's planned public acceptance of the whole experts' report, much to his frustration and annoyance.[93]

After the failure of the Anglo-American discussions, the next step was for Bevin to announce the intentions of Britain to call a conference of Arabs and Jews, an idea he had in mind since the initial decision to ask the United States to form a joint committee of inquiry. The Morrison-Grady report was to be the basis for discussion at the conference.

The London Conference

The London Conference was doomed to failure even before its start. It represented a desperate, last minute British attempt to solve the irreconcilable differences of Arabs and Jews and, thereby, maintain British influence in the country and region. By 1946, however, the Palestinian Arab demand for an independent state, to which the Arab states had become publicly and irreversibly committed, was matched by Zionist determination to create a Jewish state, which had the military strength and demographic and economic confidence to back it up.

In a concrete sense, the Arab and Jewish attitudes had not changed since the Balfour Declaration of 1917. Whatever turns diplomacy had assumed and whatever schemes had evolved during that thirty-year period, the fundamental Palestinian Arab perception that British policies and Zionist ambitions could only lead to injustice and the denial of their national rights, remained unchanged. During the Second World War, energies and attentions were diverted towards economic betterment and advancement. However, the smoldering resentment and political tension grew, while the gulf between Arab and Jewish aspirations widened. The post-war period in Palestine was characterized by the political and emotional culmination of the contending positions of Arabs and Jews.

The London Conference took place in two separate stages: the first, 10 September to 2 October 1946; and the second, 27 January to 14 February 1947.[94] The Palestinians and the Zionists both had refused to attend, because both sides rejected the provincial autonomy scheme as a basis for discussion. During the second stage, the Palestinians were in attendance, at the prodding of the Arab states and because London did not attempt to dictate the delegation's composition, as it had done before the beginning of the first stage.[95]

At the opening rounds, Bevin argued that no settlement could be achieved without Jewish consent and that, as Palestine was not ready for independence, the provincial autonomy scheme could very well constitute an experiment in coexistence that could lead to peace.[96] The British defined the advantages of provincial autonomy by emphasizing its potentiality of leading to independence and its inherent flexibility as to the type of state that might evolve. The Arabs argued that provincial autonomy would divide the country into various administrative districts; that it would leave the Jewish province open to unlimited immigration without regard to the question of whether the province could support the immigrants or not; and that it would obviously lead to a Jewish state, thus actualizing the danger of Jewish expansion.[97] It was clear to the Arabs, as it was to the British, that the Zionists wanted no less than a state, if possible comprising the entire country.

The British had known in advance what the Arab position would be, although they hoped an agreement acceptable to all sides might still be reached. While they made it clear they were willing to entertain any proposal outside the provincial autonomy scheme, they were unwilling, as they had been in 1939, to accept any agreements over Palestine without the consent of both parties (Arabs and Jews).

Of importance was an Arab constitutional proposal which essentially requested a unitary state in which Jews and Arabs would govern the country through a legislative assembly based on their electoral proportions—that is, close to three Arabs for every one Jew.[98] The Arabs were willing to recognize the Jews as a political (not just religious) community that was free to guard its own interests through a parliamentary or political bloc. Of interest to the British was Arab willingness that the Palestinian state would enter into a military agreement with Britian and that they would accept a transition period before independence was granted. (Prior to the conference the Arabs insisted on immediate independence.)

The British were willing to consider the Arab proposal (a joint sub-committee was formed to examine and clarify the constitutional points). They suggested, however, that the conference be suspended to give the Jews the opportunity to explore the matter and explain their viewpoint. During the first stage of the conference (10 September to 2 October 1946), the British simultaneously held informal discussions with the Zionists, who indicated their willingness to attend. The need for Zionist participation provided a good reason for adjourning the conference, during which time the British government's informal negotiations with them could be concluded. The Arabs rejected postponement on such a basis, but were powerless to do anything about it.

Immediately after the first stage of the London Conference in October, Bevin told the Cabinet that if negotiations failed, there were three courses of action available: to impose a solution acceptable only to one side, to terminate the mandate and withdraw from Palestine, or to propose a scheme of partition which might merge the Arab part of Palestine to Trans-Jordan.[99] One of the reasons that partition was back on the list of possible alternatives was High Commissioner Sir Alan Cunningham's strong opinion in its favor. He argued that, since a unitary or federal scheme would not solve the existing dilemmas, partition was the only solution. Additionally, Lieutenant-General Cunningham maintained that the Palestinian Arab "power for harm" was confined to the urban areas, as the peasantry not only enjoyed unparalleled prosperity but they did not relish a return "to the hardships of the Arab rebellion."[100]

In the negotiations between the Zionists and London during the interim period[101] (3 October 1946 to 26 January 1947) the former attempted to extract a British commitment on partition. But the Jews accepted partition (their minimum demand) only after British protracted consultations with Ben-Gurion (who was allowed to come to London from Paris, where he had taken refuge after the British crackdown on the Jewish Agency in 1946). Ben-Gurion and the Zionists had, in fact, revealed during the consultations their longstanding wishes and demands, a Jewish state over *all* of Palestine. They viewed their acceptance of partition as a *concession.* They also demanded unprohibited immigration under the authority of the Jewish Agency. This Jewish acceptance was another reason the British were considering partition as an option.

Before the second stage of the conference began, the government's planned tactics, under the influence of the Colonial Office, were to get Jews and Palestinians to attend, place the provincial autonomy scheme before them, and present partition as an option, although no advance pledges on it would be given to the Zionists.[102] These tactics ensured that, as throughout the mandate, Britain would be unable to take a decision on Palestine policy. The Arabs would reject partition and the Jews a unitary state. Thus, any sort of Anglo-Arab or Anglo-Zionist compromise was effectively precluded, with the Foreign Office and Colonial Office leaning towards the former and latter respectively. In such an untenable situation the provincial autonomy scheme still represented a middle ground.

The second stage (27 January to 14 February 1947) was more notable than the first for its lack of purpose. Bevin opened the conference by summarizing the three types of possible solutions:[103] the Arab plan for independence, partition, and provincial autonomy, representing the latter as a happy medium. The Arabs rejected Bevin's proposals outright. The Zionists insisted on their right to control immigration after the immediate entry of the 100,000. They intentionally did not reveal their territorial lines on partition during the private consultations because of the absurd nature of their demands. Yet neither did they believe that the British were seriously willing to implement such a scheme.

Bevin submitted a final proposal.[104] Palestine would become a trusteeship for a maximum period of five years after which it would become independent. During that period both Arabs and Jews would be given a large measure of local autonomy and both would participate in the central government, and 96,000 immigrants would enter Palestine over a period of two years, after which the High Commissioner, with the help of an Arab-Jewish advisory council, would help determine the rate of immigration on the basis of absorptive capacity for the next three years.

Again, both sides rejected the proposal. The Arabs insisted on their right to a unitary state, fearing that 96,000 Jewish immigrants, plus whatever number entered Palestine for the remainder of the trusteeship period, would immeasurably strengthen the Zionists, who might then use feeble pretexts for expansion. The Zionists, on the other hand, rejected anything that did not include the immediate entry of the 100,000 in addition to unlimited freedom in the matter of immigration. Thus, Arabs and Jews did not meet or talk to each other. The second stage was characterized by heated and emotional debates over the historical and national rights of both peoples.

*   *   *

Anglo-American policies and the London Conference contributed mightily to Palestinian (and general Arab) popular distrust of the West and its intentions. The corresponding rise of Palestinian and Arab nationalism, in their outrage over Western, particularly American, interference, reached vociferous heights in the post-war period. This nationalist sentiment was increasingly controlled and directed by the Mufti and notables who, while leading the nationalist, anti-colonial and anti-Zionist struggle, were also maintaining their power and privileges. Thus, they perpetuated factionalist divisions as they sought to create unity.

6

Notable Politics II:
External Threat, Internal Domination

The factional rivalries that we looked at in the previous chapter were exacerbated many times over by the mounting challenges from the outside. Much of Palestinian politics, especially between 1946 and 1947, therefore was concerned with constructing a coherent and united response to external pressures. In this situation, the Arab states became incontrovertibly involved with the Palestinians by way of helping them organize and unite themselves in order to deal with the barrage of policies aimed at Palestine. The Arab regimes were, of course, not without self-interest. Thus, a good deal was at stake for the Palestinians as they were buffeted by the crosscurrents of British, American, and wider Arab politicking.

By 1946, with the return of the Mufti and Jamal to the Middle East, Palestinian politics began to move towards the direction of a consolidation of power under these two, a consolidation that was meant to achieve a united leadership. But the Mufti's and Jamal's projected unity, despite their own dislike of, and disagreement with, each other, excluded the idea of a genuinely representative body which might comprise elements outside the notability. Although the balance of external forces were aligned against it, the Palestinian leadership, with the Mufti and Husaynis at the forefront, continued to be engrossed in its own conflicts over power and prerogatives.

These divisions especially concerned a compromise representative body that would lead the Palestinians internally and speak on their behalf to the outside world. The substantive challenges, as we have seen, involved the very question of the continued existence of Arab Palestine, whether it would remain a unitary state or be partitioned, and all the shades of possible solutions in between.

The Palestinians formed and reformed representative bodies in their search for a consensus, with progressive segments, including the more radicalized intelligentsia and labor unions, increasingly injecting themselves in the debate and demanding more democratic representation. The controversy and politics over a representative body to attend the London Conference in particular clearly reveals the new forces that existed, their discontent with the dominant leaders, and the notables' determination to block them out of power and decision-making.

Despite the growing disaffection with the Mufti and notability, the former especially was in a position to pursue his narrow concept of leadership without losing ground. Partly this was because of his popularity in Palestine and the Middle East upon his return. But more so, it was because almost all Palestinian social elements were in agreement over their national rights and existence. The more that existence seemed to be threatened by Western policy initiatives, the more power and political hegemony the Mufti and the traditional leadership cultivated for themselves.

Higher Fronts and Higher Committees: The Effects on Politics of Jamal's Return to Palestine and the Revival of the Mufti's Influence

During the early forties, Arab leaders made continual representations to London for the release of Jamal al-Husayni and the other Palestinian exiles. As was seen, although most of the others were allowed to return early during the war, the High Commissioner and Colonial Office were implacably against the return of Jamal and his associate, Amin al-Tamimi, both of whom were interned in southern Rhodesia. (Tamimi died in exile in October 1944 after having an operation performed on him.) Initially MacMichael, then Lord Gort, took the view that Jamal's "irreconcilable" anti-British views, coupled with the probability that he was the "only man who could become a real leader of the Palestine Arabs," made his return to Palestine undesirable.[1]

In 1944, Arab representations for the release of Jamal were revived. With the imminence of the preparatory discussions on Arab unity, Arab politicians and leaders were concerned that the Palestinians would neither be able to unite nor to send a representative to the Alexandria talks. They felt, like London, that Jamal would be the only one with the potential to unite the disparate elements in Palestinian politics. They also had learned from experience that Husayni intransigence and obstructionism would be lessened upon the return of Jamal, given the fact that the PAP made his and Haj Amin's return an obsessive precondition for co-operation.

In February 1944 Egyptian Prime Minister Nuqrashi Pasha made representations on Jamal's behalf and Nuri Pasha broached the topic with the Minister Resident, Sir E. Grigg, in late 1944.[2] In March 1945, on the eve of the signature of the Arab League pact, Nuqrashi Pasha again asked for the release of Jamal, suggesting that it was a good "psychological moment" as it would have a great effect "throughout the Arab world" whose peoples would regard it as a "noble gesture" on Britain's part.[3] The Amir Faysal, in an interview with Britain's minister in Jedda, "deplored" the absence of Jamal from the Middle Eastern scene and suggested he might be a generally moderating influence.[4] The Amir was quoted as saying that Jamal was "the most moderate of Palestinian extremists" and that he had personally witnessed Jamal's willingness to sign the White Paper proposals at the London Conference of 1939.

One reason for the increasing tempo of representations on behalf of Jamal was the Arab states' fears of a conflict in Palestine. Arab public opinion was increasingly agitated during 1944 and 1945 by the irresponsible statements emanating from the United States. The Arab leaders hoped that Jamal would be able to dampen some of the excitement among the Palestinian Arabs and so relieve any pressure on them to intervene. The Foreign Office, conscious of Britain's wider interests, also supported the release of Jamal and went to some lengths to show that he in no way was involved in the Rashid 'Ali revolt in 'Iraq.[5] But the Colonial Office was concerned that his nationalist stand would do more damage than good to British interests in Palestine.

In late 1945, with Bevin's announcement of the proposed creation of a joint Anglo-American committee, the crescendo of protests and appeals for the release of Jamal heightened. Lord Gort suggested that London wait until Arab reaction to Bevin's statement became clear. If the Palestinians rejected the AAC proposal and remained "intransigent," it would then be opportune to release Jamal as he was the only one to give the Arabs the "unity and political direction which they now lack."[6] The Palestine authorities' position had changed from the previous year. The main reason was London's concern that the Palestinians be able to represent their case to the AAC to avert the possibility of a one-sided report. Secondly, the Arab states had pressured the Palestinians to meet with the AAC and thought that cooperation among them might be attained with the return of Jamal.

Jamal's eventual release and return to Palestine in February 1946[7] came on the heels of the Mufti's arrival in Paris by car in May 1945.[8] He had arrived with twelve of his associates and was taken into French custody.[9] Although the British had requested his immediate placement under their custody, the French were reluctant to hand him over. The French explanation that they did not want to incur Muslim "odium" was not wholly believed by the British, who suspected them of using the Mufti to their advantage in Syria and Lebanon by offering him sanctuary from his enemies.[10] The French were aware of his popularity in the Arab world where he was considered a hero. The French accordingly proceeded to treat him well (they placed him in a villa outside Paris) and permitted him to have contacts with Arab ministers in Paris.

The Mufti's arrival in Paris under French custody, then, had put the British in a difficult and powerless position. It was feared that the Mufti would act as a detrimental influence in the impending Bevin announcement, instigating extremism and non-cooperation. By October 1945, London was thinking of "debunking" the Mufti, or smearing his name. However, the Palestine authorities had stated that if he were to be debunked, he would have to be attacked through his personal life, political activities in Palestine, and his war record.[11] They pointed out that, morally, there was no evidence for suitable use against him and it was uncertain whether "indeed he has ever offended against the Moslem code." The use of his political activities during the revolt would be double-edged, they accurately reasoned, as "all Arabs are united against the Zionists." Even those Palestinian Arabs who "may have had relatives murdered" at the Mufti's instigation would not command sufficient influence in the country to excite sympathy, even on the supposition that such killings could be traced to the Mufti and the motive "could be established as a private feud rather than a political act."

Finally, the Palestine authorities astutely pointed out that, regarding the Mufti's collaboration with the Axis, they doubted whether Hitler's regime would be "reprobated" on moral grounds by the Arab masses or whether there was any real awareness of the extent of Hitler's crimes. Photographs, documents and quotations proving the Mufti's faith in the Nazi cause, would "unlikely do more than to remind the Arabs that their leader made a mistake."[12] The war, they went on, was not, generally, an "Arab war." They concluded with the following insightful analysis:

> Haj Amin promised the Arabs freedom from Zionism and from British and French domination. The time may yet come when differences between British and Arabs in the Middle East will strengthen Arab belief that the line taken by Haj Amin was the only line for an honest Arab politician. Among the Palestine fellahin there is an almost religious veneration of Haj Amin and any attack on him would be regarded as an attack on a good Moslem....[13]

It was clear even to London that as long as Zionism was perceived as a danger and differences existed between the British and Arabs in the Middle East, the Mufti would remain a symbol of Arab nationalist aspirations. In such a situation, the British were in no position to "debunk" the Mufti. Thus, the Cabinet agreed, in late November 1945, to have the Mufti and his associates sent to the Sychelles as political prisoners.[14] But this depended on French cooperation, which was not forthcoming. As concerns the Mufti's wishes, he wrote Egypt and Sa'udi Arabia explaining his position and declaring his desire to leave France, assuring them that the French were ready to accept an application from an Arab country. But because of British pressure on the French and the Egyptians, the Mufti did not leave France until June 1946, by way of a successful escape.

The revival of the Mufti's influence in the Middle East also revived previously strained relations with Jamal al-Husayni. Because of 'Alami's independent activities and close association with Jamal, both men came into increasing conflict with him. As we have seen, relations between the Mufti and Jamal and 'Alami had been less than amicable ever since the pair's split with him in 1940 over the White Paper and his turn to the Axis.

Throughout 1946 Jamal and 'Alami had acted as moderating influences in Palestine. Because Jamal's return had coincided with the creation of the AAC whose investigative mission had aroused the suspicion of the Arabs, he continually visited Palestinian towns, holding conversations with local nationalist clubs and scout movements to counsel moderation.[15] During this time the Mufti apparently was in continual communication with persons in Palestine and was conducting an intensive and increasing underground political campaign which was, according to 'Alami, doing a "great deal of harm."[16] He enjoyed the freedom to correspond with Arab politicians in the Middle East and family supporters in Palestine.

The Mufti, who deeply distrusted British and Western policies in Palestine, was already trying to regain his formerly dominant position of influence and to prepare the Palestinian Arabs for armed struggle. As early as January 1946, 'Alami felt that the Mufti should be further removed from Palestine and isolated. He suggested to the Palestine authorities that Raja'i al-Husayni, the Mufti's nephew (a "moderate and level-headed" man, according to the High Commissioner) should be allowed to see the Mufti in Paris to "remonstrate" with him.[17] He also stressed that the Mufti should be allowed to leave France and live in some country, such as Switzerland, where his wife and family might join him. There he might lose the "halo of spurious martyrdom" with which large sections of the Palestinian Arabs viewed him.[18]

The more extreme the Palestinian Arabs and the Arab world perceived Western policies to be in Palestine, the more the Mufti gained credibility. The unpopular recommendations of the AAC in the spring of 1946 had placed Jamal and 'Alami at a further disadvantage and politically weakened them. Jamal toured the country and sought to stimulate further moderation (and to prevent the outbreak of premature violence), by means of demonstrations and receptions, in order to await the results of the Morrison-Grady talks in London. However, the Mufti apparently aroused opposition to Jamal from members of his own family and party leaders (younger members), who increasingly began to hamper his activities by way of calling for retaliation against Zionist violence.[19]

Jamal was under pressure not only from the Mufti but from the other notables, largely as a result of his own intransigence. Since his return to Palestine, Jamal, as head of the PAP, had begun to reassert his party's demands for total control of the AHC, formed, as was seen, in November 1945. Jamal would not give due weight to the other parties and did not accept the idea of a rotating chairman nor of rotating delegates to League sessions. Also, he wanted two PAP men for every one member of the other parties. Despite pressure and exhortation towards the need for unity by 'Izzat Darwaza (in correspondence from Syria), Jamal caused further division and aroused the factional opposition and resentment of the others.[20] He responded to Darwaza's appeals by claiming that his intention was to strengthen the AHC. Although Khalidi and 'Abd al-Hadi tried to come to terms with Jamal through discussions all three had in Cairo with Arab League Secretary-General 'Abd al-Rahman 'Azzam Bey, Jamal would not compromise.[21]

In March 1946, the AHC was dissolved, having barely survived four months. In reaction to Jamal's intransigence, the leaders of the other five parties called a popular political meeting in Jerusalem. According to al-Hut, delegates from all the districts of Palestine attended, representing workers' organizations, independents, and educated young men.[22] The attendants created an "Arab Higher Front" (AHF) composed mainly of the leaders of five familiar parties (minus the PAP).

Table 6.1 Representation on the AHF Formed In March 1946[23]

PAP: Raghib al-Nashashibi, Sulayman Tuqan
Youth Congress: Ya'qub al-Ghusayn
National Bloc: 'Abd al-Latif Salah
Reform: Dr. Husayn al-Khalidi
Istiqlal: 'Awni 'Abd al-Hadi
Independent Members: Ahmad Hilmi Pasha

It would seem, from the fact of the composition of the AHF, that the majority of attendants to the "popular" meeting perhaps represented the dominant social elite, the notability. No workers' or middle class representatives were elected to the AHF.

Jamal retained the name of the AHC and, in an effort to counter the AHF, attempted to add progressive elements on the Higher Committee. But his attempts to make the AHC more broadly representative was not just due to pressure from the opposing notables. By 1946 there was more outspoken interference in notable dominated politics by the communist Arab League for National Liberation and other left-wing parties which began to have an influence on the dominant leadership. Specifically, the AHC was increasingly criticized for being unrepresentative and undemocratic.[24] Jamal understood the need to incorporate the growing influence in Palestinian politics of labor organizations and began informal talks with these elements to that end.[25] The negotiations with the ALNL failed. The party rejected Jamal's proposed expansion of the AHC on the basis that he had no mandate from the people and that all AHC members should be installed by election.[26] However, Jamal succeeded in gaining the cooperation of the social democratic leaning Palestine Arab Workers Society led by Sami Taha and of other men representing business interests and the professional middle segment of Palestinian society.

Table 6.2: Membership on Jamal al-Husayni's AHC in April 1946[27]

Name(s)	Backbround/Affiliation
Jamal al-Husayni	
Tewfiq S. al-Husayni	
Yusif Sahyun	
Kamil al-Dajani	
Emile al-Ghury	
Rafiq al-Tamimi	All with the PAP
Anwar al-Khatib	Landlord from Hebron, associated with the PAP and 'Alami's constructive scheme
Dr. 'Izzat Tannus	A Christian medical doctor from Jerusalem of considerable business interests, politically independent
Antone 'Attallah	A leading member of the Greek Orthodox community, a Jerusalem businessman, politically independent
Ahmad al-Shukayri	A lawyer from Acre hailing from an influential family, 'Alami's friend, Arab nationalist

Table 6.2 (cont.)	
Name(s)	**Backbround/Affiliation**
Sami Taha	Head of PAWS
Dr. Yusif Haykal	Mayor of Jaffa, politically independent

Jamal's refurbished and expanded AHC was more successful than the AHF in gaining the cooperation of elements outside the fold of the notables.

Jamal's willingness to expand the Husayni dominated AHC was due to two main reasons: he wanted to counter the influence of the AHF and desired to increase and legitimize his own influence among all sections of the population as a balance to the Mufti's influence. There was perhaps a further reason for Jamal's activities. The AHF had come into a coincidental and certainly incongruous alliance with the ALNL in their appeal to boycott the AAC and to greet its arrival with a strike.[28] Although men such as Raghib al-Nashashibi and Sulayman Tuqan were never known for their unwillingness to compromise, they and 'Abd al-Latif Salah of the National Bloc identified themselves with the AHF appeal to boycott, perhaps to gain popularity and take the nationalist wind out of Jamal and the Husaynis. On the other hand Jamal, in tacit agreement with the Arab states, was afraid that a strike would hamper his efforts, as was seen, to promote moderation. Hence his alliance with PAWS's Sami Taha who, along with 'Alami, in fact met with the AAC when it visited Palestine.[29]

In all this the Mufti, too, was against Jamal's moderation and seeming cooperation with the Arab states. Jamal's goal was to achieve ascendancy over all opponents to increase the influence of the PAP in cooperation with more progressive elements. The Mufti's goal was to achieve control over all Palestinian political activity. He was not only against Jamal's perceived moderation and cooperation with the British, but also disliked Jamal's flirtation with progressive elements. In the latter sense the Mufti had more in common with Khalidi and 'Abd al-Hadi than he had with Jamal. (After mid-1946, that is after Bludan, Khalidi became a strong supporter of the Mufti.) Thus, for these reasons, the Mufti openly began to denounce Jamal and 'Alami as tools of British imperialism. In fact, things reached such a straining point between the duo and the Mufti that at the end of May 1946 'Alami paid a visit to him in Paris in the hope of reaching an amicable agreement and forestalling the ressurection of the old Arab High Command in Beirut and Syria, which was staffed by "extremists" (i.e., young nationalists) who directed the rebellion from there in 1936–39.[30] Eventually, 'Alami's trip to Paris did nothing to mend the cleavages.

The AHC and AHF lasted until June 1946 when, at Bludan, Syria, the Arab states actively assisted the Palestinians in the creation of a new representative body. The pressure on the Arab states and Palestinians to set up a unified higher committee were great. The atmosphere among Arab leaders was one of anxiety and fear. The huge demonstrations which followed the publication of the AAC recommendations had put pressure on the Arab states to show their publics that they were actively engaged in defense of Palestine. A meeting of Arab rulers at Inschass (Egypt) in May, in fact, served this purpose. Before the League meeting convened, the Arab kings and presidents who gathered there issued a communique reaffirming their support for Arab Palestine and rejecting any further Jewish immigration.[31] The League Council had met at Bludan with the intention of reconciling the AHC and AHF. The Palestinians had gone there more divided and paralyzed than at any other previous time. Political conflict continued to be centered around the jealousies and ambitions of the notability, who dragged Palestinian politics ever deeper into the quagmire of personalistic rivalries, unable, even for the briefest time, to unite in the face of what were obviously dangerous internal and external forces.

The efforts to create a new higher committee at Bludan involved long hours of meetings between Arab politicians and various influential Palestinians. A committee of fifteen was appointed to represent the Arab states at the informal discussions (which included Fayhum Ramadan Pasha of Egypt, Hamdi Pachachi Pasha of 'Iraq, Ibrahim Hashim Pasha of Trans-Jordan, Sa'ib Slam of Lebanon and Yusif Yasin representing Sa'udi Arabia), while the Palestinians who attended included the six presidents of the old parties and activists and close Mufti associates such as Subhi al-Khadra, Akram Zu'ayter, 'Izzat Darwaza, Rafiq al-Tamimi, Wasif Kamal, Farid al-'Anabtawi, and others.[32] No representatives from the working class were present.

After the grievances of both the AHC and AHF against each other were heard, a new Arab Higher Executive (AHE) was created, consisting of only four members: Jamal al-Husayni, vice chairman (the chairmanship was left vacant for the Mufti), Dr. Husayn al-Khalidi, secretary, Hilmi Pasha, and Emile al-Ghury. According to 'Abd al-Hadi, he had originally made the suggestion of creating a small executive committee of three (to consist of Jamal, Khalidi and Hilmi Pasha) in a meeting that took place in his bedroom with Sa'ib Slam, Jamal, Dr. Khalidi, and Subhi al-Khadra. Al-Hadi sarcastically implied that his suggestion, which was made rather half seriously (he described himself as staying aloof of the buffoonery of the others), was seized upon by the other Palestinians, with the proviso that a fourth member representing the Christians should be added to the committee.[33] Khalidi represented the opponents of the Husaynis, Jamal represented the PAP, and Hilmi represented the independents. Although the Jerusalem lawyer Henry Cattan and Antone 'Attallah were considered, Ghury, the staunch PAP supporter, was eventually chosen as the fourth member of the committee.

The Husaynis actually triumphed at Bludan. This was no surprise given the fact that Jamal's "moderation" was in line with the policies of the Arab states, particularly 'Iraq and Egypt. Unlike Khalidi and the others on the AHF, Jamal's cautious willingness to consider Western initiatives towards Palestine (i.e., the ACC and Morrison-Grady talks) paralleled the wishes of the Arab states, which were intent on avoiding conflict with Britain and the United States. The intention at Bludan was that the AHE should take over all Arab national and political organizations such as the Arab offices, the National Fund, 'Alami's land development scheme, the boycott machinery, and assets of the former AHC.[34] It was also intended that all Arab political elements, including labor, should be represented on a sub-committee which the AHE would set up to direct various aspects of Arab political activity.[35]

With recognition from the Arab League, the AHE attained new stature and legitimacy and firmly entrenched the Husaynis in power. Immediately after Bludan, the AHC and AHF dissolved themselves to show support for the AHE and to avoid further divisions at such a crucial period.[36] The dissolution marked an important development. It reflected the weakness of the traditional "opposition" parties, who were losing influence to the Mufti and the Husaynis. Further, it made easier the Mufti's task of appropriating all power to himself.

Although after Bludan, Jamal was made vice-chairman of the AHE under the Mufti, the former never really reconciled himself to a subordinate position. The Mufti's conflict with him and 'Alami did not cease even until the end of the mandate. However, by 1947 the two were sufficiently weakened to the point of cooperating with and enlisting the support and influence of the Mufti, who by that time had become the most powerful influence on the Palestine Arab masses. He had slipped through the hands of the French authorities and reached Egypt on 19 June 1946, from where he began to direct Palestinian Arab politics and opposition to the Zionists and the British.[37]

The Mufti had reached the Middle East after the Bludan conference and the publication of the AAC recommendations. In view of the intensification of Arab feeling over Palestine throughout the Middle East, "Haj Amin's prestige as the symbol of Arab nationalism and of Isalm. . . ." was "substantially enhanced."[38] In Palestine, all district commissioners had reported that the arrival of the Mufti in the Middle East caused celebration throughout the towns and villages and people had decorated their homes and town centers with greenery, flags and portraits of the Mufti.[39]

One district commissioner suggested that one of the major reasons for the jubilation was Palestinian Arab feeling that only when the Mufti was in power would there be greater unity among the factions and coordination in the presentation of the Arab case.[40]

Palestinian Politics in Relation to the London Conference

While the Mufti, immediately upon his arrival in Egypt, began to receive Palestinian leaders and former activists and to unify the Palestinians under his leadership, Arabs and Jews were preoccupied with London's invitation to a conference and the controversy that arose from London's stated intention to present the provincial autonomy scheme as a basis for negotiations. It will be recalled that provincial autonomy proposed dividing Palestine into an Arab and a Jewish province, each autonomous in areas concerning health and social welfare, administration, and even land sales and immigration. The central government would be under mandatory control, having power over matters such as foreign relations, defense, currency, and customs.

The fact that at Bludan the seat of chairman of the AHE was left vacant for the Mufti indicates that even at the height of differences with him, Jamal did not have enough power or support to ignore or displace him. Further, the Mufti had some populist appeal in the Arab world, which might explain why Arab states such as 'Iraq and Sa'udi Arabia did not attempt to challenge the Bludan decision to leave the chairmanship vacant.

From London, the resurgence of the Mufti's power and influence was a threat to moderation and to progressive forces within Palestine, such as the aspiring youth parties and the workers, whom London perceived as being more amenable to dialogue. From a liberal minded view, the British government thought that the replacement of the older leaders by younger and more socially progressive elements, Arab leaders more comfortable with the ideas and policies of a progressive, labor dominated Socialist state, would have a moderating influence on the direction of Palestinian politics.

From this perspective, Britain insisted, at the outset of planning its invitations to the London Conference, that the Mufti would not be accepted as part of the Palestinian delegation and questioned whether the AHE was sufficiently representative of the Palestinian people and whether they should not issue additional invitations to persons other than those on the AHE.[41] The Palestine authorities cautioned London that the AHE was regarded by most parties and sections of the Palestinian Arabs as their supreme political institution recognized as such by the League, and that it was "tactically desirable" that the AHE itself should be asked to nominate additional representatives outside itself.[42] London did not commit itself to the High Commissioner's proposals and left the issue open.

But these issues ultimately proved to be obstacles in the way of Palestinian Arab acceptance to go to London. After the High Commissioner made the invitations to the AHE, that body argued that it could not attend the London Conference if the provincial autonomy scheme were to be taken as a basis for discussion.[43] Interestingly enough, Palestinian objections to Britain's policies paralleled Jewish objections. Both rejected the provincial autonomy scheme as a basis for negotiation, both insisted on an independent state, and both rejected London's dictates as to who should be able to attend. (The Jewish Agency insisted that Jewish leaders held under detention should be freed and allowed to attend, and that Ben Gurion, then staying in Paris, should be allowed to lead any Jewish delegation.)

But the British government was anxious to get the Arabs and Jews to London and could not afford to be uncompromising in its positions. It feared that Palestine would sink into communal violence and Britain would lose its influence and position to outside powers. While reiterating its intention to place the provincial autonomy scheme before the conference, London informed all parties that they would have full liberty to present counter-proposals which would be considered by the British government.[44] Further, they were informed that London was not committed to carrying out its plan irrespective of conference results and that attendance by the AHE or the Zionists would not imply their readiness to accept London's proposals.[45] Confidentially, the High Commissioner was informed that it was not London's intention to abandon the provincial autonomy scheme if agreement was not reached at the conference. "Our action will depend on what, in the light of the proceedings of the conference, we judge will be the consequences of implementing it."[46]

In a meeting with Cunningham, Jamal accepted London's invitation on behalf of the AHE and reiterated the following Arab principles: a) That the AHE reaffirmed the decisions of the Arab League Council meeting at Alexandria in August (where the Arabs met to map out strategy for the London talks) which refused to accept the provincial autonomy scheme or any other similar scheme leading to partition and to sit with any Zionist delegation; and b) That any negotiations with the British government would have to be based on numerous previous pledges (i.e., the White Paper), the Atlantic Charter, and the Charter of the United Nations.[47] The Alexandria conference had actually urged the Palestinian Arabs to participate to ensure that rejection of any scheme of partition would be unanimous, and also that the Palestinian Arab delegation would be present when Arab counter-proposals were discussed.[48]

In the meeting with Cunningham, Jamal was informed of the desirability of wider Palestinian representation—from the municipalities, commerce, and labor. Jamal not only indicated the AHE's disfavor towards such a suggestion but insisted that the delegation should include the Mufti.[49] Jamal's stand towards wider representation was astonishing given the fact that just less than six months before he had cooperated with and co-opted men such as Sami Taha and Yusif Haykal. This indicates that Jamal's association with progressive elements was based on temporary political exigencies. Once Jamal received a share of power in Palestinian politics through the AHE, he reverted to his urban notable instincts. Further, Jamal's stand may have been influenced by the Mufti, who disliked the idea of cooperating with working class elements.

Jamal's stance hardened London's and Cunningham's position, the latter being stubbornly against the Mufti's return to Palestine or attendance at London. Prior to his meeting with Jamal, he reacted strongly to a suggestion by London that if they made any consessions to the Jewish Agency and released detained Zionist leaders, it would be impossible not to receive the Mufti. Cunningham posited the following interesting argument and observation:

> I should state most emphatically that it would be out of the question to release the Jewish leaders. Both Jamal and the Mufti would put forward extreme demands at the Conference, but Jamal's personal following accounts to less than half of the Arabs in Palestine, whereas Haj Amin is followed by nearly all....[50]

The British government now insisted on its right to issue invitations to Palestinians other than those on the AHE,[51] which prompted Cunningham to suggest the names of Musa al-'Alami, Sulayman Tuqan, Sami Taha, Antone 'Atallah, and Dr. Yusif Haykal.[52]

The AHE, through Dr. Husayn al-Khalidi, informed the High Commissioner that they would not attend the conference, insisting on the sole right to choose their political leader, which was the Mufti.[53] Khalidi adamantly pointed out that London had no right to interfere between the AHE and the leadership (i.e., the Mufti) chosen by the "free will" of the Arab people. As the AHE was the only body which represented the Arabs of Palestine, Khalidi argued, the Palestinians did not accept the government's proposals for the constitution of a delegation.[54] This, of course, represented the point of view of a notable landowning class that was trying to block out any other influence for fear that its position of power and prestige would be weakened.

The Palestine government was aware of the discontent towards the AHE of the young, professional, commercial, and labor elements in the

urban centers, which desired broader representation and more democratic participation in politics. It is of interest to point out that the last so
named on the High Commissioner's list, Dr. Haykal, had confided to Cunningham his opposition to the AHE and its dictatoral ways.[55] No doubt
part of Haykal's discontent was due to his being dropped from Jamal's
AHC upon its dissolution and his inability to obtain a role in the League-
inspired AHE.

Just before the London Conference Haykal had informed Cunningham that a new political youth movement was being formed.[56] They were
dissatisfied, Haykal stated, with the AHE because it was "impracticable
and old fashioned," particularly as witnessed by its refusal to attend the
London Conference. The new movement was being formed by younger
men in the professions and commerce, and they hoped that workers
would also join. Haykal stated that Sami Taha was asked to join but he
thought Sami had ideas of starting his own party. Some of the more progressive younger men in Jaffa had already joined, Haykal went on, and
others in the big Arab towns and communities were interested. One meeting had already been held and it decided that the movement should not
be labeled a "party" as they were clear the Arabs were tired of parties. The
new movement's program was based on a political outlook calling for cooperation between Arabs, Jews, and Britons with the hope of an eventual
creation of a joint government. The movement, however, rejected any
further Jewish immigration and was against partition. Haykal also made it
clear that the movement was not in favor of breaking with the British connection, which he said the Arabs could not live without.

Haykal had actually gone to see 'Azzam Bey to enlist League support and sympathy.[57] Probably Haykal's immediate objective was to get
the League members to put pressure on the AHE to recognize the new
youth movement and to admit their representatives to that body. This
suggests that, despite brewing middle class discontent in the urban centers, no person or movement dared challenge the Mufti, given the extreme
political and emotional situation at the time where the mass of the peasantry saw him as their protector against Zionism.[58] Finally, Haykal's
emphasis on the British connection perhaps reflected the economic ties
and interests that the commercial classes had developed during the rapid
growth of the forties.

The Mufti's residency in Egypt seems to have put a brake on the
extent of pressure the Arab states were willing to exert on the Palestinians.
Though they needed Palestinian attendance in London in order to legitimize and lend authority to their position, still the Palestinian rejection of
attendance incurred no Arab response or pressure. The Palestinian rejec-

tion probably was the work of the Mufti, for not only did he view any conference with skepticism, but he also could not get Britain to either let him return to Palestine or attend the conference. Given Jamal's resentment of the Mufti, his and the AHE's insistence on the Mufti's attendance could only have been the result of acquiescence to the latter's demands. Certainly the Arab states did not in any way intervene in the Mufti's activities nor pressure the Palestinians to attend. In Egypt the government gave him a liberal hand.

The prevailing anti-provincial autonomy opinions and the seeming harmony of Palestinian and Arab positions pushed London to soften its stand towards Palestinian representation. During the interim period of the London Conference (3 October 1946 to 26 January 1947), London again decided to invite the Palestinians but without any pre-conditions about the composition of a delegation. Also, the British government anxiously hoped that, with both Palestinian and Jewish attendance, the second stage of the conference would succeed which, as we have seen, it did not. Thus, the invitation asked Jamal to nominate a delegation to the London Conference and expressed the hope that the AHC (the AHE created at Bludan eventually was known again as the AHC) would include the five individual Palestinians ('Alami, Tuqan, Taha, 'Atallah, Haykal) to whom invitations had previously been issued.[59] The invitation tactilely recognized the AHC as the only qualified representative of the Palestinian Arabs.

The AHC nominated Jamal, Dr. Khalidi, Ghury, and Mu'in al-Madi, a close associate of the Mufti who was amnestied in 1946.[60] But before leaving for London, the delegates went to Cairo for a plenary session with the Mufti. The outcome of the meeting was a telegram stating that Madi was prevented by illness from going to London and nominating in his place Sami Taha. Dr. 'Umar al-Khalil, a left-winger who was secretary of an organization called the Village Improvement Society and an associate of Taha, Yusif Sahyun, a Catholic and an avid Husayni supporter, and Wasif Kamal, also a close associate of the Mufti and a former Axis collaborator, were also nominated.[61] Ultimately, Wasif Kamal did not attend because of London's opposition.

The change in delegates reflected a compromise by the Mufti to the pressure from various quarters that was applied against him and the Husayni dominated AHC. First, in early January 1947 the Mufti expanded the AHC from four members (Jamal, Khalidi, Hilmi Pasha, and Ghury) to nine (excluding himself) in an effort to increase his political power and reorganize Palestinian politics on more activist grounds. He added to the AHC close associates and supporters.

Table 6.3: The Mufti's Expansion of the AHC in January 1947[62]	
Original Bludan AHE mid-1946	**AHC at Beginning of 1947**
Jamal al-Husayni	The Mufti, Haj Amin
Dr. Husayn al-Khalidi	Jamal al-Husayni
Ahmad Hilmi Pasha	Dr. Husayn al-Khalidi
Emile al-Ghury	Ahmad Hilmi Pasha
	Emile al-Ghury
	Hasan Abu Sa'ud
	Izhak Darwish al-Husayni
	'Izzat Darwaza
	Rafiq al-Tamimi
	Mu'in al-Madi

This move not only aroused the hostility of old opponents of the Husaynis such as Sulayman Tuqan (the only NDP representative of significance left) and 'Awni 'Abd al-Hadi, but also attracted the criticism of the younger and educated elements in the towns.[63] The daily *Filastin,* which was a supporter of the anti-Husayni, particularly *Istiqlal*ist, camp, expressed "regrets" that no form of election was employed in the expansion of the AHC and criticized some of the persons who were chosen to go to London as being too "feudal" to appeal to the Labour government. It added that "particular regret" was felt in "proletarian circles" that no representative of Arab labor had been included (this was before the announced change of delegates).[64]

Thus, the Mufti, Jamal and others on the AHC (including Darwaza) felt that concessions would have to be made in the face of widespread dissatisfaction.[65] (It must be reiterated, however, that the concessions concerned delegates to London, not membership on the AHC. In fact, because of the Mufti's unbending attitude towards wider representation, al-Madi and Darwaza resigned from the AHC in mid-1947.) Also, in the previous month of December, the Arab states delegates to the London Conference, who had gathered in Cairo to discuss strategy for the second stage of the conference (27 January to 14 February 1947), had pressed the Palestinian leaders to send delegates to London and to admit to the AHC progressive elements such as Dr. Yusif Haykal and Sami Taha.[66] The Mufti was also told to leave 'Alami alone in his land development scheme and Arab offices, as the Mufti had warned him to bring it into line with the AHC (i.e., place it under the control of the Husaynis) or abandon it.[67] The Arab states were well aware of London's displeasure at the AHC's choice of some of the delegates and desired to do as much as possible to remove obstacles to Palestinian attendance. The Arabs also hoped they could come to an agreement with Britain. Lastly, the pressure on the Mufti emanated from 'Iraqi insistence in the League.

The Palestinians, then, had agreed to attend the London Conference first because of the recognition granted to the AHC by London, and second because of Arab states pressure. However, it would seem the latter factor was less significant in affecting their decision than the first. It was only after the British government extended an invitation in January, a month after the League meeting, that the Palestinians accepted. Under the influence of the Mufti, they were skeptical that the conference would lead to any constructive end and, in general, the Palestinian Arabs were in no mood for compromise. Instead, they were busy preparing and organizing themselves for conflict with the Zionists, whose more extreme elements were waging an unprecedented campaign of terror against Britons and Arabs.

The inability of the Arab states to exert any substantial pressure on the Palestinians at that time is further illustrated by the fact that the Mufti neither added "progressive" or labor representatives on the AHC, as was just seen, nor did he relent in his quest to control 'Alami's activities. Also, the AHC displayed unprecedented confidence when in January it made public a memorandum it submitted to the League (just after the adjournment of the conference) regarding the constitutional plan put forward by the Arab states at the conference in September (refer to the discussion of the London Conference in the previous chapter). It would seem that the constitutional plan (a unitary state in which Jews and Arabs would be proportionately represented in a legislature) was proposed without prior consultation or approval with the Palestinians. The Arab states perhaps were confident that their plan adhered to the basic demands of the Palestinians. The memorandum was notable for its intransigence, rejecting almost without exception the few elements of compromise in the proposals of the Arab states.[68] It demanded immediate independence and stoppage of immigration, accepted the Jews only as a religious minority, and recognized as Palestinian citizens only those Jews who were in Palestine prior to 1917, and their descendants.

The Palestine authorities believed that the AHC's unyielding attitude was not intended to be taken too seriously (being a retort to the excessive demands of the Zionists and the fever-pitch emotionalism the Yishuv was displaying[69]), and that the Arab states' plan would be regarded as an acceptable solution.[70] The fact that the memorandum was publicized on the eve of the departure of the Palestinian delegation to London lends credence to the theory that the rejection was a tactical diplomatic move.

Whatever the indications that the AHC's rejection was meant as a counterweight to Jewish extremism, the imprint of the Mufti's influence was as prevalent as it was in that body's memorandum of rejection of the White Paper in 1939. Firstly, there was no indication that the Mufti had any faith in conferences carried on between a colonial power and what he perceived as corrupt and subordinate regimes. Throughout the whole conference, he was actively organizing and uniting the Palestinians in preparation for rebellion, as will be seen. Also, the Arab states showed no optimism, neither at the conference nor publicly, that a solution would be found in London.

Secondly, despite the peasant revolt in 1936–39 and its challenge to the position of the dominant landowning classes, the Mufti's image was never tarnished. His escape from Palestine in 1937, his continuation of the revolt, and his consistent anti-colonialist record throughout the forties made him the preeminent leader and buttressed his unyielding nationalism and self-confidence. Zionist violence and political extremism only enhanced the Mufti's image in the Palestinian countryside. When the British authorities in Cairo inquired whether the Mufti could be returned to Palestine to stop his "mischief making" in Egypt,[71] the Palestine authorities emphatically were against the idea, stating that "his arrival would be certain to awake the now quiet Fellahin, whom he also could arouse and knit into a cohesive whole...."[72]

Thirdly, there was a more immediate factor that strengthened the Mufti's position. Britain's inability to deal with illegally armed Jewish organizations, violence, and illegal immigration, convinced many Palestinian Arabs that they would have to militarily prepare themselves and the Mufti was "regarded as the only Arab leader capable and tough enough to organize effectively any such armed Arab resistance."[73] Further, the Arab states were becoming increasingly convinced that Britain's impotence in Palestine meant that it was not in a position to "protect" the Arabs who would have to "look after themselves."[74] This and escalating Jewish terrorism, particularly after the failure of the London Conference, strongly enhanced the Mufti's leadership and weakened the opposition of the working class or other elements.

Arab Palestine throughout the mandate was a peculiar case in that the conflict with the Zionists had given the national struggle predominance over any social inequality and thus helped prolong the overlordship of the landowning classes, their families, and their local connections. In the forties this situation was magnified many times over as the notability used the nationalist weapon to deflect change in the power relationships in Palestinian society. The inherent inability of a factionalist based and organized elite to achieve broad unity became clear as the Palestinian leaders tried to organize and prepare themselves and their people for the showdown with the Zionists.

7

The Mufti, Palestinian Politics, and Efforts at Socio-Political Unity of Arab Society

To the Palestinian Arab notability of the 1940s, politics was a profession of continual conflict and little compromise. They were able neither to unite nor to organize themselves, much less lead their people. Compromise and cooperation were practically unknown, as each man pursued a destructively individualistic path and jealously guarded his prerogatives. Such was the calibre of men leading a people already harassed and exhausted by an unrelenting assault on its national existence and overwhelmed by the pervasive intervention of regional and international powers in its affairs. By 1947, the Palestinian Arab leaders had lost so much credibility as a result of their impotent maneuverings that the stage was left open for the Arab states to superimpose their disunity, dynastic intrigues, and political suspicions onto Palestine, as will be seen in Part Three.

The Mufti as Person, Nationalist Leader, and Notable

Throughout the time the London Conference was in progress, the Mufti was holding continuous sessions of the AHC in Cairo. Given the wretched state in which Palestinian politics found itself at such a critical period, the opportunity was open for the Mufti to lead the Palestinians almost as he saw fit. In a concrete way the Mufti transcended the factional (clan) rivalries of Palestinian society. Despite the variegated opposition, the Mufti represented more than a family political party or the patronage system in which urban notables like himself functioned. His political behavior was not solely motivated by the interests of his family or clan, which was not the case with Jamal. Although both indirectly guarded the ascendant position of the Husaynis, the Mufti was not as parochial as Jamal nor was he as interested in the PAP. Most of his confidants—such as

133

Subhi al-Khadra, 'Uthman Kamal Haddad, Kamil 'Areikat, and Ma'ruf al-Dawalibi—were from the time of the revolt, and they and Jamal had nothing in common. Further, Jamal was flexible compared to the Mufti, which was perhaps due to his smaller following and, secondarily, to the influence of Musa al-'Alami. Whatever the reason, Jamal certainly did not enjoy the popularity or support that the Mufti did.

In the largely agrarian society of Arab Palestine, one which was going through rapid socio-economic changes but whose social structure was only partially transformed, the Mufti symbolized the dominant nationalist-religious idiom within which the peasantry perceived its world and functioned. Because he was an urban notable of national stature and a religious functionary, he was readily understood and followed by the clannish peasantry. From this source he drew his legitimacy as a political leader.

All of this is not to imply that the Mufti was somehow above the class of urban notables he represented. His role, in fact, served to prolong the domination of that social class. The increasing turbulence in Palestine with the resultant apprehension and fear among the people helped keep the Mufti in power. The class he represented was actually rapidly losing its social power base in the forties. The traditional factions opposing the Husaynis or the Mufti could no longer muster enough support beyond their very restricted localities to act as a credible threat to the Mufti and the PAP.

This is indicated by the fact that the Husayni dominated AHC did not need the cooperation of the traditional factions to stay together. As will be seen, faction leaders, in fact, needed the AHC to exercise any power on a national level. Also, they shared the Mufti's limited conception (although not his style) of order and unity, albeit their cooperation was based on their perceived interests rather than on any good feelings towards him. Many of them actually hated the Mufti but were powerless to act against him. By 1948, for example, even Sulayman Tuqan of Nablus was trying to conciliate the Mufti. Faction leaders were compelled to follow the Mufti because of the dangers Palestine was facing and because of his influence as a result of these dangers. Furthermore, to protect their political survival, they could not align themselves with any radical opposition and, conversely, the AHC constituted the organ of their ascendancy.

What the Mufti attempted to do between 1946–48 no other Palestinian leader or party (from the notability) could do. Within his own limited view of political organization (i.e., structural and administrative organization and unity) he did what he thought best for the Palestinians. He deeply distrusted Arab regimes, whom he saw as subservient to Britain and the United States, and he looked towards the Arab masses for the effective protection of Arab Palestine.[1] A basic line of division between him and other urban notables was his willingness to resort to armed struggle to achieve Palestinian nationalist goals, regardless of the consequences for his class. While early during the Arab revolt he and the other notables had feared losing the initiative to the peasants and had wanted to put an end to the armed struggle, by the late forties the Mufti was readily preparing for armed conflict with the Zionists. In a broad sense, he represented Palestinian national interests and his actions were motivated mainly by a desire to achieve Arab nationalist goals.

The Mufti's Arab nationalist leanings were one of the primary factors accounting for his popularity and prestige in the Arab world. His struggle against the British in Palestine catapulted him into a position not entirely of his own making. The complex Palestinian problem necessitated the relative radicalization (in an anti-colonialist sense) of his political views. To be a Palestinian nationalist hardly left any room for compromise with Jewish nationalism and its backers, the Western powers. The logic of his situation and responsibilities almost dictated his position as a Palestinian and Arab nationalist. He was a major Palestinian leader and Palestine was a central factor in the rise of Arab nationalism. His convictions on Palestine, therefore, reflected the views of a younger generation of Arabs.

His attitude towards Arab regimes and their relationship with the imperialist powers was, then, remarkable. During late 1947, at the time that the United Nations was considering partition, the Mufti gave numerous interviews which revealed his unique views as compared with other Palestinian notables—views that surpassed the status quo nationalist beliefs of the *Istiqlal*ists. He not only emphatically argued against any truncation of Palestine, Zionist ambitions, and British colonialism, but differentiated between Arab regimes and the desire of the Arab peoples for unity. On Arab unity, he believed there were two opposed trends: the Arab peoples on the one hand and governments on the other. Regarding the people, he was of the conviction that unity was complete, but as a result of artificial frontiers established after 1920 and "British made thrones" the same was not true of Arab governments.[2] In the last resort, he felt that the Arab rulers would have to incline before the will of the people. There were, the Mufti argued, three influences working against Arab unity: Zionist political and territorial ambitions and designs, British duplicity, and the political ambitions and intrigues of individual Arab rulers.[3]

The Mufti's role was not purely constructive. He was determined to bring all political activity and institutions under the control of the AHC, with himself as supreme leader. He had no patience for opposition leaders or movements, and he believed that the AHC could actually direct all Palestinian national enterprises and military organization. He obstructed any call or efforts at unifying the Palestinians on a democratic basis—that is, on the basis of incorporating the diverse social elements in Palestinian society. To have accepted the participation of the workers would have been detrimental to his social power base or class. He not only resorted to intimidation of opponents, but also to assassination. His extreme nationalism and readiness to resort to armed struggle served to silence and take the wind out of his opponents. To the Mufti, cooperation and unity meant subservience to his person. His authoritarian and dictatorial styles and his intransigence and favoritism when dealing with other Palestinians hindered rather than helped the Palestinian people in their efforts to organize themselves.

Perhaps his ambitions to control everyone and everything were due to his fear of losing the initiative to the middle classes and urban workers, much as he and other notables did in the revolt just a decade previously. Whatever the case, he gave and withheld support in accordance with his interests and he did much to arouse jealousy, antagonism and division among Palestinian leaders. His uncompromising character, his habit of not bestowing confidence or delegating power to any but his associates, and his fearful reputation, coalesced to exaggerate the destructive tendencies in Palestinian politics. Ultimately, his administrative and organizational skills could not substitute for genuine unity. This was made clear when the society disintegrated in 1948. In balance, however, the Mufti did more than any other Palestinian notable to mobilize a fractured and vulnerable society, regardless of how limited his efforts may have been.

The Mufti began his attempts to organize the Palestinians scarcely a month after he arrived in Egypt. He eventually succeeded in partially doing what Jamal had failed to do. Jamal had been trying, as was shown, to unite the Arab club, scout, and youth organizations under the umbrella of the PAP. For example, the Boy Scouts, a branch of the International Scout Organization, had come into prominence because of the interest taken in them by Jamal. Enthusiasm for the movement increased rapidly in schools, where, in accordance with Jamal's wishes, political education of a strongly nationalist nature began to be disseminated.[4] The Mufti's goals were formidable, seeking to unite diverse and disparate elements under his leadership. He wanted to unify the land redemption scheme and national fund of 'Alami and Ahmad Hilmi, respectively, and to fuse the two dominant youth organizations, the *Najjada* (Helpers) and *Futuwa* (Youth). To this end, he sought to set up departments of national economy, lands, treasury, and national organizations (club and youth organizations), most of which goals did not materialize until late 1947 and into 1948. The Palestinians were trying to emulate the Jewish Agency and community.

The AHC and Political and Administrative Organization

The central weakness of the attempts by the notability to mobilize the Palestinian masses was within the dominant class itself. As mentioned, this class actually believed that the haphazard creation of schemes for institutional organizations could substitute for a coherent political and social ideology or vision. Their vision was limited to the factionalist politices that determined their place in the prevailing social order.

In addition to the limited outlook and divisiveness of the notability, however, there were more immediate factors that militated against effective organization and cooperation. One, the Mufti himself was unable to return to Palestine, particularly because of the High Commissioner's refusal to even consider the question. The Mufti repeatedly attempted to have the Arab League mediate his return to Palestine, especially in early 1947 when the Palestinians were invited to the London Conference.[5] The Palestine government was convinced that his presence would create grave security problems, if only because of his peasant following.[6] The Mufti's physical distance, and his determination to control all political activity, was another factor that made the AHC's initiatives only partially successful. It was a difficult enough proposition for the Palestinians to try to unite their resources within Palestine. It was infinitely more difficult to attempt to lead the people from outside of the country. Beside the fact that there were no coherent political parties and middle activists to mobilize the people, the Mufti's relocations from one Arab capital to another meant that the entire AHC administrative structure was moved with him. Finally, the Mufti persistently refused to grant any significant authority or power to the AHC institutions that were to be created in Palestine.

There was a considerable coming and going of Palestinian leaders to Egypt throughout 1947 as they tried to conciliate themselves with each other and with the Mufti. The AHC convened both in Jerusalem and in Alexandria, where the Mufti resided. The first major institution that the AHC wished to create, but could not resolve differences over, was the *Bayt al-Mal al-'Arabi*, the treasury of the AHC, or what was meant to be a national treasury. The *Bayt* was not only meant to serve the primary purpose of collecting taxes but to save Arab land from alienation to the Zionists.[7] To bring national enterprises under the control of the AHC, the Mufti wanted to amalgamate into the *Bayt* both 'Alami's constructive scheme and Hilmi Pasha's National Fund.

As early as July 1946, just one month after the Mufti's arrival in Egypt, the AHC held a meeting where it was agreed that the *Bayt* should exercise control over the land redemption schemes.[8] While 'Alami was more resistant, Hilmi Pasha from the outset was amenable to the Mufti's plans. One reason for this was that Hilmi was (with Khalidi) chosen at Bludan in June 1946 as one of the four original members of the AHE. Further, Hilmi was in close association with Khalidi, both of whom were in conflict with 'Alami since he initiated the constructive scheme. Thus, Hilmi Pasha responded positively to the Mufti's suggestion that sources of income from which Hilmi's National Fund were derived would be exempt from obligations to contribute to the *Bayt*.[9]

At the meeting of the Fund's administrative council in April 1947, the time the *Bayt* was officially proclaimed, Hilmi Pasha agreed to send a delegation to Egypt to hold discussions with the AHC on coordinating the Fund's activities with the *Bayt* and to invite Jamal and other Mufti associates to become members of the administrative council.[10] There is no evidence that the Fund came under the direct control of the Mufti as by late 1947 it was still functioning independently. The fact that the Fund was well established and popular, and that Hilmi Pasha was willing to cooperate and even ask for grants from the *Bayt* perhaps softened the Mufti's determination to control it.

The conflict with 'Alami was not as easily resolved. The Mufti was determined not only to put an end to 'Alami's independent activity in the constructive scheme, but to bring the Arab offices under the AHC's control. The Mufti's antagonism towards 'Alami, and his recurring bitter relationship with 'Alami's supporter, Jamal, was underlined by their political differences. The Mufti especially disliked 'Alami's political activities through the Arab offices, which the former saw as ineffective pawns of the Arab League. Also, the Mufti's dislike of the constructive scheme reflected his bitterness towards the 'Iraqi regime, the main, if not only, financial backer of 'Alami. In fairness to the Mufti, 'Alami did alienate the former because of his defiant and recalcitrant attitude. Furthermore, the 'Iraqis used their patronage of 'Alami to weaken the Mufti and (belatedly) to influence the direction of Palestinian politics in accordance with their own political/territorial ambitions.[11]

In addition to the Mufti's displeasure with him, 'Alami was particularly disliked by Hilmi Pasha and Khalidi for his association with the young and feisty Ahmad al-Shukayri. 'Alami had added Shukayri to the constructive scheme's board of directors as early as February 1946 and installed him as head of the Arab office in Jerusalem[12] There were constant rumors that Shukayri wanted to establish a socialist party. (The short-lived *Hizb al-Sha'b*, proposed in 1946, was vaguely linked to Shukayri and 'Alami.) In October 1946, Shukayri actually announced the formation of a new "socialist" party, which by the beginning of 1947 had around 200–300 members, predominantly made up of young men.[13]

Shukayri's labelling of the party as socialist reflected his hyperbolic tendencies. In all probability he was referring to the Palestine branch of the Arab Nationalist Bloc, originally formed by American University of Beirut students such as Constantine Zurayk, Taki al-Din al-Sulh, 'Adil, 'Usayran, and Fu'ad Mafraj. The Bloc was not tightly organized and was Arab nationalist; it called for unity, liberation from colonialism, and cultural and intellectual liberation from poverty and ignorance.[14] The Bloc was amorphous, had no defined structure of authority, and no formal chains of command or bureaucratic hierarchy.[15] It had a series of regional branches (Palestine, Lebanon, 'Iraq) which were weakly linked. Its members took part in the revolt of 1936–39 and the Rashid 'Ali takeover in 'Iraq in 1941. The Mufti had contacts with its leading members in Palestine and 'Iraq. Palestinians such as Farid Zayn al-Din (who was an original associate of Zurayk's in Beirut), Farid al-Sa'id, 'Izz al-Din al-Shawwa, Wasif Kamal, Khulsi al-Khayri, were all members of the Bloc.

It was in late 1946 that the Bloc was reorganized (at the same time Shuqayri made his announcement) and these men and others formed its central committee. Associated with the Bloc were Shukayri, Haykal and 'Alami (more loosely) and it had contact with Sami Taha. The Bloc supported 'Alami's schemes and 'Alami co-opted some of its men in his projects. Aside from Shuqayri, Khulsi al-Khayri was installed in the Arab office in Washington and Darwish al-Miqdadi in the Jerusalem office. Furthermore, al-Sha'b newspaper (begun in 1946 by young intellectuals)[16] was the Bloc's mouthpiece; the newspaper consistently supported 'Alami's activities. The intellectuals leading the Bloc did not have any significant impact on Palestinian politics because of its informal and amorphous character, because it was organized late in the day, and because it was unable to settle internal differences over leadership.

It should be pointed out that it was not strange that individuals such as Wasif Kamal and Miqdadi of the Arab Nationalist Bloc should also have been strong Mufti associates. The Mufti, after all, was like-minded in terms of his nationalism, though not in his attitude towards a representative leadership. Moreover, so many of the individuals active in Palestinian politics held concurrent positions on various bodies.

The sustained attack against 'Alami from the PAP and some quarters of the press (such as al-Wihda, which insinuated 'Alami was collaborating with British spies)[17] and the hostile attitude adopted towards him by the Mufti and the AHC almost made 'Alami buckle to the will of the Mufti. In January and again in September 1947, 'Alami went to 'Iraq to inform the regime of his intention to liquidate the constructive scheme and close the Arab offices, although he was persuaded by the 'Iraqis to hold out.[18]

Actually, despite the conflict between 'Alami and the Mufti, there was heavy PAP representation on the constructive scheme's administrative council, not to mention those that were PAP-leaning or close associates of the Mufti.

Table 7.1: The Constructive Scheme's Administrative Council[19]

Name	Town	Occupation
Musa al-'Alami (chair)	Jerusalem	Lawyer/landowner
Anwar al-Khatib (secretary, PAP-leaning)	Hebron	Landowner
Shaykh Mustafa al-Khayri (independent)	Ramle	Landowner/town mayor
Rafiq al-Tamimi (PAP member)	Jaffa	Landowner/merchant
Henry Cattan (independent)	Jerusalem	Lawyer/landowner
Muhammad Tewfiq al-Yahya (independent)	Haifa	Lawyer/landowner
Yusif Sahyun (PAP member)	Haifa	Lawyer/landowner
Musa al-Surani (PAP member)	Gaza	Landowner/merchant
Al-Haj 'Abd al-Rahim al-Nabulsi (independent)	Nablus	Merchant/head of Nablus Chamber of Commerce
Shaykh Raghib Abu Sa'ud al-Dajani (independent)	Jaffa	Lawyer/landowner
Jamal Hamid (independent)	Haifa	Lawyer/landowner
Dr. Tewfiq Can'an (independent)	Jerusalem	Medical doctor/head of Arab medical society
Ibrahim Sa'id al-Husayni (PAP member)	Jerusalem	Lawyer/landowner
Butros Malak (independent)	Jaffa	Lawyer/landowner
Muhammad al-'Abbushi (independent)	Jenin	Landowner/merchant
Rashad al-Shawwa (Arab Nationalist Bloc)	Gaza	Landowner/merchant
Farid al-'Anabtawi (PAP member)	Nablus	Landowner/merchant

	Table 7.1 (cont.)	
Name	**Town**	**Occupation**
Rushdi Imam al-Husayni (PAP member)	Jerusalem	Engineer and head of engineers' union

Six of the members, then, were formal members of the PAP, five of whom (except Rushdi Imam al-Husayni) belonged to the PAP's central committee, and one member (al-Khatib) was PAP-leaning. Additionally, as a gesture of reconciliation, 'Alami formed (in January 1947) a sub-committee of five (three of whom were not on the constructive scheme's administrative council at its initial formation) to act as an investigative body concerning cases of land sales. These five were Kamil Wafa al-Dajani, who acted as chair and who also belonged to the PAP's central committee, Muhammad 'Abd al-Rahim, an independent Jaffan merchant, Musa al-Surani, Mu'in al-Madi, and Darwish al-Miqdadi. Dajani, Madi, and Miqdadi were Mufti associates, the last, as was just mentioned, belonging to the Arab Nationalist Bloc.

Although 'Alami did meet with the Mufti, no reconciliation was ever effected. In March 1947, 'Alami offered to place the Arab offices under the Mufti but not the AHC. The Mufti made it clear that the offices should come under the control of the AHC with 'Alami himself as a member of that body. In that capacity, 'Alami would have a large measure of control over the offices and the constructive scheme.[20] 'Alami declined the Mufti's conciliatory offer. The gulf between the two grew, and by September 1947, al-Sha'b newspaper published details of the activities of the constructive scheme: the first LP150,000 from the 'Iraqis had all been spent, mainly on the aquisition of some 6,000 dunums in Samaria District and the purchase of a number of tractors from Czechoslovakia. A further LP100,000 had been received from 'Iraq.[21]

The Mufti's offer to 'Alami regarding the latter's projects seemed to be a sensible compromise. On the surface, the offer would entail collective, rather than private, decision making and responsibility over very important areas. However, one of the main factors accounting for 'Alami's resistance to the Mufti and the AHC was his fear that the Arab offices and constructive scheme would come under the control of the activists that dominated the AHC. Also, most of those on the scheme's administrative council and its sub-committee were independents or Arab nationalists who were, like 'Alami himself, educated professionals who represented a different and more democratic way of doing things. 'Alami, too, preferred quiet diplomacy and propaganda work. This was made clear by Jamal from a discussion he had with Stonehewer-Bird in Baghdad.[22] He told the ambassador that he preferred that the development scheme and Arab offices should be administered by 'Alami, who was "honest," and gave the following reasons in support of his opinions. One, the AHC was not permanent and it might be dissolved or suppressed at any time. Two, most members were "under the Mufti's thumb" and he, Jamal, often found himself in a minority of one. Three, he realized how "detested" the Mufti was in 'Iraq and that no help would be forthcoming if 'Alami's initiatives passed into the hands of the AHC.

There was, then, no agreement among the notability over the creation of a treasury. By April 1947, the AHC had created the *Bayt al-Mal*, despite its inability to control other enterprises that paralleled the *Bayt's* functions. The *Bayt* had a Board of Trustees or Directors consisting of 36 members, 12 of whom were appointed by the AHC and served as the Executive Board and the remaining 24 who were elected. Dr. 'Izzat Tannus, a medical doctor from Jerusalem who also was involved in business interests, acted as its head.[23] Not surprisingly, the 12-man Executive Board of Directors included, in addition to Tannus himself (he headed the *Bayt* and also served as an equal member on the Executive Board), Jamal al-Husayni, Ahmad Hilmi, and 'Abd al-Hamid Shuman. The *Bayt* set up six branch offices (Jerusalem, which also served as the national, or head office, Jaffa, Haifa, Nablus, Nazareth, and Gaza), and some sixteen branch advisory committees (ranging from 12 to 24 members) in the sub-districts, on which sat representatives of local merchants, farmers, professional men, and workers' organizations. In addition to its collection of taxes, it had three other functions, the last of which was temporary in nature:[24] to buy land, to spend on national organizations, and to prepare a study on manufacturing, commerce, and agriculture through its economic affairs section.

Contributions were described as taxes: 100 mils per head per annum for all Palestinian Arabs, LP10 for professional men, and up to LP50 for merchants.[25] The following taxes were levied on government department personnel:[26] Salaries of LP15 per month and under were exempt, LP15-24 paid LP1. per annum, LP24-40 paid LP2. per annum, and LP40 paid LP3. per annum. In addition, levies were to be applied (through a *Bayt* stamp) on transport, cinema tickets, newspapers, and tobacco.[27] By December 1947, the comparative failure of the *Bayt's* scheme of regular taxation (LP32,000 had been collected) led to an appeal by the AHC for special contributions. The first of these was a donation by the Mufti of his house in Jerusalem, valued at LP25,000.[28] According to Dr. Tannus, between 1 April 1947 and 31 March 1948, a total of LP220,000 was collected through direct and indirect taxes, all of which was paid out; while 'Arif al-'Arif maintains that, by 15 May, the total donations and taxes collected by the AHC via the *Bayt* amounted to LP156,202.[29] Whatever the case, it seems that the war, which was in full swing by January, prompted many Palestinians to give to the *Bayt*.

Besides the partially successful *Bayt al-Mal*, the other major organizations that the Mufti wanted to amalgamate under his leadership were the *Futuwa* and *Najjada* youth organizations. These were important movements, as their adherents were the young, enthusiastic, nationalist members of Palestinian society who would potentially form the nucleus of a disciplined para-military organization. As with the problems of the treasury, however, these movements were in rivalry with each other and their leaders riven with jealousy.

The *Najjada* was the first to be formed, founded by the lawyer Muhammad Nimr al-Hawari in October 1945 as an Arab Scout Movement.[30] The *Najjada* from its constitutional inception made it a goal that it not be connected with any party nor responsible to anyone but its members and by extension the people, whom it was pledged to assist through the improvement of the "educational and moral standards" of the Arab youth. Instruction included drilling, physical training, elementary military training (particularly rifle shooting) and lectures on Arab nationalist ideology and nationalism.[31] The *Najjada*'s total strength was estimated (by British reports) at 8,000, with eleven main branches in the principal towns of Jaffa (which was the headquarters), Haifa, Acre, Nablus, Beersheba, Tiberias, Jerusalem, Tulkarem, Gaza, Majdal, and Nazareth.[32] Each of these branches was sub-divided into companies, troops and patrols: the *Najjada*, which was popular among Palestinian youth, was particularly active in South Palestine.

Rivalry and divisions were aroused with the *Futuwa*'s formation by the PAP in August 1946, which was very similar in training and organization to the *Najjada*. *Futuwa* groups existed in Palestine in 1935, under the aegis of the Mufti, but were gradually dissolved during the revolt. The *Futuwa* of 1935, formed mainly through the efforts of Emile al-Ghury, was an effort by the then newly established PAP to harness the potential of youth. Its creation was influenced by the rise of militantly nationalist youth groups in Fascist Europe, just as was the *Betar* youth groups of the so-called Revisionist Zionists. The organization was reformed by Jamal al-Husayni as a rebuff to Hawari, who had refused him permission to take over the *Najjada* and affiliate it with the PAP.[33] The strength of the *Futuwa* was estimated at 5,000 members, with the bulk of its units in Jerusalem (where its headquarters was situated) and in Nablus, with other branches in Ramleh, Beisan, Safad, Tulkarem, and Tiberias.[34] Jamal was the supreme commander while the field commander of the *Futuwa* was Kamil 'Areikat, a former officer in the police as well as a former *Najjada* supporter who took a large number of *Najjada* members with him.[35]

The chief difference between the two organizations was that the

Futuwa was under the direct control of the PAP while *Najjada* refused to be affiliated or become involved in party politics, sectarianism, or clan or family rivalries.[36] It was Jamal's parochialism, intransigence and family loyalties that caused the crisis in the youth organizations. After attending a parade the *Najjada* put on in Jaffa in 1946, in which about 2,000 uniformed members marched through the streets of the city, Jamal and the PAP subsequently attacked the movement in an effort to discredit it or bring it under their control.[37] In discussions with a *Najjada* delegation, Jamal made it clear that it should dissolve itself and become incorporated into the *Futuwa* and, therefore, come under the control of the PAP's central party leadership.[38] *Najjada's* resistance to Jamal's dictatorial demands led to both organizations seeking the mediation of the Mufti.

The protracted discussions between the Mufti and each of the leaders of the two youth organizations produced ambivalent results. To militate against the dangers to Palestinian Arab unity that the rivalry between the two organizations constituted, the Mufti appointed a committee of three (Rafiq al-Tamimi, Emile al-Ghury and Hawari himself)[39] to investigate the prospect of fusing the two into one organization, to which Hawari agreed in principle. The Mufti and the committee agreed that an amalgamated youth organization would not be affiliated to any party or group on condition that the new organization would not differ with the AHC—i.e., it would follow its directives.[40] (They also agreed that the fused organization's headquarters would be in Jaffa.) This was somewhat of a victory for the *Najjada,* reflecting its numerical, democratic and popular strength. The Mufti had agreed, in essence, that neither the PAP nor Jamal would control an amalgamated youth organization. This indicated the limitations of Jamal's influence, who often used the PAP as a vehicle to enhance power for himself and his family.

The investigative committee of three was formed in October 1946. Amalgamation was stalled because *Najjada's* members constructed a variety of legal, financial, and administrative arguments against the fusion of their organization,[41] which was really an attempt to deter Tamimi (chair of the committee) and the Mufti. By April 1947, before any substance was achieved, the Mufti announced the creation of the *Munazamat al-Shabab al-'Arabi* (Arab Youth Organization). The announcement by the AHC said that the Youth Organization would be headed by a retired Egyptian officer, Mahmud Labib, and that Hawari and 'Areikat would be assistant commanders.[42] The *Bayt al-Mal* had even described the Arab Youth Organization as the Arab Army of Liberation in Palestine and promised wages of LP10 a month plus arms and food and, in the event of death in any future outbreak, a grant of LP500 to dependents.[43] While Hawari and the *Najjada* insisted that they agreed to an amalgamation in principle and that many details needed to be worked out, Mahmud Labib came to Palestine in June

1946 to begin training the youths.[44] In effect, rather than an amalgamated youth organization, which Labib was supposed to unite and head, there were three: *Najjada, Futuwa,* and the Arab Youth Organization.

The AHC managed to create more divisions and organizations. Not only was Mahmud Labib's stay in Palestine very short (from June to September 1947—the Palestine government did not renew his permit to stay), but Hawari was accused by the AHC of stirring up trouble for itself in Jaffa.[45] As late as December 1947, just days before the outbreak of hostilities between Arabs and Jews, coordination in a single command was still unachieved. However, because of the critical political situation at the time, Hawari assumed command of Jaffa defenses and was later to be on the boycott (of Jewish products) committee. Also, the AHC was forced to accept the *Najjada* as an independent scout movement. While the *Najjada* and *Futuwa* were being demoralized and losing popularity as a result of the divisions, the Arab Youth Organization was leaderless and without coherent structure or organization. The most the three organizations could achieve in the event of war was the formation of guerrilla bands.

If there was anything the AHC did with certainty, it was the convening of continuous meetings and deliberations. The AHC met on and off from the time of the Mufti's return to the Middle East in the summer of 1946 through 1947 and into 1948, when hostilities began, without ever achieving much success in its endeavors to unite its people. In essence, political events in Palestine were moving fast, and the Mufti tried to impose, within his limited conception, some semblance of socio-political and military unity and organization on Palestinian Arab society. Meetings were convened each time the Palestine problem reached a new and more complex stage in the international arena. Each stage (the London Conference, Britain's announced reference of the Palestine problem to the United Nations, the creation of the United Nations Special Committee on Palestine, partition, Britain's announcement of withdrawal) saw a flurry of activity by the AHC but little else. Repetitiously, the AHC announced its intention to merge all youth groups, unite national enterprises under the direction of *Bayt al-Mal,* and establish National Committees. All these objectives ultimately were comparative failures, if only because of the divisions in the AHC.

The pressures on the AHC and the Mufti were great. In the summer of 1947, with the announced intention of UNSCOP to investigate partition, the district commissioners reported that the more educated public opinion in the towns was doubtful whether the AHC had the ability to effectively organize its people and whether it was not out of contact with them.[46] In addition to this there were continual vocal criticisms from the ALNL over the non-representative nature of the AHC and the need for democratic methods of election.[47]

The Mufti's method of deflecting this criticism was exhortations to the people (especially villagers) to unite and to prepare themselves for conflict, although emphasizing that the time was not ripe for violence.[48] The Mufti also resorted to calling for popular conferences and in June 1947 went so far as to promise that general elections to select a new AHC would be forthcoming (the latter promise never having materialized).[49] In July 1947, four conferences actually took place: a national conference concerned with the boycott and land sales prevention; and three other conferences concerned with youth, women, and "Peace Between Brothers"— the last intended to put an end to "family" political feuds dividing the Arabs. These conferences were intended to rally public opinion around the AHC.

The result of the Mufti's efforts were predictably uncertain, tenuous, and haphazard. The Mufti opened a Jerusalem office of the AHC and appointed Jamal, Khalidi, and Ahmad Hilmi to head it. A sub-committee concerned with village affairs was established. An economic committee was formed consisting of ten advisory sub-committees on which sat merchants and manufacturers who had the task of assisting "the Arab consumer to find all his needs in the Arab market." Lastly, a Central Economic Committee for the Boycott was formed. This Committee, headed by Hawari, consisted of sixty-four members who directed the local committees and its task was to coordinate with merchants to enforce the boycott of Jewish goods.[50] (The boycott officially began close to two years earlier, in December 1945.) The conference contained numerous speeches punctuated with fiery oratory, the only practical call coming from the women's conference at which was stressed the need for agricultural and technical education.[51] There is no evidence that these conferences achieved any concrete results beyond the momentary heightening of national fervor and consciousness. Whatever organized activity resulted from them was localized, uncoordinated, fragmentary, and tenuously connected with the AHC.

Beyond the AHC's exhortations for unity, its third major focus was on the creation of National Committees. As was mentioned, the creation of NCs was continuously rumored and proclaimed as one of the major goals of the AHC at practically every one of its meetings. However, NCs did not begin to form until December 1947 (much too late), given urgency by the United Nation's partition resolution the previous month. The NCs were not only late in formation but they differed significantly from the NCs that sprouted during the 1936–39 revolt.

During the revolt, the NCs formed spontaneously as a result of the prolonged strike, and were composed of heads of all local parties. They were a product of the general radicalization of the thirties. In particular, the driving organizational force behind the NCs of the thirties was the *Istiqlal* party. But for reasons that were mentioned before, the *Istiqlal* was never able to invigorate itself after 1936, and many of its former activists were either getting old or living outside the country. In the forties, the attempts at creation of middle class parties were few and desultory. Not only did the revolt take its toll, but the difficult conditions of the forties served to hinder and prolong the formation of parties that could be active like the *Istiqlal* in its heyday.

The NCs of the thirties acted to control the strike locally, to organize collection of funds and food and to distribute these to strikers and their families, to keep the nationalist and rebellious spirit alive, and to enforce collection of funds from their richer compatriots. They acted independently of the national leaders and, in fact, became a threat to the landowning class's position.

In 1947–48, the NCs were formed at the initiative of the AHC, by way of a publication of a formal constitution for these bodies, like its other departmental creations.[52] The AHC made certain to avoid the developments of the past. Each NC was responsible for its own town or village. The AHC was concerned that the NCs be devoid of any power to elect political and military leaders, anxious to have complete authority over their activities. There was no central administrative command between NCs nor any organized line of communication between them and the AHC.[53] In short, the AHC's objective was that the NCs did not become independent local authorities outside the control of the Mufti, the PAP, and their supporters. (Later, during February 1948, when the Mufti began to see the fatal dangers in Palestine and in the halls of the Arab League, he asked that the NCs be transformed into administrative authorities upon British evacuation.)

The NCs were composed of the local parties, groups, and clubs—from workers and merchants to professionals and landlords. The villages were represented on the NCs by their shaykhs, village headmen or notables. The NCs usually formed an executive committee of smaller number, with the leader being the mayor or another person under a rotating chairmanship. Thus, local political differences and factional divisions were reflected on the NCs. The AHC intended that there would be twenty-four NCs representing all the Arab towns. They were so constituted to ensure the geographic preponderance of urban representatives.[54] This was not only an attempt by the AHC to control social organization but also to preserve its urban base and control any potential *fellah* independent action or activity. Not all the NCs were formed at the same time, mainly owing to local divisions. Those in Hebron and Ramallah, for example, were not formed until February 1948,[55] just three months before the state of Israel was proclaimed.

The NCs were burdened with more responsibility than they could handle. Their role was military, social, economic, and civil. They took on the burden of feeding, defense, collection of money, and the maintenance of order in their locales.[56] They dealt with security and crime and directed civil affairs in their jurisdiction, with some establishing courts to try criminals. Also, they attempted to prevent profiteering and to assure a continuous supply of food.[57] In the short interval between their formation and the outbreak of hostilities, the NCs were managing to gain popularity. Until January they were successful in keeping their areas quiet and restraining any attacks on Jewish areas.[58] They had in fact shown themselves to be responsible bodies, relatively disciplined, organized, and self-sufficient.[59]

Of course the NCs not only differed from each other but also reflected the socio-political conditions of their respective locales—which oftentimes meant clan and political divisions. Also, the Mufti had dealt with each NC differently, depending on the town's loyalty to him. These twin factors served to severely handicap the effectiveness of the NCs. Frequently, the membership of the NCs was unnecessarily large and burdensome. (The AHC ruled that there should be a maximum of twenty members and a minimum of five.) Acre's NC had fifty-eight members on it, twenty-six from the town and thrity-two from the adjacent villages.[60] Gaza had fifty-five members on its NC, owing to the primacy of clan factionalism.[61] In Gaza, family politics, jealousy, and divisions dictated that there be no leadership or elected leader but a continually rotating chairmanship. The Gaza NC had authority over political affairs, the treasury, and military matters. It collected money and imposed taxation and it cooperated with the military arm of the Mufti, the *Jihad al-Muqaddas*, and with the Muslim Brethren fighters from Egypt.

Although the Gaza NC was theoretically organized and functional, the reality of the town reflected a chaotic picture. In February 1948, the Gaza District Commissioner observed that "In the town there are still no local leaders, and Gaza is a medley of excitable armed men with no plan or organisation. The more one sees of the local Arab the more one realises that a determined organised Jewish operation will play havoc in this area."[62] Two weeks after this report the district commissioner reported again:

> The greatest danger to the maintenance of order in the district is the lack of control and organisation in Gaza town itself, where petty jealousies and fassad [corruption or the creation of division by gossip between families or parties] continue to obstruct the formation of an efficient National Committee. Recent Haganah Arabic broadcasts containing up-to-date gossip and scandal of Gaza have started accusations and counter accusations of pro-

Jewish activity between leaders and followers of the various factions.[63]

While Gaza's factionalism was peculiar to the town's social history, similar factionalism and disorganization most probably prevailed in the south of Palestine (Hebron-Beersheba area) and throughout small towns and villages in Palestine, particularly in the hilly region.

Another example of lack of unity was Jaffa.[64] The Jaffa NC was formed through the direct tutelage and chairmanship of Rafiq al-Tamimi and Shaykh Hasan Abu Sa'ud, both close associates of the Mufti and on the PAP's central committee. It had twenty-four members (the actual limit prescribed by the AHC) representing the PAP, Arab Front, Communists, Muslim Brethren, the Arab Club, and the Muslim People's Club. Also, five of the NC's members represented the surrounding villages. Most members were not elected but nominated by the AHC.

There were recurrent differences between Mayor Yusif Haykal, a member of the NC, and the AHC, although the Jaffa NC was treated favorably by the Mufti, mainly because of his influence in the city through his associates.[65] With the increase in hostilities in January, the NC became active and created sub-committees for economy, health, village, defense, and inflation. The defense sub-committee was under the direction of another close Mufti associate, Shaykh Hasan Salameh, who was already appointed by the Mufti to command Lydda and Ramle.

The Jaffa NC collected a total of LP135,000 for the city's defense effort. Of this amount, LP96,000 constituted contributions from townspeople, LP25,000 were obtained from the local branch of the *Bayt al-Mal* (which were taxes collected from the town), and LP13,500 was given by the Military Committee of the Arab League.

In contrast to the favorable treatment accorded the Jaffa NC, the Jerusalem and Haifa NCs were practically left on their own by the Mufti.[66] Unlike Jaffa, Jerusalem had formed local committees for the defense of the city since the November 1947 partition resolution. A central committee presided over these small local committees. The committee administered the affairs of health, treasury, and justice and cooperated with Dr. Tannus of the *Bayt al-Mal* for the collection of taxes. When the NC was formed (in January), the committee was dissolved. But the precedent of Jerusalem's independent action made the Mufti suspicious in dealing with it. The AHC refused to grant any military functions to the NC although it persisted in continuing the duties of the former central committee by helping the defenders of the city with supplies. The NC spent LP10,000 on the Arab volunteers in the city. When the Jerusalem NC asked the AHC for the allotment of its budget, estimated at LP36,000, it was wholly rejected. After the massacre at Dayr Yasin, the NC found itself spending up to LP600–LP700 daily from its budget on the wounded, the children, and the homeless. It received no help from the AHC and had to borrow from the Arab Bank and National Bank (LP5,000 for each).

Similarly, the Haifa NC was more of a spontaneous formation, initiated by the Muslim Brethern, it was composed of representatives of youths, intellectuals, various societies and clubs as well as workers. Moreover, the people of Haifa, after holding several general meetings, called on the AHC to announce the formation of a Palestine Arab government which would: create local governments in all towns; protect the civil rights of the Arabs and have the authority to collect taxes; mobilize men between the ages of 18–25; and finance training and arms acquisition on a national level (which was estimated at LP3,000,000). The leaders of Haifa also agreed on the need for the organization of doctors and nurses to care for the wounded in the event of war, and for the evacuation of women, children and the infirm to neighboring countries.[67] In Haifa, as in Jerusalem and other towns, there was a deep sense of urgency at the end of 1947, particularly in light of Britain's announcement of withdrawal in September.

These requests, made as early as October 1947, were certainly extraordinary. Although they were unimpeachable in what they sought to achieve, the Arabs of Haifa put themselves in conflict with the Mufti. In a meeting Rashid al-Haj Ibrahim, the Haifa emissary, had with the Mufti, he was told that the latter was displeased at such efforts which were initiated without obtaining his authority.[68] The AHC also made it clear that it did not accept the popularly composed Haifa resolution because it was premature and that the Arab League had taken the responsibility to defend the country on a national level—in other words, no money or help would be forthcoming. In response, the Haifa NC formed committees of defense in ten different quarters of the city and every surrounding village. It created military and civil courts, and it coordinated its efforts with the Arab merchants, workers, and police of the city.

Ultimately, the Mufti's efforts to unite the Palestinians proved to be a mixed achievement. While the notability would most certainly have continued in its destructive divisiveness, personal ambitions, and factionalism, were it not for the Mufti's uniting personality, his dictatorial methods and favoritism proved to be one more obstacle to Palestinian Arab political unity. More than any other institution, the NCs should have been accorded all the political support and resources required for their important role. They should have served as the potential local administrative nucleus for an independent Arab state, or at least as authorities who were prepared to help and coordinate the take-over of local responsibilities upon British evacuation. In essence, given the nature of Palestinian society and the divisive political situation at the national level, the NCs were the only bodies that could put up any semblance of defense and that could achieve stability and continuity in administration. They were the only bodies, moreover, that had the potential of maintaining order and morale, in coordination with municipal leaders and village councils, during a war and in its aftermath.

All this, of course, required support, coordination, links and a regular channel of communication with a national authority, notwithstanding the required authority to make immediate flexible decisions to meet complex contingencies. But such requirements and potential functions were precisely the reasons they were treated with caution by the AHC. The Mufti feared that, out of all the AHC's departmental creations, the NCs were more directly popular in content and more likely to become independent entities not easily amenable to his control and authority. In other words, they had the potential of becoming more democratically representative than the Mufti and the notables he represented would have liked.

The United Nations and the Decision to Evacuate

Earlier in this chapter, reference was made to Britain's handing over the Palestine problem to the United Nations, the creation of UNSCOP, and subsequent international events. These crucial events must now be sketched before proceeding to discuss further the Palestinian leadership's response to them.

Despite further last minute attempts at extracting Arab and Jewish concessions at the London Conference, London was already prepared for failure. Even before the conference was over, the British government had decided to refer the problem to the United Nations, at which the United Kingdom would ask for a special session of the General Assembly (which was eventually held in May 1947).

Less than a week after the conference ended in deadlock on 14 February, Bevin announced Britain's intentions in the House of Commons: Britain would submit to the United Nations various solutions which were put forward for a settlement and would not recommend any particular plan. Actually, the British did not yet intend to withdraw from Palestine and end the mandate. That would come later. Bevin and Colonial Secretary Arthur Creech-Jones told the Cabinet in mid-February that the decision to take Palestine to the United Nations did not mean Britain intended to surrender the mandate. In other words, Britain maintained a non-definitive evacuation option in the hope of staying in the country. From that point on, Britain officially and strictly adhered to a refusal to commit itself, at least in principle, to any policy that both communities did not accept.

As the League of Nations mandate was nearing its end, it was essential to transform the British presence into a United Nations trusteeship.

Bevin hoped to extend British economic and strategic presence with the United Nations' blessing. It also was hoped this presence would be guaranteed by a treaty with a unitary state, a solution that would not alienate the Arabs from Britain, and that would satisfy the commitment towards a Jewish National Home.

By February 1947, partition was supported only by High Commissioner Cunningham. The Chiefs of Staff argued that partition would destroy Britain's position in the Middle East. They also were against provincial autonomy on the basis that it would necessitate the use of British troops from other points of the Middle East and Europe (notably Germany).[69] The Chiefs wished to retain Palestine as a permanent possession to serve Britain's strategic needs in the eastern Mediterranean. Creech-Jones, formerly a consistent proponent of partition, changed his mind after being exposed to Zionist maximalist territorial demands during the London Conference. The talks with the Zionists convinced him that Jewish claims were fantastic and that partition would inevitably entail injustice to the Arabs. Finally, Bevin consistently and forecfully argued against partition, basing his opposition on the central notion that such a solution would have serious repercussions in the Arab world and alienate British influence to the advantage of Russia. Prime Minister Attlee largely concurred with Bevin's arguments.

Therefore, by February 1947, most members of the Cabinet agreed that Britain would adhere to a unitary solution—whether a binational, or federal, or whatever kind of state. This agreement put to rest at a crucial time the ongoing conflict between the Foreign Office and the Colonial Office. As mentioned before, the provincial autonomy scheme helped alleviate inter-departmental controversy because of its potential to evolve either into partition or a binational state, despite what the military minds thought of it.

Up to late 1947, British strategy at the United Nations was based on calculations of blocs and votes.[70] Bevin and the influential Harold Beeley were confident that they could win "the game" at the United Nations. It was inconceivable that the Zionists could mobilize two-thirds of the members of the General Assembly to achieve partition, much less that such an issue would produce the unlikely combination of a US-Soviet bloc. Also, it was well understood that the Arab states, as states directly concerned, would not tolerate any but a unitary solution. Thus, Bevin hoped the world body might endorse a binational or federal solution. It was almost taken for granted, even by Attlee, that, if no agreement were reached between Arabs and Jews, the United Nations would decide the issue in favor of a unitary state, meanwhile preserving Britain's appearance as an impartial arbiter.

Despite the best laid plans, hopes, and intentions of the men formulating Palestine policy, such things were not to be. The anticipated votes and alignments at the United Nations did not materialize. The binational, or federal state solution, was not supported by the world body. The United Nations Special Committee on Palestine (formed in May) recommended partition, which it submitted to the General Assembly in September. Of the eleven members of the committee, eight (Australia, Canada, Chzechoslovakia, Sweden, the Netherlands, Guatemala, Mexico, Peru) voted for partition and three (India, Iran, Yugoslavia) suggested a federal solution. It was a combination of skillful Zionist diplomacy; Jewish pressure in the United States; Arab boycott (during UNSCOP's investigations in the Middle East) and dogmatism at the United Nations; and world sympathy for Jewish displaced persons in the aftermath of Hitler's terror that produced the eight to three vote in favor of partition.[71]

In September 1947, after UNSCOP recommended partition, Creech-Jones announced before the United Nations Britain's resolute intention to evacuate the military forces and civil administration from Palestine and so end the mandate. (He repeated this announcement in mid-October.) So as not to alienate the Arabs and yet not be accused of aiding them, Britain clearly stated that it would not impose a solution by force. From that point on Britain resisted any efforts by the international community to obtain its support in the facilitation of partition, which the UN General Assembly voted in favor of (33 for, 13 against, 10 abstentions) on 29 November 1947.

Predictably, the partition proposal for a Jewish and an Arab state produced anomalous results, both demographically and geographically. The Jewish population amounted to less than one-third of the total. In terms of Jewish landownership, it ranged from 5–7 percent of the total land surface of Palestine, or some 17 (and more) percent of total cultivable land, depending on how one looks at it and whom one consults. It was, then, impossible to create a Jewish state out of Arab Palestine without that state containing a huge Arab population. In this case, the proposed Jewish state would have consisted of less than 500,000 Jews and over 509,000 Arabs; while the Arab "state" of 725,000 would have had a Jewish population of 10,000. The city of Jerusalem, which was to be internationalized, would have contained 205,000 people, 105,000 of these being Arab. Geographically, the two states would have faced each other along incredibly unnatural, twisting, and forced borders, with the Jewish state getting, in addition to the largest part of the most fertile lands in the Galilee and coastal plain, the Negev desert. The state, though not in the dimensions the Zionists would have liked (all of Palestine), was nevertheless accepted by them (some 55 percent of Palestine was given to them). Partition gave them the international recognition and legitimacy they wanted, leaving the Palestinians shocked and outraged and the Arab statesmen delivering on their behalf fiery words and scenarios of resistance.

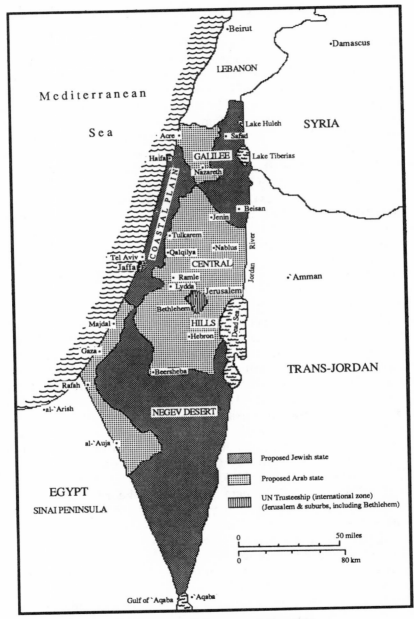

Map 3. UN Partition Recommendation, 1947

AHC Divisions in the Critical Months

During the critical months of late 1947 and early 1948, the notability within the AHC was hard put to maintain a facade of unity. For throughout the time of the AHC's belated attempts to encourage a semblance of unity in Palestine, infighting and personal conflict served to hamper effective national leadership. It would serve no purpose to present a detailed discussion of this infighting, particularly as it was devoid of ideological content. However, it is important to broadly outline some of the underlying political differences between the notables in the AHC, particularly the inconsistency between self-professed political beliefs and self-aggrandizing political behavior.

The most debilitating conflict was that between Dr. Husayn al-Khalidi and Jamal al-Husayni. These two and Ahmad Hilmi were responsible for the Jerusalem office of the AHC (which, after the Alexandria office where the Mufti resided until late 1947, was theoretically the national headquarters of the AHC). However, from its inception, the office was riddled with differences over practically every issue, small or large.[72] In particular, Khalidi and Hilmi were in conflict with Jamal over the salaries to be paid to themselves, the need for departmental clerks, and the manner in which the office should have been organized. These differences were reflected in the office's morale, in which chaos prevailed and which also prompted the Egyptian consul in Jerusalem to observe that the office workers freely displayed supposedly secret and important correspondence between the office and the Mufti.[73] Furthermore, although the office was to serve as the leading national institution in Palestine and to have directed and coordinated internal organizational contact, it was chronically short on funds.

By August 1947, Jamal left for New York to attend the plenary session of the General Assembly and did not again return to Palestine except once for a short visit. (After New York, Jamal spent his time traversing Arab capitals making certain he was not excluded from the crucial decisions reached by the Arab states over Palestine.) Khalidi and Hilmi were left to direct a virtually impotent office and stayed on until the fall of Arab Palestine.

Conflict within the AHC became particularly destructive at the time that Britain announced its intention to submit the Palestine problem to the United Nations in February 1947. Divisions as to who would attend notwithstanding, the friction centered on Musa al-'Alami's independent activities. 'Alami not only continued with his Arab offices and constructive scheme, but his more diplomatic approach and his contacts with Arab and British officials attracted the wrath of the Mufti and Khalidi. Jamal was under severe pressure from the Mufti and Khalidi over his association with 'Alami and his defense of his brother-in-law in the face of unrelenting criticism.[74] Preoccupation with the matter of 'Alami in the AHC affected the decision of nominating a delegation to attend the United Nations sessions. In the first extraordinary session of the General Assembly in April-May 1947 Jamal, who was to have led the Palestinian party, declined to go because of the unresolved differences regarding 'Alami.[75]

With the transmission of the majority and minority reports of UNSCOP to the General Assembly in September 1947, the conflict between Jamal and the Mufti and Khalidi again erupted. 'Alami's activities increasingly became a threat to the AHC, which spilled over into disagreement over the method of selecting a delegation. At first, Jamal, Khalidi, and Ghury were nominated to attend the plenary session, but this fell through on account of the attacks levelled at Jamal by Khalidi and Ahmad Hilmi, who were angered at the fact that 'Alami's schemes and activities deflected the work of the AHC.[76] Jamal was finally selected to lead a delegation which did not include Khalidi, who refused to go.[77] It would seem that Jamal scored a personal triumph over Khalidi, a major reason perhaps being the Mufti's fear that Jamal, who was incensed by the attacks against him and 'Alami, might leave the AHC and align himself with 'Alami. This reason also most probably accounts for the Mufti's restraint in dealing with 'Alami—i.e., in not ordering his assassination.

The rancor of the AHC towards 'Alami was not just due to that body's inability to control his constructive scheme and Arab offices. 'Alami was slowly gaining popular support, particularly among the younger generation and the workers—led by Sami Taha's PAWS. During the late summer when UNSCOP was still on its investigative mission, PAWS, in its annual conference, passed resolutions supporting 'Alami's work through the constructive scheme and Arab offices and favoring the formation of a workers party.[78] 'Alami's close association with Taha engendered the fear in the Mufti that the two might collaborate politically to challenge the supremacy and influence of the AHC, particularly if PAWS formed a working class party. This is borne out by the fact that immediately after PAWS's conference Taha was murdered in front of his house in Haifa. Although it was not proven, many Arabs (and Jews) believed it was the work of the Mufti. Taha's popularity was indicated by the "huge crowds, including Arab labourers from all over Palestine," who attended his funeral.[79] In a sense, the assassination of Taha was not only meant to quash the formation of a workers' party, but it also might have been the Mufti's answer to 'Alami's elusive bid for power.

'Alami never did come out into the open in his opposition to the Mufti nor form any organized following or a political party, although he refused to submit to the Mufti's dictates, a position no other notable dared assume.

'Alami's feeling towards the Mufti became clear during UNSCOP's stay in Geneva to write its report (July/August 1947). The AHC had totally boycotted UNSCOP's mission but sent Rasim al-Khalidi and Ma'ruf al-Dawalibi, close Mufti associates, to Geneva to observe, along with the Arab League liaison, Camille Sham'un, the Committee's deliberations.[80] Despite the AHC's refusal to make any official contact with UNSCOP or submit any memorandums, 'Alami had gone to Geneva, along with Cecil Hurani (secretary of the Arab office in Washington, D.C.), to make available to the Committee an independent memorandum setting down the Arab point of view.[81] The memorandum was composed by 'Alami and Hurani in the London Arab office. In a secret meeting with the British observor, Donald MacGillivary, at Geneva, 'Alami told him that he did not wish to break the boycott of the Palestinian Arabs by presenting the memorandum formally to the Committee.[82] It would be an Arab office publication addressed to world public opinion and he would either send it to the Committee under a compliments slip or have Sham'un hand it over in his capacity as liaison officer.

'Alami made clear that, although he "detested" the Mufti, he was not prepared to come out into open opposition at the time. If London produced a solution which would be accepted by the Arab states and the majority of Palestinians, then at that point 'Alami would break with the Mufti. He claimed the Mufti was determined to resist any solution which did not give him sovereign authority in all or at least a part of Palestine and that he would accept partition if his position as head of the Arab state was to be recognized. Although the Mufti most certainly had the ambition to be the supreme leader of the Arabs of Palestine, there is neither evidence nor indications to substantiate 'Alami's claim that the Mufti would have, under certain circumstances, accepted partition.

These remarks indicate that 'Alami could not totally break with the Mufti not just for fear of his life, but because the Mufti's uncompromising nationalist stand represented the mainstream in Palestine and the Arab world. These two reasons had kept any potential internal opposition at bay in the late forties. So much so that, in November 1947, many prominent members of the NDP in the Samaria district, including Nablus mayor Sulayman Tuqan, went to see the Mufti in Beirut (the Mufti secretely moved to Lebanon on 10 October 1947, without passport or visa, on an Egyptian airliner)[83] to pay "a measure of obeisance," as the Samaria District Commissioner described it, and suggested that they would compose their differences with their PAP counterparts when they returned home.[84]

Moreover, fear of the Mufti suppressed any proclivity to compromise from those who were closest to him. In November 1947, about a week before the United Nations partition resolution, Ghury, the unwavering nationalist, long-time PAP central committee member, and Husayni loyalist, privately admitted to Cunningham that he would be happy with an outcome on the line of the Morrison-Grady scheme (i.e., the provincial autonomy scheme or cantonization) or the minority proposal of UNSCOP (i.e., a federal state).[85] Of course, Ghury's weak personality and hypocritical attitude by no means represented the views of all Palestinian leaders.

*   *   *

The urban notability during the last decade of the mandate reflected a pervasive malaise that helped bring disaster to their people. Having significantly lost the social base which served as the backbone of their patronage influence, they nevertheless were determined to maintain their hold. Politics in the urban centers required broader participation, something the notables, basically the Mufti, refused to accept. The more pressure they felt, whether it emanated from more reasonable men among their numbers or from newly emerging groups and classes, the more aggressively they protected their narrow domains. Their factionalist style of politics did not fully reflect the social changes, nor the views and wishes of a very large number of discontented urbanites. However, it was these facts that caused them to intensify their factionalism as they maneuvered to maintain power.

As the Palestinian problem became rapidly entangled in the complex web of international affairs, Palestinian leaders also began to lose control of events. By the late forties, the Palestinian Arabs were subjected to incredible pressures. Very little could be done to assess and deal with these pressures with deliberation by leaders who were unable to get their own house in order.

Internal factionalism and external pressure inevitably led to confusion in Palestinian politics and society. The Arab regimes, preoccupied with their domestic political and social changes and problems and unable to cooperate effectively with each other, ensured that the Palestinians would be the recipients of the Arabs' own confusion, shortsightedness and divisions.

Part Three:

The Reaper of Disunity: External Interference and Internal Collapse, 1947–48

8

Arab Politics and the Palestinians: Nationalism, Dynastic Intrigue, and Political Ambitions

•

Palestine, Arab Nationalism, and the Arab Rulers

As we have seen, Zionist political activity in the form of maximalist statements and increased pressure in London and Washington engendered strong fears in the Palestinians, not only of Zionist designs, but of changes in British policy. The Arab states, too, became alarmed at the increasing boldness of Zionist propaganda in the United States. The Palestinians, repeatedly unsuccessful in their attempts to form either a united stand or political program, made Palestine the permanent responsibility of the Arab states. Also, Zionist aggressiveness served as a strong catalyst in arousing outraged Arab nationalist sentiment.

Despite Arab feelings over Palestine, Arab nationalism was too fractured and weak to meet the challenge of the dynamic Zionist movement. The Arab nationalist movement had no accepted ideological basis, no coherent program, and certainly no organizational framework through which to channel the raw sentiment of the masses.[1] The sublime virtues of Arab nationalism (its greatness, vitality, romanticism, and its value as a panacea to the economic, political and colonial problems and obstacles) were greatly extolled. But practical pan-Arabism was beset with divisions. In the forties, many Egyptians (intellectuals and politicians, especially of the *Wafd*) were pragmatic and cautious, preferring a leading cultural/ economic role; Ibn Sa'ud was interested more in the integrity and preservation of his sovereignty and too concerned with creating an Arab alliance system to prevent any potential aggression by one state against another (i.e., the Hashemites against his kingdom); the Lebanese (particularly the dominant Maronites) suspected and feared pan-Arabism and its potential impact on the sectarian balance; and the Syrian nationalists feared their absorption into any unity scheme.[2] They were unwilling to concede

161

leadership or right to rule to the Hashemites and, therefore, desired independence and self-rule.[3] All these states had in common the desire for the preservation of their sovereignties and political/territorial identities. Only for the Hashemites in 'Iraq and Trans-Jordan did pan-Arabism mean accretion of territory or regional integration within their conceptions of unity.

In the midst of all this stood the Palestinian Arabs. While they were closer to the Syrians in their Arab nationalist sentiments and beliefs, the majority were interested in an independent Arab Palestine within the framework of a loose unity. They desired integration, but saw it as a solution to preserve the independent and Arab character, the territorial integrity, of Palestine, and as a protection against the powerful Zionists. The Palestinians feared that conceptions of unity and federal frameworks were linked to the idea that they would be more receptive to less than a unitary Palestine. This awareness made them suspect the Arab League, when it was formed in early 1945, and its perceived colonial backers. Their interests dictated their general alignment with the Egyptain-Sa'udi-Syrian bloc. These dynamics determined the logic of Arab states policy towards Palestine and Palestinian Arab reactions to the Arab states.

In addition to the internal weakness of the Arab nationalist movement, there were external (colonial) obstacles to Arab nationalism and integration. The British feared extreme Arab nationalist sentiment and its potential "intereference" with their policies in Palestine, Egypt or elsewhere (and hence favored general Arab cooperation); the French were severely hostile and furthered sectarian divisions; and Jewish nationalism was determined to create a state in Palestine.[4]

Thus, there were serious impediments in the way of Arab nationalism. However, the creation of the Arab League did not necessarily imply that the Arab states made the best of inordinately difficult circumstances. Indeed, the general intrigue and conflicting ambitions of the Arab leaders became regulated within that institution, which had the effect of stabilizing inter-Arab relations. For Palestine, the League functioned as a legitimizing council, and it ensured that no one state, at least officially, would take steps on the issue without League consensus. The League was shaped and defined in accordance with the individual interests of the member states. No voice or influence was given to popularly representative bodies.

If there was any real potential for unity, despite the obstacles of the times, it is doubtful that the gradualist approach did any good.[5] On the contrary, with the benefit of historical perspective, it seems to have done more damage. Politically, the gradualist approach led to the strengthening of separate state structures and narrow national/territorial identities and symbols (e.g., army, flags), and to the consolidation and legitimation of territorial sovereignties. Again, despite the obstacles at the time, the idea of permanent separate state structures and territories had not taken hold. This fluidity might have enabled the Arabs to create a body that made integration a more *potential* possibility. The idea that the unity of the Arab countries was inevitable, that territories were waiting to be re-shaped, was still fresh since the break-up of the Ottoman Empire. The artificial boundaries drawn up by the colonial powers provided Arab nationalism with a powerful reason for its existence. But, socially, no popular, democratic, participative institutions were formed to encourage contact and familiarity between the Arab peoples, and to help towards the task of socialization.

There were, then, few *practical* ideas or means (or efforts) on how to begin to implement projects towards integration. There was not even a program for gradual integration, and the victory went to those regimes which desired to perpetuate the status quo. Therefore, the League mani-fested itself as a loose body of mutually suspicious states. It did not herald a new era of unity but, at most, "exhibited a common Arab front" towards Palestine and French colonialism in Syria and Lebanon.[6]

The intensity of the Palestine issue served to drive a wedge in Arab-Western relations. The Arab rulers found themselves in the greatly diffi-cult position of trying to moderate the crescendo of nationalist cries that Palestine was arousing in the general public, with their desire not to antagonize the West. Although the Palestine revolt of 1936–39 had for the first time in Palestinian/Arab states relations elicited widespread official Arab intervention, by 1945 Palestine had become firmly embedded in the emotions and consciousness of a young generation of educated Arab nationalists and the generally aware populaces of the urban centers. In the forties, public reactions were beginning to have very serious effects on Arab regimes. During Balfour day in 1945, for example, demonstrations took place in Egypt, Syria 'Iraq, and North Africa. Women's organizations, youth groups, Islamic organizations, communists, the press, cabinets and parliaments all condemned British policy in Palestine as imperialistic.[7]

The Arab rulers were fearful. In public they did not want to seem subservient to Western interests, while in private they voiced more flexi-ble opinions. But their moderation was also shaped by their fear of being dragged into a war they were unsure of winning, which led to a largely contradictory posture. They wanted to see independence for Palestine realized, yet feared they would be unable to control events in that coun-try. This aspect of their anxiety was compounded in the late forties in the face of a possible British withdrawal from Palestine. The British presence at least guaranteed order and the status quo.

Thus, most of the Arab rulers, perhaps with the exception of 'Abdul-lah, were not entirely motivated by cynical self-interest. They felt genuine outrage at what they saw as unjust Western attempts to hand over an Arab country to a basically Western minority of the Jewish religion. Too, they felt outrage at Zionist ambitions and aggressive posturing. Therefore, "it was precisely because of the sincerity of feeling over Palestine that it proved to be such a potent domestic issue in the Arab states."[8] While their interests dictated that a moderate stance be taken, then, it did not necessarily reflect their wishes towards Palestine.

But though such sentiment existed, their disunity and fear of each other led to huge blunders and miscalculations in the face of Western pressure. It was this pressure as much as their own failings and self-interest that contributed to their privately held moderate opinions. They were, after all, firmly warned by London on various occasions to be more "responsible" and to "moderate" and dampen the agitation of the "extremists."[9] In reality, the Arab regimes were in no position to demand very much. In the Arab world of the forties, the dilemma for the rulers was how to balance the spontaneity of the masses with dependence on the West. Especially in that period, the Arabs found themselves reacting to Western initiatives towards Palestine that increasingly placed them in difficulties at home.

The Arab States and Palestine Before 1947: The Fear of Intervention

Despite the British secrecy during the Cabinet discussion on partition between 1943 and 1944,[10] there was widespread talk in both Arab and Jewish circles and press of the likelihood of a partition settlement.[11] At the Alexandria deliberations for the formation of the Arab League, Arab leaders had even discussed partition. According to Nuri Pasha, the Arab delegates felt that they would oppose partition if Britain adopted it. Nuri told Sir K. Cornwallis, British ambassador to 'Iraq, that the Arab delegates felt strongly that partition would not solve the Palestine problem but would lead to more conflict.[12] He added that the Arabs realized their military weakness and they neither wanted nor planned to fight the Jews, but it would be difficult to avoid clashes.

The theme of fearing entanglement in Palestine pervaded the private utterances of almost all Arab politicians. In early 1945, Nuri told Lord Gort that he strongly opposed partition. He emphasized, however, that the situation in Palestine had reached the stage which precluded establishment of either an Arab or Jewish state.[13] Stepped-up Jewish terrorism, American intervention, and the emotional Arab response these elicited, plus London's lack of policy, influenced Nuri's opinions. He evinced extreme apprehension towards Zionist ambitions. He feared that the Arabs with their slender resources would not be able to withstand a Zionist "onslaught" on Palestine and perhaps neighboring countries. He proposed that Britain should go on ruling Palestine for another twenty-five years. If London were willing to do so, he would advocate a treaty of alliance between the Arab League members and Great Britain. The Secretary-General of the Arab League, 'Abd al-Rahman 'Azzam Bey, told Colonial Secretary George Hall the same thing: The Arabs did not mind if Great Britain continued to rule Palestine for another twenty or thirty years.[14]

But when the AAC report came out, it caused widespread popular outrage in the Arab world and attracted private and governmental denunciation. In a "secret" meeting held in June 1946, the Arabs and Palestinians came together to consider the AAC recommendations. The foreign ministers tried to formulate a united Arab response and program on Palestine. Their previous caution was transformed into a determination to fight, at least on the surface, for the independence of Palestine, largely because of public pressure. Among other things, the Arabs decided to give every form of assistance to the Palestinians to strengthen the boycott of Jewish products, to form a Palestine committee made up of all the Arab states to supervise all activities relating to Palestine, and to form a special L1,000,000 fund to which the Arab states would subscribe.[15] This money was to go to the AHE formed at this meeting.

Arab bravado was again displayed in mid-August 1946, when the Arab states met at Alexandria to prepare for the impending London Conference. There they unequivocally rejected partition in any form (including provincial autonomy), refused negotiations with the Zionists, and insisted on a unitary, independent Palestine state.[16]

Despite these seemingly unshakable pre-conference principles, the Arabs were fearful of the tense situation in Palestine and the likelihood that a breakdown in the London discussions would lead to war. Arab officials actually again repeated to the British their hope that the latter would remain in Palestine until passions cooled and dangers were minimized.[17] Arab positions, though predicated on compelling moral, legal, and historical grounds, nevertheless reflected an air of unreality, as if the Arabs' wishful thinking and hope would somehow divert—deflect—their having to contend with a task they so dearly wished to avoid.

While all the Arab states rejected the provincial autonomy scheme which the British government proposed to submit in London, only 'Abdullah was in an anxious state of excitement, interpreting the scheme in partition terms. In a conversation with the British Minister Alec Kirkbride, the King opined that an independent Palestine Arab state, like the one the Arab states were pressing for, if formed, "would be corrupted and destroyed by the Jewish minority which it would contain."[18] For a devious 'Abdullah, this was a rather lame pretext for his obvious intentions: he desired partition and an "exchange of population" as the only "just and permanent" solution to the troubles facing Palestine.[19] 'Abdullah, unlike the other Arab leaders, was certainly brutally realistic in his singleness of purpose towards Palestine.

Arab Conflict over Palestine within the Context of 'Iraqi Intrigue and 'Abdullah's Schemes

As previously shown, at the time of the creation of the Arab League, Nuri al-Sa'id's original plan was for a union of the Fertile Crescent, to exclude Egypt and Sa'udi Arabia. Nuri was never satisfied with the League, as in his view it not only failed to achieve genuine unity but also was used by the Egyptian-Sa'udi bloc, generally with the adherence of Syria, to oppose the Hashemites and their plans. By 1947, his mind was increasingly turning towards his original plan, particularly so because of the League's failure to formulate a united stand and plan towards Palestine. The need of the Palestinians for an Arab bloc that would be militarily and politically united behind them encouraged the 'Iraqis to scheme for a greater Hashemite Kingdom that would take the lead in defense of Palestine. To this end, Nuri, supported by Salih Jabr, intended to further the close and special relationship with Trans-Jordan and hoped to attract Syria to the Hashemite orbit, convinced as these two were that the majority of Syrians were opposed to their republican regime, though not necessarily in favor of 'Abdullah.

Much of 'Iraq's maneuvering on Palestine, whether as concerns the creation of a united Arab military or political command, focused on finding ways to deal with Palestine to the exclusion of the other Arab states. 'Abdullah shared the sentiments of the 'Iraqi politicians towards the Arab states and was willing to accept some form of united command and generally cooperate with 'Iraq, but his ambitions conflicted with theirs. Though Nuri wanted Fertile Crescent unity under 'Iraqi Hashemite leadership, 'Abdullah did not, and while 'Abdullah accepted a partition settlement for Palestine, the 'Iraqis did not. As 'Abdullah occasionally vented his frustrations over his ambitions, the 'Iraqis tried to placate and even deceive him to achieve their ends. This can be illustrated by a review of 'Iraqi-Trans-Jordanian relations throughout the forties, particularly those aspects concerning 'Abdullah's dreams to be king of Syria.

The 'Iraqis, principally Nuri Pasha, had consistently attempted to maneuver 'Abdullah into a neutralized position. To Nuri, 'Abdullah and his dreams of a Syrian throne were irritants and embarrassments to be handled circumspectly. Throughout the forties, 'Abdullah had provoked the Syrians and Lebanese through public proclamations about his intentions, first in July 1941, then in January 1942, in March and August 1943, and again in August 1947.[20] (In March 1947 he declared a public holiday, in commemoration of Faysal's proclamation, made in Damascus in 1920, as King of Syria.[21]) The King's last manifesto of August 1947 aroused Syrian and Lebanese ire. They issued a counter-manifesto expressing their disapproval of 'Abdullah's interference in their internal affairs and agreeing on a common front.[22]

'Abdullah, anxious over his real and imagined dreams, was usually provoked to excitement by events in inter-Arab relations which he perceived were moving toward his exclusion. In 1943–44, he was greatly perturbed by the feverish Nuri-Nahhas unity consultations which, with their popularity, made the Amir feel left out, and therefore anxious to assert himself and steal the momentum away from the other two. 'Abdullah also entertained the notion that the Regent of 'Iraq would be London's candidate as head of an Arab federation (much as the Syrians suspected that the Hashemites' ambitions over their country would be supported by the British government). To reassure the Amir, Nuri visited 'Abdullah and suggested that Arab energies should indeed be concentrated on the reunion of Greater Syria but that, given the French presence, the Amir should focus on the Palestine end.[23] To placate 'Abdullah further, Nuri added that the former's claim to the Syrian throne would not be overlooked and that, if he moved with caution, the Syrians with whom the choice lay might yet select him. Nuri either was attempting to gently deceive 'Abdullah by sustaining his hopes and so keep him quiet during his talks with Nahhas, or he saw the futility of speaking realistically to him.

By 1944, Nuri, having failed to gain ascendancy and to maneuver the Egyptians into a position wherein a union embracing Greater Syria would be a first step towards federation, subsequently endeavored to aggravate the conflict between 'Abdullah and the Syrians to attain his goals. In April 1947, shortly after the Trans-Jordanian Prime Minister visited Lebanon and Syria to improve relations, Nuri again visited 'Amman. He suggested to the King that an attempt should be made to create chaos in the Syrian territory adjacent to Trans-Jordan and 'Iraq by stirring up the Druze and the Euphrates tribes, and thereby using that as a pretext for joint 'Iraqi-Trans-Jordanian intervention.[24] Such a plan did not materialize, particularly since Nuri was not talking serious business.

By 1947, then, Arab state relations were at their worst. 'Iraqi-Syrian and Trans-Jordanian-Syrian relations were sour; the Egyptian, Lebanese, and Syrian press occassionally attacked Hashemite plans; Sa'udi Arabia feared 'Abdullah more than the Zionists; Egypt and Syria used Palestine as a propaganda weapon and as an instrument to further their prestige in the Arab world; and the Mufti aligned himself with the Syrians and Egyptians in an effort to block 'Abdullah's or 'Iraq's plans towards Palestine and to retain his position. All these complex factors and currents had determined the course of relations between the Arab states over Palestine. Matters got so bad as to have prompted a statement by the British Minister of State in the House of Commons, declaring London's strict neutrality over the question of Greater Syria.[25] Also, the Regent of 'Iraq had to send Salih Jabr to visit 'Amman, Damascus, Beirut, and Jedda to try to alleviate the tension. Jabr told the King in 'Amman, in a message from the Regent, that given the critical period which the Arabs were passing through, it was not the time for the issue of Syria to be raised.[26] 'Abdullah undertook to publish no more manifestos on the subject unless publicly provoked or unless an uprising in Syria should call for such a statement of policy.

But though the King must at times have had his doubts about the realization of his Syrian ambitions, he knew that the situation in Palestine was more conducive for the expansion of his territory. Naturally, 'Abdullah's intentions towards Palestine were known in the Arab world ever since the Peel Commission published its partition report in 1937. By the late forties, with partition again afoot, Nuri Pasha and Salih Jabr had even suspected that London was encouraging 'Abdullah in his plans to gain control of Arab Palestine. To exploit the situation to their advantage, they hoped any intervention by 'Abdullah would be a first step towards a Greater Syria. They encouraged 'Abdullah in the belief that he would have their support in the event of Arab opposition. Where 'Abdullah and the two 'Iraqis differed was in their politico-military plans. 'Abdullah was interested in obtaining the Arab part of Palestine that might be allotted through partition; whereas the 'Iraqis were hoping to take over all of Palestine. Such a development would make the task of Nuri's Fertile Crescent dream more realizable, the 'Iraqis perhaps believing that action on a joint 'Iraqi-Trans-Jordanian level would be conducive to 'Iraqi influence in Palestine.

Though there was conflict in their political ambitions, both the 'Iraqis and 'Abdullah were against the Mufti attaining any sovereignty over any part of Palestine. The Mufti not only stood in the way of either of their schemes, but also his effort to create some sort of Palestinian administrative authority in the wake of British withdrawal would hinder their task of establishing and legitimizing their presence in Palestine. Hence, as will be seen, they were opposed to the creation of a provisional Palestinian Arab government of any sort. 'Iraqi and Trans-Jordanian strategy in the League in dealing with Palestine and the Palestinians was, then, in accord with their respective schemes. Before further discussion and elucidation of these points, it is important to review British policy, first, towards the Arab states in relation to Arab intervention in Palestine and, second, to 'Abdullah's Palestine ambitions.

British Policy Towards Arab Intervention in Palestine in Late 1947

Until the time that conflict broke out between Arabs and Jews in late 1947, London characteristically left the option of staying in Palestine open. Even though they announced their withdrawal in September, the British hoped that the announcement would still have a "sobering effect" on Arabs and Jews, who might then reach an agreed settlement at the United Nations and ask Britain to remain in Palestine for a limited transitional period to put such an agreement into effect.[27] While this would not have meant a permanent presence, the hope was that Britain would reach a treaty agreement with one or both of the parties to maintain its strategic influence. Even after Arab rejection of the United Nations partition resolution of November 1947, and after the government announced in the House of Commons its withdrawal plans (in December), Britain was still ready to play the role of conciliator between Arabs and Jews.[28] The prevailing thought at the Foreign Office was that Arab fear of British withdrawal might pressure them to become conciliatory and accept a compromise. But this British attitude reflected more wishful thinking than reality. The British missions in the Arab world had continuously sounded the alarm about the tremendous public pressure on the Arab regimes to act in Palestine. This attitude nevertheless had determined the manner in which London would set its policy towards potential Arab state intervention in Palestine during the British withdrawal.

Characteristically, the British government was locked in a vise: its desire to maintain its influence in the Arab world conflicted with international pressure (particularly from the United States) calling on Britain to stop any Arab intervention. British policy centered itself in between the two poles. Throughout the withdrawal process between January and May of 1948, the government consistently warned the Arab states against intervening in Palestine. Knowing that the Arabs were unable to devise a united policy and that they were hesitant to confront the Zionists, London's warning to the Arabs oscillated between firm and soft statements designed to impress upon them the risk of confrontation between the Arab armies or irregulars and the withdrawing British troops. Whether or not the British would have actually clashed with intervening Arab armies is uncertain, though the Arab states took the British threat seriously. This was precisely the British intention.

The result was that while the Jews were well armed (relative to the Palestinians) and, after March 1948, intent on gaining as much of Palestine as possible before 15 May, when the mandate was to officially end (actually, it ended precisely at midnight, 14 May), the Arab states had decided on a policy of non-intervention as long as the British withdrawal lasted. League Secretary-General 'Azzam Bey had even told Britain's representative in Beirut that the Arab armies would only intervene if the Palestine Arabs were in the process of being defeated and that, in any case, would not occur until British withdrawal was completed. This policy indeed was strictly adhered to by the Arab states.[29] It was given definitiveness at the meeting of the League Council in December 1947, where the Arab prime ministers agreed that they were determined to avoid a clash with Great Britain.[30]

The Arab states, despite their hesitancy and disunity, were under public pressure to resist by force an imposed partition resolution. Prime Minister Riad al-Sulh of Lebanon reflected the fears of the Arab regimes when he said at the League Council meeting in December that no government in any Arab country could take a stand which could be interpreted as betraying the Arab cause without being swept away.[31] The Arab states displayed their "fervor" to help their Palestinian brethren not only through (ineffectual) meetings that officially proclaimed their determined support, but also through appearances of military preparation and maneuvers. At the League Council meeting at 'Aley in October, the Arabs declared their willingness to take military precautions on the Palestine frontiers and to allow states not bordering Palestine to participate in this duty.[32]

In response to Arab theatrics, London took every opportunity to warn and discourage the Arabs against any military incursions either by regular armies or through volunteers. The Foreign Office instructed its representatives to warn the Arab leaders that they should not attempt any direct intervention while the British were still in Palestine. They were told simply that Britain would continue to run things until further notice and that any action "prejudicial to the authority of the Palestine government would in fact be directed at HMG."[33] In Syria, where the government in particular felt compelled to carry out military maneuvers in the Quanytra area and where the Arab command and volunteer training centers were located, Britain's representative in Damascus had warned the Interior and Defense Ministers against any "military adventures." He "made it clear" to the Syrians that, until withdrawal was completed, any action against "Palestinian subjects" (i.e., Jews) or any territorial incursions would be considered as hostile actions against the British authorities in Palestine.[34]

In early December, the British government informed the Arab states and Jews of its withdrawal plans. They were told that the British would withdraw from south to north and complete the withdrawal by 1 August through the Haifa enclave (though withdrawal was completed by 31 May).[35] London took the opportunity again to warn the Arab states that they should not do anything or "permit anyone in their territory to do anything calculated to interfere with our orderly withdrawal or to oblige us while we are still in control to take measures to suppress disturbances [i.e., suppress the Arabs] in Palestine." In a second note immediately following, the Arabs and Jews were told of the exact date of the termination of the mandate.[36]

To the Arab leaders, the withdrawal plan and timetable were considered a detriment to their giving any effective help to the Palestinian Arabs. Riad al-Sulh voiced his misgivings by stating that the planned route of the withdrawal could only be to the advantage of the Jews (i.e., because the withdrawal was mainly through the areas allotted to the Jews in the partition resolution); and that the presence of British troops in north Palestine until "the last moment" would "block the Arabs and prevent them from taking effective action" at the most propitious time—that is, before the Jewish state was formed.[37] The Egyptian Foreign Minister, Fahmi Khushaba Pasha, complained that London had prevented the Arabs from obtaining arms whereas the Jews, compared to the Palestinians, were well armed and equipped, adding, rhetorically yet not without foundation, that it appeared that the Arabs were required to wait to be massacred.[38] Finally, Salih Jabr said he could see no way to avoid fighting and no Arab government could resist the demands of its people to help the Palestinians.[39]

Despite the bitter and frustrated voices of protest, and a false bravado put on in the hope that Britain would somehow change its policy in Palestine so as to keep the peace and thereby preclude any Arab intervention, these Arab leaders had in the same vein reassured the British government that Arab armed forces would not move into Palestine as long as the British troops remained.[40] The British warnings had their intended effect. The Arab states would sit it out, despite the tremendous public pressure, until after hundreds of thousands of Palestinians became refugees and the Jewish leadership proclaimed the state of Israel (14 May). Though it can be asserted with some confidence that, had the Arabs not waited, their effectiveness would have been questionable in light of their disunity, yet the possibility existed that Jewish expansion could have been checked before the military situation changed so drastically in Jewish favor. More importantly, all sides, the Zionists, the British, and the Arabs, knew how weak the Palestinian Arabs really were. Between December and May, as the British carried on with their disorderly withdrawal and prevented any Arab incursions, the task was eased for the Zionists to decisively destroy the Palestinian Arab community and to expand and consolidate borders within and beyond the limits of the United Nations partition plan.

The situation regarding 'Abdullah was more complex for the British. The King had not only been a close ally but was more directly concerned with Palestine, particularly given the fact that any collective Arab action necessitated that Trans-Jordan play a central role. It had one of the best trained armies in the Arab world (albeit small, about 8,000), two-thirds of which was stationed in Palestine, and 'Abdullah more than any other Arab ruler was determined to intervene and gain control of parts of the country. But the difficulty of dealing with 'Abdullah over intervention before British withdrawal, although important, was a secondary matter connected with the more complicated difficulties posed by 'Abdullah's political/territorial ambitions.

'Abdullah, Palestine and the British

'Abdullah's impatience over his ambitions in Palestine was particularly heightened with the UNSCOP mission. Feeling that he was getting old with nothing to his name but a well-trained army and an impoverished kingdom, 'Abdullah was willing to accept whatever he could get for the sake of expanding his domain. As recently as July 1947 'Abdullah had conveyed to London his desire for and acceptance of partition. Although in his meeting with UNSCOP in 'Amman he rejected partition and advocated the establishment of an independent state in Palestine, he subsequently told the British government that these were not the views either of his government or of himself. He explained that as Trans-Jordan was the one Arab state which stood to gain substantially from partition, it was impossible that it should also be the only state publicly to advocate this course contrary to the feelings and views in the Arab world. He felt, however, he could accept partition and any "incidental adhesions of territory."[41] He viewed partition as the only solution and he hoped that every effort would be made to ensure that it was adopted. 'Abdullah wished London to know that he would be willing to take over the Arab areas of Palestine, or whatever was left of them, after a United Nations resolution was adopted.

The prospect that a partition solution had a stronger chance of being implemented than at any other previous time, particularly in light of planned British withdrawal and seeming disinterest, had put 'Abdullah in an excited and obsessive frame of mind. He was anxious and fearful that, with a potential vacuum left behind by the British, his aspirations towards Syria and Palestine would be left uncertain. His communications with London reflected desperate attempts to gain British support for his ambitions. In a series of letters to Bevin, 'Abdullah emphasized the Soviet threat to Britain through its proxies in Egypt, Syria, and Lebanon (implying that if his kingdom were expanded he would be a determined ally) and clearly expressed his anxiety over his future position.[42] He complained that his enemies in the neighboring countries (Sa'udi Arabia and Egypt) would like to weaken him and described "how King Ibn Sa'ud is always threatening me...."[43]

The veiled reference to his territorial ambitions was conveyed to the British once before when he was in a calmer state of mind. In March 1946 'Abdullah went to London to arrange a treaty with the British as a formal successor to the mandate over Trans-Jordan, during which time he also was elevated to Kingship status. In meetings with both Attlee and Bevin, 'Abdullah made sure to impart to his hosts the exact same references concerning his ambitions.[44] On Palestine, he made it clear to Attlee that partition should be imposed on that country as it was a "reasonable and fair solution."[45]

Although London refrained from answering or encouraging 'Abdullah in the matter of partition (or Syria), the prevailing view was that Trans-Jordan was potentially of considerable strategic importance, particularly if Britain could no longer have forces in Palestine and Egypt.[46] This view had been prevalent ever since Ernest Bevin became foreign secretary in July 1945. In 1945–46, Bevin and some in the Foreign Office believed that a resolution of the Palestine problem along the lines of confederation and amalgamation of territories might provide solutions for Palestine and the Middle East, not to mention its potential ability to provide a base for British forces. In fact, only two months after assuming office Bevin proposed a federal plan. The plan would turn Palestine and Trans-Jordan into a federal state under an Arab king, which would be 'Abdullah. In this federal state there would be three provinces, the Arab and Jewish provinces of Palestine and Trans-Jordan, each with a measure of home rule.[47] Although the problems inherent in federalism were obvious, especially as Jews would not likely consent to being placed under an Arab king, this sort of thinking nevertheless gave increasing legitimacy to the idea of uniting Arab Palestine to Trans-Jordan.

But Bevin's amenability to federalism did not imply his acceptance of 'Abdullah's ambitions, at least not until 1948, whether over Greater Syria or Palestine, nor did it lead to an active pursuit of such a solution. Actually, he was consistently against partition in any form. He was against it on the basis of demographics and the principle of self-determination. His role of undermining any partition tendencies in government was the obverse of Churchill's undermining any unitary tendencies. His federalist leanings, however, were important in that, given the unhospitality of Arab nationalism in the surrounding states, it was essential to maintain excellent relations with 'Abdullah. The Trans-Jordan "option" would linger in the background until the force of events made it a possibility.

These events were rapidly approaching by the end of 1947, with partition being considered by the international community and Britain committed to withdrawal. Aware of his anxiety over his ambitions, however, London was worried 'Abdullah would militarily intervene in Palestine. Thus, the British Minister in 'Amman was instructed to calm 'Abdullah's nervousness by informing him that Britain recognized his concern about Palestinian developments and promised to consult with him about their Palestine policy. The Minister, Alec Kirkbride, was further told that London was preoccupied with the question of the possible participation of the Legion in Palestine after British withdrawal, and that the tentative thinking was that it would be necessary to withdraw the Arab Legion to Trans-Jordan and cease payments of its expenses upon withdrawal.[48] The note also made clear that if 'Abdullah were to send units of the Legion back into Palestine (that is, even after British withdrawal), London would probably have to withdraw British officers from the Legion and reconsider the provision of subsidies to the King. These things the British proposed to tell 'Abdullah in advance. These proposed intentions, however, started an internal debate, particularly with Kirkbride, over the role of Trans-Jordan in a partitioned Palestine.

Kirkbride argued against "penalising" Trans-Jordan, especially if there was a "general scramble for Arab areas of Palestine."[49] He strongly opined that albeit he agreed the Legion should be pulled back, he could not find a good reason for the stopping of subsidies, nor why Britain should try to direct Trans-Jordan's actions after withdrawal had been completed. He added that Trans-Jordan had the best claim to inherit the "residue" of Palestine and would counteract the chances of conflict between a Jewish state and the other Arab states. No other Arab leader was prepared to acquiesce to partition, Kirkbride reasoned, and it therefore was in Britain's best interest not to erect obstacles in 'Abdullah's way. The alternative of a non-viable Palestinian state under the Mufti "is not attractive and anti-Hashemites would blame us but they do so for everything else." Kirkbride's views and hopes for 'Abdullah were to come to fruition in 1948, particularly since they implied the maintenance of a British presence in the area.

On the eve of the United Nations partition resolution, London was concerned with American relations and it did not want to seem it was blocking the will and principles of the world body. However, the fear of an Arab denunciation that Britain was restraining 'Abdullah and so allowing the Zionists a free hand was not a major part of the calculations at this point. Only by February 1948, when things were not looking good for the Palestinian Arabs, did Britain have to cautiously weigh the risks involved in its client's intervention.

In the prevailing situation before the United Nations recommended partition, the British were restricted in their choices. Publicly, they adhered to their policy of a unitary state under the provincial autonomy scheme. In the event of partition, they feared (unlike Kirkbride) that an aggressive Jewish state would be a factor of instability leading to conflict with the other Arab states. They also felt that if 'Abdullah attained control over the Arab part, the Arab states would be "violently incensed" (in Bevin's words) against him and blame Britain for the outcome. On the other hand, the advantage of 'Abdullah taking over the Arab part of Palestine, perhaps including an outlet to the Mediterranean, would be the maintenance of British strategic facilities in a "fairly large part" of the country.[50] Thus, British policy towards 'Abdullah's ambitions in Palestine *at this time* was based on the pragmatic principle of "guarded approval."[51] Britain adhered to this policy in the event that it lost total influence in Palestine. As concerns the Legion, London had decided "to stop payment to that part which was rendered on the basis of the Legion's services" in Palestine.[52]

The British government's pragmatic, and perhaps devious, policy of guarded approval, particularly adhered to in view of its wider Arab interests, prompted Kirkbride to write again and urge that it was better not to communicate to the King about the Legion and that "absorption" of the Arab areas would keep 'Abdullah "busy for five years" and leave "little time or energy for Greater Syria." Moreover, the "enhancement of his prestige" would "remove the present itch for expansion."[53] Kirkbride further argued against the general policy of restricting the activities of British military missions in allied countries (in particular in 'Iraq and Trans-Jordan) and the arms embargo, which he viewed as damaging to Britain's future interests.[54] Though he did not suggest encouraging Arab state intervention, he criticized the methods employed by his government. But London stuck to its policy towards the Arab states and its intention of stopping part of its subsidies to the Arab Legion and restricting the activities of its British officers.

The most potent factor accounting for this British attitude was fear of public opinion, particularly any "damaging accusations" that might emanate from the United States.[55] Though the Foreign Office, like Kirkbride, saw "considerable advantage" in the occupation of part or whole of the Arab areas of Palestine by 'Abdullah,[56] they were, unlike Kirkbride, concerned with reactions in the Arab world and in world public opinion. A further factor in British calculations was the hope that the Arab states, desperate in their efforts to avoid conflict in Palestine, might approach London to work out a compromise before Britain's total withdrawal. This was consistently implied by Riad al-Sulh, for example, although he did not offer any clear Arab ideas to London.[57] Also, 'Azzam more than once stressed the Arab willingness to accept the Morrison-Grady proposals or even the minority recommendations of UNSCOP—but under propitious circumstances in which the Arab states might be in a position to arrange in Palestine some sort of democratically elected government.[58] Finally, Nuri Pasha indicated that the Arabs were ready for conciliation and asked Britain to play a forceful role and give the Arabs a "lead."[59] These Arab contacts were made in December, when it was clear to the Arab states that, as they could not accept partition, they would have to intervene in Palestine.

The United Nations partition resolution and subsequent events pushed the British towards a firm policy on 'Abdullah and Palestine. Because of Britain's need to "preserve American goodwill," London could not appear to be opposing the creation of a Jewish state.[60] Yet, in light of widespread Arab outrage, Bevin thought it was a propitious time to implement his vision of mutual, bilateral alliances with Arab states, a vision he brought with him to office. The implicit hopes and goals were that such alliances would temper Arab fear and vulnerability and preserve Britain's dominant position in the Middle East and prove to the world that Britain was determined to transform its imperialist role in the region. Bevin also hoped that within such a scenario of a stable Middle East, the partition of Palestine would, with the help of the Arab allies, be smoothly implemented.[61]

During January 1948, Bevin's hopes rapidly collapsed. In the early part of that month, it was fairly obvious that the Palestine situation left little room for peace or compromise. However, Bevin was still unwilling to risk alienating Arab opinion by supporting 'Abdullah. In addition, an Anglo-'Iraq treaty was being negotiated. Bevin hoped to make it a model of a new Anglo-Arab relationship. Thus, Bevin finally wrote 'Abdullah. It was an attempt to placate his sensibilities, but it was also a direct hint to 'Abdullah not to intervene in Palestine. Bevin expressed to 'Abdullah Britain's determination to remain in the Middle East and reassured him that he need not feel isolated when Britain withdrew from Palestine, as it hoped for a series of defensive alliances with the Arab states and the maintenance of some units in Trans-Jordan.[62] It was made clear that London desired to help the King maintain an efficient army and that the British government wanted to discuss its contributions to Trans-Jordan's treasury.

On Palestine, Bevin wrote that: one, the British government realized the Arabs' and King's anxiety over Palestine and wished to assist him to establish there a "stable and democratic settlement" which would enable the people of Palestine to live in good relations with their neighbors. Two, the British hoped that the King realized the risk which would ensue if Trans-Jordan were to take steps which isolated her from other Arab states. And three, it was made clear to 'Abdullah that even though London desired to contribute to a "speedy and peaceful settlement" in Palestine (i.e., partition), they would be placed in a position of considerable difficulty with the other Arab states if 'Abdullah intervened to annex the Arab part of Palestine. The ambiguity of this message is interpreted by Avi Shlaim in the following way:

. . . Fearing Abdullah's notorious indescretion and anxious to avoid the appearance of collusion in the very partition scheme it had refused to support at the United Nations or to help impose, the British government shrouded the degree to which its interests now marched with Abdullah's. Neither Abdullah's interests nor its own would be served if he took action that was so blatantly contrary to the wishes of the other Arab states that they banded against him. One way out of the dilemma was to maintain the official posture of opposition to partition while secretly encouraging Abdullah to implement it. This kind of duplicity was not entirely alien to the spirit of British diplomacy but there was always the risk of exposure.[63]

As concerns the Arab Legion, London eventually (that is, during the fast-paced events in the early part of 1948) decided not to withdraw British officers from the Legion nor, most certainly, to stop subsidies of any sort. At the end of 1947, the British feared a clash between the Legion and Jewish forces or the Legion's use in overtaking areas allotted to the Jewish state in the United Nations partition resolution. By May 1948, when they were more certain of 'Abdullah's intentions and had decided on more active collusion, the use of British officers was in fact seen as a way to insure the Legion's restraint once the British withdrawal was completed. Not only was the Legion forbidden to do anything except guard British supply lines as they withdrew, but the seventy-one British officers were instructed to withdraw from fighting if the Legion entered Jewish areas. Though the Legion was eventually withdrawn from Palestine by 15 May, some units actually remained in the UN-allotted *Arab* areas, and only those that were contiguous to the Trans-Jordanian border.[64]

By February, the British position had moved from one of caution to collusive support of 'Abdullah's ambitions. In late January the treaty with 'Iraq collapsed, largely because of vociferous nationalist opposition. This caused the parallel shattering of Bevin's vision of alliances; 'Abdullah and his kingdom became the only hope for a friendly and enduring British presence. In that month 'Abdullah sent Prime Minister Tewfiq Abu al-Huda to London to revise what was supposed to be a twenty-five year treaty signed two years earlier, to make it appear that Trans-Jordan was not under the domination of British imperialism, and yet to strengthen the British presence.

In a meeting between Abu al-Huda and Bevin, the former suggested that the Arab Legion intended to enter Palestine at the end of the mandate and occupy that part of Palestine "awarded" to the Arabs and that was contiguous to the Trans-Jordan frontier. Glubb Pasha, who accompanied Tewfiq, recalls Bevin's remarks: "It seems the obvious thing to do. . . . but do not go and invade the areas allotted to the Jews."[65] Thus, it was accepted that the Legion would play an important role in achieving 'Abdullah's objectives, preserving the British presence in Palestine as it did in Trans-Jordan, and perhaps containing Arab-Jewish fighting.

The tone of Bevin's remarks seemed to indicate thoughts that were preoccupied with the potential consequences and dilemmas, in the Arab world and internationally, of any definite British course of action on Palestine. The remarks were not made with forceful conviction, but with hesitation and a seemingly growing acceptance of the force of events. These events shaped the direct collusion between 'Abdullah and the British towards partitioning Palestine and preventing the emergence of a Palestinian Arab state. And, as far as 'Abdullah was concerned, he finally obtained his long sought go-ahead from his allies.

Arab Politics, Palestine and the Mufti: The Progressive Weakening of Palestinian Authority

In September 1947, the Political Committee of the League reluctantly convened at Sofar, Lebanon to discuss UNSCOP's report. The impetus for the League meeting came from the 'Iraqis. Though all the Arab states were under severe public pressure to act, the 'Iraqi government, in particular, assumed a leading role, given its historically aggressive posturing on Palestine.[66] In this instance as in practically all the previous ones, the 'Iraqi rulers used the question of Palestine to deflect and divert internal pressure. Popular discontent over the government's treaty negotiations with Britain were high. Consequently, the 'Iraqi Parliament, in a special joint session prior to the League meeting, went out of its way to pledge allegiance to Palestine, making clear to the government that 'Iraq, unlike other Arab states, considered the former country above its own national interests.[67]

The aggressive attitude of the 'Iraqi Prime Minister did not find a welcome reception at Sofar. He advocated economic sanctions but was opposed by the Sa'udi delegate, Yusif Yasin.[68] Salih Jabr's militant and intrepid behavior towards sanctions were, as League members knew, hypocritical and hollow. He made 'Iraq's acceptance of sanctions contingent on the acceptance of the Sa'udis, who, because of their dependence on oil revenues, had the most to lose. He knew that neither the Sa'udis nor the other Arab states would accept sanctions, therefore putting 'Iraq in a favorable public light as the champion of the Palestinian Arabs. However, at this convocation the 'Iraqi regime began an open and relentless campaign to weaken the AHC and block out its participation from League meetings and eventually to weaken its influence and independence. Jabr attacked the Palestinian delegates (Mu'in al-Madi, 'Izzat Darwaza, and Emile al-Ghury), with Trans-Jordanian support. He questioned the right of the AHC to send delegates to Arab League meetings (even though at the League's creation the Palestinians were given such a right) and refused to listen to Palestinian arguments about the AHC's legitimacy, as witnessed by its recognition by the Arab League and the United Nations.[69]

Beginning on 7 October, the Arab League Council met at 'Aley to discuss action towards Palestine. The usual discrepancy between League resolutions (for the consumption of the public) and actual policies again took precedence.[70] The Bludan resolutions were reaffirmed although no decisions were taken on their application. Arab governments were recommended to take military precautions on the frontiers of Palestine and those states that were contiguous to Palestine were asked to facilitate the participation of non-contiguous states. The governments were also recommended to give moral and material help to the Palestinians.

In accordance with the Hashemites' larger political and military schemes, Salih Jabr unsuccessfully attempted to have the Mufti barred from the meeting. The Mufti for the first time asked for the formation of a provisional government, but Jabr and Samir Rifa'i strongly opposed his request on the pretext that it would not be good for world public opinion at the United Nations.[71] The Mufti's request for a government at this time was not arbitrary. There are various reasons to explain it. First, it was just at the time Britain announced its intention to withdraw. The Mufti probably was aware of the dangers for the Palestinians if a vacuum were left behind by the British. He wanted to establish a Palestinian authority linked to the AHC government to direct the Palestinians and set a precedent of legitimacy. Second, he was apprehensive over 'Iraqi and Trans-Jordanian ambitions. It was better to have an indigenous Palestinian authority recognized by the League that would eventually deal with Arab intervention than to have the 'Iraqis or 'Abdullah establish a military occupation regime that might lead to annexation. Third, the Mufti wanted the prestige and legitimacy of a provisional government that would be able to represent the Palestinians in the League with more authority and power. In this way, decisions that the League took in the military (and financial) spheres would be more controllable by the Palestinians. That is, the Mufti wanted the volunteers to be under his command through 'Abd al-Qadir al-Husayni, his commander in Palestine. The Mufti did not relish the thought of Arab soldiers entering Palestine and was more concerned that the Palestinians receive all the material, financial and moral help they needed to conduct their own struggle.

At the 'Aley meeting the delegates, realizing the central role of Trans-Jordan in any military venture, sent 'Azzam Bey, Salih Jabr and Samir Pasha to meet with King 'Abdullah to pave the way for a reconciliation between Trans-Jordan and Syria and Lebanon. Though 'Abdullah was persuaded to invite the rest of the delegates (who subsequently left Beirut for 'Amman) at the meeting with 'Azzam and Jabr, 'Abdullah told his visitors about the folly of talking about the ejection of the Jews from Palestine and doubted the Arabs' ability to do so.[72] More importantly, the visitors agreed with 'Abdullah that the best course to follow might be to come to terms with the Zionists after a British withdrawal and to restrict them to as small a part of Palestine as possible.

At the meeting with all the Arab delegates 'Azzam claimed publicly that 'Abdullah was not to be blamed for advocating a united Syria as the union of all the Arab countries was the ultimate aim of the League.[73] But the delegates impressed on 'Abdullah the importance of not meddling in Syrian affairs. The King easily agreed to the Arabs' request as by this time his interest and obsession was singly focused on Palestine.

'Abdullah refused to hear about anything relating to a Palestinian government, whether it was led by the Mufti or not.[74] He also rejected the proposal for funding, arming, and equipping the Palestinians. It did not take much resistance from 'Abdullah to convince the delegates to keep the Mufti at bay. The main reason for this was that the Arabs were aspiring for some sort of eventual settlement with the Jews. Though there were no plans, the Arab hope was that once they contained the Zionists in a small area they would make peace with them, implying recognition of an independent Jewish state, in however small an area that may have been. These vague Arab intentions were indicated in 'Azzam's and Jabr's agreement with 'Abdullah over the need to come to terms with the Jews after the British withdrawal. It was obvious to all that the creation of a provisional government would stand in the way.

Arab thinking was exemplified by 'Azzam in his talk with the British minister in Lebanon. Though 'Azzam was one of the main proponents of a Palestinian government, in the delegates' meeting with 'Abdullah he told the British minister that the Mufti tried to "impress the Arab League with his gang leaders" but that it was made plain to him that in view of "responsible Arabs" little could be achieved that way.[75] 'Azzam said he had opposed the idea of establishing a Palestinian government but added that it might be necessary for the Arab leaders to eventually arrange for a constituent assembly to enable the Palestinians to decide on their own form of government. The Jews, he continued, might then be offered a settlement on the basis of the Morrison-Grady proposal (provincial autonomy), which the Arabs were unable to accept the previous year. Whether or not the Mufti played a part would depend on whether his "mentality changed."

The hypocrisy of 'Azzam indicated the direction of Arab thinking. He was trying to impress upon London the Arabs' willingness to compromise and therefore induce the British to use their influence in Palestine and internationally towards helping the Arabs achieve their ends. Nuri al-Sa'id had told the British minister that if "HMG adhered too rigidly to their policy of neutrality in Arab affairs," Britain would run the risk of losing that unique position of influence. The "Arab states were after all largely created by British policy."[76] In their calculations the Arabs feared that a provisional government before the end of the mandate would come in the way of their desire not to heighten or complicate the risks involved for them in Palestine. Shaykh Hafiz Wahba of Sa'udi Arabia "categorically" told Brigadier I. N. Clayton of the Cairo Middle East Office that there was "no question" of setting up a Palestinian Arab government before the mandate was relinquished and that, owing to the risk of internal (Arab) differences, no plans had yet been made for one even after the mandate's end.[77] The Arabs also were afraid that the formation of a provisional government would add considerably to the dangers of an Anglo-Arab clash in Palestine.

Despite the seeming collective Arab fear of supporting a provisional government, in the halls of the League the Arab states were in conflict over the subject, with the Hashemites consistently opposing the idea. The others, mainly Egypt and Syria, used it as a weapon against Hashemite ambitions and were at the same time under severe public pressure to support Palestine. Ultimately, Arab differences and squabbling took precedence and each state pursued its own line of policy in accordance with its interests.

At 'Aley, then, no clear political line was adopted and there were no steps taken to implement the military decisions of the League Council. A Technical Planning or Military Committee (MC) was formed at Sofar in September to consider military planning and intervention in Palestine. The MC, made up of Isma'il Safwat of 'Iraq, Mahmud Hindi of Syria, Subhi al-Khadra of Palestine, Bahjat Tabarra of Trans-Jordan, Shukri Shkayr of Lebanon, and 'Iraqi Taha al-Hashimi as inspector general of the volunteers, was to have control over the training and fighting of the volunteers until the Arab armed forces entered Palestine in May.[78] The basic premise for the MC's formation was that it would be responsible for leading, arming and coordinating the Palestinian struggle. It was not to be a substitute for an Arab Higher Command, although the latter never materialized.[79]

There was a brief attempt at 'Aley to create a special financial committee that would have responsibility of budgeting and disbursing the allocated funds, although that also did not materialize. The recommendation for the formation of the special committee came from the MC and its members were to be 'Iraq, Trans-Jordan, and possibly, Syria.[80] The MC eventually assumed the projected financial committee's task, which, along with its role of coordinating arms supply, strategy, and command, became telescoped into something approaching a Combined General Staff.[81]

The MC made numerous critical reports to the League but most of its requests were never met. At 'Aley in October, in its first report, the MC made it clear that the Palestinians were not prepared militarily, administratively, and politically to meet the Zionist challenge and that the Palestinians within the Jewish area (of a projected Jewish state) were in serious danger.[82] It asked for the immediate training and arming of volunteers; the mobilization of Arab armies on the borders of Palestine and the creation of a special command for the purpose; the creation of a unified Arab command to coordinate all state commands; the supplying to the Palestinians of at least 10,000 rifles, substantial amounts of machine guns, hand grenades and other explosives; a second L1,000,000 for the arming of the Palestinians; and the purchase by the Arab states of as much war *materiel* as possible. Again, in November, General Safwat submitted a second report in which he surveyed the strength of the Jews and pointed out the imperative for mobilizing the Arab armies at the borders and for the formation of a unified Arab command.

The Political Committee of the Arab League did not respond to the MC's reports for money, material, organization, and unity of command. To placate Safwat in particular, the MC headquarters were established in Damascus to begin the training, arming and transportation of volunteers to Palestine. The training center for the volunteers was established at Qatna, some twelve miles southwest of Damascus. It was obvious that the Arab states neither intended nor had the will to take the steps that the MC recommended. Their political differences, suspicions, and ambitions precluded any effective cooperation.

'Abdullah in particular found the MC's recommendations distasteful. He was against the irregular forces and wanted to ensure that the funds would not be channelled to the Palestinians, especially via the AHC. Despite the fact that the other Arab states tried to placate 'Abdullah through the unsuccessful attempt to form a special financial committee in which Trans-Jordan would play, with 'Iraq, a major role, 'Abdullah desired to block out any form of Palestinian representation or participation. Sour after the MC's report, 'Abdullah sent a draft of instructions and technical questions to the Trans-Jordan representative on it designed to make the MC aware of the practical difficulties which it faced.[83] The King's idea was that the general headquarters should be in Trans-Jordan under his control. According to Kirkbride, 'Abdullah (rightly) realized how little the Arab states could do in the military field and how unlikely it was that anything concrete would emerge from the MC's deliberations.

Another major purpose of 'Abdullah was to "nip in the bud the formation of armed bands under [the AHC's] command." Thus, part of the questions on the draft were more than technical. 'Abdullah suggested that bands not under the orders of General Headquarters should be prohibited; that the AHC should have no role other than representing Palestine;

and that it should be centered in Egypt to avoid friction between it and the military authorities. To further protect himself, 'Abdullah had Samir Pasha obtain Syrian and Egyptian agreement to help Trans-Jordan secure from the League as a whole the cost of maintaining the Arab Legion in case British subsidy was cut off.[84]

Although the Egyptians and Syrians naturally distrusted 'Abdullah and knew he was hankering to obtain a chunk of Palestine, they did not know what sort of military scenario he was planning to achieve his political ends. His plans, as far as he let the League know them, seemed consistent with the latter's general line of thinking. However, he was practicing deception on the other League members as his real military goals conflicted with the League's wishes. 'Abdullah knew that the Egyptians and Syrians were hesitant to send troops to Palestine owing to the difficult internal situation in each country. In any case he was certain they would send only a few token troops to their respective frontiers. The Egyptian Prime Minister, Mahmud Nuqrashi Pasha, had even made it clear at the League Council's December meeting that the Egyptian army did not desire to intervene in Palestine both because of the presence of British forces on Egyptian soil and because the Egyptian case (for the withdrawal of Britain) was still technically before the United Nations.[85]

'Abdullah naturally exploited this weakness to achieve his goals as he and the 'Iraqis were the only states outwardly willing to intervene in Palestine. At the December meeting, Samir Rifa'i asked whether any other member would object if a state found itself in a position to go to war in assisting the Palestinians.[86] With 'Iraqi support of Trans-Jordan, the others assented although they realized the point of the question. The other states (notably Syria, Sa'udi Arabia, Egypt, and Lebanon) did agree, however, that any administration set up in Palestine by another state could only be of a temporary nature pending consultation with the Palestinians. This was an indirect warning to 'Abdullah, albeit he was not bothered by it given the fact that the others were not prepared to publicly commit themselves to furnish forces.

What the League anticipated was that any intervention should be on the basis of moving into all of Palestine whereas 'Abdullah was secretly planning to enter the Arab parts allotted by the United Nations. The Arabs felt they could have partition without any effort on the part of 'Abdullah—in other words, his occupation of the proposed Arab state would be de facto recognition of partition, which they knew the Arab peoples would not stand for.[87] Thus, within these general Arab constrictions, 'Abdullah and 'Iraq proposed to the Arab states the scenario that, after 15 May, their joint forces would follow up the evacuation of British troops (which were expected to have withdrawn completely by August).[88] The greatest care would be taken to avoid any contact with British forces or even the entry into the areas of British military security.

Where Trans-Jordan's plans differed from those of 'Iraq's (mainly Nuri's, who attended the conference in the last two days) was that the former only contemplated advancing in the first place with its regular forces to the frontiers of the Arab state as defined by the United Nations. Samir Pasha argued that action inside the Jewish state would be taken by guerrillas, who would be assisted in every way. Nuri Pasha's plan envisaged the advance of Arab troops as far into the Jewish state as possible (well down into the coastal plain) without coming into contact with British forces.

The 'Iraqis wanted to legitimize, as did 'Abdullah, their entry into Palestine. But their concern was to occupy the whole country as a first step to their wider ambitions. For 'Abdullah, while he also would have liked to see the formation of a great Hashemite state, he knew that his chances of being its ruler were slim. Hence his plans for occupation markedly differed from those he made available to the League. His plan, which was in accordance with the numerous secret talks he conducted with the Zionists, and certainly with the understanding his prime minister reached with Bevin, envisaged, as a first step, the occupation of Nablus, Hebron and, *if possible,* Gaza, then the extension of his authority to all parts of Palestine *not allocated* to the Jewish state or the Jerusalem enclave.[89] A provisional military administration would be set up in the first instance, as the reason for such a move would ostensibly be the protection of Arab areas from Jewish expansion. The question of annexation would be avoided although it would be the ultimate goal. If the situation arose wherein 'Abdullah saw he could march on all of Palestine, he was willing to do so and offer the Jews a share in government on a sort of federal basis. However, 'Abdullah knew that with the means at his disposal occupation of all of Palestine was an unrealistic hope. Moreover, as will be seen, by May 1948 'Abdullah's goals dwindled considerably, reflecting the reality of the Zionist advances on the ground and the general parameters of the deal he had struck, though never conclusively, with them: he would limit his military operations to the central Palestine area (which became known as the West Bank).

Because of the differences in 'Iraqi-Trans-Jordanian political ambitions towards Palestine, there eventually was no plan of military cooperation between the two states. In fact, there were some disagreements. After the announcement at 'Aley that the Arabs would send forces to the border of Palestine, 'Iraq, unlike Syria (which could maneuver its troops on Palestine's borders), was under great pressure to send a contingent. Naturally, Trans-Jordan was the most convenient border state to send troops into. Despite repeated demands and pleas from the 'Iraqis to send at least a battalion, 'Abdullah refused to comply.[90] He was prepared to cooperate with 'Iraq regarding collective Arab schemes formed by the League but was not willing to permit any Arab troops to enter Trans-Jordan. That is, he would cooperate with the League if all troops stayed within their respective borders, thus effectively nullifying the meaning of a unified military command. Although he would have preferred specific military cooperation between 'Iraq and himself, it would had to have been outside the auspices of the League. He wrote the Regent 'Abd al-Illah that "if we permitted the entrance of forces from our sister Iraq, Saudi Arabia would demand the admittance of her forces also, perhaps even Syria might do so, and then this Kingdom of yours would be occupied before Palestine had been occupied."[91]

'Abdullah's intentions to intervene in Palestine were well known in 'Iraqi ruling circles and accepted as a first step towards broader Hashemite dreams, but they were not sure of his specific plans. They had, however, suspected 'Abdullah of wanting to annex the Arab part of Palestine in the partition plan, with London's support. In December 1947, Nuri al-Sa'id and Salih Jabr visited 'Abdullah on their way back from the League Council meeting in Cairo. As both states had just discussed ideas of intervention with the other Arab states, the 'Iraqis wanted to induce 'Abdullah into telling them his actual plans, perhaps to set their strategy towards Trans-Jordan and Palestine. They told 'Abdullah that they gathered from official circles in London that the British government was in favor of Trans-Jordan obtaining the Arab areas of Palestine.[92] The two encouraged 'Abdullah in the belief that he would have their support in the event of Arab opposition.

'Abdullah made clear his wish to secure cooperation with 'Iraq through a scheme of federal unity. Failing that, he demanded a defensive and offensive military alliance. The King's worry was to protect himself against the other Arab states. But Nuri and Jabr did not wish for 'Abdullah to have a free hand in Palestine. Thus, albeit they wished him to believe that they would back him militarily and politically, they discouraged his suggestion for political unity on the basis that the execution of such a scheme should be postponed until Palestine's future was clearer. The 'Iraqis, in their attempt to discover 'Abdullah's intentions, were perhaps overly confident that he would not succeed by himself in Palestine. They therefore might have assumed that, with their own intervention, both Hashemite states would control all of Palestine. 'Abdullah's attitude was central to the success or failure of their plans. Lastly, their rejection of 'Abdullah's suggestion for either an alliance or federal unity perhaps reflected their apprehension of being identified too closely with him and his unpopular schemes.

At the December League Council meeting in Cairo, the Arabs also discussed the nature of the Arab response to the partition resolution passed two weeks earlier. The premiers present at the meeting knew that their choices of maneuvers to evade responsibility towards Palestine had become extremely limited. The Arab states had so consistently voiced their public opposition to any form of partition that they could not now turn back. Partition, which the Arab states deeply feared, had become a concrete reality. If there was a time that political and military coordination was required, it was after the partition resolution. But even then the Arabs could not agree. Predictably, the 'Iraqi premier, Salih Jabr, continued with his aggressive attitude towards economic sanctions. Because of his blatant hypocrisy, however, the issue finally died. The gap between Arab threats and actions prevailed.

The League Council was presented with a report by the MC which in effect said that the Arabs of Palestine were in an unfavorable position compared with the Jews and that it was urgently necessary to send both arms and volunteer re-inforcements to the former.[93] The MC pointed out that while such a move might enable the Palestinian Arabs to defend themselves, only intervention by Arab armies could prevent implementation of the partition plan. The MC report asked that those men already trained at Qatna (300 of them) be sent to Palestine as instructors and a further class commenced.

But, despite the obvious shortcomings of Arab preparedness, there was agreement neither on the irregulars nor on unity of Arab command. Generally, the premiers agreed that the irregulars would operate in aid of any rising that the Palestinian Arabs might carry out. However, they were anxious that the irregulars should be restrained at least until the mandate was terminated. They feared the danger of a clash with the British if the irregulars were let into Palestine before the termination of the mandate, and even before the final evacuation was realized in August.[94] The hope of minimizing the risk of a clash was the ostensible reason Nuri Pasha gave for his policy of going into Palestine with regular forces, over which more control would (theoretically) be maintained than would be possible with irregulars.

Although the Council agreed that each Arab state would send volunteers to Syria,[95] the premiers also voiced their apprehension about their inability to control the actual number of men that went to Palestine.[96] Given the intensity of public opinion, there was little that the Arab states could do to prevent the entry of volunteers into Palestine. Recognizing that fact, the Arabs knew that, as an avenue of relieving public pressure, it was preferable and safer to have irregulars rather than Arab soldiers in Palestine. Beside these reasons, the Arab states really took no definite decision in regard to their military participation and were not to do so until May.

Eventually, it was decided to divide the supply of rifles as follows:

2,000 each from Egypt, Syria, 'Iraq, and Sa'udi Arabia, and 1,000 each from Lebanon and Trans-Jordan.[97] Syria and Lebanon offered to send an additional 1,000 French grenades and some French automatic weapons. The general military and political resolutions of the League Council were that donations from the L1,000,000 needed for the Palestine war effort (the sum first mentioned in June 1946) would be handled via the Arab governments, and that propaganda would be intensified in Britain and the United States.[98]

The pressures building up in Palestine and the panic and steady exodus of the Palestinian Arab middle class after the partition resolution in November 1947 created an ensuing sense of urgency in Arab circles. The refugee problem was becoming so visible that the Political Committee decided on the need for taxation in the form of popular contributions in the Arab world to be spent on the relief of the homeless. Isma'il Safwat outlined to the Political Committee the dangers in Palestine and made clear that the enemy positions were strengthening with each passing day, while the Palestinians were in need of military support. Safwat also complained that the fighters under the direction of the Mufti did not recognize the MC nor obey its orders and would not coordinate operations with Fawzi al-Qawaqji's Army of Liberation, technically under the control of the MC.[99] The Political Committee in response formed a special "Palestine Committee," which was to deal with the Palestine question, and a Permanent Military Committee, concerned with coordinating military cooperation between the Arab states.[100]

The latter military committee was a token move on the part of the League as it had no power or importance. Its members were the same politicians as those on the Arab League Political Committee, in addition to the Mufti. Isma'il Safwat was mandated responsibility for administering the entire military situation in Palestine and was made head of all volunteer groups (including, technically, the Mufti's *Jihad al-Muqaddas*, Holy War). The Palestine and Permanent Military Committees, whose members overlapped, actually served as a sort of Palestine or Defense Council to deal with the military-political aspects of Palestine.[101] They were partially formed in order to strip the AHC of all political and military authority and to put Palestine affairs firmly under the control of the Arab League.

The progressive trend towards the emasculation of the Mufti's powers had begun, as we have seen, at the 'Aley meeting in October, where the Arab delegates opposed his request for the formation of a provisional government. At the December meeting the Mufti was barred from attending, although he was allowed token attendance to the preliminary meeting in the morning of the first day. Given the tremendous political and military risks that the Arabs had to face after the partition resolution, it was probably felt that the fate of Palestine had to be settled without, as they saw it, the intransigent presence or demands of the Mufti. It was time for concrete action, and the stakes for the Arab states were too high to permit the Mufti to assume any influence. Although the Arab states disagreed over practically everything relating to Palestine, there was strong apprehension that the situation there would become uncontrollable if the Mufti were allowed to take full political and military command. It was, in essence, the fear of established regimes over maintaining their stability. The Mufti and the AHC, who had assumed the role of radical nationalists, had less to lose from an all-out, nationalist confrontation with the Zionists.

The exclusion of the Mufti from the discussions was largely the work of the 'Iraqi and Trans-Jordanian delegates. Although it was recognized by the Arab states that there was a need for a central authority in Palestine, particularly after British evacuation, there were no ideas as to how control and administration were to be exercised in the Arab areas of the partition scheme. This question obviously was of concern more to those Arab states other than 'Iraq and Trans-Jordan. Though these states were concerned with the practical question of administration, they were even more anxious about checking 'Iraqi-Trans-Jordanian ambitions. While Egypt, Syria, Sa'udi Arabia, and Secretary-General 'Azzam disliked the Mufti and privately opposed his political ambitions, they advocated the formation of some local administrative authority in Palestine in an effort to counter the Hashemites. At the December meeting 'Azzam, supported by the Sa'udi, Egyptian, and Syrian delegates, voiced the opinion that the establishment of a local authority was a necessary step, and Nuqrashi Pasha even mentioned the Mufti as the future ruler of Palestine.[102] Salih Jabr naturally vehemently opposed the latter suggestion, objecting on the basis that there was no need for any authority at the time, particularly as Palestine was in a situation of war. He preferred that the administration of Palestine be under some form of military command and not the Mufti.[103]

'Azzam and his supporters knew that a local authority, particularly of an administrative nature, was not necessarily synonymous with a provisional government or the enhancement of the Mufti's powers. However, they were aware of the strong possibility that any local authority would be managed and dominated by the Mufti's supporters. It was for this obvious reason that the Hashemites opposed such a scheme. Nuqrashi Pasha's suggestion was more of an off-the-cuff remark, made for reasons of Egyptian prestige. For there was no evidence that the Egyptians cared for the Mufti. It was more probable that they also opposed him assuming any power in Palestine. For one, they did not desire to see the Arabs initiate any action before 15 May that might be interpreted by London as directly provocative or precipitous. Furthermore, they displayed a continual resistance to intervention in Palestine.

Despite the efforts of 'Azzam and his supporters, then, there really was not a strong will among any of the non-Hashemite rulers to support the Mufti or a provisional government, in particular because the Hashemites were the only ones who displayed a determination to intervene in Palestine. By December, therefore, the Mufti was greatly weakened by the failure of the League to reach a decision about the establishment of a provisional government or local administrative authority, by his exclusion from the discussions in Cairo, and by the appointment of Safwat to command the volunteers. Nuri Pasha, after his return from Cairo, mentioned to Britain's minister at Baghdad that "Without Egyptian support he [the Mufti] would be nothing."[104]

Arab disagreement left a most crucial issue, the necessity of maintaining the general life of Arab Palestine, unresolved. There was a general consensus, however, that Palestine would have to be governed through some form of military administration made up of representatives of the Arab states; that this administration would be under the command of Safwat; and that the Mufti would not be allowed to direct policy in Palestine,[105] although he could not be dropped completely as his name and prestige among the masses was still valuable.[106] It was also generally agreed that the campaign in Palestine would center on the resistance of the Arab inhabitants of the projected Jewish state, supported by the Arabs of the rest of Palestine and by the volunteers. The Arab states' regular forces would be in the background ready to intervene should the irregulars be threatened with defeat. The military campaign could not start prematurely, the premiers decided, because the Arabs were neither organized nor armed. The first real move should be in May and the main effort in August.[107]

These general plans and policies towards the Mufti and Palestine were reinforced at the February meeting of the League Political Committee. The steps taken to strip the Mufti of his powers in December were given a concrete basis in February. The Mufti was not excluded from the latter meeting, perhaps because the events in Palestine, accompanied by a hysterical public and press, dictated that he be treated politely. In particular, the need to display Arab unity was paramount. The Palestinian delegation consisted of the Mufti, Jamal al-Husayni, Emile al-Ghury, and Rafiq al-Tamimi. The Mufti made his last important bid to obtain military, political and moral help for the Palestinians. In an effort to rehabilitate his power and check Hashemite ambitions and Arab irresoluteness, he made the following proposals:[108]

1. That in any general Arab command there should be a representative of the AHC who would be concerned with political affairs in Palestine;

2. That the areas evacuated by the British be transferred under the control of the national committees;

3. That a local administrative authority be established in Palestine to assume responsibilities either before or after the British termination of the mandate on 15 May;

4. That the AHC be granted funds to use as necessary for the local administrative authority he proposed, i.e., a loan to set up an Arab administration; and

5. That the Political Committee grant the AHC a specific amount of money to compensate the Palestinians for war damages, particularly for the dislocated refugees.

Despite the Mufti's emphasis on his authority as speaking for the Palestinian Arabs, the Political Committee rejected all his proposals on the basis that the AHC did not represent all the Palestinian people, although it was the Arab League that helped form that body at Bludan. The Political Committee's decisions in February in fact were meant to counter every one of the Mufti's proposals. All decisions over Palestine from that time forward were monopolized by the League and the Mufti was excluded from any meaningful decision making.

It has been mentioned that the Political Committee of the League formed a sort of Palestine or Defense Council under which two committees, the Palestine and Permanent Military Committees, functioned. The League formally relegated the Mufti to a role of equal membership with the others on both committees. He was no longer regarded as the leader of Palestine and head of a Palestinian political institution, the AHC, which theoretically represented the Palestinian Arabs. He had to adhere to the majority wishes, which majority obviously represented the Arab states in the League.

Militarily, Isma'il Safwat was made commanding general who was to report to the Palestine Council. The Mufti had been in conflict with Safwat's MC in Damascus and had attempted to obstruct its efforts to disperse and establish the regional voluntary commands in Palestine. The central reason for this conflict was that, when the MC formed the Army of Liberation (in December) under the command of the Lebanese Fawzi al-Qawaqji, the Mufti objected to this decision by the League and the MC, stating that the volunteers should come under the command of 'Abd al-Qadir al-Husayni and, by extension, himself. He argued that the Palestinians could defend their country if they were given aid, weapons, and volunteer reinforcements.[109] The Mufti's demands were firmly rejected, in particular because the Syrians, fearing Trans-Jordanian occupation of any part of Palestine even under Arab League command, wanted to ensure that Qawaqji led the irregulars.[110]

Thus, Safwat recited to the Political Committee in February numer-ous instances all over Palestine in which the Mufti's local *Jihad* command-ers and supporters refused to cooperate with the irregulars or accept detachments of volunteers under their command (e.g., 'Abd al-Qadir al-Husayni in the Jerusalem area); tried to smear and poison the name and purpose of the MC (Jenin-Tulkarem-Nablus); tried to assume commands of towns by imposing their authority (Jenin); threatened people with re-prisals if they accepted the volunteers (Hebron); and tried to openly challenge the authority of the MC (Nazareth).[111]

Because of this conflict with the MC, the Mufti was made a member of the Palestine Council, according to 'Azzam, on the condition that he would "tow the line" and fall in with the majority wishes.[112] The Mufti's "henchmen," such as 'Abd al-Qadir, would be allowed to remain in their positions of commanding certain bodies of irregulars (i.e., the *Jihad al-Muqaddas*) provided they accepted Safwat's orders. If they showed "recal-citrance" they would be removed. All funds were to be administered by the Palestine Council and none would be given to the Mufti or AHC. The Council was to be responsible for both military and civilian affairs until a Palestinian administration could be set up.

Thus, because of consistent 'Iraqi-Trans-Jordanian opposition and his conflict with the League's political and military wishes and plans, the Mufti was stripped of any practical influence, as the leader of Palestine, in the halls of the Arab League. The Palestine Council was meant to serve as a political base for the administration of Palestine until after the Arab in-tervention, if any. The irregulars, under the control of the MC which was in turn under the control of the League, were supposed to establish pre-liminary Arab military authority. The Council served a double purpose: it placated 'Iraq and Trans-Jordan, yet left open the future administration of Palestine for the Palestinians. The Mufti would theoretically be excluded from power and Hashemite attempts at expansion would implicitly be checked.

Beyond the general idea that the irregulars would support the Pal-estinian Arabs and the Arab states would be waiting in the background, there were no concrete agreements or coherent military or political plans or strategies. Even in February the Arab states were basically divided along the line of two opposing military "strategies." One party, mainly the Trans-Jordanians and 'Iraqis, thought that regular Arab forces, with irregulars, should go into Palestine perhaps all the way through to the area of the proposed Jewish state (at least so the Trans-Jordanians told their Arab brothers). The other party, mainly the Egyptians, Syrians, and Sa'udis, feared international reactions were they to openly flout the United Nations decision. They were in favor of irregular or guerrilla activity only.[113] In fact, throughout the spring of 1948, the League was eager to accept a United

Nations proposal, backed by the United States, for a truce and a trusteeship agreement. Underneath the general strategies, the Arabs wished to
bring the fighting in Palestine to an end so as not to be dragged in. The
Arab desire for a truce was one of the main reasons the Mufti practically
became a *persona non grata* by February and March of 1948. The Egyptians
in particular began to see him as an extremist.[114] Ironically, the Mufti himself distrusted the idea of the Arab armies entering Palestine.

The Arab States and Palestine
in the Final Weeks of the Mandate

As will be seen in the next chapter, the war between Arabs and Jews
in Palestine was marked by two phases in terms of the initiative of both
sides. Between December and April the Palestinians and irregulars held
the upper hand as they went on the offensive all over the country. By
April the Zionists began to gain the upper hand, particularly in mixed
towns. This was due to full mobilization and substantial consignments of
new arms. The *Irgun* massacre of the villagers of Dayr Yasin on 9 April and
the fall of Haifa on 22 April had marked the start of a strong Jewish offensive in that month. The Arabic press and public became hysterical in their
call for intervention. Military events rather than political ambitions began
to dictate the nature of the Arab response. With the general collapse of
Arab morale and the streaming of refugees, the Arab states were compelled, if not to achieve military or political unity, to at least talk to each
other on the basis of making definitive decisions.

Intensive inter-Arab consultations in Cairo, 'Amman, Damascus, and
Riyadh began after the third week in April, less than one month before the
termination of the mandate.[115] After Dayr Yasin, 'Abdullah was in an extremely excitable mood, shocked over the massacre and anxious over his
inability to control the military events unfolding in Palestine. He even
impulsively informed Kirkbride of his intention to secure Legion detachments, other than those under the command of the General Officer Commanding, for the purpose of posting them in Arab villages in Palestine.[116]
(Kirkbride subsequently talked him out of it.) In mid-April, after desperate
appeals from Qawaqji for more troops and arms, 'Abdullah sent a telegram to the League Political Committee then sitting at Cairo, inviting
them to join Trans-Jordan in the rescue of Palestine.[117] In response, Isma'il
Safwat was sent to 'Amman bearing a letter from 'Azzam, accepting the
King's offer with gratitude and asking him to coordinate details with
Safwat.[118]

Before 'Azzam's reply, however, he submitted 'Abdullah's message
to the Political Committee. The Syrian Prime Minister, Jamil Mardam, and
the Mufti were opposed to the acceptance of 'Abdullah's offer but were

"overcome" by Nuqrashi Pasha, who accused them of being prepared to sacrifice Palestine to their personal jealousies.[119] Nuqrashi Pasha was also said to have refused any longer to regard the Mufti as representing the views of the Palestinian Arabs.[120] 'Azzam told a *Sunday Times* correspondent that it was evident for some time that Qawaqji was worthless and that the Arab states were unable to supply sufficient resources to the irregulars to enable them to defend Arab Palestine.[121] Because of the military situation, 'Azzam, with Egyptian support, felt that there was no alternative to asking Trans-Jordan to lead the military initiative on the condition that all of Palestine would have to be taken over, that Trans-Jordan would not accept partition, and that Palestine would remain an Arab state.[122] But 'Abdullah and his new prime minister, Tewfiq Pasha Abu al-Huda, were determined to occupy as much of the Arab areas as they could as soon as the mandate came to an end.[123] To forestall the accusation that they were implementing the partition resolution, they would publicly say that they intended to occupy the whole of Palestine.

In the talk with Safwat, 'Abdullah made it clear that he expected the Army of Liberation to be under his command and that the Legion would not gain freedom of action in Palestine until after 15 May.[124] Safwat in turn "talked as though" the Legion should be under his command and the command of the League.[125] 'Abdullah subsequently wrote 'Azzam accepting to intervene in Palestine on the basis of the following conditions:[126]

    i. That all Arab forces in Palestine and any reinforcements would have to be under his control;

    ii. That the Legion would not be able to act independently before 15 May; and

    iii. That, as the Arab irregulars in Palestine were too few, untrained, disorganized, and short of equipment, the Legion could not be dispersed in order to protect Arab villages and therefore leave the Arabs without a striking force to cope with an enemy offensive expected after 15 May.

Obviously, 'Abdullah's military demands flowed from his political plans. The idea of not dispersing the Legion was, one, meant to protect the King by keeping his forces strong and cohesive and, two, to ensure that all his forces would be available to occupy only the Arab areas of a partitioned Palestine. 'Abdullah actually was more concerned about his rear flank than he was of the Jews, whom, according to his talks with them, he did not intend to engage beyond what was necessary to obtain the Arab areas of a partitioned Palestine. He wanted any 'Iraqi contribution in men to be used to protect the Legion's rear against Sa'udi Arabia and Syria.[127]

In late April 'Abdullah met with the Regent, the 'Iraqi ministers,

Isma'il Safwat, and Riad al-Sulh. Relations between Trans-Jordan and Syria were still strained, while 'Iraqi-Egyptian contacts were cool. It was felt that tremendous public pressure was being brought to bear on the King and Regent to intervene immediately in Palestine, as Arab morale was on the downturn and 'Amman was crowded with refugees.[128] Sulh left for Cairo bearing a letter from 'Abdullah to 'Azzam, reiterating that Trans-Jordan could not cope with the situation alone and asking for the assurance of full financial, material and troop support from other Arab states.[129] The Regent actually was in full agreement with 'Abdullah. He confided to Kirkbride that 'Iraq would not become involved unless the other Arab states participated. As regards the 'Iraqi army, the Regent said he would probably send a small force but anything like a division was out of the question in light of possible events in Kurdistan.[130] Kirkbride commented that the Regent gave him the impression that his main objective was to calm public opinion in 'Iraq rather than save Palestine and that 'Abdullah, having got what he always wanted—freedom to act—was losing his nerve.[131]

Because of Sulh's mediating efforts, the Regent went to Egypt to consult with 'Azzam, the Political Committee, and the Egyptians over 'Abdullah's conditions and requests. Given the popular mood, the Arab leaders felt the urgency of displaying initiative towards Palestine. Subsequently, the members of the Political Committee and Arab chiefs of staff met in 'Amman. The chiefs stated to the Committee the need for at least five well-equipped divisions and a squadron of fighter planes (as well as a united military command), to which the Committee responded by downplaying the need for such substantial commitment.[132] The attempt to create a supreme military command failed. 'Abdullah maintained that it should be located in Trans-Jordan under his direction and that he would not place the Legion under the existing command at Damascus. 'Azzam advocated the existing arrangement, that is, that the headquarters stay in Damascus under Safwat; the 'Iraqis wanted to keep an 'Iraqi general in command wherever headquarters were;[133] and the Egyptians were reluctant to place their army under the command of a non-Egyptian, particularly an 'Iraqi.[134] The Egyptians had already informed the Regent during his visit to Cairo that they would undertake to send troops to southern Palestine if the other states undertook to intervene at the same time.[135]

Although everyone finally agreed to commit themselves to intervene by 15 May, the implicit result of the meetings was that each state would retain its independent command and assume an operational zone in Palestine. As late as 11 May the Political Committee, meeting in Damascus, made a last belated attempt to appoint a general commander. The Committee announced that an 'Iraqi, Nur al-Din Mahmud, would be the commander of the Arab regular forces. To placate 'Abdullah, Nur al-Din was given the position of deputy general commander under 'Abdullah.[136] But nothing materialized from these decisions in that there was neither consultation nor a unified command.

The Arab invasion plan, if one can so refer to it, was prepared primarily by 'Iraqis, more specifically Nur al-Din. It was actually a revision of a more solid plan first drawn up by the young Jordanian Capt. Wasfi al-Tal, who served as operations officer for General Safwat. Nur al-Din was asked to revise and scale down the ambitious Tal plan. Thus, the resultant invasion plan, which was more within the realm of Arab capabilities, generally envisioned the 'Iraqis, Syrians, Trans-Jordanians, Lebanese, and Egyptians entering Palestine from the direction of their respective borders, and converging, perhaps in a second stage, on Haifa and Tel Aviv in a pincer movement. Specifically, it aimed at cutting "off the lines of communication between Huleh [in northeastern Galilee], Tiberias, Beisan, and other Zionist settlements along the Jordan River from cities along the Mediterranean. This was to be achieved by proceeding step by step through Jenin, Afuleh, and Nazareth so as to surround the Zionist villages and settlements to the east." Only if military conditions were favorable were the Arab armies to move ahead and occupy Haifa and Tel Aviv. Shlaim concludes that the plan was much more "modest, at least in its initial aims,"[137] than is generally believed in that its cautiousness did not imply the Arab-attributed, and more extreme objective of "throwing the Jews into the sea."

But even this plan never materialized; 'Abdullah, as late as 13 May, rejected it. He wanted to be absolute supreme commander and further wanted sweeping changes in the invasion plan. General Nuri al-Din was again forced to change the plan. Essentially, what 'Abdullah wanted, and which is what eventually took place with the actual invasion, was to leave the Arab Legion free to move to occupy central and south-central Palestine instead of going, as the plan called for, in a northerly direction to meet with the Syrian, 'Iraqi and Lebanese armies and leaving the southern and south-central flanks to the Egyptian army. Thus, what was important to 'Abdullah were the Jerusalem, Hebron, and Triangle (Nablus-Jenin-Tulkarem) areas. He was not interested in Tel Aviv or Haifa, or even the part of the Galilee assigned to the Arab state, but in Jerusalem and the central hills, in partition, in the contiguous areas he felt his Legion was able to occupy and control. And indeed, the eventual fighting done by the Legion was only in those parts in central Palestine allotted to the Arab state by the United Nations partition plan, and especially around the strategic approaches to Jerusalem. General John Bagot Glubb and the rest of the British officers ensured this fiasco by scrupulously adhering to what 'Abdullah and the British government wanted and what the Zionists were willing to tolerate, at least if they were contained.

Whereas the political objective implicit in the Arab League's plan was to prevent the partition of Palestine, Abdullah's objective was to effect the partition of Palestine by war and to bring the central part under his crown. By concentrating his own forces in the West Bank, Abdullah intended to eliminate once and for all any possibility of an independent Palestinian state and to present his partners with annexation as a *fait accompli*.[138]

'Abdullah's attitude caused panic among the other Arab states as they knew he could not be stopped. With each acting independently, with hardly any coherent plan or coordination, the stage was set for the disaster which followed. 'Abdullah's twelfth-hour change threw the entire Arab "war effort out of gear." It is no exaggeration to claim that the Arabs "were not at all sure of what they were doing."[139] Furthermore, their men, who did not amount to a total of 25,000, were poorly trained, equipped, and led. Aside from a non-existent central plan, logistics were weak, and liaison among artillery, armor, infantry, and air were faulty both within individual Arab armies and certainly between them. In the end, "The battles in each area were largely fought independently of the war elsewhere. The Israelis fought that way because they lacked mobile reserves and the Arabs because of their internal differences."[140]

The frustration and futility of Arab political maneuvering, suspicion, intrigue, and indecisiveness over Palestine, then, continued well into the last days of the mandate and thereafter. The Arab entry into Palestine on 15 May led to a prolonged war between Israel and the countries of Egypt, Syria, 'Iraq, Trans-Jordan and Lebanon. By the time the armistice negotiations (at Rhodes) ended in July 1949 (signed between Israel and Egypt, Lebanon, Syria and Trans-Jordan), much of Palestine was lost. What became Israel comprised some 80 percent of Palestine, exceeding the United Nations designated borders by far. But the story after 15 May goes beyond the scope and purpose of this book. The next, and final chapter therefore covers what we are concerned with: A detailed examination of the processes that led to the dissolution of Arab Palestine between the end of 1947 and May 1948.

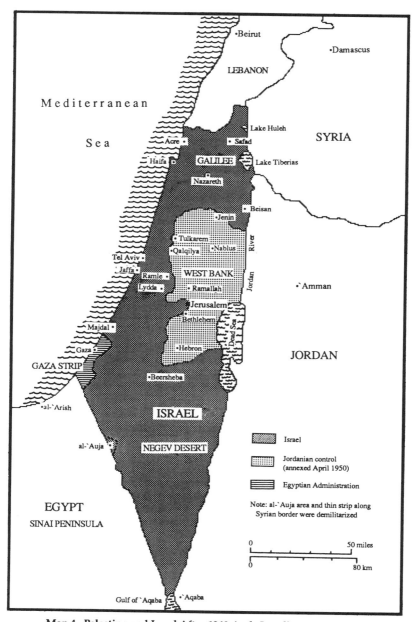

Map 4. Palestine and Israel After 1949 Arab-Israeli Armistices

9

British Withdrawal, War, and Disintegration

I n this chapter, we are not concerned with writing military history. But we need to know how the combination of Palestinian and general Arab politics and military cooperation (or lack of it) on the ground affected the disintegration of Arab Palestine. In keeping with our primary focus in this book, the underlying theme will be the fragility of Palestinian society in the face of unmanageable external pressures and divisive politico-military forces. After all, Arab Palestine, despite its internal political and social divisions, which were fundamental, eventually fell apart because of the pressure and use against it of relatively overwhelming force and terror.

Therefore, the aim of this chapter is to examine the internal and external causes of collapse. In no dimension did these two-tiered causes come together so clearly as in that of the military. Thus, we will analyze the salient features and causes of the Palestinian collapse and exodus. It is doubtful whether there will be a "last word" on such an emotional and complex controversy. However, in light of recent research, and some solidly researched work in the past, some general observations can be made and conclusions drawn.

Before launching into a discussion of the causes of collapse, we will, first, start off by setting into sharp relief Britain's waning grip on post-war Palestine in light of a Jewish rebellion and increasing disorder; second, go on to indicate Britain's actual withdrawal plans and progress and note their effects on local government; third, analyze the sociological aspect of collapse; and fourth, clarify the identity and capabilities of the Arab irregulars and the local forces, which will include a comparison to Zionist strength.

These are as brief as possible, though essential as background to the remainder of the chapter, which starts off with a description of military developments and motives behind military strategies between late November 1947 and mid-May 1948, then examines in detail, under two further

sections, Zionist political motives and tactics and internal causes of collapse. These internal causes focus on politico-military factors, that is, on
the exacerbating effect of divisive local forces on Palestinian collapse and
exodus, with Haifa and Jaffa used as small case studies. The chapter will
then end with a comment on the British role in the fall of Palestine.

Rebellion and Mandatory Administration in the Post-War Period

Between 1945 and 1948 the British were fighting a losing battle
against Jewish underground terrorism. The preoccupation with the
mainly urban-based Zionist rebellion, the need to take into account overall Arab interest in the Middle East, and international pressure all combined to render British administration ineffectual at best and chaotic at
worst. The Palestine government, in effect, was ruling under conditions of
barbed wire fences, a depleting civilian presence, and military crackdowns.

The limited nature of the British response to Jewish terrorism made
their task of imposing law and order all the more difficult. In contrast to
the response to the Arab revolt in the late thirties—collective punishment,
revocation of civil rights, the razing of homes and villages and parts of
towns, concentration camps, humiliations, and incidents of police and
military brutality—military measures towards the Jewish community
were relatively mild.

To be sure, there were roadblocks, searches and seizures (few and
short in duration), massive cordon-and-search, and a small number of
hangings of terrorists.[1] Also, in the summer of 1946 the British raided and
occupied the Jewish Agency offices in Jerusalem and Tel Aviv and
arrested most of the Jewish Agency leaders and put them in a detention
camp at Latrun, with hundreds of others.[2] The British knew that the
Haganah had itself carried out guerrilla operations (e.g., in June 1946 the
Palmach hit rail and bridge crossings all over Palestine). They also knew
that in some cases it was in complicity with the dissident terrorists of the
Irgun Zvi Leumi, IZL or *Irgun,* and *Lohamei Herut Yisrael,* LHI or Lehi (also
known as Stern) gangs (e.g., the King David Hotel outrage in July 1946).
However, the treatment accorded the Jewish leadership did not compare
with the strongly and, at times, brutally repressive measures adopted
against the AHC.[3] Perhaps the main reason for the relative British leniency
in dealing with the *Yishuv* was the sensitivity engendered by the holo-
caust and the international attention the Zionists in Palestine received.
Perhaps, also, there was an additional, more subtle, reason: unlike the Jews
who were, after all, Western, the Palestinian Arabs were, in the colonial
mind, the dehumanized "natives," reflecting a culture and religion that
Europeans feared, distorted, and despised, and whose rights and lives

could be snuffed out with more impunity.

Although the Palestine mandatory administration existed in name only, from 1945 it was on the retreat. Given Britain's dilemmas regarding its unworkable promises to Arabs and Jews, the turmoil prevailing in the last months of the mandate was inevitable. These last few years represented the culmination of an ill-conceived policy that fostered the creation of a Jewish National "Home" in Palestine against the wishes of the Palestinian Arab majority.

The British Withdrawal Plan: Effect on Local Government

The British plan of withdrawal was conceived at the end of 1947, and formalized on paper after London definitely decided to fully evacuate by August. The withdrawal process was laid out on the following general lines.[4] Evacuation was to proceed in four phases, lasting from January to 31 July 1948. The first phase was to be completed by 29 February, the second by 31 May, the third by 30 June, and the fourth by 31 July. (To reiterate, however, withdrawal was completed through the Haifa enclave by 31 May 1948.) Correspondingly, the first phase contemplated the withdrawal from the overwhelmingly Arab district of Gaza and the Negev. The second was to begin on the coast starting north of Netanya going south along a narrow strip including Tel Aviv and Jaffa, and then proceeding east (through a corridor) to include all central Palestine as far north but not including 'Affula, as far east as Tulkarem, and as far south as Al-Samu (south of Hebron). This effectively meant the inclusion of the district of Lydda and the main part of Samaria (including Jerusalem). The third phase encompassed the remainder of Samaria and the Galilee, but did not include the Acre-Haifa area. This would include a narrow finger between the coastal strip and the central area, going north and then northeast and widening to include Galilee. The final phase was to complete the withdrawal through the Haifa enclave. This was to proceed from Nahariya south to Acre and a bit east of it, down to Haifa and its surrounding environs. The plan included the evacuation of 62,000 service personnel, the removal of 240,000 tons of inventory and 19,900 vehicles, and the destruction of 7,700 tons of ammunition and explosives.[5] The forces were to be evacuated both through Egypt and through Haifa harbor.

The main problem facing the Palestine government was the evacuation of its personnel and the transfer of power to Arabs and Jews. While the *Yishuv* was self-contained and prepared to take over the functions of government, the majority of services to the Arabs was administered by the mandatory administration. The policy was to transfer these governmental and social services to local authorities. The Palestinians were practically unprepared for the speed with which the transfer process took place. The immense task of taking over government functions and properties, such as hospitals (health), schools (education), public works, electricity, water, posts, sanitation, social welfare, agricultural, vetrinary and forestry stations, was further complicated by withdrawal and war.[6] The Jewish community was organized and efficiently governed; the Palestinian side essentially was left without a functional government to maintain law and order, stability, communications, transport, food distribution, the elemental services, and defense.

The Arab effort to take over these functions therefore was feeble and they were not sufficiently organized. With no central leadership or governing institution or representative body in the country; no effective means of coordination or communication between the different regions and towns; and with lack of funds, no organized taxation, and no direction for the civil services employed by the mandatory, the transfer of government functions and services basically fell into the laps of the local authorities at municipal and village levels, that were in some cases divided against each other. In most villages, in fact, there was no statutory authority and local government followed traditional forms. In a society that was 65 percent rural, a large part of the Palestinian population was left helpless. Again, these conditions exemplified the fragility, vulnerability and weakness in traditional social and political organization.

In addition, the withdrawal process itself was complicated and lengthy. By the end of January, the police had withdrawn from Tel Aviv, Jaffa, Nablus, Hebron, and Jericho; by March there were a total of 923 officials, police and families left; by April the majority of the British staff had withdrawn (with district commissioners staying till the end), reduced to 80 in all of Palestine; and by May there were 26,000 soldiers left, mostly in the Haifa enclave, 1,700 to 2,000 tons of ammunition and explosives, some 5,000 vehicles, and 25,000 tons of inventory (which was 60 percent below target plan).[7] Actually, the six month long British withdrawal was not only lengthy, but was also confused and disorderly, having taken place under conditions of almost complete anarchy, with substantial material left behind.

The Sociological Dimension

As we shall see, the Zionists' relatively easy conquest of Arab Palestine was made possible in part by the social and factionalist divisions in Palestinian society, which greatly weakened the Palestinians' ability to withstand military/terroristic pressures. While there is no need to reiterate aspects of politics and society which were analyzed extensively in Part One and which are summarized in the conclusion, it is worthwhile to point out, albeit somewhat briefly, the conceptual relationship between sociological divisions and social disintegration.

If one were to enumerate accurately the social divisions in Palestinian society by 1947–48, regionalism, family divisions, and differences between town and country would come to the fore. There is no doubt that a degree of regionalism existed, as between the growing coastal and urban population and the more traditional hill population. The gulf here was cultural and psychological, reinforced by divergent patterns of economic development. The hill Palestinians, particularly dwellers in the smaller towns and in the villages, perceived the coastal Palestinians as remote, modern, urbane, cosmopolitan and, perhaps, more Western and less moral. They saw themselves as the protectors of the traditional, more honorable Arab culture, and were more clannish in their behavior. Regional differences might also have existed between Jerusalem and other mountainous areas such as Hebron and Nablus and even the non-mountainous Acre subdistrict.

But these divisions, particularly between mountains and coast, can also be exaggerated and their causes misunderstood. Jerusalem, for example, was as urbane and cosmopolitan as Haifa or Jaffa. Thus, what may seem like cultural and social regional divisions were really socio-economic and political. That is, regional divisions reflected the differences between agrarian and urban societies. The Nablus and Hebron (and even Ramallah subdistrict) areas and their surrounding hinterlands and parts of the Acre subdistrict were characterized by more traditional agrarian economies and the predominance of traditional elites and families. These elites actually did much to maintain regional divisions which served to protect their factionalist strongholds. Also, conflict between the Husayni elite in Jerusalem and the leaders of Haifa, for example, which manifested itself in AHC reluctance to give financial and other aid to Haifa, represented elite conflict over power and control more than wider societal divisions.

Similarly, divisions between town and country cannot easily be separated from disparities between agrarian and urban social economies. Nor, actually, can they be practically or conceptually isolated or detached from regional divisions. There certainly were social, cultural, psychological, and economic differences and disparities between the *fellah* (peasant, rural dweller) and the *madani* (urbanite), between, really, a bourgeois middle class culture and a provincial and agrarian culture. But even here there were differences. The *fellah/madani* divide might have pervaded the social outlook and behavior of the hill peasantry more than the coastal peasantry, perhaps because the villages of the latter were relatively newer in foundation and because they were economically tied to and dependent upon, more socially and culturally exposed to, the vibrant urban coastal economies. In general, however, the peasant tends to be more inward-looking, localistic, and relatively isolated, perhaps mentally more than physically, in his village world.

Underlying these social differences were the clan and familial divisions which pervaded Palestinian society. The more prominent extended families and clans played the essential role of leaders trying to organize the society that brought them forth. Though regional and urban/rural divisions did not make Palestinian Arab society at the time any more peculiar than other traditional societies, the prominence of the family gave it its special features. Perhaps it was this feature which gave *substance* to the two divisions (regionalism, town and country) discussed above. But even this feature, as we have previously shown, was reinforced by a factionalist elite which thereby maintained its influence. And because its influence was based on patronage ties which, in themself, were being weakened, the elite reverted to a strong nationalism constructed around parochial identities.

This sense of Palestinian Arab nationalism had pretty much taken root in Palestinian society by the 1940s. However, it coexisted with the predominant social divisions. Very simply, therefore, the society was not fully integrated in a national sense. Though the idea of an Arab Palestine, in its cultural and geographical dimensions, was understood by the peasantry, the world of the village and region made somewhat vague and elusive the idea and concept of a national identity which took precedence over other loyalties. Thus, mobilization, organization and fighting for the national cause were, for the people in the countryside, largely understood in local cultural and social terms, where the populist-nationalist-religious idiom predominated. This obviously impeded the ability of Palestinian Arab society to organize itself for the battle with the Zionists on a clear, coordinated, rational, and efficiently hierarchic basis.

While the 35 percent (some 500,000 people) of the urban population, particularly its middle class component, was certainly more clearly nationally conscious and pretty much defined the Palestinian national culture and ideology, it was prevented from taking control of politics and organizing itself as it should have for the prodigious tasks of 1947–48. Much of this had to do with the fact that the urban notable elite could not easily be challenged on national grounds. Therefore, preparations to meet the Zionist challenge were shaped more by the organizing dictates of urban factional leaders.

The social divisions in Palestinian society were of course aggravated and made more structurally fragile by the rapid socio-economic changes that have been analyzed. Newly emergent groups and classes, with new social and political outlooks, existed alongside a factionalist political and social structure. Vertical political cleavages and horizontal stratification patterns rendered the social structure extremely fragile. The war economy in particular, with its disruption of both agrarian and urban economies, created tension and pressure in an increasingly complex society.

However, social organization was as yet not complex or differentiated enough to have produced a stable, integrated network of mutually interdependent specializations and socio-economic relationships. The landowner and businessman, the peasant and the urban wage earner, the lawyer and the craftsman did not significantly rely on each other for goods and services. Indeed, the relatively backward economic links and communication between these groups and classes did not foster the shared experiences and interests, the shared working and social environment, that might have contributed to more cohesive social organization. Moreover, the British and Jewish presence, whether as employers or competitors, negatively affected the social structural bonds, ties, relationships, and dependencies necessary for a developed society. Palestinian Arab traditional social organization simply did not have the "staying" or "holding power" of a more complex, industrialized society, whose attributes merit brief comparison.

Industrial society is more complex in its structural differentiation and functional roles. It contains more integrated groups, classes, and occupations which make it less prone to collapse and disintegration under severe pressure. Though class division in industrial societies is more defined and focused than in pre-industrial societies and the potential for social class conflict therefore higher, there is more continuity and coherence from the psychological, social, cultural and economic aspects. Urbanization and social and geographic mobility play vital roles in this regard. This in turn means rationality and efficiency in organization, roles, specialization and communication. In industrial society, there is more coherence and cooperation, and far more superior mobilization abilities for the need, when it arises, of resistance to external pressure. This also means that these societies are better able to handle irrational fear and panic and are less susceptible to uncontrolled mass flight. These differences between modern industrial societies and traditional pre-industrial, largely agrarian societies are clearly and sharply reflected in the ways Arabs and Jews met, responded to each other, clashed, and went about achieving their objectives.

The Instruments of Force:
The Volunteers and the Local Forces

As we noted in the previous chapter, Arab disunity reflected itself in the volunteer effort. The MC in Damascus was given control over all irregulars in Palestine and was responsible for their training and armament. Training at the center of Qatna was carried out under the general control of the MC with mainly Syrian instructors, either serving officers or ex-officers of the Syrian army.[8] By February there also were about 50 Egyptian army officers in Damascus. Training consisted largely in instruction in the use and maintenance of weapons and in demolition tactics. After training many of the volunteers passed into Palestine by various routes, some through Trans-Jordan, some through Lebanon, and some directly from Syria. In a number of cases the men passing through the training center retained their local identities, for example, from Homs, Hama and Idlib.

The number of those training at Qatna at any one time did not exceed 1,000 men. According to 'Arif al-'Arif, by February 1948, 4,976 volunteers were trained at Qatna—2,987 Syrians, 800 Palestinians and 800 'Iraqis, 350 Lebanese, 50 Egyptians, and 35 Yugoslavians.[9] Of these, 2,500 entered Palestine by the month of February. In addition, there was a contingent of over 300 Egyptian irregulars in the south, mainly of the Muslim Brethren (al-Ikhwan al-Muslimun), led by Colonel Ahmad 'Abd al-'Aziz.[10] As the capacity of Qatna could not exceed 700–1,000 men, it is doubtful if another 1,500–2,000 men passed through to Palestine by April, the time of the Haganah offensive. One Israeli military historian put the number of Arab volunteers at a maximum of 4,000 men, of whom 2,000 received even rudimentary training; while Walid Khalidi, relying on AHC and Army of Liberation files, documents a total of 3,830 men belonging to eight battalions, of whom 1,000 were Palestinian.[11] Each of the battalions was comprised of about 500 men.[12]

The financing of the volunteer effort fell far short of goals. The MC did not find it easy to arm the volunteers, even those who already passed through Qatna. It collected funds from private individuals and companies, and funds were also collected by means of a special stamp affixed to all documents which normally bore fiscal stamps. Much of the expenditure on equipping and paying the volunteers was met either by the Syrian government or the Arab League funds. In many cases, out-of-date rifles and machine guns were reconditioned and issued, some of the volunteers provided their own weapons, some arms were received from Lebanon, and some were bought from private owners in Syria and Trans-Jordan.[13]

The Arab League goal of 10,000 rifles was still not reached by March. By that month, the MC received a little over 9,400 rifles from the Arab states—3,860 from 'Iraq, 2,000 from Syria, 550 from Lebanon, 1,000 from Trans-Jordan, 1,200 from Sa'udi Arabia (most of which had to be returned because of their terrible condition), and 800 from Egypt.[14] Of this, the MC reported that it gave 1,657 rifles to the AHC and 1,501 rifles to volunteers who entered Palestine.[15] Financially, by the beginning of 1948, the Arab governments gave a total of L143,294 to the AHC: L103,794 from Syria, L20,000 from Egypt, L15,000 from Lebanon, and L4,500 from Yemen.[16] 'Iraqi donations went to Musa al-'Alami's constructive scheme. This figure certainly did not even come close to the projected L1,000,000.

In the end, then, the *Jaysh al-Inqath*, or Army of Liberation, was made up of eight battalions led mainly by 'Iraqi and Syrian commanders (four and two, respectively), one Druze, and one Palestinian, Michel al-'Issa of the Ajnadin Battalion (made up of Palestinians and Druzes).[17] In addition, there were smaller companies or small battalions in different areas. Fawzi al-Qawaqji was given supreme command of the *Jaysh* in Palestine, his headquarters being in the village of Ja'ba in Central Palestine (in the center of the Triangle area, about eight miles north of Nablus). All volunteers came under the command of the *Jaysh*. The Arab states formed the *Jaysh* essentially to control and channel the tide of nationalist feelings and the spontaneous formation of organizations and committees all over the Arab world concerned with the liberation of Palestine.

In addition to the volunteers there were the fighters of the *Jihad al-Muqaddas*, formed around the end of December (at the Mufti's direction, under the command of 'Abd al-Qadir al-Husayni, the son of Musa Qazim Pasha al-Husayni, the chairman of the Arab Executive in the twenties and early thirties). The *Jihad*, although initially starting off with no more than 25 men, most of them from the Hebron area, rapidly attained respect and affection largely because of the popularity of 'Abd al-Qadir.[18] He was well thought of and looked upon as a sincere, committed nationalist who stood above family loyalty. It had most power and following in the Jerusalem-Hebron and Lydda-Ramle-Jaffa regions.

The *Jihad* was actually formed once before 1947–48. In 1934, as part of the radicalization of the thirties and in preparation for an armed revolt, it spread, under the influence of 'Abd al-Qadir and others, into secret cells of five men each and elected an organizational committee whose members were from Jerusalem, Ramallah, Lydda, and Talluzza (near Nablus).[19] Its estimated membership in 1934 was 400.[20] After the revolt the *Jihad* disbanded. As in 1936, 'Abd al-Qadir was commander of the Jerusalem-Hebron area and Shaykh Hasan Salameh the head of the Lydda-Ramle-Jaffa regions.[21] Compared to the thirties, the *Jihad*'s membership in the late forties significantly increased. By March 1948, there were 950 men of the *Jihad* and 228 irregulars (Arab volunteers) under Salameh's command; while 300 *mujahidin* (literally holy warriors, but popularly understood as fighters or strugglers), and 128 Arab volunteers were under 'Abd al-Qadir's command.[22] This made a total of 1,606 under the two *Jihad* commanders.

In addition to the two *Jihad* commanders and their men, there were other rural force units in the following geographical areas:[23] The command in Western Galilee under Abu Mahmud Saffuri; Southern and Eastern Galilee under Abu Ibrahim al-Saghir (who also played a role in the defense of Haifa); Haifa Area under 'Abd al-Haq 'Azzawi; Tulkarem Area under

'Abd al-Rahman Zaydan; and the Gaza Area under Tariq al-Ifriqi. Each of these units had an average of 150 rifles, which means a total of about 750 men.[24] There also were town garrisons which included Jerusalem, Jaffa, Haifa, Gaza, Beisan, Acre, Tiberias, and Safad. These, between them, numbered a total of over 1,500 men.[25] However, in some towns, like Jaffa, there was the spontaneous and unorganized augmentation of men as the conflict and danger intensified. Finally, the *Futuwa* and *Najjada* youth organizations between them probably had no more than a few hundred men under arms, the bulk of it in the hands of the former because of Husayni support.

Despite the *Jihad*'s popularity under 'Abd al-Qadir, the ablest of Palestinian commanders, divisions and conflict between it and Qawaqji were pervasive. Qawaqji deeply hated the Husaynis while the Mufti instructed the *Jihad* not to cooperate with or join forces with Qawaqji.[26] Additionally, Qawaqji might have even come to an informal agreement with a *Haganah* representative that he would remain neutral in the event of an attack of Jewish forces against Palestinian (*Jihad*) forces. Because of the lack of cooperation, Qawaqji and the *Jihad* adhered to an unwritten agreement: Qawaqji's irregulars mostly were stationed in the "Triangle" area (Jenin-Nablus-Tulkarem) and in the Galilee (stretching from Acre to Lake Huleh), while the *Jihad*'s area of operation was south-central. The few hundred Egyptian *Ikhwan* under 'Abd al-'Aziz operated in the south (Gaza-Beersheba area).

The total number of armed men in Palestine, before the Arab armies entered on 15 May, was less than 8,000—somewhat evenly divided between irregulars and Palestinian local forces. Also, frequently during battles local villagers came to the aid of guerrillas or joined in the fight (a spontaneous act referred to in Arabic as a *faz'a*). Al-'Arif rightly suggests that the Palestinian forces would not have held out until April if it were not for the arms they received from the AHC, which collected a total of L330,800 from Palestinian (*Bayt al-Mal*), Islamic, popular, and private sources.[27] With some of this money, the AHC purchased over 5,000 rifles, hundreds of machine guns, hundreds of grenades, and some artillery and mortars. Part of this cache must have been channelled to the Palestinians, particularly the *Jihad*.

It should be noted that the British played a central role in the Palestinians' inability to carry and accumulate significant amounts of arms during the mandate, particularly the latter half. During the 1936–39 revolt and consistently thereafter the British had confiscated large numbers of arms from the Palestinians. Between 1936 and 1945 the following arms and ammunitions were seized: 30 machine guns and submachine guns, 7,617 rifles, 4,891 pistols, 1,376 bombs and grenades, 695 shotguns, 347,375 small arms ammunition, and 3,924 shotgun ammunition.[28]

It is of interest to compare the Arab figures with Jewish forces and arms during *early 1948,* i.e., at the outbreak of hostilities, and by *15 May,* i.e., when men and arms were considerably augmented. According to Zionist and sympathetic sources, during early 1948 Jewish military capabilities were as follows.[29] The *Haganah* had some 400 full-time members while its striking force, the *Palmach,* comprised 4,500 troops (including reservists). The *Haganah* was originally composed of defensive units, or militias, to protect settlements. Many of these, some 37,000, gained experience during the war as volunteers in the British army, providing much of the organizational, training and technical background for the *Haganah.* The 37,000 were reservists, scattered throughout the Jewish settlements, and potentially available for mobilization. In addition to the full time *Palmach* force of 4,500 there were 7,500 field corps. They comprised men between the ages of 18 and 25. They were not full-time soldiers yet were given more training than the *Haganah* rank and file and were immediately mobilizable. Thus, the active (4,500 *Palmach* and 7,500 field corps) and militia forces (37,000 reservists) comprised a total of some 49,000 men. Moreover, the IZL had between 2,000 and 4,000 men, while Lehi had from 500–800. There also were some 2,000 Jewish settlement police.

To sum up, the total effective force that the Jewish population could field on a national basis at the *outbreak of hostilities* was around 15,000. By 15 May 1948 and earlier the Jewish effective forces were augmented to 27,400 fully mobilized front-line troops—i.e., 8,150 *Palmach* and 19,250 field army corps.[30] The total Jewish force that could be mobilized from a population of over 600,000 was some 50,000–60,000.

In terms of arms, Zionist sources put it thus. By *March* the Jewish forces had between 14,000 and 20,000 modern small arms (mainly rifles and some revolvers), 3,500 submachine guns, 800 light machine guns, 200 medium machine guns, 700 2-inch mortars, and 100 3-inch mortars. There were eleven single-engined light aircraft, used mainly for reconnaissance, with around forty pilots. According to Khalidi, between April and May 1948 there was a tremendous increase of arms as a result of Czechoslovakian arms consignments, one consignment of which comprised 9,300 rifles.[31] Relying on Jon and David Kimche, he quotes the following in terms of machine guns and mortars (by May 1948): 11,000 submachine guns, 1,500 light machine guns; similar amounts as above of 3- and 2-inch mortars; and, in addition, 16 Davidka 3-inch mortars, 75 PIATS (anti-tank rifles), and 4 65-mm field guns. Finally, by 15 May Khalidi documents 800 armored cars, 3 tanks, an "inexhaustible supply" of anti-tank mines; 10 fighter planes; 3 heavy transport planes; 9 medium planes; 9 light transport planes; and 25 trainers (Piper Cubs).

Compared to Arab irregulars or Palestinian guerrillas, the Jewish forces far outnumbered and outclassed them. And whereas the Jewish settlements were well fortified, self-contained military units concentrated mainly in large urban residential areas, the Palestinian population was scattered, disorganized, unmobilized, and uncoordinated. Without the irregulars, who had relatively better arms, some mobilized transport, and some artillery, the Palestinian Arab population was seriously short of arms and mobilized men, who by themselves could not have done much against the Jewish forces.

Highlights of the 1947–48 War and Motives for Strategies

It can be generally stated that up to April, the *Haganah* operated mainly in a defensive posture to prevent the fall of any Jewish settlements or towns. As over 80 percent of the Jewish forces were home guards, it took the *Haganah* at least until April to achieve substantial mobilization and obtain additional arms, including heavy artillery, mainly from Czechoslovakia. The *Yishuv* was not prepared for offensive action into Arab territory, bases or supplies as it did not have the necessary units, experience, command structure, firepower, or logistics apparatus with which to mount such operations.[32] Because the Jews were "stretched," they did not desire to widen the area of hostilities at an inopportune time, particularly since the Jewish leadership knew that the mostly small scale, unorganized, and sporadic Palestinian attacks posed no serious threat to the *Yishuv*'s existence. Especially because of David Ben-Gurion's leadership and influence, Jewish policy was one of absolute defense of settlements, regardless of the cost.

The Zionists began to plan their strategy in October 1947: to mobilize, purchase arms and start the offensive after the British sufficiently withdrew and before the Arab states entered Palestine.[33] By April these essentials were achieved. During the early months, however, the Zionists were not at a total disadvantage, despite their defensive posture. In the mixed cities they were autonomous and militarily prepared. In the countryside the settlements were excellent fortresses for defense. Also, *Haganah* tactics, not to mention Lehi or the IZL, were not all that defensive as they carried out terrorist campaigns on Arab buildings and traffic and on Arab villages.

The attacks on the villages began with what the Zionists call "retaliatory" or "reprisal" raids: These raids in essence were violent, killing mostly civilians and meant to terrorize and intimidate the Palestinians.[34] These village (mainly silent, night) raids formed "a distinct pattern of limited but powerful intimidation and preparatory terrorization...," even while making "due allowances for spontaneous reactions to Arab guerrilla attacks."[35] Although these raids, including the psychological warfare, may be interpreted as designed to make the Palestinians flee, at this early period they may also be seen as ruthless military maneuvers intended to demoralize the highly vulnerable Palestinian rural population. Certainly, it took very little provocation from the Palestinians for the *Haganah*, most of whose operations were authorized and controlled by the General Staff, to strike in a zealously massive and violent form. And David Ben-Gurion for one usually contemplated the flight of the Palestinians with great expectations.

The Palestinians from the beginning were on the offensive and gained enough experience in March to launch full-scale assaults. Qawaqji's artillery and some armored vehicles did not arrive in Palestine until April. Furthermore, because of Cunningham's insistence to London to exert pressure on the Arab League to prevent the arrival of irregulars, the latter only started to enter in substantial numbers in February, when the British could only guard the main entry routes into Palestine.[36] However, the British did engage irregulars that concentrated for an attack on a Jewish settlement. By April the British were no longer in a position to prevent any Arab entry, whether or not they desired to.

Notwithstanding these factors, the Palestinian offensive, focusing mainly on communications, managed to besiege Jewish Jerusalem and isolate pockets of Jewish colonies. During December/February the pattern of Palestinian tactical attacks basically focused on transport, settlements, and residential areas. By March the Arabs held most of the lines of communication—they were gaining the upper hand in their attempt to close mountain lanes and roads between Jewish population centers. Given the obvious fact that the Palestinians were operating in their own country and on a majority of the land surface of Palestine, they moved around with relative ease—in other words, they had most of the "geographical and tactical advantages" on their side.[37] They carried out a war of attrition which at times was mixed with frontal assaults. Qawaqji himself led various attacks in February, March and April against Jewish settlements, all of which failed.

One of Qawaqji's most "important" operations was his attack on Mishmar Ha'emek, a strategic settlement at the gateway of the coastal plain on the Jenin-Haifa road in the Marj Ibn 'Amr. After continuously bombarding the settlement with artillery, *Palmach* reinforcements arrived to help the local *Haganah* militiamen, driving back Qawaqji's forces to their headquarters. One result of Qawaqji's failed attack was a *Haganah* rejection of his proposal for a cease-fire. The consequent Jewish counterattacks saw the deliberate destruction of a string of villages around Mishmar Ha'emek and the expulsion of their inhabitants.[38] But Qawaqji's attack was in the first week of April. Although before that time, the Arabs had attained the upper hand and on occasion defeated *Haganah* infantry, the Jews also held on to all settlements and were beginning to gain the upper hand in mixed towns, such as Haifa and Jaffa, where the flight of thousands, mainly from the middle class, began to accelerate. And the conquest, destruction, expulsion, and permanent occupation methods used against the villages nearby Mishmar Ha'emek subsequently became the regular practice of Zionist forces.

In early March the *Haganah* proposed Plan D (*Dalet*), a new strategy meant not only to defend the borders of the designated Jewish state and outlying settlements, but also to conquer "Arab villages and cities," that is, in the area of the designated Arab state.[39] Whether one emphasizes the military and strategic considerations or necessities that gave rise to Plan D, considering the *Yishuv*'s problems by March, or whether or not it was a central, national plan of expulsion, which, at least explicitly, it was not, it did sanction conquest, expulsion, and destruction on a regional or district basis. These acts were carried out according to commanders' judgements, which set the precedent for wholesale expulsion in the weeks and months that followed.

The Zionists always adhered to the ultimate vision of achieving sovereignty over all of Palestine. This ultimate political/territorial vision could not be achieved without the institution of a coherent settlement policy. Especially beginning in the 1930s, with continuous manifestations of Palestinian nationalist frustration and discontent, Jewish settlements were located with such a long term view in mind; they were on the main strategic arteries, surrounding Arab towns (e.g., Jaffa, Acre, Haifa, Tiberias), and in outlying areas. The latter geographical locations were meant to constitute front-line defensive bases and a potential offensive base. Equally important, they were meant to constitute a political *fait accompli.*

This thinking, exemplified forcefully by Ben-Gurion, could only explain the fact that Plan D was decided upon (in early March) before the massacre of Dayr Yasin (9 April) and the fall of Tiberias (16–18 April) or Haifa (21–22 April). While this is not to suggest that Dayr Yasin was part of official Jewish Agency policy or that the flight of Haifa's inhabitants was planned, it is to say that the Zionists did *desire* the removal of the Palestinians and did all they could, directly or indirectly, to facilitate the achievement of this desire. Once panic struck the Arabs after Dayr Yasin and Palestinian towns fell rapidly, the Zionists, indeed, found military circumstances conducive to their goals in the second phase of the war beginning in April. (Before the fall of Haifa, the Zionists could not have foreseen nor expected a massive exodus of Arab Palestine.) Psychological and physical terror became part of Zionist tactics during that phase, tactics which cannot be easily put down to military considerations. The flight of over 30,000 Palestinians between December and March, mainly middle and upper middle classes,[40] and the fall of Haifa in April and Jaffa in April/May, encouraged the Zionists to adopt a policy of expelling or facilitating the exodus of the Palestinians from captured territory. By

April, the fall and dissolution of Arab Palestine swiftly accelerated. Also by this time, there was an increasing widespread practice of destruction and wholesale expulsion after conquest, though this was never explicitly stated by the top leaders. The political/territorial motive was given full vent.

Zionist Political Motives and Tactics as Causes of Collapse

Any discussion of the Zionist role in the Palestinian exodus is necessarily frought with subtle and complex questions concerning intent. One can confidently discount as baseless the official Israeli claim that the Arab leaders (locally and outside Palestine) asked the Palestinians to leave in order to prepare the ground for the "invasion" and destruction of the Jewish community.[41] Yet to view the exodus as a Zionist Machiavellian plan, coldly and systematically carried out by forced expulsion, rooted in fundamental ideology, is to simplify a complex and subtle event.[42] As previously noted, the *ultimate Zionist vision* was the creation of a Jewish state in all of Palestine, transforming the Palestinian majority into a minority. Implicit in Zionist ideology, whether revisionist or mainstream, was the "wordless wish" (E.B. Childers' words) that Palestine would be free of its Arab inhabitants. Despite the enigmatic professions of Zionist mainstream leaders, as personified in Ben-Gurion, over territorial/demographic designs, the Zionist leadership was always eager to accept the "transfer" or "resettlement" of the Palestinians in the numerous partition or federative schemes generated throughout the mandate either by the colonial power or by Zionist leaders in common with Britons.

The Philby federative scheme of the 1930s and early 1940s is one example. H. St. John Philby, a friend and unofficial adviser to Ibn Sa'ud, outlined an Arab federation in which Palestine and Trans-Jordan would be united under the Sa'udi monarch.[43] The idea, which contemplated the "transfer" of the Arab population from Jewish areas, actually originated with Ben-Gurion and Weizmann. Other examples (discussed in earlier chapters) include the Peel Commission's partition proposal and its recommendation for the forced expulsion of Arabs from the Galilee and the War Cabinet Palestine Committee's partition scheme of 1943–44, under which the "resettling" of the indigenous Palestinians was discussed and about which the Jewish leadership was fully aware.

Moreover, throughout the 1930s and 1940s, Ben-Gurion and other mainstream Jewish leaders contemplated, discussed, desired and envisioned with hope the emptying of Arab Palestine, sometimes through fantasized agreements with the Palestinians (or Arab states) who would leave voluntarily, at other times through the vision of forced expulsion.[44] It was always clear to the Zionists, particularly Ben-Gurion, that, no matter how they looked at it, no Jewish state could be carved out of Palestine without containing a huge Arab minority, perhaps majority, thus putting into question the viability of that state. The Zionist vision did not contemplate a pluralistic society but one of a homogeneous Jewish state, which essentially meant inherent conflict between the reality of a majority Arab population and the desire to bring millions of Jews into Palestine.

But, while the Zionists wished the Palestinians would disappear and, when they could, actively supported or pursued solutions contemplating the transfer or resettlement of the Palestinians, there was no master plan for the forcible removal of the Palestinians. More accurately, much of what happened in 1947–48 developed according to immediate circumstances. That is, it is doubtful the Zionists conceived that the Palestinians would either leave or be easily pushed out. It was during the various phases of the war, when military fortunes accelerated in Jewish favor, that the Zionist leadership increasingly did all it could to facilitate the removal of Arabs or to resort to psychological warfare, terrorism, and physical expulsion, as will be seen shortly. As military successes progressed, the ultimate and underlying or implicit political/territorial/demographic vision began to guide Zionist tactics and methods.

For the Zionists, the United Nations partition resolution and the subsequent war and confusion, though unplanned, provided the opportunity for territorial gain. While they were pretty much on the defensive through March, they knew, from their knowledge and assessment of Palestinian resistance and the ineffectiveness of Arab irregulars, that they would be able to launch a devastating offensive once they were fully mobilized and had obtained shipments of arms. It was in March, after all, that Plan D was drawn up, while the Jews were still on the defensive. Thus they were certain of their Palestinian adversary's weakness. What they were unsure of were the Arab armies. Plan D, to reiterate, did not just call for the capture of territory allotted by the United Nations, but included operations for the capture of Palestinian territory beyond the partition limits, its justification being the need to consolidate the state's borders and areas outside its borders before the Arab armies entered Palestine on 15 May.[45]

However, Plan D very soon entailed "cleaning out" Palestinians, particularly in order to establish territorial continuity between the sparsely populated and widely distributed Jewish colonies in the outlying areas and the major concentrations of Jewish populations along the coast. In effect, this meant the direct or indirect depopulation of most of Arab Palestine and the conquest of land much beyond the prospective borders of the Jewish state, something Jewish leaders and high military commanders were not unaware of. The outlying settlements, regardless of how absurdly tiny or geographically remote from the main concentration of Jewish colonies, also served a political purpose, as indicated previously. They were meant to create facts on the ground. Thus, the various partition or other schemes included them as part of a prospective Jewish state, naturally with large concentrations of Palestinians and much of Arab Palestine. Jewish settlements were meant, and succeeded in doing so judging by the United Nations partition resolution of 1947, to stake claims of Jewish statehood. And ultimately, more settlements justified expansion of borders in the name of military necessity and defense.

Hate, vengeance, and political motives could have been, and were, neatly subsumed under the all-encompassing military imperative that was the apparent logic of Plan D. Destruction of homes, villages, and crops immediately upon conquest (particularly after June, as will be noted shortly) meant non-return, and non-return meant a Jewish state without Palestinians. Therefore, the explanation for Zionist actions more realistically lies with military/strategic necessity, immediate situations, and, perhaps most importantly, ideological, political, and territorial ambitions that were either implicit in Zionist thought or, more often than not, explicitly stated.

Although Zionist methods and tactics in facilitating the exodus are clearer than Zionist motives, it should be pointed out at the outset that the nature and causes of the exodus were not uniform throughout the country.[46] The flight of Haifa's inhabitants, for example, was due to a mixture of Zionist psychological warfare, indiscriminate firing, fear and panic. The *Haganah* forces did not necessarily foresee nor actively pursue expulsion. The exodus of Jaffa's inhabitants was also more complex, resulting from a multifaceted mixture of causes: a prolonged siege, psychological warfare, IZL terrorism and looting in the early part of the assault, fear of massacres (such as Dayr Yasin and Nasr al-Din, near Tiberias), and disarray in Arab militia and irregular defense and organization. On the other hand, Lydda's and Ramle's inhabitants were terrorized (with Lydda suffering the massacre of some 250 people), outrightly expelled, and suffered a terrible fate.[47] And, as we have seen, the Palestinian villages adjacent to Mishmar Ha'emek were seized, their inhabitants expelled, and the villages destroyed. Also, in towns and villages throughout the Galilee, some fled from psychological intimidation and warfare, others left because of the war situation and hoped to return later, while most (particularly in Western Galilee) were attacked and forcibly expelled.[48] Finally, neither were Zionist motives and methods the same in the various phases of the war.[49] Between November 1947 and March 1948, the Zionists did not have much of a role in any exodus, nor should the flight of about 30,000 persons largely from the middle and upper classes (of Haifa, Jaffa, and Jerusalem) be looked at as a mass exodus. These repeated what they had done once before during the 1936–39 revolt: they left temporarily to escape the dangers, and came back to their homes and businesses when the violence was over.

But during the course of the war, and particularly at the start of the second phase (April to June), the rapid crumbling of Arab defense and morale encouraged the Zionists to actively pursue terrorism, massacres, expulsion, and psychological warfare. After June (the third phase), the Zionists became emboldened and practiced wholesale enforced expulsion. Between July and November 1948 (B. Morris's third and fourth refugee waves), conquest, expulsion, destruction, and even horrible atrocities characterized Jewish practices. This was mixed with the tendency, as from the beginning of the war, of Palestinians to flee with the appearance of Jewish forces or with their usual barrage of mortars, bombs, and gunfire. Thus, while ideology explicitly called for a Jewish state and majority over all of Palestine and implicitly hoped that that state would be free of Palestinians, forcible removal was difficult to contemplate or conceive until the war offered the circumstances for such policies in its second and third phases. Again, while there was not an explicit or formal (written) national policy to expel, and though Ben-Gurion, for obvious reasons, refused to make clear such an order, his colleagues (though not all), generals, and military commanders understood what he, and they, preferred and wanted.[50] Therefore, between April and June, and especially in July and thereafter, there pretty much was a consistent "policy" (practice, really) of direct and indirect expulsion. Whether a national policy of expulsion did or did not exist, then, is hardly morally or practically distinguishable from what the Zionists desired in their minds and hearts and, in particular, what they *did* on the ground, directly by terror and expulsion, or indirectly by encouraging fear, panic, and flight with the object of emptying the country of its indigenous people. By mid-1949 (but mostly in 1948), a total of over 700,000 Palestinian Arabs were turned into refugees.

The Zionists adopted a number of methods to drive out the Palestinians. Firstly, highly psychological broadcasts in Arabic were used by the *Haganah* such as announcing major outbreaks of diseases in Arab urban centers, reporting panic, mass flight, and demoralization, and broadcasting rumors, from information picked up by Jewish intelligence from among the Arabs, designed to sow distrust and suspicion and engender the feeling that spies were omnipresent.[51] These efforts were meant to depress Palestinian morale and spread panic and terror. Secondly, "barrel bombs," filled with a mixture of explosives and petrol, were rolled down the alleys or steplanes of densely packed Arab towns and quarters built on the slopes of the Palestine hills, causing terrific flames and explosions as they crashed into walls and doorways. Ruthless dynamiting of bazaar blocks and blind alleys were used to cause panic and flight. Usually, before and during an attack on a Palestinian town, amid the barrel bombs, mortars,

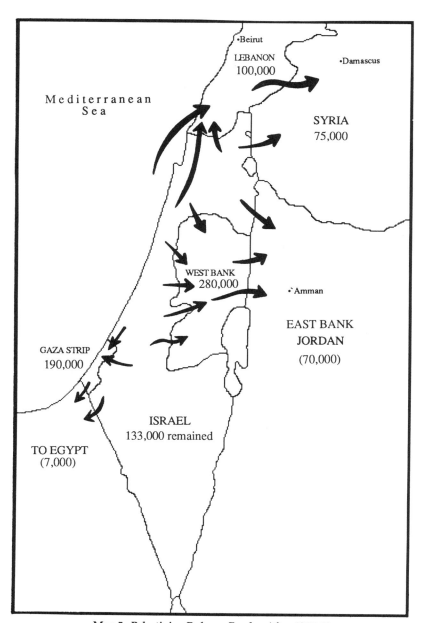

Map 5. Palestinian Refugee Exodus After 1947-48

and automatic fire, loudspeaker vans standing in the vicinity of the densely packed and terrified Arab *suqs* (town markets) would broadcast horror sounds, including shrieks, wails, anguished moans of women, the wail of sirens, and the clang of fire alarm bells. Palestinians were warned to leave and threatened with dire consequences if they did not.

These methods were used on most Palestinian Arab towns that were attacked and conquered. For example, although the Zionists did not expect an easy victory over Haifa nor the mass flight of its inhabitants, their methods certainly facilitated the Palestinians' flight. Mortars, barrel bombs, artillery, machine gun and rifle fire, including sniping at women and children, indiscriminately rained down from Mt. Carmel and Haifa's heights over the terrified Arab residential sections below, while the loud-speakers broadcast their horror sounds. In a contemporary account produced by the Israel Defense Forces Intelligence Branch on 30 June 1948, the following description is given of Zionist methods in precipitating general Arab flight and in which Haifa is specifically mentioned: " 'The factor of surprise, prolonged [artillery] barrages making loud explosive sounds, [use of] loudspeakers in Arabic [to spread frightening black propaganda messages], proved their great efficacy when used properly (as in Haifa particularly).' "[52] The flight towards the port saw the death of countless old men, women, and children as they were trampled in the panic[53] and as Zionist fire was directed towards them to help the exodus along.[54]

This discussion on Zionist methods and tactics as causes of the Palestinian exodus is strongly supported by the Israel Defense Forces Intelligence Branch report just referred to. The report, titled "The Emigration of the Arabs of Palestine in the Period 1/12/1947–1948," analyzes the number of Palestinians who fled their homes up to 1 June and enumerates the causes. The report early on discounts economic or political factors as motivating forces of the exodus. That is, there was no significant flight of people to protect their wealth, except for the 30,000 who fled at the earliest stages of the war. Secondly, the "Arabs did not leave the areas of the Jewish state because of opposition to the establishment of the state or political opposition to the prospect of life under Jewish rule."[55]

The report then goes on to enumerate what it saw as the specific causes of the exodus, assigning to those categories their percentage weights—i.e., that percent of the total exodus caused by each of the categories. Though it is somewhat impressionistic and the percentages tentative,[56] the report still sheds some interesting light on this discussion. It concludes that some 74 percent of the Palestinian exodus (300,000-400,000 people) was due to Jewish military and terrorist (e.g., Dayr Yasin) operations. These include direct, hostile operations against Palestinian towns and villages by the *Haganah*/Israel Defense Forces; the *effect* of these operations (as distinguished by direct attacks) on neighboring towns and villages; the direct operations of the dissident organizations, IZL and Lehi (especially effective around Jaffa-Tel Aviv, the coastal plain to the north, and Jerusalem); whispering campaigns ("friendly advice" by Jewish liaison officers to Palestinians to leave their homes); and ultimatums to leave. The report maintains that some 5 percent of the exodus was caused by orders and decrees to evacuate made by Palestinian leaders and local commanders, though it notes that the AHC tried to stem the flight by imposing restrictions, issuing threats, and exhorting people to stay through the radio.

Because it is difficult to "draw a clear distinction"[57] between military operations which ended in flight or direct expulsions, B. Morris suggests from this that, of the 300,000–400,000 Palestinians who became refugees by 1 June 1948 (i.e., before the expulsions in Lydda and Ramle, 9–14 July, and the subsequent widespread practice of expulsions), *direct expulsions* accounted for some 5 percent of their flight (or between 15,000 and 20,000).[58]

But this conclusion does not go far enough in its analysis. It is plausible to suggest that the exodus up to June, unlike the period afterwards, was not part of a calculated policy. However, just as it was with what the Zionists said and what they desired and did, it is hard to make a moral (or, in its effect, a practical) distinction between direct expulsion *and* provocation through psychological warfare (broadcasting of divisive rumors and of the outbreaks of diseases, the use of barrel bombs, mortars, loudspeaker vans, protracted artillery barrages), whispering campaigns (which are also a form of psychological warfare), and ultimatums to leave. The latter were designed to achieve the same objective as the former. In any case, the Zionists exploited the fear through intimidation to maximize the flight. Lastly, except for the limited exception of Haifa, in "other military operations" the Zionists "clearly desired and deliberately provoked" Palestinian flight, whether directly or indirectly.[59] Thus, it would be hard to assign a percentage to direct expulsions, which presumably was higher than Morris suggests. Jewish military campaigns were intended to fulfill the unspoken Zionist wish to make a Jewish state as free of Arabs as possible. Underlying ideology had as much, and more, of a role to play as fear of a Fifth Column within the boundaries of the United Nations delineated Jewish state. Again, this became clear from policies adopted after June, particularly between July and November, which left over 700,000 Palestinians stateless.

Politico-Military Factors and Weak Leadership as Causes of Collapse

The Palestinian and general Arab role in the fall of Palestine is, like every other contributory factor, in itself multifaceted and complex. Unequal technologies and social organization, the lack of effective local governing and administrative institutions, and politico-military divisions, all served to underline and exacerbate the weaknesses in military preparedness.[60]

The politico-military aspect itself was multifaceted in its characteristics and problems. By way of concretizing these problems, we will discuss various aspects of command, defense, preparation, and politics as these played themselves out in the fall of Haifa and Jaffa. These illustrate the general characteristics of Arab defense, whether on the part of the Palestinians or the Army of Liberation. Battles and military events will be discussed only as background to our main focus.

The controversy over the fall of Haifa concerns not only Arabs and Jews but also the British role. Up to April the pattern of fighting between Arabs and Jews in Haifa was familiar: sniping, bombings, ambushes, and gunfire. On 21 April, the British commander in Haifa, General Hugh Stockwell, commander of the Northern sector, began to redeploy his troops to the port area, opening the road for a Jewish offensive. The redeployment (and the retention of existing dispositions in Eastern Galilee) had as its objective the securing of certain routes and lanes leading into Haifa for the orderly and safe evacuation of the civil administration and armed forces during the ensuing three months. According to Arab sources, Stockwell's decision to evacuate (i.e., redeploy to the port) was made within a 24-hour notice (on 20 April), advising the *Haganah* commander, Moshe Carmel, but not Haifa's Arab leaders, thus giving the former the edge in preparing their attack.[61] The *Haganah* and IZL had their troops poised for an offensive and had carefully planned the seizure of the city upon British withdrawal in accordance with the strategy laid out for the "mixed towns" in Plan D and a specific plan for Haifa, called "Operation Scissors," conceived in late March.

On the same day (daybreak, 21 April) Stockwell began to pull his troops out, firefights broke out between Arabs and Jews, paving the way for *Haganah* and IZL attacks. These used methods that were already mentioned. By nighttime on 21 April, the Arabs were already in great panic, even before the full engagements between Arabs and Jews through the night of 21 April and into 22 April. The next day the Arab population of Haifa was in hysteria, streaming towards the harbor, not surprising given *Haganah*'s merciless actions. The Arab leaders, who went (22 April) to seek a British imposed truce, were told by Stockwell that he was not willing to enter into conflict with either party and that he was prepared to mediate a truce if the Arabs accepted its conditions.[62] Stockwell handed them a copy of the *Haganah* truce terms: surrender of all weapons, immediate curfew and *Haganah* control of the city. The Arabs rejected the truce conditions and asked for amendments to it and, later that day, met *Haganah* commanders and the Mayor, Shabatai Levi (at the town hall), in the presence of Stockwell. (It was at this time that Mr. Levi made his famous plea to the Arabs to stay.) As it was clear that the Jews refused any changes in the truce terms, the Arabs asked for time (until the evening) to consider the matter, and, according to Arab sources, were warned by Stockwell that if the Arabs did not give an answer by the appointed time (some one hour later), he would not be responsible for a bloodbath in which thousands of Arabs might die.[63] At the meeting of the Haifa NC at Victor Khayyat's house, those present (Farid Sa'd, Ilyas Qusa, Anis Nasr, George Mu'am-mar, Al-Shaykh 'Abd al-Rahman Murad, Ahmad Abu Zayd, among others) agreed that the conditions of the truce could not be accepted, upon which the meeting ended.

By informing the Jews a day before (and perhaps earlier) of his intention to redeploy, Stockwell gave them the advantage of preparing for the operation and, knowing that Arab Haifa would fall to the *Haganah*, Stockwell, in essence, "left [Haifa] to the Jews...."[64] In practical terms this meant that the Jews were able to assemble and prepare for the attack, occupying formerly held British positions and attacking with deliberate confidence the points evacuated by the British. His ostensible reasoning was that he wished to avoid a clash with either party, particularly the stronger Jewish side. This reasoning supposedly guided his refusal to permit the Arabs of Haifa any reinforcements. On the morning of 22 April, a contingent of 300–400 armed men from the neighboring village of Tira, responding to the call for aid, was refused entry into the city by Stockwell.[65]

While Stockwell should at least have warned the Jews not to commit aggression against the Arabs (Arab-Jewish clashes were mounting for weeks and the Jews were poised for attack and conquest), and definitely should have permitted the latter reinforcements or tried to stop the Jewish onslaught on the Arab quarters, the Arabs should have been prepared months before the battle of Haifa. Such an obviously important city, economically, demographically, and strategically, warranted primary consideration and preparation for its defense. The leadership in Haifa was aware of the Mufti's policies and the Damascus MC's shortcomings. Before the British redeployment, the Arabs were engaging in escalating clashes, which commenced in early April. They complacently assumed that, as the British plan was the evacuation of Haifa by August (and therefore the continuous presence of British troops in the city itself), they could risk escalation until the Arab armies might have entered in mid-May. They were confident the British presence would act as a buffer. Thus, the Arabs share some blame for the loss of their own city, notwithstanding the actions and callous behavior of the local British commander.

The Arab share of blame is indicated by what took place at the truce meetings. In the first meeting on 22 April, when the Arab leaders met with

Stockwell to seek a British imposed truce, a British report states that the Arabs *wanted* Stockwell to say that: a) he would not allow Arab reinforcements to march on the town; and b) that he would not and could not step in and attack the Jews. The Arab deputation "felt that they were in no way empowered to ask for a truce, but that if they were covered in this way by him they might go ahead."[66] It seems odd that the Arabs would ask Stockwell to say what he intended to say to them anyway. Most probably, the man who prepared the reports on Haifa, Galilee District Commissioner C. Marriott, was attempting to defend the British against any charges of carelessness and even complicity with the Jews.

At the meeting, Stockwell told the Arabs that it was not his intention to get involved with or estrange either community; that his intention was to secure routes and areas for smooth redeployment; that he would not stand for interference with his dispositions; and that he was ready to assist in any way both Arabs and Jews in the maintenance of peace and order.[67] The head of the Muslim Brethren in Haifa and member of the NC simply says that, after Stockwell told them of his refusal to get involved or let reinforcements in, he handed them the terms of the Jewish truce. However, Shaykh al-Khatib maintains that the Arabs asked Stockwell to use his authority "to help" the Arabs and "stop the Jewish attack."[68] This hardly constitutes a truce meeting, nor a request for a British "attack" on the Jews. Whatever the Arabs said at the meeting, it is plausible to assume that the fear of being labeled traitors (which also was the case with the Jaffa leadership) by the AHC might have indeed pushed them to ask Stockwell to "cover" them to enable them to sue for a truce, which they did by meeting with the Jews at the town hall.

In the third (and last) truce meeting (that is, after the second town hall meeting with the *Haganah*, Mayor Levi, and the British), when the Arabs returned to give their final answer in the late evening of 22 April, the British report reveals more interesting details. Arab sources do not mention that the NC returned to give a final answer, but that, after the three-party town hall (second truce) meeting in which it was clear the Jews rejected any amendments to the truce, the Arabs met among themselves (at Victor Khayyat's house) and decided not to accept the Jewish conditions.[69] According to the report, the Arab deputation *did* resume the meeting (but only with the British side), and told Stockwell that they were in no position to sign the truce as they had no control over the Arab military elements in the town and that they could not fulfill the terms of the truce if they did sign.[70]

The report further states that the Arabs also asked for military assistance in the "evacuation" of the Arab population. The Marine Commando and British Police were organizing the refugees and "Movement Control" was shipping them by Royal Navy Z-Craft to Acre. By 24 April, the report maintains, the Arabs had even formed with the Jews a joint Arab-Jewish Committee under the chairmanship of the mayor to facilitate the "confusing mixture" of flight and evacuation. By the beginning of May, 3,000 Arabs out of a population of about 70,000 Arabs were left in Haifa, some thousands from the middle and upper classes having left earlier in the year. It is significant to note that al-Hut sarcastically concludes her discussion on Haifa by saying that, given the bitter reality of the Arab weakness and situation, the "noble Haifa residents" (i.e., the leaders) exposed their city and the children to continuous flight and annihilation because of their fear of being accused of treachery.[71]

By the time the last meeting took place in the late evening of 22 April, then, the Arabs were in a state of panic and flight, helped along by Zionist terror tactics. The Arab leaders asked for British help in evacuation *after* the mass flight and tragedy was in full swing. This is not the same as giving orders to their people to evacuate. What they wanted was British protection against continuous and indiscriminate Jewish harassment and gunfire. From the perspective of hindsight, however, it would seem the Arab leaders should have accepted a truce, thereby potentially stopping the fighting and slowing down or stopping the flight of their people.

Certainly, the Arab leadership did not do anything to persuade its people to stay put, regardless of Haifa's loss to the Jews. It is true that *Haganah* and IZL behavior during the week of the exodus was horrific (beatings, looting, humiliation), and that, as a result, not many Arabs relished the prospect of living under the Jews, but Arab acceptance of the truce would have at least made the emptying of Arab Haifa a difficult proposition. After all, after 22 April, there was little or no fighting in Haifa. Even on 22 April, the district commissioner reported that fighting continued in a "desultory fashion" and, as far as the British could determine, there were on that day 16–20 Jews killed, 30–40 wounded, and 100 Arabs killed, 150–200 wounded.[72] Despite the relatively minor fighting, however, this indicates that the armed defenders of the city (the Palestinian militias who by this time were acting independently of their political leaders) were still active during the mass flight. But if the leaders were determined at least to slow down the flight of their people by agreeing to a truce, the "armed elements" would not have been able to resist any Arab-Jewish agreement and could have been easily disarmed. (Of course, to be fair, even a truce would not have, in the end, prevented the *Haganah* from breaking it.)

The Arab leaders, then, played an important role in helping to depress Arab morale. This includes the Arab states. Firstly, the Military Committee in Damascus had not only neglected Haifa and had no worthwhile presence in the city (i.e., a strong contingent of well-equipped men with a coordinated strategy for defense), but it typically did not respond to appeals for reinforcements.[73] Secondly, the 400 to 600-man local Palestinian contingent[74] was chronically short of arms, dependent on outdated rifles, and possessed very few revolvers.[75] Thirdly, Haifa was defended by a motley of groups.[76] There were two Army of Liberation commanders to train and lead the fighters: Muhammad Hamad and Muhammad al-Hunayti. (The former died early in a *Haganah* ambush while supervising an arms shipment on the Acre-Haifa road.) In addition, there were independent fighters and men under the influence of the AHC, commanded by Abu-Ibrahim al-Saghir. The third command or group of leaders was the National Committee. Thus, there were three commands in Haifa, who usually were in conflict with each other: There was conflict between the Haifa NC and AHC commanders on the one hand, and the Army of Liberation commanders and those of the AHC on the other. There was, then, little or no unity of command.

Lastly, beginning on 21 April, some of the Arab military and political leaders fled Haifa, which had a demoralizing effect on people and irregulars. Ahmad Bey al-Khalil, Chief Magistrate and a prominent AHC representative in Haifa, a "man who had considerable influence," escaped by sea; Amin Bey 'Izz al-Din, the commander who took over Muhammad Hamad's place, left town (ostensibly to procure arms, but really to save himself) and never returned; and Yunis Naf'a, another local militia commander, left on 22 April.[77] Some of the "fighting" leaders, then, left Haifa immediately on or before the clash. The burden was borne by the young men of the town. By 4 May, no leader was left except Victor Khayyat and George Mu'ammar.[78]

The circumstances surrounding the fall of Jaffa, as far as the internal Arab politico-military factors were concerned, were similar to those which caused the fall of Haifa (as indeed most of the Arab towns until May). Jaffa more than any other Arab town was almost thoroughly surrounded by Jewish settlements. By 1948, there were around 80,000 Arabs in Jaffa with a minority of between 10,000 and 15,000 Jews. In the Tel Aviv-Jaffa complex there were about 213,000 Jews, with about 82,000 in the surrounding settlements.[79] The only strategic outlet for Jaffa was along the Tel Aviv-Jerusalem road, on which, just southeast of Jaffa, lay the villages of Yazur, Bayt Dajan, Salameh, and others.

As in all of Palestine, the fighting around Jaffa began at the time of the partition resolution, although the Zionist forces were unable to make any advances until late in April. Heavy assaults by joint IZL-*Haganah* forces were repulsed but by 20 April, communications between Jaffa and the outside were totally blocked. On 25 April, the IZL forces commenced their steady bombardment of Jaffa with heavy mortars and artillery, under which cover they made an assault followed by the *Haganah*. By 28 April the Manshiye quarter (north) of Jaffa was captured although the

Jews were repulsed from Tel al-Rish. The IZL forces continued their heavy bombardment of Jaffa's center from Manshiye, while they carried on with their supplementary psychological warfare as the troops looted, carrying anything and everything they could find.

In the minds of the people of Jaffa, as in most other towns, was the massacre at Dayr Yasin, and Haifa had just fallen and its people were in a state of panic and flight. During the three day assault and bombardment and continuing to the beginning of May, Jaffa's residents carried on their flight. Yazur and other villages also fell to a planned *Haganah* assault which began on 28 April, and their inhabitants fled and/or were expelled. But the gradual depression of morale was not just due to Zionist military tactics nor to uncontrollable panic and fear. Again, as in Haifa, internal divisions and the flight of commanders (the non-Palestinian commanders usually fled in the face of mass flight), as well as the Military Committee's reluctance to help, had their toll. Besides this, the usual shortages of equipment, munitions, and transport were endemic.

From an administrative aspect Jaffa was run by the local NC, which encompassed all groups within a national front, and by commanders sent by the MC in Damascus and commanders from the Army of Liberation (and by extension, Damascus). Militarily, its defense was dependent on Hasan Salameh's *Jihad* contingent which, in any case, hardly distinguished itself in the defense of so important a city. Also, it seems the delegation by the Military Committee of the city's defense to, first, an 'Iraqi officer, 'Abd al-Wahhab al-Shaykh 'Ali, and, later, to an Army of Liberation commander, did not sit well with Salameh.[80] Jealousy and division between the *Jihad* and the *Jaysh* was not to be easily overcome even in the face of overriding dangers. In addition to these, there were a number of fighters from the local Muslim Brethren and the Mufti's *Munazamat al-Shabab*. There also were some Sa'udis and Yemenis who had lived in Jaffa before the fighting started, and from the outside came a sprinkling of Egyptians, 'Iraqis, North Africans, and Yugoslavians.[81]

By February, there were a total of 540 men defending Jaffa, 175 of whom were Arab irregulars.[82] Scattered throughout the city were mobile units totalling 165 men, representing the following groups: Sixty men under *Munazamat al-Shabab* commander 'Abd al-Rahman al-Saksak, carrying 15 rifles, 1 machine gun, and 7 Tommy guns. These men represented the last-minute amalgamation of the *Futuwa* and *Najjada*. Thirty men, carrying 30 rifles, 1 machine gun, and 1 Tommy gun, represented the Muslim Brethren under the command of Hasan 'Abd al-Fattah and Al-Haj Ahmad Dawleh. There was the Al-'Ajami group, which included 15 men who carried 16 weapons and who were under the direction of Muhammad al-Tib al-Dajani. There were 30 men of the *Haras al-Lajneh* (NC guards) who carried 25 rifles and 2 machine guns, commanded by Halim

Abu Khadra. And the town's center was guarded by 30 men, headed by 'Abd al-Rahman al-Qaddumi, who carried 30 rifles and 1 machine gun. By the end of March, Jaffa was defended by 1,500 fighters scattered throughout the city's outskirts, carrying a total of 574 rifles and 74 machine guns. The men included 300 fighters of the *Jihad* and about 300 irregulars. The rest were local Jaffans.

The mixture of fighters and groups was neither well trained nor armed, and there certainly was no central, united command. This was recognized by the Military Committee delegated commander, 'Abd al-Wahhab (who took part in Rashid 'Ali al-Kilani's rebellion in 1941). He resigned after failing to convince local leaders and the Military Committee of the necessity of sending the Jaffa defenders to Qatna for better training. He left also because of the conflict between followers of the Mufti and Mayor Haykal, both of whose men continually interfered with his work and who caused general confusion and rumors of treachery and spying. The Military Committee sent 'Adil Nijm al-Din as his replacement, who promptly set himself the task of replacing with his own men (the irregulars) those officers whom the Jaffa NC originally installed, thus alienating the Palestinians and injecting divisions between them and the Arab volunteers.[83]

As soon as the heavy Jewish assault began on 25 April, the local commanders (the head of the Jaffa garrison, commander of the Ramle garrison and Hasan Salameh) appealed for reinforcements from Qawaqji, who (according to himself) quickly responded and sent (Palestinian) commander Michel al-'Issa of the Ajnadin Battalion. Al-'Issa, under protection of a convoy and Hasan Salameh's assistance, reached Jaffa on the morning of 28 April.[84] In addition to the Ajnadin Battalion, an artillery unit earlier was placed in Yazur, which commenced to bombard Tel Aviv (on 27 April) to relieve pressure on Jaffa. Al-Hut contends that the artillery unit suddenly pulled out, not only leaving Jaffa helpless to stop Jewish bombardment but rendering vulnerable and exposed the strategic villages along the Tel Aviv-Jerusalem highway.[85] Al-Qawaqji maintains that the artillery unit fired all the sixty shells available to it.[86]

A day after the artillery unit's shelling of Tel Aviv (28 April) the British intervened with minor air and ground bombardment and the entry of British troops into Jaffa. Al-'Arif says that the artillery unit's retreat was due to British intervention, the latter being asked by the *Haganah* to help them with Qawaqji's forces.[87] From Qawaqji's cable to the High Command, it *seemed* to him that Jaffa was aerially bombarded.[88] But there is no evidence, and certainly would have been no reason, that the British hit the Arabs. British sources contend, however, that, with the IZL assault on 27 April (i.e., cutting through Manshiye), a British tank battalion and artillery regiment were rushed off to Jaffa, and other reinforcements came by sea from Cyprus, whereupon British artillery began to shell Jewish positions.[89] What happened was that the British, sensitive to the fall of Haifa and the row created over it between the military and the Foreign Office, decided to intervene before Jaffa faced the same fate. After the Zionist offensive momentarily halted, the British then probably had to stop Qawaqji's artillery, if it even existed, perhaps at the *Haganah*'s request. It is probable also that it wasn't the British at all who stopped Qawaqji, but he quit just before the *Haganah* attacks (28 April) on Yazur and the other villages. In any case, Arab morale rapidly sank with the fall of Manshiye on 28 April.

Upon al-'Issa's entry into Jaffa on 28 April, the Damascus High Command ordered the removal of al-Nijm and his replacement with the former. Although al-Nijm was to be given some other duty, by 30 April he and his men ('Iraqis and Yugoslavs) escaped Jaffa by sea.[90] The panic and flight gripped the whole population, and the Arab irregulars and their commander fled along with the mass of people. The Ajnadin had even resorted to armed clashes with al-Nijm and his men to prevent them from taking their arms with them.[91] According to commander al-'Issa's cables, even the "Ajnadin [was] infected by panic and flight."[92] The people and fighters of Jaffa (or what was left of them) must have watched this demoralizing spectacle of a commander (al-Nijm) fleeing to save his life, thus reinforcing the tendency of mass flight. Salameh also pulled out, with his men, on 28 April, two days before Nijm. Even by the end of April, al-'Issa was losing ground to the Jewish forces, and by that time supplies of food and water were cut off. Al-'Issa sent desperate telegrams to the Military Committee and to Qawaqji, calling for reinforcements of regular soldiers, asking for clear ideas and instructions, and describing the continuous stream of refugees.[93]

One of the reasons for the Ajnadin's demoralization was the High Command's incompetence, its inability or unwillingness to supply weapons, reinforcements or any other type of aid, and its useless directives. This made overwhelmingly clear the dire need for a united, central Palestinian political authority and military leadership, which was never forthcoming.

Finally, deputations were sent to 'Abdullah and the MC in Damascus, but to no avail. Even the *khatib* of Jaffa's biggest mosque, Muhammad Fawzi al-Imam, met with Taha al-Hashimi and returned empty handed. The Arab attitude is best exemplified by the meeting between Palestinians Hikmat al-Taji al-Faruqi and Hashim Saba' with the MC in Damascus. Mardam Bey promised all efforts towards the struggle; Hashimi said there was not enough supplies; and Ahmad Sharabati lectured on the difficulty of defending Jaffa, explaining that the military situation there was hopeless as defending it would require a big army and a safe line of communication.

In the circumstances, Sharabati suggested that the people evacuate Jaffa.[94]

By the beginning of May, the Lydda District Commissioner estimated that some 5,000 to 8,000 were left of Jaffa's population of 80,000. The remaining National Committee and Municipal Council leaders were considering the idea of declaring Jaffa an undefended city so as to protect it from further Jewish attacks. These had formed an Emergency Committee to deal with matters. In a meeting with the district commissioner the Arabs (Mayor Yusif Haykal, Edward Beiruti, councillor, Ahmad Abu Laban, councillor, NC members Mustapha Tahir, Muhammad 'Abd al-Rahim, Rashid Riahi, Rafiq Asfar, Salah Nazir, Sa'id Khayyat, and commander Michel al-'Issa) welcomed the idea but no one wished his name to be associated with the suggestion in case he should be branded a traitor by "absent Arab leaders."[95] The only one ready to commit his name was Michel al-'Issa. After leaving the meeting with the district commissioner they again met later and wished to delegate authority to negotiate with the Zionists with Edward Beiruti, Ahmad Abu-Laban, and al-'Issa. But when the chosen delegates asked that minutes be taken of the meeting, other members opposed it. It is difficult to understand the fear of these men at a time when the situation was hopeless and practically the whole town had left. It only indicates the extent to which the Mufti had monopolized the Zionist danger and silenced any internal opposition to him.

Despite the district commissioner's appeal to the remaining members to help stop the exodus, evacuation and flight continued. On 4 May, Mayor Haykal himself left, leaving behind a handwritten note to the district commissioner saying: "As the situation requires that His Majesty King Abdullah be kept acquainted therewith, it has been considered in the interest of the town that I go to acquaint His Majesty with the situation and get the view of His Majesty thereon. It is my desire to return to Jaffa if the road to it is safe and free from the Haganna."[96] Haykal refused to commit himself to anything and, after delegating authority for negotiations, fled town.

By 9 May, the remaining members of the Emergency Committee declared their neutrality and asked for international protection. By 15 May, one out of twenty-four NC members and one of eleven city council members remained. Although Jaffa was finally surrendered to Tel Aviv, even these last two members were uncertain of their authority in such a chaotic and hopeless situation, particularly when all the others were afraid of being put in the limelight as having negotiated with the Jews. It remains to be said that many of the internal factors and circumstances that contributed to the fall of Haifa and Jaffa were prevalent in the fall of other Arab towns and areas, such as Acre and the Galilee.

The British Role in the Fall of Palestine

The British role in the fall of Arab Palestine in the last months of the mandate does not seem to have been guided by any underhanded policy in helping either Jews or Arabs. It is true, however, that by May the British had already been in active collusion with 'Abdullah (who was in turn colluding with the Zionists) to prevent the emergence of a Palestinian Arab state. Moreover, they were determined *not* to obstruct the realization of the partition lines and that meant actually preventing the Arab Legion, through the use of Glubb Pasha and the British officers, from blocking Jewish expansion under Plan D. Lastly, with the British following a withdrawal pattern that coincided with the partition lines, and with the Arab states prevented from entering until mid-May even though the Zionists were advancing, the practical result was the ensurance of Palestine's partition. This was consistent with British policy, which preferred the division of the country between the Zionists/Israelis and 'Abdullah. All this does not convincingly prove that the British withdrawal, and British policy, made the Zionist conquests more advantageous. But I cannot agree with Cohen's assertion that, because it was from east to west, the British withdrawal worked to the detriment of those Jewish settlements in the outlying areas (e.g., the Etzion Bloc south of Jerusalem.)[97]

In fact, British withdrawal was not strictly from east to west but a complicated mixture that also saw movement from west to east and then eventual evacuation through Haifa. It began with the evacuation of the south (Gaza and the Negev), which was overwhelmingly Arab; then proceeded west-northwest from Jaffa-Tel Aviv through central Palestine then up to 'Affula (one of two points at which the proposed Arab and Jewish states exactly met); then west back to east through the Galilee and the Haifa enclave. It can be argued that the second phase of the withdrawal (Netanya-Jaffa/Tel Aviv, proceeding central-east), which was to be completed by 31 May (but was actually completed much earlier), worked to protect the Jews from Arab attack as a huge part of the Jewish population was surrounded by British forces. However, the Palestinian Arabs did not have the capability, and the Arab states were certainly too divided, to attack the coast. Furthermore, the reverse could be argued: as the British forces stood between and among the Arabs and Jews, the Palestinian centers of Jaffa-Ramle/Lydda-Jerusalem-Samaria also were theoretically protected. It is perhaps more accurate to say that British withdrawal was more of a mixture, and generally left the Arabs and Jews in control of their own territory rather early. This could explain the ability of the Palestinians to maintain an offensive until April. It also might explain why the

Zionists waited until April to launch their offensive: British withdrawal had reached a point where the former felt free to activate their plans of conquest.

There are, in fact, numerous examples in which both Jews and Arabs waited until British withdrawal and then proceeded to take over or replace them. There are also numerous examples in which the British intervened on one side or another. For example, they made Qawaqji's artillery unit withdraw from the Jaffa area; they stopped his attack on the settlement of Kfar Szold (close to the Syrian border) in February; and they made him withdraw (in April) from the Nabi Samwil ridge northwest of Jerusalem, from where he had shelled the Jewish quarter of old Jerusalem. On the Arab side, they shelled, however briefly, IZL positions north of Jaffa; they also briefly shelled the Jewish flank with mortar in their initial attack on Acre in late April; and they prevented the *Haganah* from holding on to the villages it captured along the road to Jerusalem, thus prolonging the Arab siege of that city. The British insisted on keeping the routes of their withdrawal open. The major blunder of the British (mainly of the local commander) was in Haifa. And that indeed cost the Arabs dearly.

Generally, one of the main considerations affecting British withdrawal plans was the need to minimize conflict (however unsuccessful that was) by withdrawing from predominantly Arab and Jewish areas that were not contiguous and containing the smallest possible minority population clusters. It must be asserted, however, that the British were conscious and apprehensive of the negative effects of helping the Arabs: that "would have invited the opprobrium of the international community and possibly the responsibility for a new Jewish dispersion, even massacre, in which British officers would have been incriminated."[98]

But this was underlying and theoretical. In practice, it is difficult to conclusively judge the British on partiality. British withdrawal plans and interventions, "or lack of them, were motivated primarily by security and logistic considerations, and at times by the inclination of the local commander. There was *not* any high policy of aiding one side or another."[99] In the end, however that may have been, the primary responsibility for the defense of Palestine lay with the Palestinians themselves and the Arab states. For the former, the combination of military, political, and sociological factors coalesced to cause widespread communal collapse and disintegration.

Conclusion

The Reasons for the Disintegration of Palestinian Society with an Emphasis on the Persistence of Factionalism

The history of Palestine and the fate of its people cannot be fully understood without taking into account the multiplicity of internal and external variables that shaped and determined that small country's course. That course might even have been manageable had it taken a path similar to the other Arab, and indeed Third World, states: colonial domination, nationalism and decolonization, and the subsequent colonial legacy. But that was not to be. A new factor, Zionism, that complicated the history of Palestine and the life of its people, came into the picture. At a time when the Palestinian Arabs, and Arabs generally, began to develop a national consciousness, another group of people began to colonize the country, animated by their own nationalist goals, which were based on a religious identity. Add to this Britain's nurturing of the Zionist movement (basically for imperial reasons), and the direct effects on Arab Palestine of its colonial policies, and one has an extremely complex mixture and interaction of factors that shaped the outcome of Palestinian politics and society during the mandate period.

When the British took over the mandate, they found a society that was already undergoing social, economic, and political changes. These changes had begun under Ottoman rule, accelerated by internal, regional, and international economic factors as well as by the impact of religious missions from the West. Too, the British found a strongly entrenched urban notable elite that had been, in the previous century, consolidating its power and privileges through a gradual process of land accumulation, a process made favorable by the Ottoman state's policies and, equally, its impotence. Finally, the British found a difficult agrarian situation, again perpetuated by the Ottoman state. The Arab agrarian economy, already based on highly unequal relationships between landowner and peasant, was being gradually subjected to socio-economic processes whose dynamics were slowly having a dislocating effect on the rural social economy and society.

The colonial state, not surprisingly, did not have much intention of changing the relationships it had encountered. These political and socioeconomic relationships were characterized by regional, familial, local, and social divisions, shaped by the Ottoman *millet* system and administrative practices. The prevailing divisions were actually encouraged by the Ottoman state in its feeble efforts to control its empire through the deliberate perpetuation of traditional social organization. The central state's weak authority and reliance on local notables in turn reinforced that sociopolitical organization. Politics was carried out on a factional basis, under which the notables were secure in their roles as possessors of landed wealth and as intermediaries between state and society, a society over which they had influence but a state they were never allowed to control.

For the British not to have dealt with the local, traditional elite would of course have been foolish, not to mention the fact that, at the beginning of the mandate, there were no other leaders. But to insist on maintaining traditional social and political relationships throughout the mandate in the face of countervailing socio-economic change and the impact of Zionist colonization, was destructive, at least for the Palestinian Arabs.

And this change was inevitable. If nothing else, imperial intrerests dictated a communications infrastructure, including ports, harbors, roads, and airports. When the population rebelled, as the Palestinian Arabs frequently did, the colonial power took to building a security system, basically police stations and prisons. Too, much building had to be done to house the colonial government and its administrative structure, in addition to military needs, needs that exploded during the mandate's last decade.

While the British were thus having an unintended impact on Arab society, the Zionists, with their importation of capital and skills and land buying, were also causing and effecting changes in Palestinian society. Money was spent in Palestine on rent, construction, and agricultural products, not to mention the employment of Palestinian workers in Jewish plantations, construction sites, and factories, at least during the early part of the mandate.

The Arab social and political economy also was changing itself, so to speak. Expanding population, migration to urban centers and the coast, investment in industry and citrus, increased agricultural productivity, the expansion of commerce, tourism and trade, all these factors were having a phenomenal impact on Palestinian society. A new commercial elite was growing, a conscious and relatively cohesive working class made its presence felt, and a middle class of varied background predominated in the cities. All this while the urban notable elite's basis for power and factional politics, the patronage system, was being rapidly undermined.

But these complex, interlinked factors combined to the Palestinians' disadvantage. They coalesced to weaken the society by causing sharply uneven change and ongoing dislocation in the countryside, thus increasing the structural fragmentation in rural society; by inhibiting the growth and consolidation of a new elite; and by ensuring a contradictory developmental path for those migrants who were being turned into workers.

So what does all this mean for factionalism in Palestinian society? First, as to the role of the British in this regard, the disjointed changes occurring in Palestinian Arab society were encouraged by mandatory social and economic practices and policies. Colonial programs in the countryside, towards migrant labor, and towards the nascent urban working class, tended to exacerbate the tension, confusion, division and contradictory processes in the social structure. The pursuit of social order and minimum government involvement in social policy sharply conflicted with socio-economic changes. The Arabs became increasingly dependent on the state for jobs and social justice, a role the state was unwilling to fulfill. (Though some may argue that it wasn't the colonial state's business to meet Palestinian needs and expectations, the answer is that it should not have been the colonial state's business to forcibly rule others, implant a competing community in their midst, and tax them in order to finance its control over them.)

The rapid transformations of the forties heightened rural social mobility and awareness. But the state also was unwilling and unable to accommodate these changes. The impermanent and insecure nature of the newly emerging strata left them greatly weakened. The resultant aggravation of uneven development at the lower levels of the social structure contributed to the lack of cohesion in Palestinian rural society, leaving a severely disrupted traditional social organization vulnerable and fragile in the face of enormous external pressures. And it should be recalled that these processes in the forties came on the heels of a three-year rebellion in the late thirties which, with its sacrifices and the brutal repression it elicited from the British, had already severely weakened and exhausted Palestinian society and communal unity.

The British therefore attempted to maintain the rural society as they found it, and their policies towards migrant workers and labor were also meant to perpetuate the status quo. The net effect was the erection of impediments to wider social and structural integration. Rather than helping along the inexorable processes of change, the state tried to contain them, and thus served to hinder the trend towards national integration. That hindrance was to be seen in policies towards education, economy, local politics, and social programs in general. Given the need to maintain control and protect imperial interests, as well as to fulfill promises made to the Zionists, it would have been surprising indeed if the British did install a progressive regime concerned solely with the welfare of the indigenous people.

Aside from the direct role of the state, its support of the demographic minority had negative consequences on Palestinian society. Despite attributes of interdependence there really was no harmony between Arab and Jewish economies and societies. The benefits the Arabs accrued from Jewish colonization were incidental. Zionism, for political/ideological reasons, really never did have any intentions of either integrating in the wider society or accepting it in its vision of a Jewish state. This, more than the socio-cultural chasm between the two societies and Arab rejection of Jewish aspirations, determined the largely self-contained and competitive nature of the Jewish community in Palestine.

The autonomous nature of the *Yishuv* and British furtherance of its aims (in land, immigration, and industry) implied many things for Palestinian structural fragmentation and political factionalism. It is without doubt that the full potential development of the Arab economy and industry was inhibited by the Jewish presence. Arab capital could not compete and utilize all its resources. Colonial tariff and fiscal policies ensured the growth of Jewish-owned industry, which was able to directly compete with the fledgling Arab manufacturing sector and even sell a large array of consumer products in the Arab market. This had a retarding effect on the growth of a new, non-factionalist based elite.

Too, the presence of the Jews indirectly engendered an uneven development that exacerbated tension in the social structure. In the first half of the mandate, a significant part of Arab migrant labor became dependent on employment in Jewish plantations (and less so in Jewish industry). Simultaneously, the Arabs were increasingly being blocked from employment in Jewish concerns. By the opening decade of the forties, Arab employment in Jewish industry was practically non-existent. Additionally, Jewish competition for jobs with the state sector hurt the development of Arab labor. It depressed wages and took jobs away from the less skilled Arab workers. This situation was magnified during the forties (because of the vast number of jobs available). Without the presence of Jewish workers in the big cities, the growth of the skilled Arab working class would have been more significant.

Lastly, Jewish land purchases also strongly affected the Palestinians in a number of ways. Because purchased land became permanently alienated, this contributed to landlessness, severe fluctuations in employment, land scarcity, congestion, and frustration in the countryside. While the relationship between Arab landowner and peasant had indeed been unequal, characterized by exploitation through work and debt and leaving a rapidly growing rural population in a continued state of underdevelopment, this situation was mitigated by communal farming arrangements and an interdependent web of socio-cultural relations. Zionist colonization, on the other hand, was underpinned by an ideology which directly pursued religio-ethnic exclusivity in land ownership, and whose dislocating effects were traumatic.

Land purchases also had an indirect effect on Palestinian factionalism, although this was a problem many Arabs brought upon themselves. As almost all relied on the Jewish sector for funds from time to time, land sales had a divisive influence on the national movement. The suspicion, mistrust, cynicism, resentment, antagonism, and demoralization that was engendered at all levels of Palestinian Arab society by land sales cannot be overemphasized. The issue of land sales and accusations and counter-accusations regarding it continued throughout the mandate and formed an ongoing basis for conflict.

The state also aggravated factionalism at the national and elite level. Politically, the state refused to accept or recognize the Palestinian Arabs as a national entity or people. This began with the Balfour Declaration. Many features of the Ottoman *millet* system were incorporated into the mandate; the various communities could obtain government right to administer their own religious, cultural, and educational establishments. Thus, an *Arab* community, unlike a Jewish community, was not legally recognized.

But this alone did not faze the development of a national movement or strong national identity. The government also increased tension in the national movement in another way. It failed to develop self-governing institutions except for the few municipal councils, relying on the traditional leadership of men like the Mufti and town mayors. Although the Palestinians boycotted the first legislative council proposal made in early 1922 and an offer for an Arab agency in 1923, they subsequently (in the late 1920s and throughout the rest of the mandate) were ready to consider and/or accept some form of self-government as a step towards effective representation. During the mandate's last decade, this was seen through the futile efforts to get Britain to adhere to its own policy, the White Paper.

However, the Palestinians wavered continually and were deeply fearful of the long term implications of any self-governing proposal which was ambiguous towards the Jewish National Home policy and which would leave Zionist ambitions unchecked. The British commitment to a Jewish National Home and its vague formulation led to ambiguity and contradictions about legal status, the political system, and independence. The dilemmas and pressures posed for the Arab leadership by such a situation led to continual disagreement about strategy and decision-making and aggravated mutual suspicions and factionalist conflict. Also, the lack of representative institutions denied Palestinian society a truly democratic voice, a situation which allowed the notability to continue with its infighting.

More fundamentally than self-governing institutions, the lack of effective power over the state meant that the Palestinian Arab notability which headed the national movement would be unable to use the resources of the state to centralize power in its hands and thereby develop into a cohesive stratum. The elites could not use their access to state resources to advance themselves and hasten the process of differentiation in the notability. Unlike the elites in the surrounding countries, the Palestine Arab elite's power, like Palestinian society in general, was curbed by extraordinary factors. There was no continuity between economic wealth and ultimate political power. The colonial state did not mediate and protect the indigenous elite's economic interests. Rather, it protected and nurtured the advanced economy and industry of a competing community. Also, the lack of central power further factionalized the national movement, whose autonomous (i.e., notable family) components fought each other for predominance. If they had had a stake in national power, their interests might have dictated their cooperation in the maintenance of stability and power among themselves.

Aside from exogenous socio-economic and political factors that directly and indirectly contributed to the continuation of Palestinian Arab factionalist politics and structural factionalism and fragility at the lower levels of Palestinian society, there is the internal process, concerned with the impact of social change on national integration, to consider.

It is clear that traditional vertical cleavages were being subjected to rapid social change in which the society was in the uncertain transition between old and new social groups and classes and old and new politics. It is without doubt that the traditional urban notable elite was losing, and lost in some regions, its patronage social power base. Despite the contradictory and prohibitive effects of external variables on Palestinian social change, family ties and personal followings competed with clearly newly emerging social groups and classes. A remarkably conscious and relatively socially cohesive Arab urban working class was taking shape. Also, there was a landless peasant work force neither rooted in the urban social and political economy nor permanently attached to the rural countryside. Finally, there was the growing entrepreneurial or commercial elite that had the potential to challenge the urban notability. This elite, located largely in Jerusalem and the coastal towns, especially Jaffa and Haifa, differed from urban notables in the sense that it did not derive its income from land nor was it dependent on a factional base.

An additional challenger to factionalist-based politics and the notability was the bourgeois middle class. As understood here, the term "bourgeoisie" not only includes traders, merchants, manufacturers and businessmen, but also the professionals, intellectuals, and bureaucrats. These elements were marked by socio-economic as well as social and cultural similarities. Their lifestyles, world outlook, dress, consumption habits, and political perceptions and expectations contrasted dramatically with the urban notable or provincial elites. Along with the commercial elements, they formed the discontented middle and lower middle segments in the towns and villages (as teachers, civil servants). They gave the bourgeoisie as a whole much of its self-consciousness as a class. Throughout the mandate they articulated and gave substance to Palestinian cultural nationalism. By the late forties, in concert with commercial elements, they were beginning to make attempts at party organization (*Al-Sh'ab*, Arab Front in Jaffa, Arab Nationalist Bloc) and cooperated with the workers and such men as Ahmad al-Shuqayri, Musa al-'Alami, and Yusif Haykal. They were in a better position to come together via the medium of political parties than any other group or class, except the workers. It took an alliance of the professional middle class (particularly the intellectuals) and the working class (FATU) to create a radical political party (ALNL).

Despite the dramatic changes of the forties, there were, as we have pointed out numerous times, countervailing forces, external and internal in nature, that prohibited the full potential development of these changes. The working class was still structurally (i.e., economically, though not socially or politically) feeble, and its development uneven and overly tied and dependent on the colonial state. The migrant wage laborers constituted a huge, "floating" element that was moving from place to place in search of jobs, even up to 1947–48. And the elite came mostly from middle/upper Muslim and Christian families of commerce who had no power in society and no continuous socio-economic connections. Its most important members, the manufacturers, faced additional impediments to their growth and transformation into a middle/upper middle class bourgeoisie. Also, this commercial stratum was not economically or socially cohesive, reflecting the different backgrounds of its members.

Finally, the middle class elements (professionals, intellectuals, and bureaucrats) were not a socially integrated stratum, mainly because of their different socio-economic backgrounds, though they shared similar occupations. Some were the children of landed families and continued to be an integral part of these families. Others belonged to small families who pursued retailing and trade. Still others were members of the new commercial elite.

But even in the face of these realities, social change had become inexorable and proceeded very far, far enough to have weakened, openly challenged, and perhaps replaced, within a few short years, the power and position of the urban notables who, contrary to what is generally believed, did not form a socio-economic continuum (in privileges, wealth, control). By the forties they no longer represented an economically and socially secure elite whose landed, rentier wealth was conceived by some to have been heirarchically connected to the countryside in an unbroken chain. Patronage by this time could no longer serve as a stable context for factionalist politics.

The urban notable elite, actually the Mufti and those individuals connected with him in the AHC and based in Jerusalem, maintained their hold on power because of nationalist sentiments and also through the use of the threat of Zionist danger to mute internal opposition and delay the formation of an independent opposition. In the last decade of the mandate, everyone's energies were supposed to be directed towards the national cause. And the national cause was double-edged, being an added reason for the potential loss of power by the notables. If the notables did not assume an aggressive vanguard role in the national movement, then that movement would easily have come under the control of an educated new generation of middle class elements and, though small, a very socially and politically aware working class, groups who were discontented with the notables' perennial factionalism.

The urban notables were practically sustained because of the symbol and leadership of the Mufti. For he was, and by extension those of his social class, except the factionalist opposition (NDP), were preeminent Palestinians whose lives were spent in national, anti-colonial, and anti-Zionist struggles. As is made clear in this book, because the notability was never allowed national power, and was therefore not connected to the colonial state as in the other Arab countries and most countries of the Third World, it found itself leading the national movement. Its monopoly on nationalist sentiment became its primary source for legitimacy, even though it was resented and occassionally attacked by almost all the other urban elements.

That the notability used nationalism to maintain power is an indicator of the strength of nationalist sentiment in Palestinian society at the time. Palestinian national thought and expression evolved from a patriotic to a pan-Arab (and perhaps pan-Islamic) to a Palestinian national form, this evolution being partly shaped by the intensity of the struggle with Zionism. Though there was no national institutional foundation and no ideological clarity or agreement (not unusual), it was quite clear that almost all called for Palestinian national self-determination in the territory of mandate Palestine. The idea of nationalism had taken hold, and nation-building was, relative to the region, quite developed. Institutional development, by which I mean the development and running of state institutions and power, was never allowed to assume its course by the colonial authorities (though it was allowed to do so in the other Arab countries, overseen by the colonial presence). Palestinian political organization and coordination of the national movement, however, were national in their reach and scope.

But though a national political culture became widespread, with its attendant national organization and articulation, the national movement was fragmented by the elites who led it, who could not unite in the face of very difficult challenges. This elite factionalism was partly a result of urban notable manipulation of nationalist sentiment, not necessarily because the elite reflected the true nature of the society it led. That society, as we have seen, had changed relatively dramatically. Also, the traditional elite was sustained in power (local, not state) directly by the colonial authorities, and indirectly through the denial of institutional development and democracy at the formal (state) national level.

All this is not to say that there were not concrete social divisions that might have helped prolong the leadership of the urban notables. Though the urban strata were pretty much at the forefront of Palestinian nationalist thought and organization, the countryside certainly was more divided by vertical, mainly familial and kin, cleavages. These cleavages were encouraged by the provincial and rural families who were relatively better-off than the rest. These lesser families served as the backbone of the factionalist and clientelist system in the countryside and as the connections or intermediaries of the urban notable elites. In the forties, the elites' links to these elements were based more on socio-cultural and traditional loyalties than on economic power.

The peasantry could not be expected to see things with the clarity of the middle strata or working class. Social and religious prestige, ascription, illustrious family histories, all these factors helped determine the light in which the peasantry viewed the traditional elite. The peasantry did understand, however, the idea of a Palestinian national identity based in a defined territory. This is evidenced by the 1936–39 revolt and the strong support given in the forties to the Mufti, who, as was mentioned at numerous points, appealed to the peasantry on the basis of a nationalist-populist-religious idiom. He was the kind of authority and leader that they understood and followed. While rural classes therefore had a sense of national identity, though elusive, the mobilization and organization of the countryside was based on personal appeals and connections and on the immediate experience of dislocation caused by Zionism. National identities existed side by side with familial or local identities and loyalties. Obviously, this very much hindered full national integration.

It must also be emphasized that the role of the family, kinship, and the network of social relationships by which these were characterized, was part of Arabic and Middle Eastern culture. This culture was as much a part of urban as it was of rural life. There were, in addition, rural/urban divisions and regional divisions, the latter mostly reinforced by the factional elites, as well as socio-economic differences between the coastal and mountainous regions.

But in describing traditional social organization, one can go on indefinitely about the kinds of vertical cleavages and segmentation that existed. This was no more unusual in late mandatory Palestine than it was in other Middle Eastern and Third World countries. Therefore, Palestinian Arab society in the forties was no less (in fact, more) nationally aware or integrated than other peoples living under similar socio-economic conditions. While this is not unique, then, it did make nation and state building for the Palestinian Arabs a more problematic venture than it was for the Zionists. Moreover, it must be reemphasized that Zionist colonization was unique in many ways and the colonial state did all it could to nurture the development of the Jewish community and block the Palestinian Arabs from obtaining national self-determination.

Taking all these factors into consideration, in addition to the fact that Arab Palestine was being subjected to enormous disruptions and tensions caused by rapid social change and conflictual colonial policies, it can be readily seen that Palestinian society in the forties was in unstable flux, vulnerable to collapse under severe pressure. Arab Palestine was experiencing dislocation on a wide scale. The transitional social structures uneasily coexisted with a factionalist system prolonged by an insecure traditional elite. This rendered the society extremely fragile. With an absent (Arab) central authority, Arab society did not have the social resources to organize and unite itself. Moreover, during the mandate's last decade the urban notable elites led a disjointed society without the solid factional base that they once held. Their popular support was not really widespread and their hold over Palestinian society was much more tenuous than appeared. Thus, aside from structural factionalism, the forties also were characterized by much distrust and cynicism, despite the strength of national sentiment.

This socio-political context did not auger well for the Palestinians when conflict finally erupted between them and the Zionists. The fragmentation in Palestinian society, which was intensified both by external and internal political and socio-economic factors, was worsened by the existing divisions among the Arab regimes. The mistrust centered around various dynastic intrigues and individual state interests. It cannot be said, however, that, except for the Hashemites, there were any sinister Arab motives or ambitions towards Palestine. Even among the Hashemites, Nuri Pasha and the 'Iraqi branch reflected a more genuine interest in the unity of the Arab East. All of Nuri's intrigues revolved around this central pivot. His vision was rooted in a more realistic potential for unity in the area of the Fertile Crescent. Despite 'Iraqi territorial ambitions, however, there was no proclivity to accept partition as 'Abdullah was willing to do.

'Abdullah adhered to a vision of expansion of territory and crown; Nuri al-Sa'id reflected a broader Arab nationalist vision.

In addition to Arab intrigue, the disorganization among the Arabs was rooted in the social backwardness and fractured nature of Arab society in general. The divisions in Arab politics were mirrored in the state of nationalism and the pan-Arab national movement. The Arab regimes tried to monopolize the unorganized national sentiment in general, and towards Palestine in particular, in an effort to sustain their legitimacy and deflect internal dissent.

The weaknesses in the Palestinian ranks were compounded by Arab opposition to a Palestinian authority. The Hashemites' campaign against the Mufti and AHC was relentless. They opposed a Palestinian authority in Palestine because the leadership of the Mufti obstructed their plans and ambitions towards Palestine. Though the Egyptians-Syrians-Sa'udis supported the creation of a provisional government and an administrative authority in Palestine, it was mainly because of their attempt to block Hashemite ambitions. The other Arab states were concerned as much with 'Abdullah's duplicity as they were with the Zionists. It was the balance of power, not warm feeling towards the Mufti, that dictated their posture.

But even this posture began to wane in the last weeks of the mandate, and it eventually turned into one of opposition to the Mufti. The central reason for the change in attitude was Arab fear and reluctance to intervene in Palestine. This was especially true for the Egytpians and Sa'udis. It became increasingly important to control the Palestinians as the Arab states found themselves sucked into the Palestine conflict. As the tide of war turned against the Palestinians and the Arab public became restless, the non-Hashemite bloc, particularly the Egyptians, felt compelled to cooperate (militarily) with 'Abdullah. It was easier and safer to deal with a regime which would react in a measured response to war in Palestine, than it was to deal with the unpredictable Mufti and his followers in Palestine. In other words, they were apprehensive that the Mufti's power and influence in Palestine would become an impediment to the political, diplomatic, and tactical flexibility required in dealing with the Palestine conflict. Thus, by spring 1948, there was an unwitting congruence of interest between the Hashemites and the non-Hashemite bloc.

It seems paradoxical that the Mufti's influence began to wane so rapidly in the halls of the Arab League, given his popularity within Palestine and in the Middle East. But his strength and influence in Palestine was not the same as it was outside of Palestine. His weakness outside reflected the fractured and disorganized state of the national movement in the Arab world. Nationalism was amorphous and could not be easily organized and mobilized at a pan-Arab level, despite spontaneous nationalist outbursts. The Mufti's popularity existed, but there was no coherent organization to translate it into action. In addition, the regimes monopolized the sentiments of Arab nationalism over Palestine in their bids to outdo each other and therefore took the wind out of the Mufti. The Arab regimes' need for survival and caution outweighed the risk with the public of stripping the Mufti of any influence within the Arab League. Moreover, the divisions in the Palestinian leadership and their dependence on the Arab states exposed them to weakness, control, and manipulation from the outside.

The British, too, helped weaken the prospect of a Palestinian administrative authority before the mandate's end in mid-May. Because the British, anxious about retaining their influence in the area, concretely and otherwise, distrusted the Mufti's nationalist opposition to imperialism, they also put their lot in with 'Abdullah. The prospects for a British base and rights in an independent Arab Palestine (that is, a partitioned Palestine, but under Palestinian authority) did not seem promising under the Mufti, who was perceived as a potential destabilizer in the area. All sides, therefore, did not desire an effective Palestinian authority.

Blocking the emergence of a Palestinian Arab state, as called for in the United Nations partition resolution, was the especial preoccupation of the British/Zionist/Trans-Jordanian triangle, the Zionists' connection in this triangle being their intensive negotiations with 'Abdullah, from which the British benefited. The Zionists and 'Abdullah had been talking since the early 1920s, the inevitable and explicit logic of their aims being to prevent the legitimate expression of Palestinian nationalism. When British interests converged with the interests of the other two, the Palestinians actually faced tremendous odds in preventing their own suppression and the loss and division of their patrimony.

The Hashemite-Zionist collusion would of course provide 'Abdullah with an enlarged crown and the Zionists with their state. The deal with 'Abdullah meant that the Zionists were left free to defeat the Palestinians and the Arab states and so establish their state. But the Zionists were not truly interested in a deal with 'Abdullah or anyone else if it meant checking their expansionist ambitions. The collusion with the Hashemites served to neutralize a potentially powerful foe. When things on the battlefield went in Jewish favor, as they did beginning in April, then it mattered little whether their ally was in a difficult position, and certainly agreements were not meant to be kept by them if there was a chance at more land-grabbing. The limited fighting 'Abdullah's Legion did around Jerusalem was more because of Jewish aggression than because of the monarch's design.

For the British, by the third month of 1948, they were in active duplicity with 'Abdullah, aware of his talks with the Zionists. Their preeminent goal was the maintenance of the British presence in the Middle East. To this end, they also colluded with 'Abdullah by politically supporting his plans, by blocking any Arab interventions, by suppressing the Palestinians, by subsidizing (along with the Jewish Agency, which regularly gave 'Abdullah money) his Legion and crown, by protecting his regime, and by using British officers on the Arab Legion to secure, through a defensive and inactive posture, their political/imperial aims and 'Abdullah's political/territorial ambitions.

Given Arab disunity, the Palestinians were not only almost totally vulnerable but also would have needed a miracle to save them. However, no doubt the fact that the Palestinians were unable to create any sort of administrative structure or authority influenced British thinking and strategy and Arab states policies. For the Palestinians also weakened themselves. Throughout the mandate, the notables were unable to achieve for any significant length of time a united political program or to cooperate in effectively creating local autonomous institutions that would have served as a basis for governing their people. Despite the fact that they were denied legislative councils and national self-rule, the Palestinians could have developed self-governing institutions at the community level at their own initiative. However, the notability worried that such institutions would mean wider participation and more democratic representation and therefore a weakened grip.

Partly because of a lack of well-developed community level institutions, the elite fought for domination over and created an amorphous and fractured national movement and helped block the emergence of more effective political and administrative organization. In the last few critical months of the mandate, no real thought or concrete plans were being worked out for the assumption of local control upon British evacuation, regardless of what the Arab states did or did not do in this matter. With the AHC out of the country, and with no strong interim government or authority, social disunity was bound to ensue in the resulting vacuum. Certainly, both the Mufti from the outside and the AHC members and followers in Palestine (Jamal, Khalidi, the PAP) were continually hostile to wider representation (from workers and the middle classes). The full potential of the Palestinians was not utilized precisely because of narrow factionalist interests.

Factional division among the Palestinian Arabs was aggravated by the politico-military disorganization and disharmony of the Arab states. Almost everything was lacking among the volunteers, particularly arms and effective central command. There was no coherent strategy for defense. Training among the irregulars was short in duration and late in activation, and there were not enough well-trained and disciplined commanders. This had its toll: treachery and desertion took place in many towns. It also had a demoralizing effect on the Palestinians.

As concerns the wider Arab effort, the Military Committee in Damascus either was dangerously naive or strapped by its masters (it would seem it was a mixture of both). Also, there was a tendency to believe, whether among the Palestinians or the MC, that what was lost might yet be retrieved. This might have accounted for the readiness to evacuate and retreat, in the belief that it was temporary. A dangerous complacency, as it turned out.

Finally, the Arab effort would have been much more effective if the Palestinians themselves had taken primary military and political command in their own country. Despite the difficulties, the Palestinians displayed little ability to contend with the enormous task at hand. Though the Mufti pleaded with the Arab states that, if supplied with money and weapons, the Palestinians could deal with the situation militarily, he failed to foster the kind of unity needed to support his contention. This indicates, at the very least, that the Palestinians seriously underestimated the strength of their adversary. More importantly, the Mufti could have allowed more flexibility to local bodies such as the NCs. Instead, the Mufti showed favoritism towards one town or faction over the other by disbursing funds according to loyalty. This engendered further alienation and demoralization.

Having said all this, it is important to consider the practical effects on events of a more united and effective Palestinian leadership. What would have changed? For one thing, a united leadership would have gained more credibility, legitimacy, and authority among the Arab states. If the Palestinians developed a local administrative structure and authority, with a united leadership speaking on their behalf to the outside world, they would have been better equipped to deal with all external parties. They might also have been more effective in their resistance and avoided the rapid disintegration of their society. There seems to have been a law of direct proportionality at work: The more the Palestinians were divided, the easier it was for the Arab states (and others) to control them and sap their legitimacy and strength. Certainly, a leadership that could not develop the necessary cooperation (or undertake flexible and tactical political postures) was inviting trouble for its people.

But all of this belongs to the realm of speculation, considering the rapid development of politico-military events at the mandate's end. Much of what happened to Palestine between 1947 and 1948 was beyond the Palestinians' control. First, after the partition resolution, the British would have preferred a Palestinian leadership that accepted some form of partition settlement and showed amenability to their presence. Effective local administration or not, what motivated the British was their need for a continuing presence in the area. Palestinian nationalism was too hostile to British colonialism, especially because of the latter's support of Zionism.

Second, the Mufti wisely feared the entry into Palestine of Hashemite troops and vainly attempted to pre-empt this eventuality. He knew the Palestinians would be unable to stop the occupation of any part of Palestine either by Hashemite or any other Arab troops. Even if the Palestinians used their organizational, administrative and military capabilities to their full potential, which they were capable of doing, the subsequent loss of Palestine to a powerful enemy would have, and did, make this supposition meaningless. The Palestinians were powerless to do anything about 'Abdullah's Arab Legion. Though the Mufti obviously did not foresee the loss of Palestine, what he tried to get from the Arab League was a commitment that would guarantee the authority and legitimacy of the AHC once Arab soldiers entered Palestine. Again, even if the Palestinians were united and organized, they needed a collective Arab guarantee that they would respect the right of the Palestinian people to govern themselves. With Hashemite ambitions and Arab disagreement, this was nearly impossible.

Even more impossible to have been able to deal with was Zionist military power and ambitions. For in the end, when all is said and done, the Palestinian Arabs lost Palestine because of the brutal realism, single-mindedness, and determination of their enemy to get what it wanted. Realizing this, perhaps the Palestinians should have been "realistic" and compromised with their enemies by accepting the "right" of the Jews to establish a state in Palestine. While in hindsight this now seems the wise thing to have done, it is enormously difficult to judge them either way on this count. It would have taken prophetic powers to have foreseen what eventually happened, and a vision wider than humanly possible to succumb to and accept the idea that, by giving away more than half of their country, as the United Nations partition plan called for, they would have acted realistically. How realistic indeed it would have been to accept the loss of the most fertile parts of one's country, to have some 500,000 of one's people come under hostile (Zionist) sovereignty, to have lost fields, homes, farms, and towns, and to have been sandwiched between powerful neighbors east and west, is not easy to say.

When the Zionists made "concessions," it was to agree to take less than the entire country. They were, after all, losing nothing, despite their own perceptions and beliefs over their right to Eretz (the Land of) Israel. And in the sweeping emotions, hatreds, fears, distortions, and profound mistrust between Palestinians and Jews, Zionist arguments over right—that they had a religious attachment to and identity with the land that gave birth to their heritage and culture, that they lived on that land long ago, that the Palestinians should weigh their claims as against the entire

Jewish people, that the Jewish people deserved a "home" after limitless years of persecution—could hardly be expected to fall on receptive ears. The Jewish experience and sentiments simply could not be internalized or empathized with, meaning very little to most Palestinians, who, through their daily experience, saw an aggressive Zionism which consistently denied their very peoplehood, and which was intent on taking their land. Besides, the Palestinians had their own legal, moral, and historical arsenal, an arsenal that prevented them from coolly and clearly assessing their situation. It would, therefore, have taken a lot more than such Jewish arguments for them to concede Jewish rights, which, as the Palestinians well knew, really meant a Jewish state in their midst.

But it wasn't merely a matter of Palestinian rejection or even mutual denial. The logic of Zionist ambitions, as aggressively advanced and symbolized in Ben-Gurion, really left very little room for the continued existence of a Palestinian nation. It is by now a matter of historical record that the *mainstream* Labor Zionists, not to mention the so-called Revisionists (who also demanded Trans-Jordan and other Arab lands), would not have been content with anything short of dominating the entire country. Partition and its limits, whether in 1937 or 1947, were seen by Ben-Gurion as a stepping-stone for expansion. He considered neither boundaries nor agreements sacred. They were to be broken when convenient—the inherent maximalist aims of Zionism's vision were not to be lost sight of.

It is certainly true that the Palestinian leaders, notably the Mufti, were generally intransigent in the sense that they refused to consider any sort of *modus vivendi* short of a constitutional state based on the strength of the respective proportions—which basically meant Palestinian control and the Jewish minority remaining that way. It is quite as true, however, that the most Zionism offered the Palestinians was the "opportunity" to exist as a subordinate minority and to eschew any ideas of existing as a nation. And that was Zionism's good side. Ben-Gurion quite forcefully made it clear that, should the Palestinians resist, then the Zionists, or the Jewish state, would know what to do with them.

The Zionist leadership did not indicate what its acceptable boundaries were; how the Palestinians would fit into a state defined by Jewishness; how, indeed, they would fit into a state that would insist on making way for millions of Jews yet did not have the land to absorb them; how, within this scenario, Palestinian property, political, and civil rights would even be protected; and what would happen to Palestinians in a Jewish state and to those outside it—assuming they accepted partition and created a state of their own—once the millions of Jews were brought in. The point is, there was absolutely nothing in Zionist ideology that would have prevented the realization of the kind of state (Greater Israel) that the movement envisioned.

Even if the Palestinian national movement had accepted the idea of a Jewish state, it is highly improbable that this state would have welcomed those Palestinians who would have come under its jurisdiction or been contained by the neighboring Palestinian state. It was a difficult proposition to create a viable Jewish state, with the Palestinians remaining within it and next to it, on the basis of such notions as pluralism, political democracy, and justice. From its inception, Zionism refused to define the limits of what it wanted, nor to truly come to grips with the implications of its own program, particularly the place of Palestinians in a Jewish state. Basically, it denied the existence of a Palestinian nation as vigorously as the Palestinians refused to concede its claims. Equally, Zionism denied the implications of the realities of its own aspirations and the possibility that it didn't quite represent the most enlightened or beneficial intrusion into the Palestinians' lives.

The logic of the Zionist vision as it worked itself out was made clear in 1948. The determination to produce the state that was promised in the 1947 partition resolution was rapidly overtaken by an inexorable dynamic: security, the fear of a Fifth Column, and the need for consolidation became blurred and indistinguishable from visions of a Greater Jewish State, free from as many Palestinians as possible. Thus, when it became clear that conquest and expulsion were working out extremely well, these pretty much became a widespread practice by April 1948. Fear, the tendency to flee in the face of Jewish advances, the effect of Zionist assaults, Arab incompetence, tactical evacuation, all these were not necessarily related to direct Zionist action, nor could the Zionists possibly have foreseen the ease with which they sliced through Palestine and the collapse of its people. However, there existed the overpowering temptation to "transfer" the Palestinians once the opportunity presented itself, which was the underlying object of Plan D. And that opportunity arose from April onwards. Expulsion, physical and psychological terror, destruction of villages and crops to prevent return, atrocities; all were part of the Zionist menu as they sought to take advantage of the transformations that were occurring before their eyes.

Certainly, as the Palestinian people were pretty much denied by both Revisionists and Laborites, they were already dehumanized, the Zionist mentality and psyche seeing little injustice in wanting to clear out the local natives (not very different from the experience of colonial-settler societies). (This of course did not apply to the Zionist left across the board, but more to the Ben-Gurionist-led and inspired part.) Therefore, of the 400,000 Palestinians who became refugees from December 1947 through May 1948, a large majority were pushed out by direct and indirect Zionist actions. From the beginning of June onwards, the additional 300,000-plus refugees became so through deliberate policy. Again, security and legitimate existence became blurred and subordinate to the euphoric possibility of realizing the political/territorial/demographic vision. In the end, internal Palestinian weakness, fragmentation, and division were not by themselves enough to have caused the disintegration of the society. A very weak and vulnerable society still needed military/terroristic pressures to cause its collapse.

*　　*　　*

The fundamental character of the Palestine problem began as early as the late nineteenth century with Zionist colonization and was accelerated with the beginning of colonial rule. The political, economic, social, and diplomatic complexities that confronted the Palestinian Arabs during the mandate reached their apex in the forties. In this last decade, these pressures finally culminated in the disintegration of Palestinian society. Effective social and political organization is difficult enough to achieve in traditional societies. However, from the beginning, Arab Palestine was subject to nique internal and external forces that it really could not contend with or control.

Notes*

Introduction

1. For example, Bernard Wasserstein, *The British in Palestine, the mandatory government and the Arab-Jewish conflict 1917–1929* (London, 1978).
2. For example, Yehoshua Porath, *The Emergence of the Palestinian Arab National Movement, 1918–1929* (London, 1974) and *The Palestinian Arab National Movement, 1929–1939* (London, 1977); Ann Mosely Lesch, *Arab Politics in Palestine, 1917–1939* (Ithaca, 1979); and Abdul Wahab Kayyali, *Palestine: A Modern History* (London, 1978).

Chapter 1. State, Society and Politics in Late Ottoman and Early Mandatory Palestine

1. Moshe Ma'oz, *Ottoman Reform in Syria and Palestine 1840–1861* (Oxford, 1968).
2. For an understanding of Ottoman Palestine see M. Ma'oz, ed., *Studies on Palestine During the Ottoman Period* (Jerusalem, 1975). For a recent discussion of the subject-matter in this chapter, and particularly of the notables in late Ottoman Palestine, see Muhammad Y. Muslih, *The Origins of Palestinian Nationalism* (New York, 1988), pp. 56–58.
3. Marwan R. Buheiry, "The Agricultural Exports of Southern Palestine, 1885–1914," *Journal of Palestine Studies,* 10 (1981), p. 61.
4. Y. Porath, *The Emergence,* pp. 5–7; see also Ma'oz, *Ottoman Reform,* pp. 32–34.
5. William R. Polk, David M. Stamler, and Edmund Asfour, *Backdrop to Tragedy: The Struggle For Palestine* (Boston, 1957), p. 232.
6. Buheiry, "The Agricultural Exports," p. 65.
7. For a description of the ruling clan families in early 19th century Ottoman Palestine, see M. Abir, "Local Leadership and Early Reforms in Palestine," in Ma'oz, *Studies on Palestine.*
8. *The Emergence,* pp. 5–7.
9. Henry Rosenfeld, "From Peasantry to Wage Labor and Residual Peasantry: The Transformation of an Arab Village," in Louise Sweet, ed., *Peoples and Cultures of the Middle East* (New York, 1970), pp. 143–44.
10. Talal Asad, "Anthropological Texts and Ideological Problems: An Analysis of Cohen on Arab Villages in Israel," *Review of Middle East Studies,* 1 (1975), p. 11. Asad says more than half of the surplus was appropriated. But this cannot really be known as the amount depended on the balance of power between peasant and tax-farmer.
11. Polk *et al., Backdrop to Tragedy,* p. 233.
12. Rosenfeld, "From Peasantry to Wage Labor," p. 144.

---

*All Arabic sources cited in the notes are translated in the bibliography.

13. See Y. Firestone, "Crop Sharing Economics in Mandatory Palestine," *Middle Eastern Studies,* parts I & II, vol. 11, nos. 1 & 2 (Jan. 1975 & May 1975), pp. 3–23 and pp. 175–94.

14. Roger Owen, *The Middle East in the World Economy 1800–1914* (London, 1981), p. 35. For a detailed discussion of this system's origins, forms, development or changes over time, and geographical spread, see pp. 256–59, 269 of Owen's book. The system itself was extremely complex: little is known about its development and geographical spread and the number of variables seeking to explain changes within it are large.

15. James Reilly, "The Peasantry of Late Ottoman Palestine," *Journal of Palestine Studies,* 5 (1981), pp. 82–97.

16. *Ibid.,* p. 92.

17. Rosemary Sayigh, *Palestinians: From Peasants to Revolutionaries* (London, 1979), pp. 13–17.

18. This insight was suggested to me by Mr. 'Aziz Shahin of Ramallah in an interview in March 1983. For an excellent analysis of socio-political conditions of *Qays-Yaman* factionalism, see M. Hoexter, "The Role of Qays and Yemen Factions in Local Political Divisions: Jabal Nablus Compared with the Judean Hills in the First Half of the Nineteenth Century," *Asian and African Studies,* IV (1973), pp. 249–312. Hoexter interestingly distinguishes between two regional patterns of alliances: the Nablus area, where the town landlords participated in and led clan conflicts; and the Jerusalem area, where notables served as mediators and arbitrators. Unlike Nablus notables, Jerusalem's notables did not rule the hinterland because of the city's relatively independent economic base.

19. Owen, *The Middle East in the World Economy,* pp. 173–74.

20. Porath, *The Emergence,* p. 10; also see Kenneth W. Stein, *The Land Question in Palestine, 1917–1939* (Chapel Hill, 1984) p. 7.

21. Porath, *ibid.,* pp. 9–10.

22. A. Scholch, "European Penetration and the Economic Development of Palestine, 1856–82," in Roger Owen, ed., *Studies in the Social and Economic History of Palestine in the Nineteenth and Twentieth Centuries* (London, 1983), p. 49. The following description is based on Scholch. For the economic development of Palestine in the periods 1850–1880 and after, see also Owen, *The Middle East in the World Economy,* pp. 175–79, 265–66. Finally, for the period 1885–1914 see Buheiry, "The Agricultural Exports," esp. pp. 64–65.

23. From Y. Ben-Arieh, "The Population of the Large Towns in Palestine During the First Eighty Years of the Nineteenth Century According to Western Sources," in Ma'oz, *Studies on Palestine During the Ottoman Period,* p. 68.

24. PG, *A Survey of Palestine* (Jerusalem, 1946), ii, pp. 719–21.

25. Stein, *The Land Question,* p. 6.

26. *Ibid.,* p. 10.

27. *Ibid.,* p. 22.

28. A. Scholch, "European Penetration," p. 22.

29. Joel Migdal, "Urbanization and Political Change: The Impact of Foreign Rule," *Comp. Stud. in Soc. and His.,* 19 (1977), p. 331.

30. Porath, *The Palestinian Arab,* p. 81.

31. Scholch, "European Penetration," pp. 23–24. Also Stein, *The Land Question*, p. 26. Stein says the peasants owned the land either completely or partially or enjoyed only cultivation rights.

32. A. Granott, *The Land System in Palestine* (London, 1952), pp. 38–39. These and the following figures are mostly from Zionist and sympathetic sources, including Stein. Despite the unreliability and perhaps dubiousness of the information and figures, they should be taken as rough indicators of the inequality in land ownership.

33. *Ibid.,* p. 39.

34. See Owen, *The Middle East in the World Economy*, p. 268.

35. Stein, *The Land Question*, p. 26.

36. Granott, *The Land System*, p. 81. Also on the Sursuqs see Scholch, "European Penetration," pp. 24–25. The other rich families were probably the Beiruti business families of Butros and Farah, whom Scholch says purchased 17 villages from the Ottomans in Marj Ibn 'Amr and near Nazareth in 1869.

37. Granott, *ibid.,* p. 81. Again, these figures should be approached with caution, as they are probably exaggerated.

38. Calculated from Stein, *The Land Question*, appendix 1, pp. 223–25. The list of large estates is based on Zionist sources for *that year* (1919) and is not, presumably, meant to be complete. Hence any discrepancies with earlier figures. There were an additional 89,000 *dunums* which were co-owned between Palestinians and non-Palestinians which I did not figure into the calculations. Finally, the non-Palestinian owners hailed mainly from Beirut, Damascus, and Alexandria.

39. See Albert Hourani, "Ottoman Reform and the Politics of Notables," in William R. Polk and Richard L. Chambers, eds., *Beginnings of Modernization in the Middle East* (Chicago, 1968), pp. 333–51. See Porath, *The Emergence*, p. 13, for some examples of Palestinians holding high posts in the Ottoman administration.

40. See J. Migdal's contribution in Migdal, ed., *Palestinian Society and Politics* (Princeton, 1980), p. 20. The Husaynis since Ottoman times held various posts as mayors, administrators of *awqaf* for the al-Nabi Musa mosque near Jericho, and district and sub-district governors and administrators.

41. See, for example, John D. Powell, "Peasant Society and Clientelist Politics," *Am. Pol. S. Rev.,* LXN (1970), pp. 411–25.

42. See Rene Lemarchand and Keith Legg, "Political Clientelism and Development," *Comparative Politics,* IV (1972), pp. 149–78.

43. For an elaboration of these concepts see Jeremy Boissevain, "Patronage in Sicily," *Man,* I (1968), pp. 18, 29; also Powell "Peasant Society," pp. 412–13.

44. David Waines, "The Failure of the Nationalist Resistence," in Ibrahim Abu-Lughod, ed., *The Transformation of Palestine* (Evanston, Illinois, 1971), p. 218.

45. See E. Z. Sabella, "The Leading Palestinian Hamayil (Families) and Socio-Economic and Political Organization in Palestine 1917–1948" (Univ. of Virginia M.A. thesis, Dept. of Sociology/Anthropology, Aug. 1971), pp. 41–42, for a description of the *hamulah* alignments.

46. *Ibid.,* p. 42. Sabella, p. 41, says some village potentates, such as the 'Amru family in the Hebron mountain range, ruled without opposition and without

any need to form associations with urban families. They allied themselves with one or another faction, however, bacause they were not strong enough to "adopt a course of neutrality."

47. Lesch, *Arab Politics,* p. 59.

48. Sabella, "The Leading," pp. 26–27.

49. Sabella, *ibid.,* p. 27. The actual number of families (in all of Palestine) the author gives is 200. But then, it is obvious the figures would not add up. He does not indicate what origins the other 80 families might have claimed or what other kinds of origins there were.

50. Phillip S. Khoury, *Urban Notables and Arab Nationalism: The Politics of Damascus 1860–1920* (London, 1983), p. 48. Khoury is here describing the patronage resources of the notables of Damascus, which applies just as well to Jerusalem.

51. Sabella, "The Leading," p. 35.

52. On this see Firestone, "Crop-Sharing Economics in Mandatory Palestine," Part II, pp. 184–85.

53. Salim Tamari, "Factionalism and Class Formation in Recent Palestinian History," in Owen, *Studies,* p. 229.

54. M. F. Abcarius, "The Fiscal System," in S. B. Himadeh, ed., *The Economic Organization of Palestine* (Beirut, 1938), table on p. 546. Of course, this was an unusual year, the high point of the revolt. Abcarius, however, provides figures for the years 1918–38.

55. See Migdal's contribution for an overall picture of the processes that took place, in Migdal, *Palestinian Society.*

56. See Lesch, *Arab Politics,* chap. on "Social and Economic Setting."

57. See Adnan M. Abu-Ghazaleh, "Arab Cultural Nationalism in Palestine During the British Mandate," *Journal of Palestine Studies,* 1 (1972), pp. 37–63.

58. See *A Survey of Palestine* (Jerusalem, 1946), i, pp. 114, 157–58. These figures are probably underestimates. The Department of Statistics calculated an Arab population of 1,176,571 (plus 500,000 Jews) at the *end of 1943,* and 1,257,037 Arabs (plus 543,000 Jews) by the *beginning of 1945.* See Janet L. Abu-Lughod, "The Demographic Transformation of Palestine," in I. Abu-Lughod, *The Transformation,* p. 152.

59. *Survey,* i, p. 159.

60. *Survey,* i, pp. 155–58.

61. *Survey,* ii, pp. 719–20, calculated from tables 21 and 22. Any apparent discrepancies with figures from Table 1.1 (see note 23) is explained by the fact that these figures exclude Jews.

62. Migdal, *Palestinian Society,* p. 27, table 3.

Chapter 2. Socio-Economic Change During the Latter Part of the Mandate: Peasants, Workers, and Factionalism

1. W.J. Johnson and R.E.H. Crosbie, *Report of a Committee on the Economic Conditions of Agriculturists in Palestine and the Fiscal Measures of Government in Relation Thereto* (Jerusalem, 1930), p. 29. Johnson was government Treasurer, Crosbie was Southern DC.

2. Abu-Lughod, "The Demographic Transformation," p. 155.

3. By 1923 nearly 75 percent of musha' lands were owned by individuals who lived in the towns. Somewhere between 2.6 million to 3.3 million dunums of musha' land were owned by absentee landlords. See Stein, The Land Question, p. 15.

4. Sarah Graham-Brown, "The Political Economy of the Jabal Nablus, 1920–48," in Owen, Studies, p. 109.

5. HC to CO, 30 Apr. 1941, CO 733/76048/41/42/43.

6. Sayigh, From Peasants to Revolutionaries, p. 48. Italics in original.

7. For a detailed discussion of all the issues relating to land tenure and agricultural production, see Graham-Brown, "The Political Economy," pp. 113–37.

8. Ibid., p. 121.

9. Although there is controversy over Jewish ownership, Stein's work, The Land Question, is the most recent and best researched on the issue. See appendix 2, p. 226. The figures are based on registered purchases and exclude government concessions.

10. See Stein, ibid., p. 83, and pp. 105–08.

11. CO memo, 1943, FO 371/35040. 4,807,260 dunums of the total was uncultivable land.

12. Stein, The Land Question, p. 157, says the final tally of 899 landless made by Lewis French and the Development Department in the early 1930s was not "demonstrative of anything except a Jewish Agency political victory." The Department, formed to deal with the landless problem, relied heavily on the J.A. for documentation and opinions and all claims went to the J.A. before a final decision was taken. Nevertheless, Stein does not venture to give estimates of Arab landlessness caused by Jewish land purchases. It is instructive to note, however, that the purchase of Wadi Hawarith lands (an area about 30 miles south of Haifa) in 1929, alone caused the eviction of 900 (out of 1,200) tenants (Stein, pp. 76–79). Polk et. al., Backdrop to Tragedy, pp. 236–38, say 8,000 peasants were evicted in one sale alone in 1921; while Porath, The Palestinian Arab, p. 90, thinks the total figure "did not exceed a few thousand."

13. Calculated from Stein, ibid., p. 182, table 13.

14. Lesch, Arab Politics, p. 69.

15. Porath, The Palestinian Arab, p. 129. The word is Porath's. The Jewish population increased from 175,000 in 1931 to 355,000 in 1935.

16. PG, Dept. of Stat., "Survey of Social and Economic Conditions in Arab Villages, 1944," Gen. Month. Bul. of Cur. Stat. (Jerusalem, Dec. 1945), p. 756.

17. Sir John Hope-Simpson, Report on Immigration, Land Settlement and Development (London, 1930), p. 143. Hope-Simpson extrapolated the landless figure on the basis of the Johnson-Crosbie survey. The latter is based on a sample of 104 villages representing 23,573 families. It was found that 6,940 families, or 29.4 percent, were laborers (landless). Stein, The Land Question, pp. 108–11, criticizes this extrapolation and argues that endogenous socio-economic dynamics were overlooked.

18. R.R. Nathan, O. Gass, and D. Creamer, Palestine: Problems and Promise (Washington, D.C., 1946), p. 196. The figure was given without clarification as to how it was arrived at. For our purpose it is used as a rough indicator.

19. This assumption is borne out by the following figures from a table on size of ownership in Stein, *The Land Question*, p. 28 (collected from Rural Property Tax records): In the Safad subdistrict, out of a total of 4,657 owners, a mere 76 owned over 500 *dunums*. The corresponding figures for the Acre and Haifa subdistricts were 57 out of 9,308 and 25 out of 3,276, respectively.

20. Ylana Miller, "Administrative Policy in Rural Palestine: The Impact of British Norms on Arab Community Life, 1920-1948," in Migdal, *Palestinian Society*, p. 129.

21. The following short discussion is based on Y.N. Miller, *Government and Society in Rural Palestine 1920-1948* (Austin, 1985).

22. See Miller, *ibid.*, pp. 79-86, on the lack of government social and economic services and programs. Also Stein, *The Land Question*, pp. 16-18, 146-47.

23. On educational policy see especially Miller, *ibid.*, pp. 90-97. The British also emphasized elementary education but purposely neglected secondary education for fear it would upset occupational patterns and stability.

24. In addition to Miller, see Tarif Khalidi, "Palestinian Historiography: 1900-1948," *Journal of Palestine Studies*, 10 (1980), esp. pp. 68-70.

25. Miller, *Government and Society*, p. 97. In March 1940, HC MacMichael appointed a committee to investigate social conditions. He expressed "shock and embarrassment" at its finding: 56 percent of all applicants for education in towns were rejected on account of lack of accommodation and 85 percent of the *fellahin* were still illiterate. See HC to CO 30 Apr. 1941 CO 733/76048/41/42/43.

26. George Mansur, *The Arab Worker Under the Palestine Mandate* (Jerusalem, 1937), p. 14, estimated 11,000 migrant workers alone lived in the shantytowns of Jaffa.

27. On the subject of the rise of Arab nationalism during this time, see C. Ernest Dawn, *From Ottomanism to Arabism* (Urbana, Ill., 1973); and Zeine N. Zeine, *The Emergence of Arab Nationalism* (Beirut, 1966). Most recently, See Muslih's discussion on Arabism and Ottomanism in his *The Origins of Palestinian Nationalism*, p. 58-68.

28. Bernard Wasserstein, " 'Clipping the Claws of the Colonisers': Arab Officials in the Government of Palestine, 1917-48," *Middle Eastern Studies*, 13 (1977), pp. 171, 174.

29. See Aida Ali Najjar, "The Arabic Press and Nationalism in Palestine, 1920-1948" (Syracuse Univ. Ph.D. thesis 1975), chap. 2. A leading role was played by the two dailys, *Filastin* and *al-Karmil*, both published by Christians, 'Isa al-'Isa brothers in Jaffa and Najib al-Nassar in Haifa, respectively. For this and the political significance of the Arab press reaction to Zionism between 1908-1914, also see Muslih, *The Origins*, pp. 65, 78-87.

30. See Kayyali, *Palestine: A Modern History*, pp. 54-56, 107-09, 157-59.

31. See in this regard Miller, *Government and Society*, pp. 22ff; also Stein, *The Land Question*, pp. 65-70.

32. Quoted in Kayyali, *Palestine*, p. 157.

33. Rachelle L. Taqqu, "Arab Labor in Mandatory Palestine, 1920-1948" (Columbia Univ. Ph.D. thesis 1977), p. 58.

34. *Survey*, i, pp. 336-42.

35. The Jewish Nesher Cement works employed some 300 Arabs (the Jewish

labor only policy was not successful until after 1936, at the time of the Arab rebellion) and Palestine Potash Ltd. (British-Jewish) employed up to 700. See CO 852/499/1941. Jewish sources say up to 8,000 Arabs worked on Jewish-owned groves at the peak of the season, no doubt an exaggerated figure. See Taqqu, "Arab Labor," p. 59.

36. See Taqqu, "Arab Labor," pp. 84–98, 106–12 for a detailed discussion of this and related points.

37. First Interim Report of Employment Committee, 27 Oct. 1944, CO 733/469/76284/45.

38. *Ibid.*

39. Nathan *et. al.,* *Palestine: Problem and Promise,* p. 213.

40. Memo on food production by Director of Department of Agriculture, Sept. 1942, CO 852/469/5/42.

41. See *Survey,* i, pp. 364–68, in which a study of eight sub-districts was made.

42. Taqqu, "Arab Labor," pp. 187–88 or Taqqu, "Peasants into Workmen: Internal Labor Migration and the Arab Village Community Under the Mandate," in Migdal, *Palestinian Society,* p. 281. "Incomplete and inconsistent" are her words.

43. Taqqu, "Arab Labor," pp. 223–24.

44. In Jaffa, out of a population of 72,000 by 1945, 70 percent lived in slum conditions; in Haifa, with an Arab population of over 65,000 by the same year, 41 percent lived in slum conditions. See the statistics and descriptions in *Survey,* ii, pp. 691–96.

45. For an account of the history of PAWS and the Arab labor movement and its political interaction with the established leadership, see 'Abd al-Qadir Yasin, "al-tabaqa al-'umaliya wa al-haraka al-siyasia fi filastin," *Shu'un Filastiniya,* 33 (1976); and Hani al-Hindi, "malahathat hawl awda' al-tabaqa al-'arabiya al-'amila fi filastin fi 'ahd al-intidab," *Shu'un Filastiniya,* 32 (1974).

46. See a confidential note from CS to HC, 14 Aug. 1942 ISA, R.G.2, I/LAB/31/42. The CS wrote the HC that "Government attaches great importance to the encouragement and development . . . of Arab trade unionism. . . ."

47. Annual Report of the Department of Labour, 1942, CO 733/441/75430/42–43.

48. Note on "Progress of the Palestine Arab Trade Union Movement During 1943," by Inspector of Labour for Jerusalem Region, E.M. Chudleigh, 13 Sept. 1943, ISA, R.G.2, I/LAB/31/42.

49. *Survey,* ii, p. 764.

50. Memo from the Central Committee of PAWS, meeting at Nazareth, to HC, 14 Jan. 1946, ISA, R.G.2, G/41/45, 1945/46.

51. From Arab Labor Society Secretary Jamal Hamid, Safad, to Safad DC, 24 Feb. 1937, R.G. 27, S225:27-2681.

52. See district commissioners' reports (under "Societies") from the Galilee District in ISA, R.G.27, on the formation of numerous PAWS branches. The government and CO were suspicious of these developments, albeit they did not try to stop them. The CS wrote the HC that: "it is difficult to see the object of trade unions in villages, and it will be recalled that other prima facie harmless organizations (e.g., the Boy Scouts) have been turned in the past to illicit purposes." CS to HC, which was forwarded to Galilee DC, 28 Sept. 1943, ISA R.G.2, I/LAB/31/42.

53. Miller, *Government and Society,* pp. 147–48. *Mukhtars* included a wide range of individuals: men of little status as well as large landowners; some who represented a whole village or villages; and others who represented narrow kinship or religious groups. See Miller, p. 146.

54. Miller, "Administrative Policy in Rural Palestine," in Migdal, *Palestinian Society,* p. 140.

55. I. Khattar, Assistant Inspector of Labour, Haifa, to Inspector for Northern Region, 19 May 1945, ISA, R.G.2, I/LAB/31/42.

56. A note on FATU by E.M. Chudleigh, Inspector General of Jerusalem Region, 15 July 1943, ISA, R.G.2, I/LAB/31/42.

57. *Ibid.*

58. PG report on the development of Communism in Palestine, 27 Apr. 1946, FO 371/52621. Also see Y. Porath, "'Usbat al-Taharrur al-Watani (The National Liberation League), 1943–1948," *Asian and African Studies,* 4 (1986), pp. 7–9.

59. PG report, *ibid.* 'Amr headed the League at the same time he was on the Executive Committee of the Arab Workers Congress, made up of independent—PAWS branches—labor groups.

60. See Taqqu, "Arab Labor," p. 300.

61. The following discussion on government policy is based largely on Taqqu, *ibid.,* pp. 212–21, with whose conclusions I am in agreement.

62. On the Communist party see J. Beinen, "The Palestine Communist Party, 1919–1949," *MERIP,* 55 (Washington, 1977).

63. PG report on the development of Communism in Palestine, 27 April 1946, FO 371/52621. On the League see also Walter Z. Laqueur, *Communism and Nationalism in the Middle East* (New York, 1956), pp. 110–12; and Porath, "'Usbat al-Taharrur," pp. 7–11ff.

64. See statement by Emile Tuma at the Arab Office Press Conference, 6 June 1947, C.I.D. Headquarters, Jerusalem, 12 Aug. 1947, CO 537/2281.

Chapter 3. Notables, Merchants, and Capitalists in the Arab Political Economy

1. Himadeh, "Industry," in Himadeh, *Economic Organization,* p. 216.

2. D. Horowitz and R. Hinden, *Economic Survey of Palestine with Special Reference to the Years 1936 and 1937* (Tel Aviv, 1938), p. 208.

3. Great Britain, *Report of the Palestine Royal Commission* (London, 1937), p. 210.

4. See Horowitz and Hinden, *Economic Survey,* pp. 9–14.

5. *Ibid.,* p. 209. The authors do not make it clear, however, how much of this money went to non-Palestinian absentees.

6. See Asad, "Anthropological Texts," pp. 15–21.

7. HC to CO, 3 July 1943, CO 733/75873/5/42–43/pt. 2.

8. From Accountant General's Office, Jerusalem, to Chief Secretary, 19 Sept. 1946, ISA, R.G. 2, F/205/46.

9. Fu'ad Saba's evidence, at the 59th and 62nd meetings, to the Peel (Royal) Commission, 16 Jan. 1937, *Minutes of Evidence Heard at Public Sessions* (London, 1937). Saba served as secretary to the AHC.

10. Evidence of George Mansur (Arab labor spokesman) to the Peel Commission, *ibid.*

11. Royal Commission, *Report*, p. 129. The average share of customs and excise duties as between Arabs and Jews was: Jews, 61 percent; Arabs, 39 percent. See HC to CO on a report by the Financial Secretary, 10 Sept. 1946, CO 733/472/3.

12. In 1943 the Jews paid 61.7 percent of the income tax; Arabs, 14.4 percent; foreign companies, 18.8 percent; and "others" the balance. See note by Financial Secretary on financial policy, 15 Feb. 1945, CO 733/450/75005/45.

13. Taqqu, "Arab Labor," p. 62.

14. Minutes of meeting of War Supply Board Members, Jerusalem, 18 Sept. 1942, with visiting Minister of State from Cairo, CO 852/506/21/42.

15. M.A. Novomeysky, co-director of Palestine Potash Ltd., in a pamphlet entitled *Quo Vadis?*, summarizing the advances of Jewish industry, Jerusalem, 1945, CO 852/576/11/46.

16. *Survey*, i, pp. 446, 506.

17. See minutes of War Supply Board meeting, 18 Sept. 1942, CO 852/506/21/42.

18. From Haifa Chamber of Commerce to Chief Secretary, 30 Sept. 1945, complaining about the high cost of Jewish made products as compared to British products, CO 733/471/76436/46.

19. PG, *Statistical Abstract of Palestine, 1944-45* (Jerusalem, 1946), pp. 52-53.

20. Article by M.A. Novomeysky, 1945, CO 852/576/11/46.

21. *Statistical Abstract*, pp. 52-53.

22. *Ibid.*, pp. 52, 58.

23. Article by M.A. Novomeysky, CO 852/576/11/46.

24. *Statistical Abstract*, p. 52.

25. *Ibid.*, pp. 52-53, 58.

26. The Arabs accumulated more than $157,000,000 in foreign assets, "almost exclusively in sterling assets." Deposits in the two banks grew from a total of $5,300,000 in Dec. 1942 to $27,884,000 in Oct. 1945. See J.C. Hurewitz, *The Struggle for Palestine*, 2nd ed. (New York, 1968), p. 189.

27. The first is from Salim Tamari, "Factionalism and Class Formation," in Owen, *Studies*, p. 239; the second is from Shulamit Carmi and Henry Rosenfeld, "The Origins of the Process of Proletarianization and Urbanization of the Arab Peasants in Palestine," *Annals of the NY Acad. of S.*, 220 (1974), pp. 470-85.

28. Taysir Nashif, "Palestinian Arab and Jewish Leadership in the Mandate Period," *Journal of Palestine Studies*, 24 (1977), p. 117. In addition, 1 was a tribal chief; there was no information on the other, thus totalling 32.

29. Bayan N. al-Hout, "The Palestinian Political Elite During the Mandate Period," *Journal of Palestine Studies*, 9 (1979), p. 103, table 9. The sample exceeds 100 because the author counted those that were actively engaged in more than one occupation.

30. *Ibid.*, pp. 104-07, on which the following description and quotes of income levels are based.

31. See, for example, S.D. Goitein, *Studies in Islamic History and Institutions* (Leiden, 1966), pp. 217-41. For a similar, "Marxist Orientalist" approach which demonstrates the amenability of Islam to commercial relations, see Maxime

Rodinson, *Islam and Capitalism* (Harmondsworth, England 1974).

32. HC to CO, 28 Sept. 1936, ISA, R.G. 2, C/320/36.

33. From Arab Chamber of Commerce, Jerusalem, to Chief Secretary, 23 Apr. 1947, ISA, R.G. 2, C/80/46/X.

34. From Jaffa Chamber of Commerce to Commissioner of Trade and Industries, 13 June 1946, ISA, R.G. 9, DCI/1-6-4/1:9 1348.

35. Director of Labour to Chief Secretary, 3 Nov. 1945, ISA, R.G. 2, I/LAB/1/45. A report by the Regional Inspector on a conference of Arab Trade Union Congress held in Jerusalem to discuss unemployment.

36. See Samih Farsoun and Karen Farsoun, "Class and Patterns of Association Among Kinsmen in Contemporary Lebanon," *Anthropological Quarterly*, 47 (1974), pp. 93-111, for the use of such concepts in the case of Lebanon.

37. See Hanna Batatu, *The Old Social Classes and the Revolutionary Movements of Iraq* (Princeton, 1978), pp. 271-72.

38. It should be noted, however, that in countries like Syria and 'Iraq the self-ruling governments helped put the merchants on their feet through guaranteed markets or preferential state contracts and various exemptions from taxes and import duties, policies that in Palestine applied to Jewish industry.

39. Calculations based on figures in Taqqu, "Arab Labor," p. 228.

40. *Ibid.*, p. 228.

41. Graham-Brown, "The Political Economy," p. 138.

42. Tiberias Chamber of Commerce to District Officer, 1 Nov. 1944, ISA, R.G. 27, T495: 24-2692.

43. Graham-Brown, "The Political Economy," pp. 141-42.

44. Migdal, "Urbanization and Political Change," esp. pp. 335-46.

Chapter 4. The Backdrop: British Policy and Palestinian Politics in Regard to the White Paper, 1939-41

1. Lesch, *Arab Politics*, p. 217.

2. Lesch, *ibid.*, p. 220.

3. For descriptions of the partition proposal and its impact on Arab opinion, see the following: Kayyali, *Palestine*, p. 207; Porath, *The Palestinian Arab*, p. 228; and Howard M. Sacher, *Europe Leaves the Middle East* (New York, 1972), pp. 79-81. For the Zionist reaction (they also rejected the proposals) see Avi Shlaim, *Collusion Across the Jordan* (New York, 1988), pp. 57-65.

4. For example, of some 135,000 *dunum*s of Arab-owned citrus plantations, 87,000 *dunum*s would fall under the Jewish state. The rural Arab population living in the citrus area (that is, dependent on the industry) of the proposed Jewish state would have been 60,000 alone, not to mention 80,000 in towns, chiefly Haifa. In addition, many absentee owners, transport workers, and shippers living outside the citrus area but inside the Jewish state (a population of 165,000) would be at a severe disadvantage. See CS Ormsby-Gore to HC, Sir Arthur Wauchope, 14 Sept. 1937, ISA, R.G. 2, X/69/37.

5. HC to CO, 2 Jan. 1939, CO 733/398/75156.

6. See the Tegart Papers at St. Antony's College Personal Papers Collection

(Oxford) for documentation of the things enumerated. Also see CO 733/406/75872/123B for cases and complaints. Phillip Mattar, *The Mufti of Jerusalem* (New York, 1988), pp. 83, 90, also documents these practices, and adds that the British and Zionist forces indiscriminately bombed and shot civilians, "used suspects as human minesweepers," executed Palestinians for minor offenses, and cooperated with the Nashashibis to assassinate rebels.

7. Michael J. Cohen, *Palestine, Retreat From the Mandate: The Making of British Policy, 1936–45* (London, 1978), p. 66.

8. Lesch, *Arab Politics,* p. 178.

9. Ahmad M. Gomaa, *The Foundation of the League of Arab States: War Time Diplomacy and Inter-Arab Politics, 1941 to 1945* (London, 1977), pp. 9–10.

10. Great Britain, *Statement of Policy Presented by the Secretary of State for the Colonies to Parliament* (London, 1939), para. 10 (4).

11. *Ibid.,* para. 10 (6).

12. Cohen, *Retreat,* p. 83.

13. See Lesch, *Arab Politics,* p. 176, footnote 71.

14. Cohen, *Retreat,* p. 86.

15. See CO memo on these points by H.F. Downie, 21 Feb. 1941, CO 733/426/75872/85.

16. Cohen, *Retreat,* pp. 82–85. Also see Thomas Mayer, *Egypt and the Palestine Question, 1936–1945* (Berlin, 1983), pp. 127–33.

17. See reports of increasing activity among rebels and reports of political developments: HC to CO, 23 Feb. 1939, CO 733/406/75872/6; HC to CO, 5 July 1939, CO 733/398/75156; HC to CO, 28 Sept. 1939, CO 733/415/75984.

18. See report of Junieh meeting, from H̄C̄ to C̄O, 27 Feb. 1939, CO 733/398/75/75156. The minimum demands were: restricted Jewish immigration—perhaps 5,000–10,000 a year—restriction on land sales, and establishment of an elective assembly whose members would be proportionate to the strength of the respective communities.

19. From Consul-General Havard in Beirut to FO, 7 June 1939, FO 371/23237, submitting translation of AHC's rejection.

20. Khairiah Qasmiah, ed., *'Awni 'Abd al-Hadi: Awraq Khassa* (Beirut, 1974), p. 118. The Arab states privately also tried to convince the Palestinians to accept the White Paper. 'Ali Maher Pasha argued it was the best the Arabs could hope for in the present "miserable situation." See summary of Arab-Palestinian discussions in Cairo, Lampson to FO, 17 May 1939, FO 371/23236. Also Qasmiah, pp. 116–18.

21. HC to CO, 28 May 1939, CO 733/398/75156.

22. 'Abd al-Latif Salah declined to accept the AHC's offer of advisory status to the Palestinian delegation. "He expected a separate British invitation and denied the Mufti the right to select the Delegation." Porath, *The Palestinian Arab,* p. 282.

23. This is what Ghusayn in effect said when he asked in a conversation with Heath of Palestine Police whether it was possible to give assurance to those willing to cooperate that they would be the persons appointed to heads of departments. Sir M. Lampson to FO, 3 June, FO 371/23237.

24. Qasmiah, *'Abd al-Hadi,* p. 123.

25. See Sir M. Lampson to FO, 15 June 1939, FO 371/23237, and Cairo British Embassy to FO, 15 June 1939, FO 371/23238.
26. HC to CO, 14 Jan. 1940, FO 371/24565.
27. From British Embassy to FO, 22 July 1939, FO 371/23239, enclosing report by K. Heath on his conversations with 'Awni.
28. Cairo to FO, 29 July 1939, FO 371/23239, enclosing conversation between 'Abd al-Hadi and Oriental Secretary.
29. 'Abd al-Hadi's word, *ibid.*
30. From Lampson to FO, 3 Dec. 1939, FO 371/24565, according to report of a conversation between 'Awni and Oriental Secretary.
31. Gomaa, The *Foundation*, p. 22.
32. *Ibid.*, p. 22. On the Newcombe mission and the Mufti's collaboration with 'Iraqi nationalists, see also Mattar, *The Mufti*, pp. 92–93.
33. Newcombe to FO, 24 June 1946, FO 371/52587. Newcombe was writing in defense of the Mufti, whom the British by then (1946) wanted because of his Axis activities.
34. Oriental Minister Moyne to CS Stanley, 2 Oct. 1944, FO 371/45411, recounting the 1940 events in order to establish that Jamal was worthy of return to Palestine from his exile.
35. See situation report, HC to CO, 27 Feb. 1939, CO 733/398/75156.
36. MacMichael's description—HC to CO, 27 June 1940, CO 733/426/75872/85/40.
37. HC to CO, 27 Feb. 1939, CO 733/398/75156.
38. HC to CO, 11 July 1939, CO 733/406/75872/12.
39. *Ibid.*
40. See HC to CO, 30 May 1939, on MacMichael's meeting with the NDP delegation, CO 733/406/75872/12. The delegation included Raghib Bey, who had returned to Palestine by May 1939, Sulayman Tuqan of Nablus, Haj 'Adil al-Shawwa of Gaza, 'Abd al-Ra'uf Bitar of Jaffa, Farid Irshayd of Jenin, and representatives of the municipal authorities of Shefa 'Amr (in Galilee) and Hebron.
41. HC to CO, 30 May 1939, CO 733/406/75872/12.
42. HC to CO, enclosing NDP signed by Raghib, 15 Aug. 1939, CO 733/406/75872/12.
43. HC to CO, 30 May 1939, *ibid.*
44. See report on Muzaffar and others, HC to CO, 27 June 1940, CO 733/426/75872/85/40.
45. See Kirkbride's report dated 14 June 1940 as it was dispatched to London, HC to CO, 27 June 1940, CO 733/426/75872/40.
46. *Ibid.*
47. Kirkbirde's comments, *ibid.*
48. Lloyd to HC, 14 Aug. 1940 and 9 Sept. 1940, CO 733/426/75872/85.
49. *Ibid.*
50. See HC to CO, enclosing record of interview with S. Tuqan, 27 Jan. 1941, CO 733/44/75872/114/1941.
51. Tuqan's version of the discussion, *ibid.*
52. Tuqan's comments to HC, *ibid.*

53. MacMichael's talk with Tuqan, *ibid.*

54. See HC to CO, 24 Mar. 1941 and 23 June 1941 on reports of meetings and lists of individuals who attended and the districts they hailed from, CO 733/44/ 75871/114/1941.

55. Porath, *The Palestinian Arab*, p. 66.

56. *Ibid.*, p. 67.

57. See *ibid.*, pp. 73–74. It is of interest to note that, regarding the Peel Commission partition proposal of 1937, the NDP, basically Raghib Bey, quickly publicly dissociated itself from 'Abdullah when the Amir publicly announced his acceptance. See Mary C. Wilson, *King Abdullah, Britain and the Making of Jordan* (Cambridge, England, 1987), p. 123.

58. See Porath's discussion on the *Istiqlal, The Palestinian Arab*, pp. 124–26.

59. Lesch, *Arab Politics*, pp. 105–06.

60. Porath, *The Palestinian Arab*, pp. 163–65; also see Kayyali, *Palestine*, p. 189.

61. Lesch, *Arab Politics*, pp. 105–06.

62. Porath, *The Palestinian Arab*, pp. 124–25.

63. *Ibid.*, pp. 75–77.

64. *Ibid.*, p. 79.

65. *Ibid.*, p. 77.

66. See *al-Difa'*, 1/3/4 May, 1944. *Al-Difa'*, which in the thirties reflected the opinions of *Istiqlal*, became a strong Husayni supporter. See also Hurewitz, *The Struggle*, p. 185. Thirty-nine delegates attended the meeting in Jerusalem.

67. For examples of these branches and their correspondence with Jerusalem, see ISA R.G. 65/3, files 1851, 1885, 1866, 3508, 3600, in Arabic.

68. ISA, R.G. 65/3, file 2411 ("Central Office: Meetings and Names of Members, 1945–46," in Arabic).

69. Bayan al-Hut, *al-qiyadat wal-mu'assasat al-siyasiya fi filastin, 1917–1948* (Beirut, 1981), appendix, doc. no. 58, p. 900. The eleven were: Farid al-'Anabtawi (Nablus), Musa al-Surani (Gaza), Ibrahim Sa'id al-Husayni and Muhammad Rafiq al-Husayni (Jerusalem), Rafiq al-Tamimi (Jaffa), Kamil al-Dajani (Jaffa), Muhammad al-Ja'bari (Hebron), Rashad al-Khatib (Hebron), Yusif Sahyun (Haifa), Michel 'Azir (Jaffa), and 'Abdullah Samara (Tulkarem). Eight of these were landowners/merchants.

70. HC to CO, 27 Jan. 1942, CO 733/439/75156/1943/1942–43.

71. Hurewitz, *The Struggle*, p. 185.

Chapter 5. Notable Politics I: Futile Exercises in Leadership

1. See Gomaa, *The Foundation*, pp. 69–70; also Y. Porath, *In Search of Arab Unity, 1930–1945* (London, 1986), pp. 151–52.

2. James Jankowski, "The Egyptian Wafd and Arab Nationalism, 1918–1944," in Edward Ingrams, ed., *National and International Politics in the Middle East* (London, 1986), p. 176.

3. Mayer, *Egypt and the Palestine Question*, p. 181.

4. Qasmiah, *'Awni 'Abd al-Hadi*, pp. 128–29. However, 'Abd al-Hadi, along with Musa al-'Alami, al-Haj Ibrahim, and Ahmad Hilmi, disagreed with the un-

clear implications of Jewish immigration contained in Nuri's semi-autonomy scheme for the Jews. See 'Abd al-Hadi's letter to Nuri, Qasmiah, pp. 129–30.

5. HC to CO, 27 May 1943, CO 733/439/75156/1943/1942–43.

6. HC to CO, 25 Feb. 1943, *ibid.*

7. Al-Hut, *al-qiyadat,* p. 470.

8. *Ibid.,* p. 471.

9. *Ibid.,* p. 471. Al-Hut relies on Husayn Fakhri al-Khalidi's unpublished memoirs, held in a "private library" in Beirut, for her information.

10. *Ibid.,* p. 471.

11. HC to CO, 31 Jan. 1944, FO 371/39987. Nuri told these things to Amir 'Abdullah on 29 Jan. on his way back to Baghdad.

12. Lydda DC to CO, 18 May 1945, CO 733/456/75156/119/ pt.1.

13. Al-Hut, *al-qiyadat* p. 473.

14. Lydda DC to CO, 18 May 1945, CO 733/456/75156/119/ pt.1.

15. Jerusalem DC to CO, 6 Oct. 1945, CO 733/75156/119/45/pt. 2.

16. See Najjar, "The Arabic Press and Nationalism in Palestine," p. 175.

17. HC to CO, 30 Oct. 1945, CO 733/456/75156/143/44.

18. Jerusalem DC to CO, 6 Oct. 1945, CO 733/75156/119/45/pt. 2.

19. Samaria DC to CO, 8 Oct. 1945, CO 733/456/75156/119/pt. 1.

20. Jerusalem DC to CO, 6 Oct. 1945, CO 733/75156/119/45/pt. 2.

21. Jaffa DC to CO, 6 Oct. 1945, CO 733/456/75156/119/pt. 1.

22. See al-Hut, *al-qiyadat,* for a summary of the party, pp. 473–74.

23. See a letter from al-Nimr to HC, 7 May 1945, ISA, R.G. 2, Pol/16/44.

24. *Ibid.*

25. Ihsan al-Nimr, Nablus, to HC, 10 Dec. 1944, ISA R.G. 2, Pol/16/44.

26. See al-Hut, *al-qiyadat,* p. 542. The telegrams were from Tewfiq Salih. They were vague and confused, saying the PAP desired Arab opinion on "present affairs" and then asking for the release of Jamal who was, according to Salih, "giving up on life" in his exile, i.e., desperate and despondent.

27. 'Izzat Darwaza, *al-qadiya al-filastiniya fi mukhtalaf marahilha* (Sidon, 1960), sec. 2, pp. 39–40. Also al-Hut, *ibid.,* p. 542, and appendix, doc. no. 56, p. 899.

28. See following files on such representations: ISA, R.G. 2, Pol/15/44; ISA, R.G. 2, Pol 3/45; ISA, R.G. 2, Pol/12/45; and ISA, R.G. 2, Pol/15/45.

29. From Tewfiq Salih al-Husayni to HC, 1 June 1945, ISA R.G. 2, Pol/15/45. The party held a similar mass rally and other meetings in November 1944. See *Al-Difa',* 1 Dec. 1944 and 28 Feb. 1945; also *Filastin,* 10/13 Nov. 1944.

30. See PG memo on Palestinian Arab politics, 24 July 1945, FO 371/45417.

31. See memo on the National Fund from HC to CO, 9 July 1947, CO 537/2281.

32. *Ibid.*

33. Gaza DC's fortnightly report to CO, 6 May 1945, CO 733/456/75156/119/ pt. 1.

34. *Ibid.*

35. See a "Note on potential Arab political violence in Palestine," by the PG, Apr. 1946, FO 371/52526.

36. *Ibid.*

37. See CO 537/1707, DC reports.

38. A "Note on potential Arab political violence."
39. Galilee DC's fortnightly report to CO, 6 May 1945, CO 733/456/75156/119/pt. 1.
40. *Ibid.*
41. PG memo on 'Alami's Land Development Scheme, 9 July 1947, CO 537/2281.
42. Memo on National Fund, HC to CO, 9 July 1947, CO 537/2281. The others were Muhammad Yunis al-Husayni (Gaza), Ahmad al-'Aki (?), 'Issa Bsisu (Gaza), Muhammad 'Ali al-Ja'bari (Hebron).
43. *Ibid.*
44. Jerusalem DC to CO, 5 June 1945, CO 733/456/75156/119/pt. 1.
45. Memo on Palestinian Arab politics, 24 July 1945, FO 371/45417.
46. *Ibid.*
47. *Ibid.*
48. Muhammad Khalil, ed., *The Arab States and the Arab League* (Beirut, 1962), ii, p. 61.
49. On 2 Apr. 1945 Tewfiq Salih, 'Abd al-Hadi, 'Abd al-Latif Salah, and Ghusayn met at Raghib al-Nashashibi's house to formulate a response to the Annex on Palestine. They argued on a number of legal points, including that Palestine was prepared for self-rule, as was the ostensible *raison d'etre* of the mandate, and on the natural rights of the Arabs. See Qasmiah, *'Awni 'Abd al-Hadi,* pp. 130 (including footnote 8)–31.
50. Al-Hut, *al-qiyadat,* pp. 539–40. In the "Special Resolution" on Palestine of the Alexandria Protocal, made in Oct. 1944, the League Council maintained that Palestine constituted an "important" part of the Arab world; that "cessation" of immigration, "preservation" of Palestinian lands, and "achievement" of Palestinian independence were "permanent" Arab rights. See Khalil, *The Arab States,* ii, p. 55.
51. Al-Hut, *ibid.,* p. 540.
52. Mayer, *Egypt and the Palestine Question,* p. 293.
53. *Ibid.,* p. 293.
54. Memo on 'Alami's Land Development Scheme, 9 Aug. 1947, CO 537/2281.
55. Memo on Palestinian Arab politics, 24 July 1945, FO 371/45417.
56. Al-Hut, *al-qiyadat,* p. 548.
57. Memo on Palestinian Arab politics, 24 July 1945, FO 371/45417.
58. Memo on 'Alami's Land Development Scheme, 9 July 1947, CO 537/2281.
59. Memo on Palestinian Arab politics, 24 July 1945, FO 371/45417.
60. Memo on National Fund, HC to CO, 9 July 1947, CO 537/2281.
61. Al-Hut, *al-qiyadat,* p. 548.
62. Memo on Palestinian Arab politics, 24 July 1945, FO 371/45417.
63. Al-Hut, *al-qiyadat,* p. 550.
64. Memo on National Fund, HC to CO, 9 July 1947, CO 537/2281.
65. Mayer, *Egypt and the Palestine Question,* pp. 291–95.
66. Memo on National Fund, HC to CO, 9 July 1947, CO 537/2281.
67. A clipped article from *al-Wihda* (no title indicated), 16 June 1945, FO 371/45417.
68. See the reproduced documents of Churchill's memos and correspondence in Gavriel Cohen, *Churchill and Palestine, 1939–1942* (Jerusalem, 1976).
69. Churchill to Eden, 30 May 1941, doc. reproduced in *ibid.*

70. For a full discussion of the background to the Biltmore program, see Evan M. Wilson, *Decision on Palestine: How the U.S. Came to Recognize Israel* (Stanford, 1979), chap. 1.

71. Halifax to FO, 9 Jan 1944, FO 371/40133.

72. See Evan M. Wilson, "The Palestine Papers, 1943–1947," *Journal of Palestine Studies*, 2 (1973), p. 43.

73. See meeting of War Cabinet on 2 July 1943, CO 733/444/75872/A/43. The WCCP was created in July 1943 and was composed of the following men: Herbert Morrison (in chair), Home Secretary; Viscount Cranborne, Lord Privy Seal; Oliver Stanley, Colonial Secretary; L.S. Amery, Secretary of State for India and Burma, an avid exponent of partition; Archibald Sinclair, Secretary of State for Air; and Richard Law, Parliamentary Under Secretary of State for Foreign Affairs. Law represented the FO view against partition.

74. See WCCP report on partition, 19 Dec. 1943, CO 733/461/75872/44/pt. 3. Partition, the breaking up of states, federation schemes, and the founding of satellite colonies for the Jews in North Africa (which Churchill suggested the WCCP consider, as an additional dimension of the Jewish state in Palestine) represented the surreal yet dangerous mentality of the colonial mind, prompting one FO official to comment on the discussions that "The general atmosphere was that the Zionists should take over Palestine and Trans-Jordania and most of the North African continent. When it gets down to hard tacks probably it won't be so wild." R.A. Butler's minute on the first meeting of the WCCP, 7 Aug. 1943, FO 371/35036.

75. See summary of views at conference, which took place on 6/7 Apr. 1944, in CO 733/461/75872/44/pt. 2.

76. See Grigg's memo to War Cabinet, 4 Apr. 1945, CO 733/461/75872/45/pt. 1.

77. See CO 733/461/75872/45/pt. 1.

78. Memo by D.G. Harris, 1 Sept. 1945, CO 733/463/75872/132/45.

79. From Gort to CO, 15 Dec. 1945, CO 733/463/75872/132/45.

80. Gort to CO, 15 Dec. 1945, *ibid.*

81. Memo by CS Hall, Sept. 1945, CO 733/463/75872/132/45.

82. Kenneth Ray Bain, *The March to Zion: United States Policy and the Founding of Israel, 1945–1948* (College Station, 1979), p. 71.

83. M.J. Cohen, *Palestine and the Great Powers, 1945–1948* (Princeton, 1982), pp. 45–48, maintains the theme that, because of Truman's provincialism and wide knowledge of domestic politics, and as a non-elected (and indeed highly unpopular) president during his first term, eager to succeed, he had more "mundane" (i.e., domestic politics, Jewish votes) reasons for "airing his sympathies for the Jewish victims."

84. Martin (FO) to Howe (CO), 10 Jan. 1946, FO 371/52504; and Bain, *The March*, chap. 4.

85. For a balanced discussion of the recommendations see Wilson, *Decision*, pp. 87–88.

86. Washington to FO, 30 Apr. 1946, FO 371/52519; and Bain, *The March*, pp. 120–21. The statement was written for him by Bartley Crum (one of the six Americans on the AAC and a pro-Zionist demogogue) and David Niles. See Wilson, *Decision*, p. 89.

87. Prime Minister to President, 26 May 1946, FO 371/52526.

88. Cohen, *Palestine and the Great Powers*, p. 121.

89. See Cohen, *ibid.*, pp. 116–34, for detailed analysis of the experts' committee discussions, or what became known as the Morrison-Grady report.

90. Wilson, *Decision*, p. 93.

91. Cohen, *Palestine and the Great Powers*, pp. 122–23.

92. *Ibid.*, pp. 123–24; and Bain, *The March*, p. 131.

93. Cohen, *ibid.*, pp. 128–32; Wilson, *Decision*, p. 94, and Bain, *ibid.*, pp. 128–30. Cohen says that "hanging over everything" was the "domestic political situation"—congressional elections in autumn. It should be added that part of Truman's non-acceptance of the scheme was due to opposition to it from the six members of the AAC, whom Truman consulted, on the basis that t would lead to partition.

94. See CO 537/1722; 1775; 1779; 1781; 1783; 2323; and 2324 for the detailed events and minutes of the Conference.

95. Refer to chap. 6, the section titled "Palestinian Politics in Relation to the London Conference."

96. See Bevin's opening remarks at the first and second meetings, 10 Sept. 1946 and 11 Sept. 1946, respectively, CO 537/1775.

97. Faris al-Khuri's remarks at the second meeting, *ibid.* Khuri at the time was president of the Syrian Chamber of Deputies.

98. The full text of the constitutional proposal is found in CO 537/1778.

99. Extract from conclusion of a Cabinet meeting held on 25 Oct. 1946, CO 537/1779.

100. HC to CO, 20 Sept. 1946, CO 537/1783.

101. On British-Zionist negotiations during the interim period see Choen, *Palestine and the Great Powers*, pp. 151–62. Also see meetings between FO, CO and Zionist officials, 1 Oct. 1946, CO 537/1779.

102. Meeting of CO officials, 27 Nov. 1946, CO 537/1783.

103. Conference minutes, ninth meeting, 30 Jan. 1947, CO 537/2324.

104. Cohen, *Palestine and the Great Powers*, p. 220.

Chapter 6. Notable Politics II: External Threat, Internal Domination

1. Eastwood of CO to Baxter of FO, 13 Apr. 1945, FO 371/45411.

2. *Ibid.*

3. Killearn)Cairo) to FO, 28 Mar. 1945, FO 371/45411.

4. Jedda to FO, 4 July 1945, FO 371/45411.

5. Lord Moyne, Oriental Secretary (in Egypt) to CS Oliver Stanley, 2 Oct. 1944, FO 371/45411.

6. Officer Administering the Government of Palestine (O.A.G.) to CO, 17 Nov. 1945, FO 371/45412.

7. Jamal entered Palestine on 4 Feb. through Ras al-Naqura (near the Lebanese border). He went by car from Acre to Nablus down to Ramallah then to Jerusalem. The PAP staged a big welcome at Naqura. According to the PAP's semi-official organ *al-Difa'*, motorcades and taxis carrying people from all

over the country went to greet him. Included were Muslim and Christian functionaries, notables, village *shaykh*s and the Boy Scouts. See *al-Difa'*, 4/7/8 Feb. 1946.

8. Paris to FO, 23 May 1945, FO 371/45420.

9. Paris to FO, 30 Aug. 1945, FO 371/45420. Those with him were: Hasan Abu Sa'ud, Mufti of Nablus; Safwat Husayn, landowner; Sa'd al-Din 'Abd al-Latif, journalist; Salim al-Husayni, *waqf* director (all from Jerusalem); Dr. Farhan Jandali, eye doctor from Homs; Dr. Zafer Rifa'i, lawyer from Aleppo; Yusif Ruessi, journalist from Tunis; Baha' Taba, merchant from Beirut; and Khalid Ramadan, chauffeur from Beirut.

10. *Ibid.*

11. O.A.G. to CO, 29 Sept. 1945, FO 371/45421.

12. *Ibid.* The British had the following evidence against the Mufti: 1) that he had broadcast from Berlin, Bari, Athens, and Rome "violently" attacking the British oppressors and hailing the German liberators; 2) that he was photographed with Hitler in Berlin and in 1942 sent a message to the Japanese Emperor assuring him that the Arabs were praying for a Japanese victory; 3) that the Italians tried to use him to influence Muslims of Hertzogovina and Croatia in favor of Italy. In 1944 he was sent to Yugoslavia to persuade Muslims to break with Marshal Tito, and in the same year he was photographed inspecting Arab quisling troops in Bosnia. See a memo to the Cabinet by the CS, Nov. 1945, FO 371/45421; also Mattar, *The Mufti*, p. 104.

13. *Ibid.*

14. Cabinet meeting, 27 Nov. 1945, FO 371/45421.

15. DC, Samaria, to CO, 4 Mar. 1946, CO 537/1707. See also *al-Difa'*, 8/9/11 Feb. and 2/3/5 Mar. 1946.

16. HC to CO, 21 Jan. 1946, FO 371/52585. 'Alami had visited the HC in order to get the authorities' support in his and Jamal's attempts to keep things cool until the AAC made its recommendation public. I found no record of who the Mufti's contacts were.

17. *Ibid.* Raja'i was an assistant secretary in the Government Secretariat and later joined the London Arab Office.

18. *Ibid.*

19. HC to CO, 2 Apr. 1946, FO 371/52528; and HC to CO, 12 July 1946, FO 371/52585. Again, no record of these people was found.

20. For the infighting and Darwaza's correspondence as seen through 'Abd al-Hadi's memoirs, see Qasmiah, *'Awni 'Abd al-Hadi*, pp. 141–42.

21. Al-Hut, *al-qiyadat*, p. 543.

22. *Ibid.*, p. 543. The author does not specify or list either names of individuals or organizations.

23. Darwaza, *al-qiyadat*, sec. 2, pp. 57–58; al-Hut, *ibid.*, appendix, doc. no. 52, p. 899; and Qasmiah, *'Awni 'Abd al-Hadi*, p. 142, footnote 6.

24. HC to CO, 2 Apr. 1946, FO 371/52514.

25. *Ibid.*

26. PG, "An Outline of Recent Developments of Communism in Palestine," 27 Apr. 1946, FO 371/52621.

27. Al-Hut, *al-qiyadat*, appendix, doc. no. 52, p. 899; and Darwaza, *al-qiyadat*, sec. 2, p. 57.
28. PG, "An Outline of Recent Developments of Communism," 27 Apr. 1946. FO 371/52561.
29. *Ibid.* Robert John and Sami Hadawi, The Palestine Diary (Beirut, 1970), ii, p. 41, say Jamal and 'Adb al-Hadi testified in front of the AAC as "representatives" of the AHC.
30. HC to CO, 20 May 1946, FO 371/52585. The quoted words are the HC's, supposedly expressed by 'Alami in his conversation with the former.
31. The White Paper immigration quota (75,000) was supposed to come to an end in March 1944 but the British prolonged it until the end of 1945 on the basis that it was not yet exhausted. At the announcement of the formation of the AAC in Nov., Bevin also asked the Arab states for a continuation of immigration above and beyond the quota, at 1,500 per month, pending a permanent settlement. Because the League answer was vague, HMG unilaterally renewed the quota in Jan. 1946. See CO 733/461/75872/45/pt. 5; and FO 371/52503.
32. See Qasmiah, *'Awni 'Abd al-Hadi*, p. 143.
33. *Ibid.*, p. 143.
34. HC to CO, 29 June 1946, CO 537/1772; also Darwaza, *al-qiyadat*, sec. 2, p. 58.
35. *Ibid.*
36. Al-Hut, *al-qiyadat*, p. 585. Significantly, in a resolution on the "higher Arab Executive" (12 June 1946), the Arab League strongly recommended the dissolution of the AHC and AHF, saying that their adherents should consider the AHE as the only representative body of the Palestine Arabs. See Khalil, *The Arab League*, ii, p. 162.
37. See FO 371/52587. The Mufti had left France on 8 June and travelled overland through Syria and Lebanon then by ship to Egypt.
38. HC to CO 12 July 1946, FO 371/52585.
39. See CO 537/1707 for DC reports.
40. Gaza DC, 20 June 1946, in CO 537/1707.
41. CO memo (by CS George Hall) to Cabinet, 26 July 1946, CO 537/1772.
42. HC (Cunningham) to CO, 28 July 1946, CO 537/1172.
43. Meeting between Jamal and Cunningham, 8 Aug. 1946, CO 537/1772.
44. CO to HC, 9 Aug. 1946, CO 537/1772.
45. *Ibid.*
46. *Ibid.*
47. HC to CO, 26 Aug. 1946, CO 537/1772.
48. Jamal's description of the Alexandria Conference to Cunningham, *ibid.*
49. *Ibid.*
50. HC to CO, 17 Aug. 1946, CO 537/1772.
51. CO to HC, 27 Aug. 1946, CO 537/1772.
52. HC to CO, 28 Aug. 1946, CO 537/1772.
53. *Ibid.*
54. *Ibid.*
55. HC to Co, 7 Sept. 1946, FO 371/52557, on a meeting he had with Haykal.

56. HC to CO, 28 Aug. 1946, CO 537/1772.

57. *Ibid.*

58. HC Cunningham, commenting on the Mufti's influence in connection with the London Conference, again reiterated his familiar views: "the Mufti is looked on throughout the whole country as a national hero and should he be in a position to bring his influence to bear on the Arabs of Palestine, I believe they would follow him almost to a man in whatever way he directed." HC to CO, 20 Sept. 1946, CO 537/1783.

59. HC to CO, 4 Feb. 1947, FO 371/61767. The invitation was conveyed by the PG on 10 Jan. 1947.

60. HC to CO, 4 Feb. 1947, situation report, CO 537/2281. Jamal's reply of acceptance said the AHC did not feel able to put forward any names suggested by the HC, reiterating that the AHC alone should be entirely free to nominate its own men. See HC to CO, 13 Jan. 1947, CO 537/2323.

61. HC to CO, 23 Jan. 1947, CO 537/2323. The HC referred to Sahyun as an "unpleasant nonentity," to Kamal as a "renegade," and to Khalil as "level headed" and "well balanced."

62. CO note on Mufti's activities, 14 Jan. 1947, FO 371/61834; and Qasmiah, *'Awni 'Abd al-Hadi,* p. 143, footnote 7.

63. HC to CO, 4 Feb. 1947, FO 371/61767.

64. *Filastin,* 17 Jan. 1947. The HC said that members of the NDP, "which is still influential in certain restricted localities" (meaning Nablus), were deeply offended (meaning Tuqan). See HC to CO, 18 Jan. 1947, CO 537/2323.

65. HC to CO, 4 Feb. 1947, CO 537/2281.

66. HC to CO, 29 Dec. 1946, CO 537/2294. It is worth noting that, in the second stage of the conference, nothing was said, debated, or suggested by either Sami Taha or 'Umar al-Khalil. Perhaps this reflected their inexperience, timidity and lack of confidence among an experienced gathering of British and Arab diplomats.

67. *Ibid.*

68. HC to CO, 4 Feb. 1947, CO 537/2281.

69. *Ibid.* The cycle of violence initiated by the *Irgun* and Stern gangs, and the British response of military curfews and control, was causing hysterical outcries from the Jewish community, as the HC described it.

70. HC to CO, 4 Feb. 1947, FO 371/61767.

71. Cairo to FO, 28 Jan. 1947, FO 371/61834.

72. HC to CO, 23 Mar. 1947, FO 371/61834.

73. Cairo (Oriental Minister) to FO, 11 Jan. 1947, FO 371/61834.

74. Azzam's words to Oriental Minister, *ibid.*

Chapter 7. The Mufti, Palestinian Politics, and Efforts at Socio-Political Unity of Arab Society

1. HC to CO, 5 Dec. 1946, CO 537/1707.

2. Beirut to FO, 21 Nov. 1947, FO 371/61836, from an interview the Mufti gave Pakistani Sir Firoz Khan Noon in 'Aley, Lebanon. Sir Firoz was a prominent

pro-British Indian Muslim politician who was serving as India's HC in London. See also secret interview in 'Aley with two officers of the Palestine police, A.F. Giles, Departmental Inspector-General, and J.A. Briance, Departmental Superintendent of Police, 22 Sept. 1947, FO 371/61835.

3. *Ibid.*

4. Foreign Office Research Department (F.O.R.D.) report on youth movements in the Middle East, 12 Feb. 1947, FO 371/61542.

5. Cairo (Campbell) to FO, 28 Jan. 1947, FO 371/61834.

6. HC to CO, 23 Mar. 1947, FO 371/61834.

7. The role of brokers and middle men in land sales throughout the forties was outrageous. In late 1946 DCs were reporting that the Mufti himself ordered the assassination of land brokers and other "traitors." HC to CO, 5 Dec. 1946, CO 537/1708.

8. PG report on the Arab National Fund and Constructive Scheme, HC to CO, 9 Sept. 1947, CO 537/2281.

9. *Ibid.*

10. *Ibid.*

11. Darwaza maintains that 'Alami's attitude and association with the 'Iraqis heightened the division in Palestinian politics. See *al-qiyadat*, sec. 2, p. 58.

12. HC to CO, 4 Feb. 1947, CO 537/2281.

13. HC to CO, 5 Nov. 1946, CO 537/1708; and HC to CO, 9 Sept. 1947, CO 537/2281.

14. For a detailed discussion of the Bloc, see al-Hut, *al-qiyadat*, pp. 491–96. A listing of its members is found in appendix, doc. 59, p. 900.

15. The Bloc is actually the antecedent of the Arab National Movement from which the Marxist fronts of the Palestinian Resistance branched in the 1960s. It was influenced by Zurayk's thoughts. See Walid Kazziha, *Revolutionary Movements in the Arab World* (New York, 1975).

16. On *al-Sha'b* newspaper see Najjar, "The Arabic Press and Nationalism in Palestine," pp. 180–81. The daily's staff was young and educated, among them Kan'an Abu Khadra, founder, Edmond Rock, Michel 'Azir, Hilmi Hanun, 'Umar 'Azzuni, Yusif Hanna and 'Abd al-Ghani al-Karmi. In Feb. 1948 it was shut down, along with *al-Ittihad*, by the government.

17. See copy of article by *al-Wihda*, no date, enclosure in HC to CO, 11 Oct. 1947, CO 537/2281.

18. HC to CO, 4 Feb. 1947; and 9 July 1947, CO 537/2281.

19. This table is based on PG report on the National Fund and Constructive Scheme, HC to CO, 9 Sept. 1947, CO 537/2281, and on al-Hut, *al-qiyadat*, appendix, doc. no. 63, p. 904, who provides towns of origin and occupations.

20. HC to CO, 3 Apr. 1947, CO 537/2281.

21. See *al-Sha'b* article enclosed in HC to CO, 9 Sept. 1947, CO 537/2281. 'Arif al-'Arif says the 'Iraqi regime eventually gave a total of L500,000 to Musa for his scheme and propaganda offices. See al-'Arif, *al-nakba: nakbat bayt al-maqdis wal-firdaws al-mafqud 1947–1952* (Sidon, 1956), i, p. 47.

22. Baghdad to FO, 10 Mar. 1947, FO 371/61913.

23. For a full description of the *Bayt* by its "Secretary General" himself, see Izzat Tannous (as his last name is transliterated on his book), *The Palestinians* (New York, 1988), pp. 386–92. Also HC to CO, 12 Feb. 1947, CO 537/2294.

24. Al-Hut, *al-qiyadat,* p. 594.

25. Tannous, *The Palestinians,* pp. 390–91, does not indicate how much was levied against merchants, whom he groups with two other categories, "companies and industries." The LP50 figure is from HC to CO, 12 Feb. 1947, CO 537/2294.

26. This is based on Samaria DC to CO, 3 Sept. 1947, CO 537/2280. Dr. Tannous, *ibid.,* only says that "officials" paid LP1.50 "each."

27. Tannous, *ibid.,* and HC to CO, 12 Feb. 1947, CO 537/2294.

28. HC to CO, 12 Dec. 1947, CO 537/2280.

29. See budget figures in his book, *The Palestinians,* pp. 390–92; and al-'Arif, *al-nakba,* i, p. 47. Dr. Tannous's figures actually contain a discrepancy: on his "payments" side of the budget the total comes out to LP127,000, rather than LP220,000.

30. See F.O.R.D. special secret report entitled "Youth Movements in the Middle East," 12 Feb. 1947, FO 371/61542. See Hawari's own recollection of events at the end of the mandate in a very polemical and bitter diatribe against the Palestinian struggle and the Mufti: *sir al-nakba* (Nazareth, 1955).

31. F.O.R.D. report, *ibid.*

32. *Ibid.* Al-Hut, *al-qiyadat,* leaves out Acre, Tulkarem, Beersheba, Tiberias and Majdal in her account, p. 509.

33. F.O.R.D. special report, 12 Feb. 1947, FO 371/61542.

34. *Ibid.* Al-Hut, *al-qiyadat,* gives an estimated membership of 3,500 for the *Futuwa,* p. 511.

35. F.O.R.D. special report, 12 Feb. 1947, FO 371/61542.

36. Al-Hut, *al-qiyadat,* p. 511.

37. *Ibid.,* p. 510. People from all over the country attended; also the leaders of Jaffa. Notables included Khalidi, Ahmad Hilmi, and Dr. Haykal. See also Hawari, *sir al-nakba,* p. 20.

38. Al-Hut, *ibid.,* p. 511.

39. *Ibid.,* p. 511; and F.O.R.D. special report, 12 Feb. 1947, FO 371/61542.

40. Al-Hut, *ibid.,* p. 511.

41. *Ibid.,* pp. 511–12. The *Najjada* representatives argued, for example, that a legal change of name which would require the change of uniforms, flags, emblems, etc., would cost an estimated LP20,000. They also argued that the change might alert the authorities to the fact that *Najjada* was not purely a scout organization, and might depress morale.

42. Lydda DC to CO, 2 Apr. 1947 and 3 June 1947, CO 537/2280. Actually, Labib was commander of the Muslim Brotherhood's (Egypt) military section.

43. Galilee DC to CO, 3 July 1947, CO 537/2280.

44. HC to CO, 7 June 1947, CO 537/2281.

45. HC to CO, 9 Sept. 1947, CO 537/2281. Labib did actually get a chance to do some training. The Haifa DC, 5 Aug. 1947, CO 537/2280, wrote that there was training of youth in the mainly Christian village of Bassa.

46. HC to CO, 5 July 1947 and HC to CO, 15 Nov. 1947, CO 537/2294.

47. See, for example, HC to CO, enclosing a declaration by the ALNL in which was demanded the creation of a supreme Arab body, vested with a mandate from the people through popular elections, 12 July 1947, CO 537/2294.

48. HC to CO, 22 Nov. 1947, CO 537/2294.
49. HC to CO 11 June 1947, CO 537/2294.
50. See HC to CO, 5 July 1947; 12 July 1947; 19 July 1947; and 14 Sept. 1947 in CO 537/2294.
51. HC to CO, 19 July 1947, CO 537/2294.
52. Al-Hut, *al-qiyadat*, p. 599.
53. *Ibid.*, p. 600. Al-Hut comments that each NC resembled an independent democracy.
54. HC to CO, 30 Nov. 1947, CO 537/2294.
55. Samaria DC to CO, no date, CO 537/3853.
56. Al-Hut, *al-qiyadat*, p. 599; also al-'Arif, *al-nakba*, i, pp. 94–95, on the functions of the Jerusalem NC.
57. Galilee DC to CO, 4 Mar. 1948, CO 537/3853.
58. See CO 537/3853.
59. This was the observation of the PG intelligence. HC to CO, 20 Dec. 1947, CO 537/2294.
60. Galilee DC to CO, 4 Mar. 1948, CO 537/3853.
61. See al-Hut, *al-qiyadat*, pp. 600–01.
62. Gaza DC to CO, 16 Feb. 1948, CO 537/3853.
63. Gaza DC to CO, 1 Mar. 1948 CO 536/3853.
64. The following discussion is based on al-'Arif, *al-nakba*, i, pp. 226–32.
65. When the AHC called for a three-day general strike in the early days of Dec., Haykal, leading the NC, insisted that the strike should wait until the orange crop was sold. *Ibid.*, p. 228.
66. The following discussion is based mainly on al-'Arif, *ibid.*, pp. 94–95 (esp. footnote 1, p. 94) and 209–10.
67. Galilee DC to CO, 17 Oct. 1947, CO 537/2280.
68. *Ibid.*
69. William Roger Louis, *The British Empire in the Middle East 1945–1951: Arab Nationalism, the United States and Postwar Imperialism* (London, 1984), pp. 456–57.
70. The following discussion of British policy and strategy at the UN is a summary of Louis, *ibid.*, chap. 4. See also Louis, "British Imperialism and the End of the Palestine Mandate," in Louis and Robert W. Stookey, eds., *The End of the Palestine Mandate* (Austin, 1986), pp. 10–19.
71. See Fred J. Khouri, *The Arab-Israeli Dilemma* (New York, 1968), chap. 2.
72. For a full discussion of the problems at the Jerusalem office, based almost entirely on the personal papers of Dr. Khalidi, see al-Hut, *al-qiyadat*, pp. 587–89.
73. *Ibid.*, p. 589.
74. HC to CO, 29 Apr. 1947, CO 537/2294.
75. *Ibid.* The delegation that finally went consisted of four: Raja'i al-Husayni, Henry Cattan and 'Issa Nakhleh, two Jerusalem advocates, the first being particularly prominent, and Ghury.
76. Samaria DC to CO, 3 Sept. 1947 CO 537/2280.
77. *Ibid.* The delegation again consisted of Raja'i al-Husayni, Cattan, and Nakhleh, plus another close Mufti associate, Wasif Kamal.

78. Galilee DC to CO, 16 Sept. 1947, CO 537/2280.
79. This is what the Galilee DC related, *ibid.*
80. Al-Hut, *al-qiyadat*, p. 571.
81. From MacGillivary to FO, 4 Aug. 1947, FO 371/61876.
82. *Ibid.* The meeting took place at the Hotel Victoria in Geneva.
83. See FO 371/61835. The Mufti was accompanied by Ahmad Hilmi, Subhi al-Khadra, 'Uthman Kamal Haddad, and Nujhad Husayn. There followed on a second MISR airline flight Shaykh Hasan Abu Sa'ud (then the Mufti of Jerusalem), Ma'ruf al-Dawalibi, Majdi Ja'uni, and Ishaq Darwish al-Husayni.
84. Samaria DC to CO, 3 Nov. 1947, CO 537/2280. Others who paid homage to the Mufti were the Muslim Brethren, including Shaykh Nimr al-Khatib, head of the Qassamites. See HC to CO, 20 Dec. 1947, CO 537/2294.
85. HC to CO, 22 Nov. 1947, CO 537/2294.

Chapter 8. Arab Politics and the Palestinians: Nationalism, Dynastic Intrigue, and Political Ambitions

1. For a discussion of these points, see Gomaa, *The Foundation,* p. 266–67.
2. See Patrick Seale, *The Struggle for Syria: A Study in Postwar Arab Policy, 1945–1958* (London, 1965).
3. Porath, *In Search of Arab Unity,* p. 56.
4. For these ideas, see Gomaa, *The Foundation,* Conclusion.
5. Cecil A. Hourani, "The Arab League in Perspective," *Middle East Journal,* 2 (1947), is one of those who argue that the Arab League was a victory for "moderate" Arab nationalism.
6. Porath, *In Search of Arab Unity,* p. 318. Gomaa, *The Foundation,* p. 271, concludes much the same thing: "Arab nationalism developed mainly in reaction against foreign domination and influence."
7. See FO 371/52521.
8. Barry Rubin, *The Arab States and the Palestine Conflict* (New York, 1981), p. xvi.
9. See FO 371/52506 for numerous examples of British pressure.
10. Refer to chap. 5 under section "British Schemes for Settlement During the War."
11. Office of Minister of State (Lord Moyne) in Cairo to FO, 1 Mar. 1944, CO 733/461/75872/44 pt. 2.
12. Baghdad to FO, 5 Dec. 1944, CO 733/461/75872/44 pt. 3.
13. Baghdad to FO, 19 Jan. 1945, CO 733/461/75872/45. Lord Gort was on a visit to 'Iraq.
14. Note of interview between 'Azzam and Hall in London, 17 Oct. 1945, FO 371/52574.
15. British Legation, 'Amman, to FO, 23 July 1946, FO 371/32551. The other resolutions committed the Arabs to decline to grant new economic concessions to nationals of Britain and the U.S. and to oppose Anglo-American political interests at international meetings. See Darwaza, *al-qadiya,* sec. 2, pp. 55–57.
16. See HC to CO, 26 Aug. 1946, CO 537/1772.

17. 'Azzam Bey, speaking to the Oriental Minister in Cairo, Sir R.J. Campbell, said that a few more years of the British presence might allow things to cool down; while Nuri Pasha, in conversation with Ambassador Busk, wanted to see HMG "spin the matter out" until the November 1948 elections in the US, which he hoped might end Truman's presidency and with it Zionist pressure. Cairo to FO, 30 July 1946, and Baghdad to FO, 20 Aug. 1946, both in CO 537/1772.

18. 'Amman to FO, 29 July 1947, FO 371/52551.

19. Prime Minister Ibrahim Pasha's words, who spoke for 'Abdullah, in *ibid.* See also 'Amman to FO, 27 Aug. 1946, FO 371/52556.

20. See HC to CO, 24 July 1943, FO 371/34960. Also Damascus to FO, 15 Aug. 1947, FO 371/61494. For a more detailed treatment of the subject of 'Abdullah's Syrian ambitions, see Wilson, *King Abdullah,* p. 136–42ff.

21. 'Amman to FO, 10 Mar. 1947, FO 371/61492.

22. See FO 371/61495. Ibn Sa'ud also issued a manifesto on 31 Aug., attacking 'Abdullah's Hashemite plans.

23. HC to CO, 24 July 1943, FO 371/34960. Also Wilson *King Abdullah,* p. 142.

24. 'Amman to FO, 21 Apr. 1947, FO 371/61493.

25. The statement was made on 14 July 1947. See file in *ibid.*

26. 'Amman to Baghdad, 15 Sept. 1947, FO 371/61496.

27. FO to HMG's representatives in the Middle East, 17 Oct. 1947, FO 371/61882.

28. FO to HMG's representatives in the Arab states, 15 Dec. 1947, FO 371/61890.

29. Beirut to FO, 16 Oct. 1947, FO 371/61883.

30. 'Amman to FO, 21 Dec. 1947 FO 371/61583.

31. Brigadier I.N. Clayton's report on the proceedings of the League Council in Cairo between 8–17 Dec. 1947. Clayton to FO, 23 Dec. 1947, FO 371/68634. Clayton went on to say that Samir Rifa'i (Trans-Jordan) and Yusif Yasin (Sa'udi Arabia) said that if their governments attempted to take a moderate stand, their lives and the lives of their respective kings would be in danger.

32. Damascus to FO, 11 Oct. 1947, FO 371/61882.

33. FO to HMG's representatives in the Arab states, 17 Oct. 1947, FO 371/61882.

34. Damascus to FO, 11 Oct. 1947, FO 371/61882.

35. FO to HMG's representatives in the Middle East, 5 Dec. 1947 FO 371/61890.

36. *Ibid.* The first note was on 5 Dec., the second on 10 Dec.

37. Beirut to FO, 6 Dec. 1947, FO 371/61891.

38. Cairo to FO, 6 Dec. 1947, FO 371/61580 and to Dominion countries, 13 Dec. 1947, FO 371/61893.

39. FO to Dominion countries, 13 Dec. 1947, *ibid.*

40. The 'Iraqi government had even officially informed HMG that, one, 'Iraq would not take any action calculated to complicate British withdrawal and, two, it would not send troops into Palestine while the British authorities remained in control. See Baghdad to FO, 9 Dec. 1947, FO 371/61892, for this and similar assurances by other Arab officials.

41. 'Amman (C.M. Pirie-Gordon) to FO, 30 July 1947, FO 371/61876. Pirie-Gordon's words.

42. 'Abdullah to Bevin, 30 Aug. 1947, FO 371/62226. He had actually written

previous letters to Bevin, on 10 May 1947 and 28 July 1947.

43. *Ibid.*

44. See Louis, *The British Empire,* pp. 356–57.

45. Talks between Attlee and 'Abdullah, 13 Mar. 1946, FO 371/52574.

46. See note by Burrows of FO to CO, 11 Oct. 1947, FO 371/61960. For a fuller discussion of the theme that Britain's concern was with maintaining a presence in the Middle East—hence 'Abdullah's importance—see Wilson, *King Abdullah,* chap. 9, esp. p. 162.

47. See minutes of a meeting held at FO, 10 Sept. 1945, FO 371/45379.

48. FO to 'Amman, 26 Oct. 1947, FO 371/61882. Also see Shlaim, *Collusion Across the Jordan,* p. 110.

49. Kirkbride to FO, 29 Oct. 1947, FO 371/62226. Also Shlaim, *ibid.,* p. 103.

50. Bevin to all HMG representatives in Arab capitals, 11 Nov. 1947, FO 141/1182. This was in answer to Kirkbride.

51. Bevin's instructions, *ibid.*

52. *Ibid.*

53. Kirkbride to FO, 17 Nov. 1947, FO 371/61584.

54. Kirkbride to Orme-Sargent at FO, 18 Nov. 1947, *ibid.*

55. FO to Kirkbride, 22 Dec. 1947, *ibid.*

56. *Ibid.*

57. See Beirut to FO, 28 Dec. 1947, FO 371/61584, in which Sulh suggested to the British minister (Boswall) that it was a psychological moment for an understanding between HMG and the Arab states; and Beirut to FO, 12 Oct. 1947, FO 371/61880, in which Sulh said the Arab states hoped some sort of *modus vivendi* might be found.

58. See Beirut to FO, 16 Oct. 1947, FO 371/61883; and Beirut to FO, 19 Dec. 1947, FO 371/61583.

59. *Ibid.*

60. Louis, *The British Empire,* p. 367.

61. *Ibid.,* p. 365.

62. Bevin to 'Abdullah, 11 Jan. 1948, FO 371/62226. Also Shlaim, *Collusion,* pp. 131–32.

63. Shlaim, *Collusion,* pp. 132–33. Whereas I emphasize *events* in shaping British policy which, in its ambiguity and cautiousness towards 'Abdullah, was driven by the need to maintain a flexible set of options in order to guarantee British presence in the area, Shlaim forcefully interprets British actions as being clearly based on duplicity and collusion, thus implying a consistent and clear set of goals in British policy-making regarding 'Abdullah.

64. See Shlaim, *ibid.,* pp. 221–24, and Wilson, *King Abdullah,* pp. 169, 171, on which this paragraph is based.

65. Louis, *The British Empire,* p. 372, quotes this from Lieutenant-General Sir John Bagot Glubb's book, *A Soldier With the Arabs.* For other angles of the Bevin-Abu al-Huda exchange, see Cohen, *Palestine and the Great Powers,* pp. 330–31, Shlaim, *Collusion,* pp. 136–39, and Wilson, *King Abdulah,* p. 167.

66. Thousands of telegrams were received by Arab leaders from opposition parties, associations, and leading figures throughout the Arab world. The

press was particularly aggressive in its call for the use of force to resist the plans of Zionism and its defenders at the United Nations. See FO 371/61878 and 61880 for numerous examples.

67. American State Department to its London Embassy (a report on 'Iraqi Parliament proceedings), 28 Mar. 1947, FO 371/61874.

68. See FO report on what went on at the Political Committee meeting, 25 Sept. 1947, FO 371/61881. Also see Darwaza, *al-qadiya*, sec. 2, pp. 98–101. The meeting ended mildly and economic sanctions were referred to the League Council.

69. Al-Hut, *al-qiyadat*, p. 572.

70. See League resolutions, FO minute, 15 Oct. 1947, FO 371/61886. See also Darwaza, *al-qadiya*, sec. 2, pp. 101–07.

71. Al-'Arif, *al-nakba*, i, pp. 15–16. The Mufti actually tried, but never met with Jabr, the latter refusing to talk to or acknowledge him.

72. 'Amman to FO, 11 Oct. 1947, FO 371/61881.

73. 'Amman to FO, 14 Oct. 1947, FO 371/61882.

74. Al-Hut, *al-qiyadat*, p. 580; al-'Arif, *al-nakba*, i, p. 16.

75. Beirut to FO, 16 Oct. 1947, FO 371/61883.

76. Beirut (Houston-Boswall) to FO, 19 Dec. 1947, FO 371/61583.

77. From British Middle East Office in Cairo to FO, 19 Dec. 1947, FO 371/61583.

78. Al-'Arif, *al-nakba*, i, p. 16; al-Hut, *al-qiyadat*, p. 605.

79. Al-Hut, *ibid.*, p. 607.

80. See FO minute on Oct. League meeting, 15 Oct. 1947, FO 371/61886.

81. Beirut to FO, 3 Dec. 1947, FO 371/61580.

82. The following paragraph on the MC's military reports to the League are based on: al-Hut, *al-qiyadat*, p. 605; Darwaza, *al-qadiya*, sec. 2, pp. 101–07; and al-'Arif, *al-nakba*, i, pp. 18–21.

83. 'Amman to FO, 22 Oct. 1947, FO 371/61885.

84. FO minute on League meeting at 'Aley, 15 Oct. 1947, FO 371/61881.

85. 'Amman to FO, 21 Dec. 1947, FO 371/61583, giving report on the League Council meeting in December. The meeting was held in Cairo but Samir Rifa'i gave the full details of what went on to Kirkbride.

86. *Ibid.*

87. Beirut to FO, 28 Dec. 1947, FO 371/61583.

88. Brigadier Clayton's report on the League Council meeting in Cairo from 8–17 Dec., 23 Dec. 1947, FO 371/68634.

89. 'Amman to FO, 23 Dec. 1947, FO 371/61583. The rest of the para. is based on this reference. The plan was in line with 'Abdullah's secret contacts with the Jewish Agency. In the middle of November 1947, the King met with Golda Myerson in the upper Jordan valley. Both agreed the Mufti was their common enemy, and 'Abdullah made clear his intentions to annex the Arab part of Palestine and not attack the Jews. On this and subsequent 'Abdullah-Jewish contacts, see Cohen, *Palestine and the Great Powers*, pp. 331–34, and Shlaim, *Collusion*, pp. 110–21, 205–14. Shlaim offers the best and most detailed account of the entire (i.e., from 1922–52) Hashemite-Jewish relationship. His chaps. 2–9 cover the period of this book (1939–48).

90. See Baghdad to FO, 10 Dec. 1947; 'Amman to FO, 4 Dec. 1947; and 'Amman to FO, 29 Nov. 1947, all in FO 371/61580.

91. 'Abdullah to Regent, 29 Nov. 1947, *ibid.*

92. 'Amman to FO, 20 Dec. 1947, FO 371/61583.

93. 'Amman to FO, 21 Dec. 1947, FO 371/61583; also see al-'Arif, *al-nakba*, i, p. 100.

94. Brigadier Clayton to FO, 23 Dec. 1947, FO 371/68364.

95. Al-Hut, *al-qiyadat*, p. 581.

96. 'Amman to FO, 21 Dec. 1947, FO 371/61583.

97. Al-'Arif, *al-nakba*, i, p. 36. Also see report in *ibid.*

98. Al-Hut, *op. cit.*, p. 581. Darwaza, *al-qadiya*, sec. 2, pp. 58–59.

99. Al-'Arif, *al-nakba*, i, p. 128; al-Hut, *al-qiyadat*, p. 607.

100. Al-'Arif, *ibid.*, p. 108; al-Hut, *ibid.*, p. 504.

101. The members of the Palestine Committee were 'Azzam Bey, chairman, 'Iraqi Nazif al-Shawy, Jamil Mardam, Riad al-Sulh, 'Abd al-Qadir Pasha al-Jundi, Khayr al-Din Zarkaleh of Sa'udi Arabia, the Mufti, Isma'il Safwat, and general Taha al-Hashimi, the 'Iraqi military expert. The Permanent Military Committee members were Hamdi Pachachi, Riad al-Sulh, 'Ali al-Mu'ayyad, Sa'id al-Mufti, Ahmad Khushbe, and the Mufti. See al-Hut, *ibid.*, doc. nos. 65 and 66 in appendix, p. 905. Also see al-'Arif, *ibid.*, p. 108.

102. See 'Amman to FO, 21 Dec. 1947, FO 371/61583; also al-'Arif, *al-nakba*, i, p. 36.

103. Al-'Arif, *ibid.*, p. 36; al-Hut, *al-qiyadat*, p. 502.

104. Baghdad to FO, 23 Dec. 1947, FO 371/61583.

105. From British Embassy in Cairo to FO, 29 Dec. 1947, FO 371/68365. This was a summary of the Arab discussions at Cairo, supplied to the Embassy by "a most reliable source" who obtained it direct from 'Azzam Bey and the Mufti.

106. Clayton to FO, 23 Dec. 1947, FO 371/68364.

107. British Embassy in Cairo to FO, 30 Dec. 1947, FO 371/68365.

108. Al-Hut, *al-qiyadat*, p. 583. See also Cohen, *Palestine and the Great Powers*, p. 306. Cohen relies for his information on Joseph Nevo, *Abdullah and Palestine* (in Hebrew) (Tel Aviv, 1975).

109. Al-'Arif, *al-nakba*, i, p. 41.

110. Damascus to FO, 24 Dec. 1947, FO 371/62226.

111. See Safwat's statement in al-Hut, *al-qiyadat*, doc. no. 65, appendix, p. 839, and al-'Arif, *al-nakba*, i, p. 129.

112. 'Azzam's discussion with Clayton. British Middle East Office to FO, 17 Feb. 1948, FO 371/68381.

113. Clayton (Cairo) to FO, 17 Feb. 1948, FO 371/68381. 'Azzam's description to Clayton.

114. Thomas Mayer, "Egypt's 1948 Invastion of Palestine," *Middle Eastern Studies*, 22 (1986), p. 23.

115. For a more detailed discussion of inter-Arab politico-military policies in the month before the termination of the mandate, see Shlaim, *Collusion*, pp. 172–74 and chap. 7, esp. pp. 196–204, 224–230.

116. 'Amman to FO, 15 Apr. 1948, FO 371/68527.

117. 'Amman to FO, 16 Apr. 1948, FO 371/68527.

118. *Ibid.*

119. 'Amman to FO, 19 Apr. 1948, FO 371/68527. Trans-Jordan P.M., Tewfiq Abu al-Huda, conveyed the substance of the Political Committee talks to Kirkbride.

120. HC to CO, 20 Apr. 1948, FO 371/68527. Cunningham was informed of the substance of the Nuqrashi-Mufti exchange by a "good Arab source."

121. This is what the *Times* correspondent told General Glubb Pasha in 'Amman. 'Amman to FO, 15 Apr. 1948, FO 371/68527.

122. 'Amman to FO, 16 Apr. 1948, FO 371/68527.

123. 'Amman to FO, 14 Apr. 1948, FO 371/68367.

124. 'Amman to FO, 17 Apr. 1948, FO 371/68527.

125. *Ibid.*, Kirkbride's words.

126. 'Amman to FO, 21 Apr. 1948, FO 371/68527.

127. HC to CO, 20 Apr. 1947, FO 371/68527.

128. 'Amman to FO, 25 Apr. 1948, FO 371/68370.

129. *Ibid.*

130. *Ibid.*

131. *Ibid.*

132. Al-Hut, al-qiyadat, p. 610.

133. 'Amman to FO, 29 Apr. 1948, FO 371/68370.

134. Al-Hut, *op. cit.*, p. 610; also al-'Arif, *al-nakba*, i, p. 110.

135. 'Amman to FO, 29 Apr. 1948, FO 371/68370.

136. Al-Hut, *al-qiyadat*, p. 610; also al-'Arif, *op. cit.*, pp. 108–09.

137. Shlaim, *Collusion*, p. 201. Bith quotes are from Shlaim, pp. 197–201. Shlaim offers a fine discussion of the plan and other details, including maps of what he refers to as the "Damascus plan" in comparison to its actual implementation, or invasion route.

138. *Ibid.*, p. 202.

139. J. Bowyer-Bell, *The Long War: Israel and the Arabs Since 1946* (Englewood Cliffs, NJ, 1969), p. 131.

140. *Ibid.*, pp. 128–129, 131.

Chapter 9. British Withdrawal, War, and Disintegration

1. See Bowyer-Bell, *The Long War*, pp. 19–47; and Cohen, *Palestine and the Great Powers*, pp. 229–50.

2. Bowyer-Bell, *ibid.*, p. 25.

3. *Ibid.*, p. 25.

4. See CO 537/3917 on British withdrawal plans and the subsequent reports of the HC as to its progress.

5. Chief of Staff report on withdrawal, 26 Jan. 1948, CO 537/3917.

6. Don Peretz, "Palestinian Social Stratification: The Political Implications," *Journal of Palestine Studies*, 7 (1977), p. 56, slightly touches on this theme.

7. See Palestine to Cabinet, 25 Jan. 1948, 28 Jan. 1948, 17 Mar. 1948, 24 Mar. 1948, 22 Apr. 1948, 23 Apr. 1948, and 25 May 1948, all in CO 537/3917.

8. British Legation, Damascus, to FO, 19 Feb. 1948, FO 371/68368. The following description of Qatna is based on this report.

9. *Al-nakba,* i, pp. 102–03.

10. Cairo British Embassy to FO, 19 Feb. 1948 FO 371/68368—"Egyptian aid to the 'Liberation of Palestine.' "

11. Colonel Natanel Lorch, *The Edge of the Sword: Israel's War of Independence, 1947–1949* (New York, 1961), p. 264; also Walid Khalidi, ed., *From Haven to Conquest* (Beirut, 1971). appendix VIII, p. 860. Lorch does not make clear whether these figures included Palestinians.

12. See al-'Arif, *op. cit.,* p. 39. Darwaza, *al-qadiya,* sec. 2, p. 119, estimates the volunteers at 5,000 men.

13. British Legation, Damascus, to FO, 19 Feb. 1948, FO 371/68368. See also John Kimche and David Kimche, *Both Sides of the Hill: Britain and the Palestine War* (London, 1960), pp. 81–82.

14. Al-'Arif, *al-nakba,* i,p. 60. Egypt claimed it gave another 1,200 rifles to the Mufti.

15. *Ibid.,* i, p. 58. See also Kimches, *op. cit.,* footnote 1, p. 82.

16. Al-'Arif, *ibid.,* p. 46; Darwaza, *al-qadiya,* sec. 2, pp. 58–59. These figures exclude another L46,175 donated by three large Arab companies which chose to remain anonymous.

17. For the battalions see Khalidi, *From Haven,* appendix VIII, p. 860. See also al-'Arif, *al-nakba,* i, pp. 38–39.

18. Al-'Arif, *ibid.,* pp. 156–59.

19. Porath, *The Palestinian Arab,* p. 131.

20. *Ibid.,* p. 131.

21. See Lesch, *Arab Politics,* pp. 291, 224.

22. Al-'Arif, *al-nakba,* i, pp. 128–29.

23. See Khalidi, *From Haven,* appendix VIII, pp. 856–60.

24. *Ibid.,* pp. 858–60.

25. *Ibid.,* pp. 858–60.

26. See the recounting of the meeting between Qawaqji and Yehoshua Palmon, an officer in the *Haganah* Intelligence Service, in Shlaim, *Collusion,* pp. 154–59. Also see Porath, *The Palestinian Arab,* footnote 246, chap. 7, pp. 350–51. According to both Shlaim and Porath, both of whom base their information on interviews with Palmon, the latter went away with the understanding that Qawaqji: would not (and actually did not) coordinate with the *Jihad;* he would not (and actually hardly did) aid them if (when) their forces were attacked by the Jews—he would (and actually mostly did) remain neutral; and the Jews would concentrate their military efforts against the *Jihad* and not against Qawaqji. The agreement was never carried out to the letter, judging from the Qawaqji-*Haganah* clashes, though indeed such clashes were very limited.

27. Al-'Arif, *al-nakba,* i, p. 47. This figure excludes the Arab states donations mentioned earlier. It is of interest to note that King 'Abd al-'Aziz donated L40,000.

28. See Khalidi, *From Haven,* appendix III, p. 845. Khalidi got his figures form *A Survey of Palestine,* ii.

29. Unless otherwise indicated, the following statistics on Jewish men and arms

are from the following sources, from which I gleaned the highest figures on each item from each source: Trevor N. Dupuy, *Elusive Vistory: The Arab-Israeli Wars, 1947–1974* (New York, 1978), pp. 8, 10; Chaim Herzog, *The Arab-Israeli Wars* (New York, 1982), pp. 18–21; Zeev Schiff, *A History of the Israeli Army*, tr. by A. Rothstein (San Francisco, 1974), pp. 28, 33; and Bowyer-Bell, *The Long War*, pp. 74–75.

30. See Khalidi, *From Haven*, appendix IX, pp. 861–66. Khalidi rigorously compares and analyzes Zionist works on the subject. He documents an additional 9,000 in the *Gadna* or Youth Battalions.

31. *Ibid.*, pp. 861–66.

32. See Cohen, *Palestine and Great Powers*, pp. 302–44.

33. Lorch, *The Edge of the Sword*, pp. 87–88.

34. See Erskine B. Childers, "The Wordless Wish: From Citizens to Refugees," in Abu-Lughod, *The Transformation*, p. 182.

35. *Ibid.*, p. 182. Benny Morris, *The Birth of the Palestinian Refugee Problem* (New York, 1987), pp. 30–36, generally argues that the Jewish leadership's policy was based on restraint so as not to widen the scope of the conflict in the early months of the violence, but also that the *Haganah*'s massive "reprisals, sometimes excessive, sometimes misdirected," tended to widen the "circle of violence" (p. 36).

36. Cohen, *Palestine and the Great Powers*, p. 310. Qawaqji himself entered Palestine in March 1948 (across the Allenby Bridge). In his memoirs he maintains, paradoxically, that he entered in "broad daylight" and was even welcomed by a British officer, on behalf of the British High Command, upon reaching his headquarters in Central Palestine. See "Memoirs, 1948: Part 1," *Journal of Palestine Studies*, 4 (1972), pp. 29–30. His name in this article is transliterated as "Fauzi al-Qawuqji." I will use this spelling when I cite him.

37. Bowyer-Bell, *The Long War*, pp. 83, 93.

38. See Qawuqji, *op. cit.*, pp. 37–47, for a detailed description of the battle, which really lasted ten days, 4–14 April. While Qawaqji's claim that the British conspired with the Jews to reinforce the settlement is questionable, he convincingly shows that, despite his pleas, the MC in Damascus did not supply him with badly needed arms and ammunition. See Morris, *The Birth*, pp. 115–18, for the account of the Arab villages' destruction by the *Haganah*.

39. Cohen, *Palestine and the Great Powers*, p. 335. For a recent, sympathetic discussion of plan D, see Morris, *The Birth*, pp. 61–64. Unlike Cohen, and as demonstrated by Khalidi (see note 45 below), Morris does not make it clear if the plan called for the conquest and destruction of Arab towns and villages *outside* the borders of the UN-designated Jewish state, though he *seems* to be saying it *did not* make such inclusion. He does say and imply, however, that the plan, because it called for "securing" Jewish settlements outside the state's borders, this, in effect, meant conquest of substantial portions of Arab Palestine beyond the state's partition limits. Also Shlaim, *Collusion*, p. 159.

40. See Peretz, "Palestinian Social Stratification," pp. 48–74. Morris, *The Birth*, p. 30, puts the figure at 75,000, "mostly from the urban upper and middle classes of Jaffa, Haifa, and Jerusalem, and from villages around Jerusalem and in the Coastal Plain. . . ." Morris, however, does not offer an accounting for his figure.

41. On the contrary, Arab governments and the AHC actively tried to prevent

the exodus. On the different ways this was done see, as a small sample: E.B. Childers, "The Other Exodus," *The Spectator*, No. 6933 (12 May 1961), pp. 672–75, reprinted in Walter Laqueur and Barry Rubin, eds., *The Arab-Israeli Reader: A Documentary History of the Middle East* (New York, 1984), pp. 143–51; John and Hadawi, *The Palestine Diary*, ii, pp. 383–84; and Morris, *The Birth*, pp. 66–70, *passim*.

42. For more or less this view, see Walid Khalidi, "Plan Dalet, The Zionist Blueprint for the Conquest of Palestine," *Middle East Forum*, 37 (1961), pp. 8–22; Childers, "The Wordless Wish," esp. pp. 165–83; and, more recently, Nafez Nazzal, *The Palestinian Exodus from Galilee, 1948* (Beirut, 1978).

43. For a detailed account of the Philby scheme see Porath, *In Search of Arab Unity*, pp. 80–106.

44. Morris, *The Birth*, pp. 23–28, discusses the notion of "transfer" among Jewish leaders in the 1930s and 40s.

45. See Khalidi, *From Haven*, appendix VIII, pp. 856–77, for the thirteen operations included in Plan D.

46. The exodus is finely discussed by Steven Glazer, "The Palestinian Exodus in 1948," *Journal of Palestine Studies*, 9 (1980), pp. 96–118; for geographic distinctions, pp. 109–10. Again, also refer to Morris's work, *The Birth*. Morris throughout his book emphasizes the military or strategic imperative, punctuated with numerous references to political/territorial motives, and leaves an ambivalence or ambiguity in his conclusions.

47. See Benny Morris, "Operation Dani and the Palestinian Exodus from Lydda and Ramle in 1948," *Middle East Journal*, 40 (1986), pp. 82–109. Also *The Birth*, pp. 203–12.

48. In addition to Nafez Nazzal's book, *The Palestinian Exodus*, see his "The Zionist Occupation of Western Galilee," *Journal of Palestine Studies*, 3 (1974), pp. 58–76.

49. Again see Glazer, "The Palestinian Exodus," pp. 103–07, for a discussion of this aspect. Most authors who discuss the 1947–48 war distinguish the phases. See also Morris, *The Birth, passim*, whose "phases" (or "waves") of refugees) I follow. It should be noted that the commonly accepted phases of the war do not necessarily coincide, timewise, with the phases, or waves, of refugees (e.g., the *second phase* was between March to 15 May, while the *second wave* of refugees was between April and June).

50. Morris, *The Birth*, p. 292 and *passim* for Ben Gurion's policies. The operations between July and November 1948 caused, according to Morris, the flight of up to 250,000 people, much of the flight precipitated by an aggressive policy (i.e., of terrorism, atrocities, expulsions), whose object was to empty the country.

51. The following paragraph on Zionist psychological and physical terror is based on Childers, "The Wordless Wish," esp. pp. 187–89. This article still remains the best and essentially most accurate summary account of Zionist terror tactics to date.

52. As quoted by Benny Morris, "The Causes and Character of the Arab Exodus from Palestine: the Israel Defence Forces Intelligence Branch Analysis of June 1948," *Middle Eastern Studies*, 22 (1986), p. 6. The brackets of explanation are also Morris's. See also his *The Birth*, pp. 76–77.

53. See the descriptions of the tragedy in Walid Khalidi, "The Fall of Haifa," *Middle East Forum*, 35 (1959), pp. 22–32.

54. This is corroborated by C. Marriott, Galilee DC, to FO, 26 Apr. 1948, FO 371/ 68505. The DC says British forces engaged Zionists who were harassing with gunfire the flow of refugees, killing several Jewish fighters and a senior *Haganah* officer.

55. Morris, "The Causes and Character," p. 8. In this article published prior to his book, *The Birth*, Morris pretty much maintains, as in his book, the general tenor that the Palestinian flight was so multifaceted and complex, that it is extremely difficult to pin down any general patterns. He argues, however, that the basic causes were three: Arab-initiated evacuation, flight before the advancing Jewish armies, and direct expulsion, always making sure to interject the military imperative.

56. The following discussion and quotes are based on *ibid.*, pp. 8–13. Morris, p. 14, says: "there is no reason to cast doubt on the report's integrity... in the production of this analysis."

57. *Ibid.*, p. 15.

58. *Ibid.*, p. 18. The report assigns 10 percent of general fear; 8 percent to "local factors" (loss of morale, loss of confidence in Arab strength); 1 percent to fear of Jewish retaliation after an Arab attack; and another 1 percent to pressure from Arab irregulars, fear of Arab invasion, or the isolation of some villages in mostly Jewish areas.

59. Morris's conclusion, *ibid.*, p. 15.

60. For a succinct description of Palestinian shortcomings, see Musa Alami, "The Lesson of Palestine," *Middle East Journal*, 3 (1949), pp. 373–405, esp. 374.

61. See Khalidi, "The Fall of Haifa," for details of events. The following pages on Haifa (and Jaffa) were written before the publication of B. Morris's book, *The Birth*. I decided, after careful review of Morris on Haifa (pp. 73–95), that I would not change my account in light of any discrepancies with Morris's more detailed account. The Haifa affair was much too complicated and the sources contradictory. My general, essential account is accurate, and my emphases and interpretations, right or wrong, remain my own.

62. Al-Hut, *al-qiyadat*, p. 629. For the sequence of events see Muhammad Nimr al-Khatib, *min athr al-nakba* (Damascus, 1951, pp. 266–70. Shaykh al-Khatib was the Muslim Brethren leader in Haifa. In his book he offers a first hand-account of the fall of his city.

63. Al-'Arif, *al-nakba*, i, p. 222; and al-Khatib, *ibid.*, p. 269.

64. Cohen, *Palestine and the Great Powers*, p. 341.

65. Al-Khatib, *min athr*, p. 266.

66. Galilee DC to FO, 26 Apr. 1948, FO 371/68505.

67. *Ibid.*

68. Al-Khatib, *min athr*, p. 268.

69. *Ibid.*, p. 270; also al-'Arif, *al-nakba*, i, pp. 222–23. Al-Khatib says he never did find out if the Arab delegation returned to give its answer to the Jews and British.

70. Galilee DC to FO, 26 June 1948 FO 371/68505.

71. *Al-qiyadat*, p. 630.

72. Galilee DC to FO, 26 Apr. 1948, FO 371/68505.

73. Galilee DC to FO, *ibid.*, The DC specifically mentions this point in his assess-

ment of Arab weaknesses.

74. Al-'Arif, *al-nakba*, i, p. 218, maintains there were 450 Arabfighters and some 4,000 *Haganah* and IZL men. Al-Hut, p. 268, also mentions there were no more than 400 Arabs defending Haifa. However, C. Marriott, the Galilee DC, exaggeratedly says there were about 2,000 Arab fighters and about 400 Jews backed by "an undeterminate number of reserves."

75. See al-Khatib, *min athr*, pp. 134, 138–39, 174 ff.

76. Al-'Arif, *op. cit.*, i, pp. 20–109.

77. Galilee DC to FO, 26 Apr. 1948, FO 371/68505; also al-Khatib, *op. cit.*, p. 265.

78. Galilee DC report, *ibid.*

79. Janet L. Abu-Lughod, "The Demographic Transformation of Palestine," p. 153.

80. Al-'Arif, *al-nakba*, i, p. 228. Also see al-Qawuqji, "Memoirs, Part I," pp. 50–58 on Jaffa. Again, for an Israeli account of Jaffa see Morris, *The Birth*, pp. 95–101.

81. Al'Arif, *ibid.*, p. 239. The Yugoslavians comprised 50–60 men.

82. *Ibid.*, pp. 232–34, 239, 245, esp. table, on which the following para. is based.

83. *Ibid.*, pp. 238, 247.

84. Al-Qawuqji, "Memoirs, Part I," pp. 53–54.

85. *Al-qiyadat*, pp. 631–32. On the Yazur artillery, see also al-'Arif, *al-nakba*, i, pp. 256–57.

86. Al-Qawuqji, *op. cit.*, p. 54.

87. Al-'Arif *op. cit.*, pp. 257, 261.

88. Al-Qawuqji, "Memoirs, Part I," p. 55, cable dated 29/4. Morris makes no mention of British attacks on Jaffa, but only that 4,500 British troops with tanks entered Jaffa and that IZL positions and headquarters were briefly shelled. And he certainly makes no mention of Qawaqji's shelling of Tel Aviv or anywhere else. See his *The Birth*, pp. 100–01.

89. Galilee DC to FO, 10 May 1948, FO 371/68507; also al-'Arif, *al-nakba*, i, p. 261.

90. Al-'Arif, *ibid.*, p. 259; also al-Qawuqji, "Memiors, Part I," p. 56.

91. Al-Qawuqji, *ibid.*, cables dated 2/5 and 3/5, pp. 56–57.

92. *Ibid.*, cable dated 2/5, p. 56.

93. Al-Hut, *al-qiyadat*, p. 632.

94. *Ibid.*, p. 632.

95. Fuller Hanging File, St. Antony's College Personal Papers Collection, Oxford. The meeting took place on 3 May. The following description of events is based on this file.

96. *Ibid.*, The note is dated 4 May 1948.

97. *Palestine and the Great Powers*, p. 341.

98. *Ibid.*, p. 343.

99. *Ibid.*, p. 343, Cohen's emphasis.

Chronology

1936–1939 The Palestine Arab Revolt and Concurrent Events
— April-October 1936 First stage of national strike and rebellion
— April 1936 Creation of the AHC
— July 1937 Palestine Royal (Peel) Commission issues its partition report
— September 1937 AHC and Arab states condemn partition proposal; revolt rekindled; AHC outlawed; members exiled to Seychelles; Mufti escapes to Lebanon, Jamal al-Husayni to Egypt (eventually also exiled to Seychelles)
— September 1938 Woodhead Commission of Inquiry finds partition unfavorable
— May 1939 White Paper issued after London Conference
— June 1939 AHC, under Mufti's influence, rejects White Paper

1939–1940 Moderate members of AHC carry on inconclusive secret talks with British over their acceptance of White Paper

Summer 1940 Jamal al-Husayni and Musa al-ʿAlami hold talks in Baghdad with "official" British envoy Col. Stewart Newcombe; White Paper accepted by them and reluctantly by Mufti; subsequently, Newcombe recalled, scheme collapsed, pushing Mufti towards Axis

(Summer) 1940–1941 Government held unsuccessful private talks with NDP men who were interested in gaining PG support for eliminating Husayni influence; *Istiqlal*ist Rashid al-Haj Ibrahim and Ahmad Hilmi Pasha joined, interested in constitutional provisions of White Paper

1942–1945 Sporadic Attempts at Palestinian Arab Unity
— December 1942 Rashid al-Haj Ibrahim, at conference of Arab chambers of commerce, initiated the idea of forming a political body
— February 1943 A conference held in Haifa elected al-Haj Ibrahim head of a committee charged with organizing and convening general Arab meeting to elect a permanent body to represent the Palestinians; efforts came to nothing, largely because of PAP opposition
— Spring 1943 Discussions in Jerusalem initiated by *Istiqlal*ist ʿAwni ʿAbd al-Hadi and Ahmad Hilmi Pasha with Yaʿqub al-Ghusayn of Youth Congress and Dr. Khalidi of Reform party concerning formation of representative political committee made up of factions; vehemently opposed by PAP

— October 1943 'Iraqi Nuri Pasha al-Sa'id went to Jerusalem to help unite Palestinian factions in time for Arab unity discussions; attended by leaders of the factional, political parties; unsuccessful because of PAP opposition

— Mid-1944 Revival of Arab National Fund by Ahmad Hilmi Pasha; organized to counter Zionist land buying and as a vehicle to form a new AHC independent of Husaynis; changed board of directors of Fund to detach Husayni influence

— Late 1944-Early 1945 Musa al-'Alami sent to Egypt as representative of Palestinians at Arab unity talks; March 1945 publication of Covenant of Arab League Special Annex on Palestine; most Palestinian Arabs upset over mildly worded statement, dashing hopes of nationalists who wanted full representative status for Palestine on League; 'Alami's return to Palestine in March caused much criticism against him from all quarters; his land development scheme and propaganda offices, supported by League, specially 'Iraq, were seen as substitutes for more effective action; 'Alami's constructive scheme also competed with Ahmad Hilmi's National Fund; much acrimony between all sides, especially against 'Alami

— March-July 1945 Talks held between Ahmad Hilmi and opposition parties (to PAP) to form a new AHC; included were Dr. 'Izzat Tannus and 'Issa al-'Issa, proprietor of *Filastin* newspaper; Hilmi's National Bank was also used in an attempt to weaken Husayni influence on the Bank's board of directors by adding opposition individuals on the board; initiatives and talks over AHC came to nothing, partly because of lack of NDP cooperation

— May 1945 Rashid al-Haj Ibrahim initiated a popular meeting in Jaffa for purpose of organizing an Arab Front; Front created but short-lived; its formation was in response to the divisions between Ahmad Hilmi, 'Alami, and PAP; a meeting was also initiated with Jaffa clubs by Ghusayn at his house where unity was called for

— June 1945 PAP held "national" meeting in Jerusalem; claimed 5,000 attendants; called for return of Jamal, reaffirmed Mufti's leadership, and demanded independence and stoppage of land sales and Jewish immigration

— November 1945 Syrian Jamil Mardam Bey sent to Palestine by Arab League Council to help Palestinians form a united body; visit encouraged by PAP; a new AHC was formed, consisting of the six factional political parties with Ahmad Hilmi and 'Alami acting as independents; membership dominated by PAP; the other parties resentful

1942-1945 Concurrent Developments in British Policy Making
— Up to 1943 Churchill as Prime Minister throughout war period acted

as main pillar of opposition to White Paper of 1939; blocked promise of independence contained in it; he was in conflict with Foreign Office, which was aware of wider Arab interests; Churchill interested in Zionism and American Jewry's help in obtaining American support in war

— July 1943 War Cabinet Committee on Palestine created to examine various partition schemes

— January 1944 WCCP report: called for three states: Jerusalem, an Arab state as part of Southern Syria, and a Jewish state

— April 1944 Report opposed by Palestine HC Harold MacMichael, Foreign Office and Chiefs of Staff in meeting in Cairo

— Late 1944 Lord Moyne, Resident Minister in Middle East, murdered by Jewish terrorists; his replacement, Lord Grigg, against partition; attempt also on MacMichael's life, replaced by HC Lord Gort, also against partition

— Spring 1945 Grigg offered solution for settlement: local autonomy scheme within a unitary state; severely criticized Jewish Agency and called for its abolishment

— Fall 1945 Sir Douglas Harris of Colonial Office proposes provincial autonomy scheme; midway between unitary state and partition

— Winter 1945 Lord Gort rejected provincial autonomy; desired Palestine remain a united country (status quo) and also criticized Jewish Agency for undermining Arab-Jewish coexistence

1945–1947 Developments in Western Policy Towards Palestine

— Up to 1945 Zionists in May 1942 congregated in New York at Biltmore Hotel and announced need for "Jewish commonwealth" in Palestine; increasing Zionist hostility to Britain as war nears end; late 1944 whirlwind of support for Zionist goals by American politicians, presidential contenders, and media; much Jewish pressure in American politics; outrage at reports filtering out of Europe

— May 1945 End of war; Zionist terrorism launched against Britain in Palestine

— April 1945 Harry Truman ascends presidency upon Franklin Roosevelt's death; unrelenting Jewish pressure pushed Truman towards pro-Zionist policies

— July 1945 Truman begins to insist on need for London to rescind immigration restrictions under White Paper and for immediate entry into Palestine of 100,000 displaced European Jews; Labour assumes office in Britain, Ernest Bevin becomes Foreign Secretary; Bevin decides to involve Americans in British policy and to link Jewish refugees with Palestine settlement; he announces continuation of Jewish immigration even after exhaustion of White Paper quota

— Late 1945 Creation of Anglo-American Committee of Inquiry; given 120 days to make recommendations for a Palestine settlement and resolve question of 100,000

— April 1946 AAC makes recommendations: Palestine to be neither Arab nor Jewish; final government established to protect right of all three faiths, and continuation of mandate pending trusteeship agreement at UN; also recommended Britain grant authority for immediate entry of 100,000 Jewish displaced persons and the rescinding of the land-buying restrictions in White Paper; End of April Truman, reacting to Jewish pressure, unilaterally makes statement that focused on the 100,000, giving himself credit for proposal, and evincing his happiness over call for White Paper's abrogation; in June repeats his hopes for the 100,000

— Summer 1946 British angry; Prime Minister Clement Attlee sends terse notes to Truman; July, Anglo-American experts' meeting convenes in London to discuss all aspects and implications of implementing AAC report; British submit provincial autonomy scheme which American side accepts; a plan devised to transport to Palestine the 100,000; result of agreement called Morrison-Grady report; U.S. unhappy that American team accepted that the 100,000 be worked out *after* entire plan was accepted by both Arabs and Jews; experts' discussion eventually got nowhere because Truman's planned acceptance of report was checked by Jewish lobby and allies in Congress

— July 1946 Zionist terrorist acts continue and escalate through the winter; July 22, Jerusalem King David Hotel blown up by *Irgun*; about 89 killed

— Sept. 1946-Feb. 1947 London Conference; Britain submitted provincial autonomy scheme; first round (10 Sept. to 2 Oct. 1946) only Arab states in attendance; second round (27 Jan. 1947 to 14 Feb. 1947) Palestinians and Zionists attended; Arabs rejected provincial autonomy, propose constitutional, unitary state; negotiations during interim period between Zionists and British; former made *concession* by not insisting on whole of Palestine but on partition, rejecting provincial autonomy; in second round Arabs insisted on unitary state, Zionists on partition; British offered provincial autonomy; discussion got nowhere

1945–1947 Palestinian Politics: Formation of Higher Committees

— May 1945 Mufti arrived in Paris by car; revival of his influence in Palestine and the Middle East

— February 1946 Jamal al-Husayni allowed to return to Palestine; acted as moderating influence in Palestine during spring 1946, at

time of AAC recommendations; 'Alami worked with him; Jamal under pressure from Mufti from France; both men in conflict with him
— March 1946 AHC formed in Nov. 1945 by Mardam Bey was dissolved, largely because of Jamal's intransigence, who wanted to control it through PAP; leaders of other five parties formed an Arab Higher Front; Jamal retained name of AHC
— April 1946 Jamal attempted to counter influence of AHF by adding progressive elements to his AHC, including labor (PAWS's Sami Taha) and independents
— June 1946 Arab states at Bludan, Syria assisted Palestinians in creating an Arab Higher Executive composed of Jamal, Khalidi, Ahmad Hilmi, and Emile al-Ghury, secretary of PAP; intention was that AHE control all Palestinian national and political organizations; AHC and AHF dissolved themselves; Mufti arrives in Egypt, secretly leaving France; all DCs in Palestine reported jubilation; Mufti began to receive Palestinian leaders and activists and to take control of AHE, whose seat of chairman was left vacant for him; he was refused return to Palestine by British
— Summer 1946 Talks between British and Palestinians over a delegation to London Conference; HC Cunningham tried to dictate to Jamal composition of delegation and need for wider representation; Jamal resisted; Palestinians did not attend first stage of conference
— Late 1946-Early 1947 British invited Palestinians to attend second stage without pressure, accepting the AHE as the only representative body; in January 1947, Mufti expanded AHE and it became known again as the AHC; associates such as 'Izzat Darwaza, Amin al-Tamimi, and Mu'in al-Madi were added to the body; its numbers expanded from four to ten; no labor, independent, or opposition elements were added on; Mufti rapidly became the preeminent leader, particularly because of his consistent anti-colonial stance

1946–1947 Mufti's Attempt to Unify Palestinian Leadership and Society
— April 1946 *Bayt al-Mal* proclaimed; Hilmi Pasha's National Fund continued to function separately but Hilmi made clear his readiness to cooperate with the *Bayt* and to invite Jamal and other Mufti associates to be on Fund's administrative council; conflict with 'Alami unresolved, who refused control of AHC over his scheme, was supported by 'Iraqis, and was in conflict with both Hilmi Pasha and Dr. Khalidi
— Late 1946-1947 Sustained attack by press on 'Alami, who buckled and tried to come to terms with Mufti; no reconciliation achieved because 'Alami offered to place Arab offices and constructive scheme

under Mufti, but not AHC; Mufti suggested 'Alami run his programs but as member of the AHC, which 'Alami rejected; he continued with his independent activities

— April 1947   Mufti announces creation of Arab Youth Organization; it came after protracted arbitration by AHC between *Najjada*, founded in Oct. 1945 by Muhammad Nimr al-Hawari, and *Futuwa*, formed by Jamal and the PAP in August 1946; both were bodies of nationalist youth; ultimately there was no fusion of youth organizations, though Arab Youth Organization was supposed to represent their unity; *Najjada* refused PAP control, Jamal was intransigent; in end, three youth groups functioned separately and single command remained unachieved

— Summer 1947   Popular conferences were held; economic and boycott committees were established; Mufti exhorted Palestinians to unite

— December 1947   Beginning of formation of National Committees; formed by AHC decree, not spontaneously; AHC concerned to control them; divisions and Mufti favoritism; NCs still being formed as late as February 1948; burdened with military, social, economic, and civil roles yet were not all fully supported by Mufti; their important role was undermined

1947   Concurrent International Events Concerning Palestine

— February 1947   Failure of London Conference; Bevin announced British intention to submit to UN various solutions on Palestine and would not recommend any particular plan; the British government supported a unitary state, in whatever form

— May 1947   Special session of General Assembly on Palestine; appointment of UNSCOP (eleven members)

— September 1947   Publication of UNSCOP report; majority recommends partition; minority report recommends federal solution; Britain (Colonial Secretary Arthur Creech-Jones) announces its intention to terminate mandate

— November 1947   UN General Assembly voted in favor of partition (33 for, 13 against, 10 abstentions) after long debate and much US pressure; Palestinians reject partition; Zionists accept it

1947   Palestinian Factional Politics in Relation to International (Western) Policies

— Summer 1947   Conflict between Dr. Khalidi and Jamal over the role of the Jerusalem office of the AHC, supposedly to serve as the national headquarters; Ahmad Hilmi, also responsible for the Jerusalem office, sided with Khalidi; conflict was over salaries, need for departmental clerks, and organization of office; disorganization prevailed and morale low in office

— July-August 1947 'Alami was in Geneva while UNSCOP was there writing its report; despite AHC's refusal to make official contacts with UNSCOP, 'Alami contacted UNSCOP and give them a memorandum submitting Arab point of view; he criticized Mufti to Donald MacGillivray, British observer at Geneva, and wrongly claimed Mufti would accept partition if he were made supreme leader

— August 1947 Jamal left for New York to attend plenary session of General Assembly; did not return again to Palestine except for a short visit; Khalidi and Hilmi left to direct office; stayed on till fall of Palestine

— September 1947 Conflict over who would attend UN sessions, first in February, then in May, and again in September; 'Alami's activities spilled over to matter of delegate selection to UN; Jamal eventually led (late August) a delegation that did not include Khalidi or Ahmad Hilmi; Jamal supported 'Alami and was a reason why the Mufti was restrained to act against him, fearing Jamal's defection from the AHC and his alignment with 'Alami

— November 1947 A week before UN partition resolution, Emile al-Ghury privately told Cunningham that he would be happy to accept provincial autonomy scheme on UNSCOP's minority proposal

1946–1948 Concurrent Developments in Arab States Policies

— Up to 1945 Between 1944 and 1945 Arab politicians and leaders repeatedly told Britain of their desire that British remain in Palestine to keep peace and maintain status quo; that they had no intention of intervening or fighting; and that they were apprehensive over Zionist policy; individual and collective Arab efforts in Britain and U.S. on behalf of Palestine; at same time Arab regimes were divided and intriguing towards each other and Palestine

— May 1946 Arab League heads meet at Inschass, Egypt; warned U.S. and Britain not to "transgress" Palestinian Arab rights

— June 1946 "Secret" meeting of Arab League Council at Bludan, Syria; decide to help Palestinians financially and materially; adopt unpublicized resolutions warning Britain and U.S. that their policies might have adverse effect on commercial and political relations in Middle East; protest proposals of AAC

— August 1946 Arab League Council meets at Alexandria, Egypt to prepare for London Conference; partition was rejected; negotiations with Zionists refused and insistence on unitary Palestine state; at same time Arab officials hoped Britain would remain in Palestine

— September 1947 Arab League Political Committee convenes at Sofar, prodded by 'Iraqis; discussed UNSCOP's report; 'Iraqi representative hypocritically demanded economic sanctions against the West, making it contingent on Sa'udi acceptance; Military Committee established and money committed; 'Iraqis begin relentless campaign to weaken AHC

— October 1947 Arab League Council meets at 'Aley, Lebanon; Bludan resolution reaffirmed; Arab governments recommended to undertake military manuevers on frontiers of Palestine; Mufti asked for formation of provisional government but vehemently opposed by 'Iraqis and Trans-Jordanians; Military Committee points to dangers of Arab weakness and asks for money, material, organization, and unity of command, all not responded to by League Political Committee

— December 1947 Arab League Council meeting at Cairo; Arab states especially Egyptians reluctant to intervene in Palestine; agreed that volunteers should take initiative, but did not decide to intervene; Hashemites had their own ambitions; Arab states feared clash with Britain if either volunteers entered or they intervened before the mandate's end; indirectly made clear to 'Abdullah that any military administration set up in Palestine would be of temporary nature; Mufti barred from meeting, his proposal for a provisional government under him definitely rejected, and he was denied from directing policy towards Palestine

— February 1948 Meeting of League Political Committee; Mufti made last bid to obtain military, political, and moral help for the Palestinians and to check Hashemite ambitions; attempted to gain backing for AHC's control of all affairs in Palestine; Political Committee rejected all of his proposals on the basis that AHC did not represent Palestinian people; all funds would be administered by League's Palestine Council and not given to Mufti or AHC (although some money eventually was)

— April 1948 Intensive inter-Arab consultations and heightened anxiety over situation in Palestine, Palestinians losing and volunteers being routed

— Late April-Early May Political Committee was meeting between Damascus and 'Amman; as late as 11 May there was no agreement concerning unified command, but 'Abdullah was made general commander

— May 13 Days before this date invasion plan drawn up; 'Abdullah sabotaged it, insisting on being supreme commander and wanting sweeping changes in the plan; he wanted to leave Arab Legion free to occupy central Palestine, consistent with his secret agreements with the Zionists and collusion with the British

— May 15 Arabs entered Palestine with no plan nor coordination; each acted independently; they were suspicious of each other, and 'Abdullah did not cooperate with the rest of them; some 20,000 to 25,000 total Arab soldiers; result: disastrous war, loss of Palestine

1948 Events Leading to the Fall of Palestine

— January British evacuation begins; disorderly, under widespread Zionist rebellion and terrorism (since 1945); fighting between Palestinians and Jews (since December 1947); at this time, some 15,000 total effective Jewish forces

— February Some 5,000 volunteers (Arab irregulars) trained at Qatna (Syria); of these 2,500 entered Palestine by this month; also 300 Egyptian irregulars in the south, mainly of Muslim Brethren

— Up to Early March Palestinians held communications, besieged Jewish Jerusalem, and attacked transport, settlements, and residential areas; Zionists also carry on terrorist campaigns on Arab buildings and traffic and on Arab villages, the last being violent, night raids, killing mostly civilians

— March Fawzi al-Qawaqji enters Palestine; head of Army of Liberation; headquarters in central Palestine; launches a few minor offensives; Arab League goal of 10,000 rifles still not reached; MC in Damascus gave 1,657 rifles to AHC and 1,501 to volunteers; financially, Arab regimes gave some L143,294 to the AHC, in addition to the rifles, a figure that was far from the promised L1 million; by this time there were some 950 men of the *Jihad* (in addition to 228 volunteers) under Hasan Salameh's command and 300 *mujahidin* and 128 volunteers under 'Abd al-Qadir's command; some 300 men made up the *Futuwa* and *Najjada*; Enmity between Qawaqji and *Jihad*, particularly 'Abd al-Qadir; Qawaqji met with a *Haganah* intelligence officer upon his entry to Palestine, agreeing that he would not coordinate with the *Jihad*, would not aid them, and Zionists would concentrate their forces against the *Jihad*, not against Qawaqji's forces; *Haganah* works out Plan D, designed to defend designated Jewish state's borders and to expand by conquering Palestinian towns and villages

— April Some 8,000 armed men in Palestine, divided evenly between volunteers (which included a big number of Palestinians) and all-Palestinian local forces; British no longer in position to block entry into Palestine; Qawaqji launches assault on Mishmar Ha'emek and is eventually driven back; *Haganah* destruction of a string of villages nearby Mishmar Ha'emek and the expulsion of their inhabitants; massacre at Dayr Yasin (9 April); fall of Tiberias (16–18 April); fall of Haifa (21–22 April) beginning of assault on Jaffa (end of April)

— April/May Some 50,000–60,000 total effective Jewish forces; siege of Acre; Palestinian exodus; fall of Jaffa; fall of Safad; assault on Western Galilee; fear, panic, direct and indirect expulsion, psychological/ physical terror; Palestinian forces in disarray; volunteers ineffective; local (town) military and political leaders divided; volunteer commanders in towns (Haifa, Acre) and regions (Galilee) left; some national committee members in fallen towns leave

— May Some 350,000–400,00 Palestinians became refugees by June; proclamation of the state of Israel (14 May); end of Palestine mandate and administration (15 May); Arab forces (Egyptian, Syrian, Lebanese, Trans-Jordanian, 'Iraqi) invade Palestine; Palestinian disaster continues; another 300,000–350,000 Palestinians become refugees after June 1948; Israel is in control of 80 percent of historic Palestine by beginning of 1949

Bibliography*

Unpublished Sources

1. Archives

A. Arab Studies Society, Jerusalem (Faisal Husseini, Director) *Jihad al-Muqaddas*

B. Israel State Archives, Jerusalem, Prime Minister's Office, Record Group (R.G.) 2, Chief Secretary's Office:
  Accounts, Finance: F
  Labour: I/Lab.
  Local Government: G
  Moslem Affairs, Press: K
  Political Activity: V
  Railways, Ports: R
  Village Administration: Y
  R.G.   9: Department of Commerce and Industry (DCI)
  R.G.   23: District Commissioner's Office, Jerusalem
  R.G.   24: District Commissioner's Office, Lydda
  R.G.   25: District Commissioner's Office, Haifa
  R.G.   27: District Commissioner's Office, Galilee
  R.G.   65 (3): Arabic Documents
  R.G. 112: District Commissioner's Office, Samaria

C. Public Record Office
  CO 733: Colonial Office, Correspondence, Palestine
  CO 537: Colonial Office, Supplementaries, Palestine
  CO 852: Colonial Office, Economic Affairs
  CO 859: Colonial Office, Social Services
  FO 371: Foreign Office, Political

2. Manuscript Sources

A. Theses

Abu Ghazaleh, Adnan Mohammad. "Arab Cultural Nationalism in Palestine, 1919–1948," Ph.D. (New York University, 1967).

---

*This bibliography includes *most* works cited in the text and *additional* sources (primary and otherwise) useful to the subject.

Najjar, Aida Ali. "The Arabic Press and Nationalism in Palestine, 1920–1948," Ph.D. (Syracuse, 1975).

Sabella, E.Z. "The Leading Palestinian Hamayil (Families) and Socio-Economic and Political Organizations in Palestine 1917–1948" M.A. (Univ. of Virginia, 1971).

Seikaly, May, "The Arab Comminity of Haifa, 1918–1936: A Study in Transformation," D. Phil. (Oxford, 1983).

Taqqu, Rachelle L. "Arab Labor in Mandatory Palestine, 1920–1948," Ph.D. (Columbia, 1977).

3. *Private Collections*

A. St. Antony's College Personal Papers Collection, Middle East Centre, Oxford

Fuller Hanging File. This file contains many details by the Lydda District Commissioner on the politico-military situation in the most important Arab city, Jaffa, at the time of its fall and conquest.

MacGillivray Papers (Sir Donald). This file by the Deputy Under-Secretary, with long experience in Palestine, analyzes the politico-administrative aspects of British withdrawal. It discusses the practical financial, military, and economic considerations involved in British withdrawal. It also looks at the possible impact of withdrawal on the Arabs' capability to govern themselves.

Macmichael Papers (Sir Harold). These copious papers are very useful for understanding British political/diplomatic policy, especially towards Jewish immigration, during the war period. They also contain information on colonial development policies at the opening of the war.

Tegart Papers (Sir Charles). These papers of the head of Palestine Police vividly describe the harsh British measures against the Palestinian Arabs during the time of the revolt. They also contain interesting intelligence and police information on Palestinian political activity, organizations, and individuals. Important in comprehending the debilitated state of Palestinian society at the opening of the complex, post-1939 period.

Printed Sources

1. *Primary*

A. Documents, Great Britain

Parliamentary Papers. Command

Cmd. 3683–3687. *Report on Immigration, Land Settlement and Development* by Sir John Hope Simpson. London: HMSO, 1930.

Cmd. 5854. *Report of the Palestine Partition Commission* [Woodhead]. London: HMSO, 1938.

Cmd. 5479. *Report of the Palestine Royal Commission* [Peel Commission]. London: HMSO, 1937.

Palestine Royal Commission. *Minutes of Evidence Heard at Public Sessions.* London: HMSO, 1937.

Cmd. 6019. *Statement of Policy Presented by the Secretary of State for the Colonies to Parliament* [White Paper]. London: HMSO, 1939.

Cmd. 6175. *Statement of Policy on Colonial Development and Welfare.* London: HMSO, 1940.

Cmd. 6180. *Land Transfer Regulations.* London: HMSO, 1940.

Cmd. 6873. *Palestine: Statement of Information Relating to Acts of Violence.* London: HMSO, 1946.

Cmd. 7044. *Proposals for the Future of Palestine: July, 1946–February, 1947.* London: HMSO, 1947.

B. Documents, Palestine Government

A Survey of Palestine (prepared for the information of the Anglo-American Committee of Inquiry), 3 vols. Jerusalem: Government Printer, 1946.

Census Office. *Census for Palestine, 1931,* by E. Mills. 2 vols. Alexandria, 1931.

Department of Labour, *Annual Report.* Jerusalem: Government Printer, 1942–46.

Report of a Committee on the Economic Conditions of Agriculturists in Palestine and the Fiscal Measures of Government in Relation Thereto [Johnson-Crosbie Report]. Jerusalem: Government Printer, 1930.

Report of the Committee on Village Administration and Responsibility [Bailey Committee Report]. Jerusalem: Government Printer, 1940.

Report on Agricultural Development and Settlement in Palestine, by Lewis French. Jerusalem: Government Printer, 1st report, 1931, supp. report, 1932.

Department of Statistics. *General Monthly Bulletin of Current Statistics.* Jerusalem: Government Printer, 1945–46.

Department of Statistics. *Vital Statistics Tables, 1922–1945.* Jerusalem: Government Printer, 1947.

Department of Statistics. *Statistical Abstract of Palestine, 1944–45.* Jerusalem: Government Printer, 1946.

C. Newspapers

al-Difa': 1942–48
Filastin: 1940–48

2. *Secondary*

A. Books

Abcarius, Michael F. *Palestine through the Fog of Propaganda.* London: Hutchison, 1946.

Abu-Lughod, Ibrahim, ed. *The Transformation of Palestine.* Evanston: Northwestern Univ. Press, 1971.

Al-'Arif, 'Arif. *al-nakba: nakbat bayt al-maqdis wal-firdaws al-mafqud, 1947–1952. (The Disaster: The Disaster of the Holy House and the Lost Paradise, 1947–1952)* vol. 1. Saida: al-maktab al-'asriya lil-tiba'a wal-nashr, 1956.

Al-Hawari, Muhammad Nimr. *sir al-nakba (The Secret of the Disaster)* Nazareth: matba'at al-hakim, 1955.

Al-Hut, Bayan N. *al-qiyadat wal-mu'assasat al-siyasiya fi filastin, 1917–1948. (Political Leadership and Organization in Palestine, 1917–1948)* Beirut: Institute for Palestine Studies, 1981.

Al-Khatib, Muhammad Nimr. *min athr al-nakba. (On the Disaster's Effects)* Damascus: al-matba'a al-'umumiya, 1951.

'Allush, Naji. *al-muqawama al-arabiya fi filastin, 1914–1948. (The Arab Resistance in Palestine, 1914–1948)* Beirut: Palestine Research Center, 1967.

Andrews, Fannie Fern. *The Holy Land Under Mandate.* 2 vols. Boston: Houghton, Mifflin, 1931.

Antonius, George. *The Arab Awakening.* New York: Capricon, 1965.

Bain, Kenneth Ray. *The March to Zion: United States Policy and the Founding of Israel, 1945–1948.* College Station: Texas A & M Univ. Press, 1979.

Barbour, Nevill. *Nisi Dominus: A Survey of the Palestine Controversy.*

London: George Harrap, 1946.

Cohen, Michael J. *Palestine, Retreat From the Mandate: The Making of British Policy, 1936–45.* London: Holmes and Meier, 1978.

Cohen, Michael J. *Palestine and the Great Powers 1945–1948.* New Jersey: Princeton Univ. Press, 1982.

Darwaza, 'Izzat. *al-qadiya al-filastiniya fi mukhtalaf marahilha. (The Palestine Problem in its Various Stages)* Saida: al-maktabeh al-'asriya, 1960.

Dawn, C. Ernest. *From Ottomanism to Arabism.* Urbana: University of Illinois Press, 1973.

ESCO Foundation for Palestine. *Palestine: A Study of Jewish, Arab and British Policies.* 2 vols. New Haven: Yale Univ. Press, 1947.

Finn, Elizabeth Ann. *Home in the Holy Land: A Tale Illustrating Customs and Incidents in Modern Jerusalem.* London: J. Nisbet, 1866.

Flapan, Simha. *The Birth of Israel: Myths and Realities.* New York: Pantheon, 1987.

Furlonge, Geoffrey. *Palestine is My Country: The Story of Musa Alami.* London: John Murray, 1969.

Gomaa, Ahmad M. *The Foundation of the League of Arab States: War Time Diplomacy and Inter-Arab Politics, 1941 to 1945.* London: Longmans, 1977.

Granott, A. *The Land System of Palestine.* London: Eyres & Spottiswoode, 1952.

Hadawi, Sami. *Bitter Harvest: Palestine between 1914–1967.* New York: New World Press, 1967.

Hattis, Susan Lee. *The Bi-National Idea in Palestine during Mandatory Times.* Haifa: Shikmona, 1970.

J.B. Hobman, ed. *Palestine's Economic Future.* London: Lund Humphries, 1946.

Hertzberg, Arthur, ed. *The Zionist Idea: A Historical Analysis and Reader.* New York: Atheneum, 1986.

Himadeh, S.B., ed. *The Economic Organization of Palestine.* Beirut: American Univ. Press, 1938.

Horowitz, D. and R. Hinden. *Economic Survey of Palestine with Special Reference to the Years 1936 and 1937.* Tel Aviv: Jewish Agency, 1938.

Hurewitz, J.C. *The Struggle for Palestine*. 2nd ed. New York: Greenwood Press, 1968.

John, Robert and Sami Hadawi. *The Palestine Diary*. 2 vols. New York: New World Press, 1970.

Kayyali, Abdul Wahhab. *Palestine: A Modern History*. London: Croom Helm, 1978.

Kedouri, Eli and Sylvia G. Haim, eds. *Zionism and Arabism in Palestine and Israel*. London: Frank Cass, 1982.

Kendall, Henry, and K.H. Baruth. *Village Development in Palestine during the British Mandate*. London: Crown Agents for the Colonies, 1949.

Khalidi, Walid, ed. *From Haven to Conquest*. Beirut: Institute for Palestine Studies, 1971 (Republished in 1987.)

Khalidi, Walid. *Before Their Diaspora: A Photographic History of the Palestinians, 1876–1948*. Washington, D.C.: Institute for Palestine Studies, 1984.

Khalil, Muhammad, ed. *The Arab States and the Arab League*. 2 vols. Beirut: Khayats, 1962.

Khouri, Fred J. *The Arab-Israeli Dilemma*. New York: Syracuse Univ. Press, 1968.

Khoury, Phillip S. *Urban Notables and Arab Nationalism: The Politics of Damascus 1860–1920*. London: Cambridge Univ. Press, 1983.

Kimche, Jon and David Kimche. *Both Sides of the Hill: Britain and the Palestine War*. London: Secker & Warburg, 1960.

Kirkbride, Alec S. *A Crackle of Thorns*. London: John Murray, 1956

Laqueur, Walter Z. *Communism and Nationalism in the Middle East*. New York: Fredrick A. Praeger, 1956.

Laqueur, Walter Z. and Barry Rubin, eds. *The Arab-Israeli Reader: A Documentary History of the Middle East*. New York: Penguin, 1984.

Lesch, Ann Mosely. *Arab Politics in Palestine, 1917–1939*. Ithaca: Cornell Univ. Press, 1979.

Louis, William Roger. *The British Empire in the Middle East 1945–1951: Arab Nationalism, the United States and Postwar Imperialism*. London: Oxford Univ. Press, 1984.

Louis, Wm. Roger and Robert W. Stookey, eds. *The End of the Palestine Mandate*. Austin: University of Texas Press, 1986.

Mandel, Neville J. *The Arabs and Zionism before World War I.* Berkeley: University of California Press, 1976.

Mansur, George, *The Arab Worker Under the Palestine Mandate.* Jerusalem: Commercial Press, 1937.

Ma'oz, Moshe. *Ottoman Reform in Syria and Palestine 1840-1861.* Oxford: Clarendon Press, 1968.

Ma'oz, Moshe, ed. *Studies on Palestine During the Ottoman Period.* Jerusalem: Magness Press, 1975.

Mayer, Thomas. *Egypt and the Palestine Question, 1936-1945.* Berlin: Klaus Shwarz Verlag, 1983.

Migdal, Joel, ed. *Palestinian Society and Politics.* Princeton: Princeton Univ. Press, 1980.

Miller, Ylana N. *Government and Society and Rural Palestine 1920-1948.* Austin: University of Texas Press, 1985.

Monroe, Elizabeth. *Britain's Moment in the Middle East, 1914-1956.* Baltimore: Johns Hopkins Press, 1963.

Morris, Benny. *The Birth of the Palestinian Refugee Problem, 1947-1949.* New York: Cambridge Univ. Press, 1987.

Muslih, Muhammad Y. *The Origins of Palestinian Nationalism.* New York: Columbia Univ. Press, 1988.

Nathan, R.R., O. Gass, and D. Creamer. *Palestine: Problems and Promise.* Washington: American Council on Public Affairs, 1946.

Nazzal, Nafez. *The Palestinian Exodus from Galilee, 1948.* Beirut: Institute for Palestine Studies, 1978.

Oliphant, Laurence. *Haifa or Life in Modern Palestine.* New York: Harper, 1887.

Owen, Roger. *The Middle East in the World Economy 1800-1914.* London: Methuen, 1981.

Owen, Roger, ed. *Studies in the Social and Economic History of Palestine in the Nineteenth and Twentieth Centuries.* London: Macmillan, 1983.

Patai, Raphael. *On Culture Contact and Its Working in Modern Palestine.* American Anthropological Association, No. 67, 1947.

Polk, William R., David M. Stamler, and Edmund Asfour. *Backdrop to Tragedy: The Struggle for Palestine.* Boston: Beacon Press, 1957.

Porath, Yehoshua. *The Emergence of the Palestinian Arab National Movement, 1918–1929.* London: Frank Cass, 1974.

Porath, Y. *The Palestinian Arab National Movement, 1929–1939.* London: Frank Cass, 1977.

Porath, Y. *In Search of Arab Unity, 1930–1945.* London: Frank Cass, 1986.

Qasmiah, Khairiah, ed. *'Awni 'Abd al-Hadi: Awraq Khassa. ('Awni 'Abd al-Hadi: Private Papers)* Beirut: PLO Research Center, 1974.

Sayigh, Rosemary. *Palestinians: From Peasants to Revolutionaries.* London: Zed Press, 1979.

Segev, Tom. *1949: The First Israelis.* New York: Free Press, 1986.

Shlaim, Avi. *Collusion Across the Jordan: King Abdullah, the Zionist Movement, and the Partition of Palestine.* New York: Columbia Univ. Press, 1988.

Stein, Kenneth. *The Land Question in Palestine, 1917–1939.* Chapel Hill: University of North Carolina Press, 1984.

Tannous, Izzat. *The Palestinians.* New York: I.G.T. Press, 1988.

Taylor, Alan R. *Prelude to Israel: An Analysis of Zionist Diplomacy, 1897–1947.* Beirut: Institute for Palestine Studies, 1970.

Teveth, Shabtai. *Ben-Gurion and the Palestine Arabs.* Oxford: Oxford Univ. Press, 1985.

Tibawi, Abdul Latif. *Arab Education in Mandatory Palestine: A Study of Three Decades of British Administration.* London: Luzac, 1956.

Wasserstein, Bernard. *The British in Palestine, the mandatory government and the Arab-Jewish conflict 1917–1929.* London: Royal Historical Society, 1978.

Wilson, Evan M. *Decision on Palestine: How the U.S. Came to Recognize Israel.* Stanford: Hoover Institution Press, 1979.

Wilson, Mary, *King Abdullah, Britain and the Making of Jordan.* Cambridge: Cambridge Univ. Press, 1987.

Yasin, Subhi. *al-thawrah al-'arabiya al-kubra fi filastin, 1936–1939. (The Great Arab Revolt in Palestine, 1936–1939)* Cairo: dar al-katib, 1967.

Zeine, Zeine N. *The Emergence of Arab Nationalism.* Beirut: Khayats, 1966.

B. Articles

Abboushi, Wasef F. "The Road to Rebellion: Arab Palestine in the 1930's." *Journal of Palestine Studies*, 23 (1977).

Abu-Ghazaleh, Adnan M. "Arab Cultural Nationalism in Palestine During the British Mandate." *Journal of Palestine Studies*, 1 (1972).

Alami, Musa. "The Lesson of Palestine." *Middle East Journal*, 3 (1949).

Al-Hout, Bayan N. "The Palestinian Political Elite during the Mandate Period." *Journal of Palestine Studies*, 9 (1979).

Al-Qawuqji, Fauzi. "Memoirs, 1948: Part I." *Journal of Palestine Studies*, 4 (1972).

Al-Qawuqji, Fauzi. "Memoirs, 1948: Part II." *Journal of Palestine Studies*, 5 (1972).

Asad, Talal. "Anthropological Texts and Ideological Problems: An Analysis of Cohen on Arab Villages in Israel." *Review of Middle East Studies*, 1 (1975).

Beinen, J. "The Palestine Communist Party, 1919-1949." *MERIP*, 55 (1977).

Bowden, Tom. "The Politics of the Arab Rebellion in Palestine 1936-39." *Middle Eastern Studies*, 11 (1975).

Buheiry, Marwan R. "The Agricultural Exports of Southern Palestine, 1885-1914." *Journal of Palestine Studies*, 10 (1981).

Carmi, Shulamit and Henry Rosenfeld. "The Origins of the Process of Proletarianization and Urbanization of the Arab Peasants in Palestine." *Annals of the New York Academy of Sciences*, 220 (1974).

Childers, Erskine. "The Other Exodus." *The Spectator*, 6933 (12 May 1961).

Farsoun, Samih and Karen Farsoun. "Class and Patterns of Association Among Kinsmen in Contemporary Lebanon." *Anthropological Quarterly*, 47 (1974).

Firestone, Ya'cov. "Crop Sharing Economics in Mandatory Palestine." *Middle Eastern Studies*, pt. I, 11 (Jan. 1975).

Firestone, Y. "Crop Sharing Economics in Mandatory Palestine." *Middle Eastern Studies*, pt. II, 11 (May 1975).

Glazer, Steven. "The Palestinian Exodus in 1948." *Journal of Palestine Studies*, 9 (1980).

Haddad, Elias N. "Political Parties in Syria and Palestine (Qaisi and Yemeni)." *Journal of the Palestine Oriental Society*, 1 (1921).

Hoexter, M. "The Role of Qays and Yemen Factions in Local Political Divisions: Jabal Nablus Compared with the Judean Hills in the First Half of the Nineteenth Century." *Asian and African Studies*, IV (1973).

Hourani, Albert. "Ottoman Reform and the Politics of Notables." In William R. Polk and Richard L. Chambers, eds. *Beginnings of Modernization in the Middle East.* Chicago: Chicago Univ. Press, 1968.

Hourani, Cecil A. "The Arab League in Perspective." *Middle East Journal*, 1 (1947).

Hurani, Hani. "malahathat hawl awda' al-tabaqa al-'arabiya al-'amila fi filastin fi 'ahd al-intidab." ("Observations Concerning the Conditions of the Arab Working Class in Palestine During the Mandage Era") *Shu'un Filastiniya*, 32 (1974).

Jankowski, James. "The Government of Egypt and the Palestine Questions, 1936–1939." *Middle Eastern Studies*, 17 (1981).

Karpat, Kemal H. "The Transformation of the Ottoman State, 1789–1908." *International Journal of Middle East Studies*, 3 (1972).

Kedourie, Elie. "Religion and Politics: The Diaries of Khalil Sakakini." *Middle Eastern Affairs*, 1, St. Antony's Papers, 4 (1958).

Khalidi, Rashid. "Revisionist Views of the Modern History of Palestine: 1948." *Arab Studies Quarterly*, 10 (Fall 1988).

Khalidi, Tarif. "Palestinian Historiography: 1900–1948." *Journal of Palestine Studies*, 10 (1980).

Khalidi, W. "The Fall of Haifa." *Middle East Forum*, 35 (1959).

Khalidi, W. "Plan Dalet, The Zionist Blueprint for the Conquest of Palestine." *Middle East Forum*, 37 (1961).

Lesch, A.M. "The Palestine Arab Nationalist Movement under the Mandate." In William B. Quandt, Fuad Jabber, and Ann Mosely Lesch, *The Politics of Palestiinian Nationalism.* Berkeley: University of California Press, 1973.

Lesch, A.M. "The Origins of Palestine Arab Nationalism." In William W. Haddad and William L. Ochsenwald, eds. *Nationalism in a Non-National State: The Dissolution of the Ottoman Empire.*

Columbus: Ohio State Univ. Press, 1977.

Mandel, Neville. "Turks, Arabs and Jewish Immigration into Palestine, 1882–1914." *Middle Eastern Affairs*, 4 (1968).

Mayer, Thomas. "Egypt's 1948 Invasion of Palestine." *Middle Eastern Studies*, 22 (1986).

Migdal, Joel. "Urbanization and Political Change: The Impact of Foreign Rule." *Comparative Studies in Society and History*, 19 (1977).

Morris, B. "Operation Dani and the Palestinian Exodus from Lydda and Ramle in 1948." *Middle East Journal*, 40 (1986).

Morris, B. "The Causes and Character of the Arab Exodus from Palestine: the Israel Defence Forces Intelligence Branch Analysis of June 1948." *Middle Eastern Studies*, 22 (1986).

Nashif, Taysir. "Palestinian Arab and Jewish Leadership in the Mandate Period." *Journal of Palestine Studies*, 24 (1977).

Nazzal, Nafez. "The Zionist Occupation of Western Galilee." *Journal of Palestine Studies*, 3 (1974).

Peretz, Don. "Palestinian Social Stratification: The Political Implications." *Journal of Palestine Studies*, 7 (1977).

Porath, Y. "Usbat al-Taharrur al-Watani (The National Liberation League), 1943–1948." *Asian and African Studies*, 4 (1968).

Porath, Y. "Al-Hajj Amin Al-Husayni, Mufti of Jerusalem—His rise to Power and the Consolidation of His Position." *Asian and African Studies*, 7 (1971).

Porath, Y. "The Political Organization of the Palestinian Arabs under the British Mandate." In Moshe Ma'oz, ed. *Palestinian Arab Politics*. Jerusalem: Jerusalem Academic Press, 1975.

Reilly, James. "The Peasantry of Late Ottoman Palestine." *Journal of Palestine Studies*, 5 (1981).

Rosenfeld, Henry. "From Peasantry to Wage Labour and Residual Peasantry: The Transformation of an Arab Village." In Louise Sweet, ed. *People and Cultures of the Middle East*. New York: Natural History Press, 1970.

Shoufani, Elias. "The Fall of a Village." *Journal of Palestine Studies*, 4 (1972).

Wasserstein, Bernard. " 'Clipping the Claws of the Colonizers': Arab Officials in the Government of Palestine, 1917–48." *Middle Eastern Studies*, 13 (1977).

Wilson, Evan M. "The Palestine Papers, 1943–1947." *Journal of Palestine Studies,* 2 (1973).

Yasin, 'Abd al-Qadir. "al-tabaqa al-'umaliya wa al-haraka al-siyasiya fi filastin." ("The Working Class and the Political Movement in Palestine") *Shu'un Filastiniya,* 33 (1976).

Zureik, Elia. "Towards a Sociology of the Palestinians." *Journal of Palestine Studies,* 6 (1977).

Index

DATE DUE